RELATIONS IN PUBLIC

RELATIONS IN PUBLIC

Microstudies of the Public Order

Erving Goffman

HARPER TORCHBOOKS
Harper & Row, Publishers
New York, Cambridge, Hagerstown, Philadelphia, San Francisco
London, Mexico City, São Paulo, Sydney

This book was originally published by Basic Books, Inc. in 1971.

RELATIONS IN PUBLIC

 For information address Harper & Row, Publishers, Inc., 10 East 53rd Street, New York, N.Y. 10022. Published simultaneously in Canada by Fitzhenry & Whiteside Limited, Toronto.

First HARPER COLOPHON edition published 1972

ISBN: 0-06-131957-0

80 12 11 10 9 8 7 6

DEDICATED

TO THE MEMORY OF

A. R. Radcliffe-Brown

WHOM

ON HIS VISIT TO THE

UNIVERSITY OF EDINBURGH IN 1950

I ALMOST MET

If, disregarding conduct that is entirely private, we consider only that species of conduct which involves direct relations with other persons; and if under the name government we include all control of such conduct, however arising; then we must say that the earliest kind of government, the most general kind of government, and the government which is ever spontaneously recommencing, is the government of ceremonial observance. More may be said. This kind of government, besides preceding other kinds, and besides having in all places and times approached nearer to universality of influence, has ever had, and continues to have, the largest share in regulating men's lives.

Herbert Spencer, *The Principles of Sociology*

Preface

I

The realm of activity that is generated by face-to-face interaction and organized by norms of co-mingling—a domain containing weddings, family meals, chaired meetings, forced marches, service encounters, queues, crowds, and couples—has never been sufficiently treated as a subject matter in its own right. In fact, a convenience has often been made of it. Whenever a concrete illustration has been needed of how it is with a social establishment, or a bit of social structure, or even a society, interaction vignettes have been fetched in to provide vivid evidence and, incidentally, a little obeisance to the fact that there are people out there moving about. Thus interaction practices have been used to illuminate other things, but themselves are treated as though they did not need to be defined or were not worth defining. Yet the nicest use for these events is the explication of their own generic character.

Recently this neglected field—the field of public life [1]—has begun to receive very active attention, this being an aspect no doubt of a complex unsettling expressed variously in the current unsafety and incivility of our city streets, the new political device

[1] This choice of terms is not much better than any other. "Public life" can mean the career associated with political office, a definition here to be excluded, and can exclude face-to-face interaction within a private domestic establishment, here definitely to be included. Current alternatives—proxemics, micro-sociology, face-to-face interaction, human ethology—all have weaknesses, too.

of intentionally breaking the ground rules for self-expression during meetings and contacts, the change in rules of censorship, and the social molestation encouraged in the various forms of "encounter group" and experimental theater. Indeed, concern about public life has heated up far beyond our capacity to throw light on it.

The realm of face-to-face interaction, then, which was a field to borrow from, has become one to do battle in. In both cases an account is drawn upon that hasn't yet been established. It would seem a good time to develop the interaction ethology needed if we are to study this domain naturalistically.

In this book I want to focus on one issue, a conceptually delicate one: the connections between an element of social structure, in this case social relationships, and public life. Attention will be given to those aspects of social relationships that figure when the related persons are in one another's immediate presence. A double care will therefore be required, ours being a dual subject matter commonly accorded none. Before beginning, however, I would like to add a brief note about public order and about method.

II

The dealings that any set of actors routinely have with one another and with specified classes of objects seem universally to become subject to ground rules of a restrictive and enabling kind. When persons engage in regulated dealings with each other, they come to employ social routines or practices, namely, patterned adaptations to the rules—including conformances, by-passings, secret deviations, excusable infractions, flagrant violations, and the like. These variously motivated and variously functioning patterns of actual behavior, these routines associated with ground rules, together constitute what might be called a "social order."

The study of social order is part of the study of social organization; however, a weakened notion of organization is involved. The concern is with the conditions and constraints placed upon the manner in which ends are sought or activity carried out and with patterned adaptations associated with these pursuings, with little concern for the choice of ends or the manner in which these ends may be integrated into a single system of activity. A certain atomization is involved: the interest is in the norms and practices employed by any particular participant in the channel of mutual dealings and not in the differentiation and integration of participants.[2] Ground rules are an important organizational device, but only one component of an organization. Moreover, ground rules can regulate dealings when those who participate share hardly any additional organization at all.

It should be apparent that thinking about social orders has been subject to a conservative bias, a bias that many would see as operative in the very selection of the topic and title. There is the political doctrine that order is "natural," that any order is good, and that a bad social order is better than no order at all. There is also the belief that the rules of an order are such as to make mutual dealings possible. And in truth, the rules of an order *are* necessarily such as to preclude the kind of activity that would have disrupted the mutual dealings, making it impractical to continue with them. However, it is also the case that the mutual dealings associated with any set of ground rules could probably be sustained with fewer rules or different ones, that some of the rules which do apply produce more inconvenience than they are worth, and that some participants profit considerably more than others from the order. It is also the case that a large number of infractions are compatible with maintaining an order and that the issue of how many this might be is a nice theoretical problem that has exercised passions, not minds. Finally, in a complex society the disorganization of a social order is a breakdown in but one component of the whole, and the whole is not so closely integrated as to break down because of this.

[2] The rules of an order may themselves, of course, form a system and exhibit typical system properties such as mutual consistency and exhaustiveness.

In spite of the fact that there is much to suspect in an interest in order, the subject matter has a defense. It is possible to imagine a society without many of the ground rules sustained by Americans. Indeed, it is easy to imagine a society being the better off for this. But it is not possible to imagine a society that does not make extensive use of various sets of ground rules. Furthermore, the seventeenth-century model of the state which justifies constraints on the grounds that everyone profits from them does have some validity in regard to orders. Unlike many organizations and structures, an order can benefit almost all of its participants individually, often equitably, and sometimes immensely compared to the individual cost, and in fact may be consciously supported (even established) because the mutual benefits are apparent. Persons *can* come together and voluntarily agree to abide by certain ground rules, forming a norm-generating coalition, the better to free attention from unimportant matters and get on with the business at hand.[3] Also, when an order actually does break down, a great flood of social disturbance can result, the participants then being forced to appreciate all the uses they had made of the prior order and all the

[3] Of course, nice issues are involved here. Agreement to conform can be arrived at tacitly as well as openly, and this increases the number of possible cases. But the conditions that could provide the individual with self-interested warrant for adhering to a rule are sometimes ineffective because no device is available through which each participant can assure the others that he appreciates the circumstances, believes they appreciate the circumstances, and is confident that they are aware of his appreciation and belief. In actual life, the notion of enlightened self-interest seems more important as an argument than as an analysis. When an individual finds himself dependent on the operation of a ground rule, he can tell himself—or be told by others—that he must not break it, for if everyone were to, he himself would suffer from the consequences. And so he would. However, in many circumstances his breaking the rule would not appreciably undermine the support which others give it, and should their support be undermined for other reasons, his maintenance of the rule would be unlikely to bring it back into force. In fact, pure self-interest should lead the individual to encourage others to guide their conduct by an image of what would happen were everyone to cease to support the rule, and while thus encouraging the others, he himself should quietly disregard the rule. Note, if everyone else were to follow *this* maxim, his not doing so would still be unlikely to have an appreciable effect.

dependency they had developed on it. And these claims about order are valid in spite of the fact that the imagery involved seems to have been used to justify the doing of every unnecessary and coercive arrangement in the world, and that feelings about a breakdown in order can be excited in connection with minor disturbances whose consequences are largely restricted to this overreaction.

Ground rules can be found in channels of mutual dealings that allow the participants to be outside of each other's immediate physical presence. An example is the etiquette governing business correspondence, or the regulations governing stock market transactions, or the syntax of a written language. My concern in this volume is with the ground rules and the associated orderings of behavior that pertain to public life—to persons co-mingling and to places and social occasions where this face-to-face contact occurs. My special concern then is with "public order."

It is possible to study public order in domestic establishments and other places where entree and the desire to enter are restricted, for these settings certainly have rules and practices regarding co-mingling.[4] But on the whole, our concern with households has been in how they manage their relationships and not their passageways. And on the whole (and no doubt properly), interest in public order has focused on those situations where the unacquainted and the merely acquainted become physically accessible to one another—situations where order as such may be a central issue.

III

Throughout the papers in this volume unsubstantiated assertions are made regarding the occurrence of certain social practices in certain times and among peoples of various kinds. This description

---

[4] In the Project on Human Communication at Bronx State Hospital, Albert E. Scheflen is directing the videotaping of hundreds of hours of

by pronouncement is claimed to be a necessary evil. I assume that if a broad attempt is to be made to tie together bits and pieces of contemporary social life in exploratory analysis, then a great number of assertions must be made without solid quantitative evidence. (Admittedly this license has greater warrant in traditional ethnographic work than in the study of "small behaviors." Face-to-face interaction generates many natural indicators nicely subject to measure and count. Further, much of expressive behavior disappears from mind as soon as it is observed, and only a randomly scheduled use of appropriate recording equipment is likely to be fully successful in sampling it.)

A second weakness, perhaps not necessary, is the effort made to correct for the first. Verbal hedges are involved.

One hedge, rightly notorious, is the occurrence qualifier. Instead of making absolute generalizations or ones in statistical form, I will assert that a given practice occurs among a set of individuals "routinely" or "often" or "on occasion," thereby admitting to a want of organized evidence even while pretending carefulness. Statements qualified in this way are hard to prove false, which is nice, but the same qualification weakens the sense in which they might be true, which isn't.

The second hedge is the distribution qualifier known familiarly as "In our society. . . ." Thus, I use the phrases "In Western society," "In the American middle classes," and so forth. The issue here is deeper than that of the questionability of using a pat device to guard against ethnocentric overgeneralizations. To say that a particular practice is found *in* a given place (or a given class of places) leaves a great deal unspecified even when systematically collected data are available. For it is often unclear whether it is claimed that the practice occurs throughout the place or only somewhere in it, and if throughout, whether this is the only place it occurs. Furthermore, the social arrangements and small behaviors considered in this book have the awkward property of per-

---

kitchen mingling in several working-class households, and for the first time—for good or bad—has made possible the close study of public order in private places.

taining not to a set of individuals that can be bounded nicely, like the citizens of a particular nation state, but to groupings whose boundaries we know very little about. Class, region, ethnic group, and age-grade are involved, and these are familiar enough. But the other reference units cause trouble. There is "epoch," which carries the difficulty that persons in certain parts of the world are more old-fashioned than their age mates in other parts. And the other reference units are not much better. There is the English-speaking world, the Anglo-American community, West European nations, Protestant countries, Christian society, and the West. Such are the units we are led to if we are interested in the *full* location of the practices to be considered in this volume. In any case, the reference unit, "American society" (which I use throughout), is something of a conceptual scandal, very nearly a contradiction in terms; the social unit "civilization" (whatever that might mean) is as relevant as that of nation state.

So the problem is not merely that of having to make statements about groups and communities without sufficient data, but that of not knowing very much about the identity and boundaries of the groupings about which there are insufficient data. I employ the term "our" but do so knowing that in regard to small behaviors the "our" cannot be conventionally or conveniently specified. I can with least lack of confidence make assertions about my "own" cultural group, the one with which I have had the most first-hand experience, but I do not know what to call this grouping, what its full span or distribution is, how far back it goes in time, nor how these dimensions might have to be changed, according to the particular bit of familiar behavior under question. (But note, in making claims about what various half-defined groups consider proper and improper, I do not mean to be read as agreeing with any of them, although often my sentences will allow this reading. I mean to make statements from within other people's point of view without repeatedly explicating the frame, and ask to be accused of laconicity, not morality.)

Certainly, then, the method that often is resorted to here—unsystematic, naturalistic observation—has very serious limitations. I claim as a defense that the traditional research designs thus far employed in this area have considerable limitations of their own. In spite of disclaimers, the findings of these studies are assumed to hold more broadly than the particularities of their execution can immediately warrant; in each case a second study would be necessary to determine of whom and what the results are true. The variables which emerge tend to be creatures of research designs that have no existence outside the room in which the apparatus and subjects are located, except perhaps briefly when a replication or a "continuity" is performed under sympathetic auspices and a full moon. Concepts are devised on the run in order to get on with setting things up so that trials can be performed and the effects of controlled variation of some kind or other measured, the science of which is assured by the use of lab coats and government money. The work begins with the sentence, "We hypothesize that . . . ," goes on from there to a full discussion of the biases and limits of the proposed design, reasons why these aren't nullifying, and culminates in an appreciable number of satisfyingly significant correlations tending to confirm some of the hypotheses: as though the uncovering of pattern in social life were that simple. A sort of sympathetic magic seems to be involved, the assumption being that if you go through the motions attributable to science then science will result. But it hasn't. (Five years after publication, many of these efforts remind one of the experiments children perform with Gilbert sets: "Follow instructions and you can be a real chemist, just like the picture on the box.") Fields of naturalistic study have not been uncovered through these methods. Concepts have not emerged that reorder our view of social activity. Frameworks have not been established into which a continuously larger number of facts can be placed. Understanding of ordinary behavior has not accumulated; distance has.

Finally, a note is necessary about the use of ethological suggestions. In contemporary social science, the only students as a group who seem to have the capacity to study the small behaviors of their own society and to treat the conduct of their own familiars objectively are linguists, the traditional drawback of these scholars for my concerns being the relatively narrow range of theirs. They are strong on supplying methodological inspiration but weak in regard to content. The work of ethologists provides a trickier model.

Social groups of animals—bands, flocks, herds, prides, troops, packs—have the special feature that the members of any particular group usually remain in perceptual range of one another. Thus, almost all activity is socially situated; social life and public life are coterminous. Therefore, ethologists perforce end up being students of face-to-face interaction. So they are a source. More important, they have developed a field discipline that leads them to study animal conduct in very close detail and with a measure of control on preconception. In consequence, they have developed the ability to cut into the flow of apparently haphazard animal activity at its articulations and to isolate natural patterns. Once these behavioral sequences are pointed out to the observer, his seeing is changed. So ethologists provide an inspiration. It must be said that many ethologists are quick to apply a Darwinian frame, accounting for any behavioral routine in terms of its current (and even vestigial) survival value, and that earlier work was rather quick in making species-wide imputations. When these biases are brought to the study of human behavior, some very unsophisticated statements result. But if we politely disattend this feature of ethology, its value for us as a model stands clear.

Author's Note

The six papers that form the body of this book deal with a single domain of activity and were written to be published together. Moreover, they are sequentially related; each is somewhat dependent on the terms defined in the prior ones. Yet—except for the two on interchanges—each develops its own perspective starting from conceptual scratch. And taken together, the six do not purport to cover systematically, exhaustively, and without repetition what is common to them. I snipe at a target from six different positions unevenly spaced; there is no pretense at laying down a barrage. The result is chapters, but wayward ones. The paper placed in the appendix was published separately and meant to stand on its own. It considerably repeats some of the arguments developed in the text and can be read as one application of them.

The collection as a whole continues the consideration of face-to-face interaction developed in three previous books, *Encounters* (1961), *Behavior in Public Places* (1963) and *Interaction Ritual* (1967).

I would like to thank Lee Ann Crawford for an immense amount of help with a wide range of editorial work.

E.G.

Philadelphia, 1971

Contents

RELATIONS
IN
PUBLIC

[1]

The Individual as a Unit

I *Introduction*

In discussions of face-to-face interaction, the term "individual" (or an equivalent such as "person") is inevitably used, as I shall also. However, this easy and necessary use covers multiple sins of imprecision.

For example, in talking about a social setting such as a suburban residential street or a fashionable New York store, it is possible to speak of someone present as being properly or improperly dressed for the time and place. It will be half understood that clothing as an aspect of decorum pertains to the scene as a whole, being a sign of respect (or disrespect) for it. An individual could, of course, dress in a particular way with malice aforethought, because he anticipates a conversational encounter with particular others, but if he does, and wants to be effective, he may have to disguise his intent, since dress is defined as not properly pertaining to what occurs in conversations. Obviously, however, there are matters that properly pertain to encounters. There are rules for taking and terminating a turn at talking; [1] there are norms synchronizing the

[1] Recently given extensive treatment by Starkey Duncan, Jr., of the University of Chicago, in a yet unpublished research report, "Towards a

process of eyeing the speaker and being eyed by him; there is an etiquette for initiating an encounter and bringing it to an end.[2] Here, too, we can speak of an individual conducting himself properly or improperly, but this time relative to encounters, not settings.[3] The "system of reference" has changed and so, I believe, do

---

Grammar for Taking Speaking Turns in a Conversation: A System Approach to Face-to-Face Interaction." Duncan demonstrates that a speaker ready to give up his role employs signals through multiple channels: content, syntax, intonation contour, paralinguistic behavior, and bodily gesture. Studies such as Duncan's point up the awesome competency both with respect to performance and interpretation which seems to be required by all those who are able to exchange a few remarks with a friend or pass someone on the street without colliding with him. It follows that the presumably technical use of terms such as "undersocialization" may have been a little premature. Illiterate graduates of American slum schools may not have learned some things that are useful in getting ahead, but to say that they are unassimilated to the wider society is stretching it a bit. It is becoming increasingly clear that the difference in interactional competence between the crude and the cultivated is slight compared to the similarities, however fateful the consequence of this difference.

[2] There is the complication that although some practices pertain properly to only one frame of reference, others pertain officially and directly to more than one system. For example, the obligation to refrain from smoking may be owed a setting such as a church or court of law, but also an encounter in which one's fellow interactant is a female or a superordinate; technical considerations, such as fire hazards, may also impose restrictions on smoking. The fact is that the corpus of ritualized expressions of any society is limited, and although each system of activity can put together its own selection of ritual elements, these must be drawn from the available idiom.

[3] The simultaneous management of both these systems is a wondrously complex matter and understandably subject to failures of various sorts. When several individuals become deeply involved in a conversation in the presence of a non-participant, they may begin to fail to sustain the reserve and respect that accessible encounters owe the surround and cause the bystander to suddenly feel as though he were in the presence of something that had gotten out of control. Individuals with a long-settled relationship who sustain few pretenses before each other and who find themselves alongside an honored guest at a reception but not in an encounter with him, may attempt to sustain a conversation of their own but painfully find that their talk has utterly failed to engross them. Yet they must enact their engrossment because of what bystanders can properly see about their situation. And even should they manage to convince the gathering, they can

the constitutive units to which the system applies. It is too easy to say merely that the individual plays different roles. The somethings that participate in different systems of activity are in some degree different things.

With the idea in mind, then, that in interaction studies the individual can be different things, I want in this paper to briefly consider two things an individual can be: a vehicular unit and a participation unit.

II *Vehicular Units*

Of the various sets of ground rules that provide the normative bases of public order, one class will concern us here: traffic codes. The matter at issue was nicely formulated at the turn of the century in the opening paragraph of a famous book by Ross:

---

find themselves humiliated by knowing that each knows the other knows of the contrivance yet cannot admit to the other that he is ready to engage in this sort of pretense. Similarly, on a public bus: a bedraggled passenger hallucinates the need for a fix and receives studied civil inattention from fellow passengers; an unsuspecting arrival sits down beside him, is greeted with a profusion of disarrayed, voluble requests, and responds by words that are addressed as much to the other passengers as to the troublesome one. The newcomer thereby gives all those within range a clear sense of the pacification he is attempting, of the awkwardness of the attempt, of the sense of a conversation improperly opened up to the gathering, of the patronizing tone characteristically employed when this is done, and yet no one will be able to say just what items of conduct produce this tremor of uneasy witness in them. So, too, in stage productions where the script requires the assembled company to break from a single focus of attention and fall into separate two- and three-person talks that are not to be heard, it is very often apparent to the audience that something false is in progress, namely, encounters sustained entirely from without. In all of this we can see that those in a conversational encounter are not merely allowed to let their joint involvement carry them away from bystanders; they are likely to be disapproved of if this does not occur. A participant's failure to sustain sufficient involvement and failure to sustain sufficient check on involvement can both cause properly disinterested bystanders to feel that something is not going right.

> A condition of order at the junction of crowded city thoroughfares implies primarily an absence of collisions between men or vehicles that interfere one with another. Order cannot be said to prevail among people going in the same direction at the same pace, because there is no interference. It does not exist when persons are constantly colliding one with another. But when all who meet or overtake one another in crowded ways take the time and pains needed to avoid collision, the throng is *orderly*. Now, at the bottom of the notion of social order lies the same idea. The members of an orderly community do not go out of their way to aggress upon one another. Moreover, whenever their pursuits interfere, they make the adjustments necessary to escape collision and make them according to some conventional rule.[4]

That is probably enough theory for the time. What is needed now is description. Take, for example, techniques that pedestrians employ in order to avoid bumping into one another. These seem of little significance. However, there are an appreciable number of such devices; they are *constantly* in use and they cast a pattern on street behavior. Street traffic would be a shambles without them. Yet until very recently no student anywhere gave them a thought, most being involved in studies not subject to modest, naturalistic observation.

A vehicular unit is a shell of some kind controlled (usually from within) by a human pilot or navigator. A traffic code is a set of rules whose maintenance allows vehicular units independent use of a set of thoroughfares for the purpose of moving from one point to another. The arrangement is that collision and mutual obstruction are systematically avoided by means of certain self-accepted restrictions on movement. When adhered to, a traffic code provides a safe passage pattern.

Thoroughfares may be in the air, on the land, on water, under the waves, on ski slopes, and soon, no doubt, in outer space. Vehicular units themselves vary according to the thickness of their skins. There are ships, submarines, trains, and armored cars, all of

---

[4] Edward Alsworth Ross, *Social Control* (New York: The Macmillan Company, 1908), p. 1.

which have thick skins, being guided by men who are well hidden and in some ways well protected. There are buggies, open cars, sedan chairs, rickshaws, bicycles, and sporting devices such as skis, surfboards, toboggans, kayaks, skates, and skateboards, which leave the navigator relatively exposed. The more protective the shell, the more, on the whole, the unit is restricted to simple movements. Note, a road and its traffic will support shells of somewhat different kinds—cars, bicycles, horse-drawn carts, and, of course, pedestrians. Viewed in this perspective, the individual himself, moving across roads and down streets—the individual as pedestrian—can be considered a pilot encased in a soft and exposing shell, namely his clothes and skin.

Road traffic has interesting features: relative uniformity of rules across regional and national boundaries, and this in spite of the limited span of particular police jurisdictions; relative lack of differentiation of rights by sex, class, age, race, or wealth; relative explicitness and exhaustiveness of rules accompanied by strict, formal social control; a widespread sense that it is all right to break a rule if you can get away with it. In addition, road traffic rules serve as something of an ideal case in arguments regarding the nature and value of ground rules.

Road traffic, of course, has an interface with sidewalk or street traffic, officially at crosswalks and driveways. And the two systems have points of similarity. In both cases what is ordered is passings-by of unacquainted pilots—or at least ones who need not be acquainted—thus providing one source of material for the study of the social relations binding strangers.[5] In both cases, the participant must trustfully put himself into the hands of others. And in both cases, as will be seen, something like the same informally patterned routing practices are employed.

Differences between the two kinds of traffic are obvious. On the

---

[5] As Harvey Sacks, of the University of California at Irvine, has recently pointed out (unpublished lectures), the term "strangers" is a troublesome one. One usually means "fellow user of a public place," not merely any unacquainted other—for example, ordinarily not a policeman or a shop clerk.

road, the overriding purpose is to get from one point to another. (The minor exceptions would include joyriding, pickup cruising, and police surveillance.) On walks and in semi-public places such as stadiums and stores, getting from one point to another is not the only purpose and often not the main one; individuals who are vehicular units will often be functioning in other ways, too, for example, as shoppers, conversationalists, diners, and so forth, and the social order sustained by walkers provides a basis for all of these activities, not merely that of moving from point to point. Also the role of unintentional physical contact differs in the two systems, collision apparently being a matter of more concern on the road than on the sidewalk. Pedestrians can twist, duck, bend, and turn sharply, and therefore, unlike motorists, can safely count on being able to extricate themselves in the last few milliseconds before impending impact. Should pedestrians actually collide, damage is not likely to be significant, whereas between motorists collision is unlikely (given current costs of repair) to be insignificant.[6] Further, a pedestrian who walks aggressively or drops in his tracks or collides with another can hardly produce a traffic jam, although, of course,

---

[6] There are many pretty illustrations of these collision contingencies. For example, waitresses moving in a crowded dining room carrying large service trays on the flat of one hand find they must use the other hand and their voice to ensure a much wider spatial margin of safety than unencumbered pedestrians require or patrons seem immediately ready to provide. A heavily loaded tray increases the size of its carrier and decreases her capacity to turn or to stop quickly. Other persons must not only provide more than usual leeway but also must accept more than their usual share of the avoidance task, since they are the better able to maneuver. If the unencumbered are to make these provisions effectively, they must give—or be caused to give—evidence that they have seen what is needed of them; and they must give these signs earlier in their approach than would be required of them in ordinary pedestrian traffic. Systematically altered traffic conditions thus prevail. Individuals pushing clothes carts in wholesale business districts create something of the same problem for themselves and the pedestrians around them.

In terms of collision contingencies, ships are to cars somewhat as cars are to pedestrians. Ships can be maneuvered much less nicely than can cars, requiring more lead time for each desired outcome and, in addition, producing greater loss per unintended contact.

he can produce a considerable audience. Those who want to pass almost always will have room to do so, and, in any case, they can take to the road or the fields if need be. Cars, of course, are more easily held up. So, too, an improperly conducted motorist is likely to be in unobstructed sight of an offended party longer than an improperly conducted pedestrian is in sight of those he offends. Road traffic, in consequence, seems a more competitive, less fore-bearing system than does street traffic, the one compensation being that a driver can avoid eye-to-eye confrontation relatively easily simply by staying in his car, looking straight ahead, and moving off when traffic allows, knowing that he can hardly be chased after effectively by anyone other than the police. Note, in road traffic, formal understandings seem central, although, of course, many informal understandings are operative; in pedestrian traffic, informal understandings dominate, often appearing to copy loosely the formal rules of road traffic.

A few comments about pedestrian traffic seem possible.[7] In American downtown streets, traffic tends to sort itself out into two opposite-going sides. The dividing line is somewhere near the middle of the sidewalk but is subject to momentary shifting (to accommodate sudden bunching of traffic in one direction) and to longer term displacement caused by the tendency for the journey to and from work to involve a large volume going in one direction in the morning and the reverse at night. As in road traffic, the side going in one's direction tends to be on the right of the dividing line. However, pedestrians on either side who desire to walk

---

[7] A useful consideration of pedestrian routing problems is available in an unpublished treatment by Lynette H. Lofland, "In the Presence of Strangers: A Study of Behavior in Public Settings" (The University of Michigan: Center for Research in Social Organization, May 1966), pp. 131–134. Lofland introduces the notion of "collision course" and its avoidance and raises the issue of the principles that ought to be discoverable by which collisions are avoided. A valuable study was done by Michael Wolff and Verena Hirsch at City University of New York, partly reported in an unpublished paper by Hirsch, "A Study of Pedestrian Behavior" (1970), and in one by Wolff, "The Behavior of Pedestrians on Forty-Second Street, New York City" (1970).

quickly sometimes move to the curb and there manage two-way flow. The innermost part of the street tends to be slowest, perhaps because of the obstruction produced by window shoppers and those entering and leaving buildings.[8] Apart from these considerations, lane formation *within* the right- or left-hand side tends not to be marked, although when an individual momentarily shifts from a lane to facilitate traffic flow, he is apparently likely to shift back into it after the interference is past.[9] It might also be added that at crosswalks the side-division tends to break down, and those going in one direction will take up both sides at the curb, thus facing across the street a broad front of others ready to come toward them.[10] Contrariwise, there are steps and tunnels that physically mark and thereby consolidate two-lane flow.

When routing by divided two-way flow is not used to avoid collision during opposite-direction passing, pedestrians tend (in America) to use the road traffic device of veering to the right,[11] although this practice is breached for many reasons, among which are the principled ones that males should take the road side when passing females [12] and that pedestrians have the right to cut across

[8] Suggested by Hilary Callan.

[9] Described by Hirsch, *op. cit.*, p. 10. Ronald Goodrich of the Department of Psychology, City University of New York, has suggested to me that pedestrians may return to their original lane because it is from there that they have taken long-range scanning of approaching traffic; by returning, they can take up a preparedness already established. If prevented from returning to their old place, presumably a long-span orientation would have to be re-established.

[10] *Ibid.*, p. 14. But after the curb is left, divided flow may be re-established temporarily.

[11] Apparently pedestrians tend also to keep to the right in passing cyclists; incidentally, in case of uncertainty, pedestrians sometimes employ the tack of "freezing" so that the cyclist can see in time that it is he who is to make the decision. (Here I draw on an unpublished paper by William A. Cozzens, "The Bicycle" [1969].)

[12] There are other sex-role differences. For example, Hirsch (*op. cit.*, p. 9) suggests that women wait longer than do men before yielding to an oncomer, perhaps on the assumption that gallantry can be relied on, providing, of course, the oncomer is a male.

the sidewalk at any point, there being no full equivalent of periodic road intersections.

The workability of lane and passing rules is based upon two processes important in the organization of public life: externalization and scanning.

By the term "externalization," or "body gloss," I refer to the process whereby an individual pointedly uses over-all body gesture to make otherwise unavailable facts about his situation gleanable. Thus, in driving and walking the individual conducts himself—or rather his vehicular shell—so that the direction, rate, and resoluteness of his proposed course will be readable. In ethological terms, he provides an "intention display." By providing this gestural prefigurement and committing himself to what it foretells, the individual makes himself into something that others can read and predict from; by employing this device at proper strategic junctures—ones where his indicated course will be perceived as a promise or warning or threat but not as a challenge—he becomes something to which they can adapt without loss of self-respect.[13]

The term "scanning" does not have to be defined, but the way it is done in pedestrian traffic needs to be described. When a pedestrian in American society walks down the street, he seems to make an assumption that those to the front of a close circle around him are ones whose course he must check up on, and those who are a person or two away or moving behind his sight-line can be tuned out. In brief, the individual, as he moves along, tends to maintain a scanning or check-out area. (By angling his own head so as not to be directly obstructed visually by the head of the pedestrian ahead of him, he can ensure his maintenance of this view.) [14] As oncom-

---

[13] We must expect that if the individual is able to produce a reading of his physical intent through body gesture then he will also be able intentionally to induce misreadings. Ronald Goodrich, in correspondence, has suggested that in football, offensive ends are expected to acquire skill in providing false intention displays, that classification of these moves is attempted, and that an offensive end who acquires skill at this sort of misdirection is said to have "good moves."

[14] Suggested in Wolff, *op. cit.*, p. 11. Wolff, in correspondence, argues that the individual may indeed have appreciable concern about nearby per-

ers enter the individual's scanning range—something like three or four sidewalk squares away—they are commonly glanced at briefly and thereafter disattended because their distance from him and their indicated rate and direction of movement imply that collision is not likely and that no perception by them of him is necessary for his easily avoiding collision. A simple "body check" is involved, albeit one performed more circumspectly (at present) by women than by men. This check tends to occur when the individual making it can introduce a large directional change through a small and therefore undemeaning angular correction.[15] Once others have been checked out satisfactorily, they can be allowed to come close without this being cause for concern. Thus the individual can generally cease to concern himself with others as soon as they have come close enough abreast of him so that any interference from them would require a very abrupt turn. And further, since he apparently does not concern himself with oncomers who are separated from him by others, he can, in dense traffic, be unconcerned about persons who are actually very close to him. Therefore, the scanning area is not a circle but an elongated oval, narrow to either side of the individual and longest in front of him, constantly changing in area depending on traffic density around him. Note that even as the individual is checking out those who are just coming into range, so they will be checking him out, which means that oncomers will be eyeing each other at something of the same moment and that this moment will be similarly located in the course of both; yet this act is almost entirely out of awareness.[16]

---

sons who have passed behind his sight-line, but in many circumstances relies on the appearance of those approaching him as an "early-warning system." Faces that reflect an oncoming danger provide a rear-view mirror (to use Wolff's term) for a person who is moving just ahead of the danger and in the same direction.

[15] Hirsch (*op. cit.*, p. 10) thus suggests that once this face-saving distance is breached, oncoming pairs may sometimes rigidly refuse to give way, apparently because personal space has become openly threatened.

[16] Scanning is a human adjustment practiced apart from traffic systems; as in traffic it usually occurs in well-structured moments and places in the course of the individual's movement.

When an individual deems that a simple body-check is not sufficient, as when a collision course is apparent or there is no clear indication of the other's course, then additional assurances are likely to be sought. He can ostentatiously take or hold a course, waiting to do this until he can be sure that the other is checking him out. If he wants to be still more careful, he can engage in a "checked-body-check"; after he has given a course indication, he can make sure the signal has been picked up by the other, either by meeting the other's eyes (although not for engagement) or by noting the other's direction of vision, in either case establishing that his own course gesture has not likely been overlooked. In brief, he can check up on the other's eye check on him, the assumption here being that the other can be relied on to act safely providing only that he has perceived the situation.[17] Finally, a brief face engagement may be initiated in which one party signals what he proposes they do and the other party signals agreement. (A strategic device here is to signal a collaborative routing in which the other has a slight advantage, this usually assuring agreement.) In all of this maneuvering, two special moments can be found. First, there is the "critical sign": the act on the part of the other that finally allows the individual to discover what it is the other proposes to do. Second, there is the "establishment point": the moment both parties can feel that critical signs have been exchanged regarding compatible directions and timing, and that both appreciate that they both appreciate that this has occurred. It is then that movements can be executed with full security and confidence; it is then that those involved can feel fully at ease and fully turn their attention elsewhere.

There are, then, pedestrian routing practices.[18] Somewhat the

---

[17] This is one example of the moral faith that is systematically built into traffic systems at certain junctures—faith that all others will know how to act and will so act—and provides a hint of the vulnerability of these social orders to circumstances that produce mistrust.

[18] Of which only a few illustrations have been supplied. There are others. For example, a *Time* (May 11, 1970, p. 66) review of the Wolff and Hirsch study states:

same devices are employed in car traffic and in car-pedestrian traffic. (Checked-body-checks, for example, are especially noticeable in the conduct of pedestrians as they begin to traverse a crosswalk in the immediate face of cars ready to move with a change in light.)

As often noted in the literature, these routing signals generate the possibility of gamesmanship. By not allowing pedestrians to catch his eye, a driver can keep them in a hesitant condition. By ostensibly failing to read a course sign that has been pointedly given him, one driver can force another driver to fall back or accept a "chicken" challenge. By "catching" the eye of a driver, another can gesture a request (for example, to cut into a line of cars from a side road, or pull out into traffic) for which no effective body gesture is available.

Routing practices can involve near-simultaneous, parallel adjustments on the part of relevant parties, thereby avoiding the appearance that one participant is deferentially giving way to another. This control of impressions is often helped by the close presence of third parties whose accommodative movements introduce complicating expressions. (Not only may *C* be adapting to *B* while *B* is adapting to *A*, but also *C*, when behind *B*, may often find it expedient to adapt now to what he assumes *B* is about to do to avoid *A*—a coordination of adjustment easily seen on film but hard to elicit verbally from those who daily manage it.) In circumstances where these accommodations are not practicable—for example, during heavy snow when only a narrow path has been cut in the

---

A popular maneuver in busy traffic [to avoid collision] was what Wolff dubbed the "step-and-slide"—a slight angling of the body, a turning of the shoulder and an almost imperceptible sidestep, all of which is reciprocated by the oncoming pedestrian.

Wolff also noted behavioral patterns among pedestrians walking in the same direction. Generally, they move in a sort of formation that permits them to see over the shoulders of the people in front. When one person in a cluster of individuals changes position, the others adjust theirs to accommodate the new "over-the-shoulder" relationship. Walking directly behind somebody is usually saved for congested sidewalks, when the person ahead is used as a sort of blocking guard.

walk, or around a construction site when again the path may be one-person wide, or at an entranceway that has a heavy door—then another set of mechanisms is available, a set that is employed in such circumstances throughout our society, a set identified with the term "gallantry." Here physical weakness attributable to age, sex, or medical condition is given priority, the understanding being that the preference is going to something worthy but not strong.[19] When no safe basis for this gallantry exists, one party can elect to use broad gestures in a display of mock deference, which here can have the functional effect of deference without its subordinative implications. (Whether the individual gives way in a serious or mock fashion, the other can be expected to complete the interchange by externalizing a display of speed, thereby both minimizing the other's sacrifice and demonstrating that it has been duly appreciated.) When the parties are too evenly matched to manage a narrow passage with these devices, *both* may step out of the cleared way simultaneously, a nice example of wasting a resource in order to avoid an expression.[20] Circumstances sometimes allow another diplomatic solution: once both parties have seen that someone will have to give way, the first to reach an only (or at least an evident) shunting spur—a clearing to the side of the path—can wait there for the other to pass, on the assumption that had the other reached this point first, he would have acted in the general interest also, and that he appreciates that that is the basis of his current advantage. Given these practical occasions for civility, it should be quite obvious that if one or more participants are intent on it, then the streets can nicely provide the ingredients

---

[19] See "Fun in Games," in Goffman, *Encounters* (New York: Bobbs-Merrill, Inc., 1961), p. 32.

[20] Road traffic provides parallel possibilities except that stepping out of the path may require a bit more doing, as Clark W. Thayer illustrates in *Diplomat* (New York: Harper & Row, Publishers, Inc., 1959), p. 225:

> A happier solution was found about the same time [the mid-seventeenth century] in The Hague when the Spanish and French ambassadors' carriage met in a narrow street and each solemnly refused to pull over for the other. After a long dispute it was finally decided to pull down a fence at the side of the road so that they might pass without either giving way to the other.

for a character contest.[21] One need only veer into the course of the other while holding his eye, and he will be forced to press his claims or to accommodate under conditions where his giving way will be seen as a submissive response to a challenge; indeed, all accommodative arrangements generate this possibility.

I have so far considered only those pedestrian traffic practices that are interpersonal (or rather intervehicular) in character. There are, of course, single unit practices. For example, as the individual proceeds along his course, he scans the flooring immediately in front of him so that he will have time to sidestep small obstructions and sources of contamination.[22] Here, too, is a structured scanning that is performed without much awareness. Within the oval scanned for oncomers, then, is a smaller region that is also kept under eye.

All in all, then, it is possible to argue that there is such a thing as a pedestrian traffic system, the individual himself being the vehicular unit. One incidental value in isolating this system within interaction is that we are then able to follow the operation of other elements more rigorously. Take, for example, rules about touching. In ordinary circumstances, a physical contact can be seen as an intimacy, either warranted by the relationship or deemed an offense. It is clear that when a medical perspective is available or some other technical "frame" such as that which a make-up man must employ, then touching can occur without its ritual implications holding sway. Interestingly, the same can be true with regard to traffic. A man passing to the inside of a female, between a wall and

---

[21] The structure of character contests is described in Goffman, *Interaction Ritual* (New York: Anchor Books, 1967), pp. 239–258.

[22] The nice statement concerning the flooring scan is Orwell's description of an Indian prisoner in Burma walking to his hanging, shackled between two guards, who sidesteps momentarily out of the path to avoid a small puddle. In this little act of dissociated, unforegone orientation, Orwell saw testimony that a fully qualified human life was about to be taken. In Orwell's seeing we are to see that step-monitoring is deeply enough a human act to serve as a brutal reminder of humanness. George Orwell, *Shooting an Elephant and Other Essays* (New York: Harcourt Brace Jovanovich, 1950; London: *Collected Essays*, Secker & Warburg, 1950), p. 15.

her person, can manage his passage by touching her arm or shoulder as though to minimize contact and collision. And the more closely she is accompanied by those who can openly claim her—such as children and husband—the more, it seems, he can be sure of the reading given his act and the more license he can take in regard to physical contact.

Just as there are acts that are permissible because they are associated with vehicular requirements, so there are acts that serve to divide the vehicular function from other ones. Given the requirements for conducting conversational encounters, we can expect that devices will be employed to accommodate these demands to bodies in motion. For example, when two individuals are talking to each other and a third races by to whom one of the talkers owes a few greeting comments, the engaged individual may hold the arm of his fellow participant while turning to address the person passing by. The arm hold serves, as it were, to hold the conversation, to fix it, out of real interaction time while the other work gets done. Similarly, a person walking down the aisle of a subway coach, accidentally stepping on the toe of a seated passenger, can maintain his rate of movement, turn his head back and hold out his arm and hand while he verbally excuses himself. The held-out hand, in effect, holds the offender in the remedial encounter even while his body is rapidly leaving it.

A final note about pedestrian traffic. City streets, even in times that defame them, provide a setting where mutual trust is routinely displayed between strangers. Voluntary coordination of action is achieved in which each of two parties has a conception of how matters ought to be handled between them, the two conceptions agree, each party believes this agreement exists, and each appreciates that this knowledge about the agreement is possessed by the other. In brief, the structural prerequisites for rule by convention are found.[23] Avoidance of collision is one example of the consequence.

---

[23] Usefully considered in David K. Lewis, *Convention: A Philosophical Study* (Cambridge, Mass.: Harvard University Press, 1969; London: Oxford

The basic prerequisites for rule by convention are assumed in Meadian social psychology but are never made quite explicit. Among trusting individuals, these assumptions can be fulfilled in various circumstances: open discussion at one extreme and blindly effected coordination—in the manner considered by Thomas Schelling—at the other. In pedestrian (and apparently automobile) traffic, trust can be treated as problematic and coordination seen to depend neither on discussion nor tacit communication. As the two parties approach each other, each provides progressive evidence to the other, a small step at a time, that each is adhering to a proper course and to the one he has been indicating. And since ordinarily the gain to be achieved here by inducing confusion or by outright trickery is not great, trust can be—and is—sustained.[24] Of course, the conditions that allow one to develop trust anew at each contact expose one at all times to sudden cause for doubt.

University Press, 1969). See also Thomas J. Scheff, "Toward a Sociological Model of Consensus," *American Sociological Review*, XXXII (1967): 32–46. Both Lewis and Scheff draw on Thomas C. Schelling's analysis of coordination of action through tacit communication, as in his *The Strategy of Conflict* (Cambridge, Mass.: Harvard University Press, 1960; London: Oxford University Press, 1960), pp. 89–118. I might add that the mutually held glance seems to provide a very special and very efficient means through which consensual coordination can be achieved. Apparently when one individual meets the eyes of another he can indicate a position, perceive the other's response to his taking this position, and show his own response to the other's response all in a brief moment. The two individuals are thus collapsed into interaction. It is understandable, then, that looking into the eyes of another is in many circumstances considered to be an incursion.

[24] The study of the social circumstances within which various public agreements, bargains, and conventions must be sustained—involving factors such as accountability, maneuverability, duration of contact, giving and withholding eye engagement, cost of alternative routes—has hardly begun. Here see a very suggestive paper by Thomas C. Schelling, "On the Ecology of Micromotives" (October 1970), forthcoming.

I might suggest one example. When two lines of same-direction traffic merge into each other and no clear right of way is present, a solution, formalized in some traffic codes, is for the lines to interweave, a car from each at a time, so no great advantage goes to either line; and this can be so seen by those in both lines. When two-way traffic must maneuver in one lane

III *Participation Units*

Individuals navigate streets and shops and attend social occasions either unaccompanied or in the social company of others, that is, they appear in public either in a "single" or in a "with." These are interactional units, not social-structural ones. They pertain entirely to the management of co-presence. I take them to be fundamental units of public life.

A single is a party of one, a person who has come alone, a person "by himself," even though there may be other individuals near him and he has cause for talking to them. A single, then, is an individual, but not all individuals are singles, those who are being active in a special capacity.

A with is a party of more than one whose members are perceived to be "together." They maintain some kind of ecological proximity, ensuring the closeness that ordinarily permits easy conversation and the exclusion of nonmembers who otherwise might intercept talk. At least one member, and usually all, has the right to initiate talk within the with at will. The conversation sustained by the members is available to all members but not necessarily joined by all members—indeed, two different conversations can be sustained by those in the same with. Members have the obligation to exhibit ritual concern when joining and withdrawing and can expect to be deferred to by outsiders who would make contact with one of the members. In contemporary practice, any set of in-

---

to pass a few feet of sudden narrowing, this, too, can often be handled by turn-taking. However, if a two-way, two-lane road becomes obstructed over a distance of several cars, then the first line of cars through the obstruction is likely to continue to pass through it for the simple reason that there is no way for the car behind the one that has just taken a turn to hold off and wait for one from the other line to pass. Line turn-taking would only be possible if each line stopped *before* the obstruction began and then took turns, but this would require a special signalling system. Thus, unintended unfairness results.

dividuals in a with are in a "personal" relationship to one another; however, this does not tell us anything specific about the character of the relationship.[25]

The family flock is an example of a with from the animal world. Note, just as some animal withs involve the trailing out of members in a kind of single file, so also in some cultures, such as middle-European Jewish, a family with in a public place will sometimes walk in partial file, or spaced abreast more than a foot apart, making talk a little difficult, except for the functional correlate that in this group private talk is sustained across relatively large distances. And in societies where females have low status, a woman may be obliged to walk a few steps behind her husband.[26]

In American society, most withs in streets and stores contain only two persons, although three-person and even four-person withs are found. On busy city streets large withs can disrupt pedestrian traffic and are often forced into temporary segmentation; in any case, when withs are on the move, any size above three persons restricts easy entrance into talk, since mutual orientation and orientation to the path become incompatible, and increasingly so with size.[27] (Understandably, cyclists who go riding together have a difficult time maintaining a with.)

A single is relatively vulnerable to contact, this being the grounds presumably why the ladies who inhabited traditional eti-

---

[25] Formal etiquette of a generation ago allowed for the possibility of a gentleman offering his arm to an unacquainted lady in contexts where it was felt to be undesirable for her to be unescorted, as when passing between her doorstep and a cab. The nicest handling of this courtesy allowed the lady to act as though no extension of her acquaintanceship circle had been made.

[26] See, for example, Harold B. Barclay, *Buurri al Lamaab* (Ithaca, N.Y.: Cornell University Press, 1964), p. 114. Hilary Callan has suggested that this sort of spacing between husband and wife in Arabic societies allows the male to make sociable contact with other males without the latter coming into untoward contact with his wife.

[27] In American cities, traffic requirements seem to take precedence over conversational ones. Thus at crosswalks and at elevator entrances, individuals involved in two-person conversation will often hold their talk in temporary abeyance as they orient fully to movement contingencies.

quette manuals did not appear in public unaccompanied; members of a with, after all, can count on some mutual protection. Withs, especially all male ones, have considerable choice in where they sit; singles have less, since they must be alive to the invitation or to the overture their positioning might seem to be making.[28] So, too, a member of a with is freer to approach a stranger in order to obtain or offer help than is a single. Withs might be approached more safely also, except that more than one person's time will have to be taken; further, a natural ambiguity may be generated as to which member of the with is to answer, and an undesired show of dominance when one does answer. Singles suffer a further vulnerability: those who behave in a prankish or questionable manner are judged more harshly than are members of a with. Apparently if others seem willing to accompany one and are relatively at ease in this participation, then it is taken that one's antics cannot be a sign of extreme aberrancy. Singles, in consequence, more than those who are accompanied, make an effort to externalize a legitimate purpose and character, that is, render proper facts about themselves easily readable through what can be gleaned by looking at them.

The usual informational contingencies of one's participation unit are well known. To attend alone is to expose oneself as possibly not being able to muster up companionship, but conceals who it would be were one to be accompanied. To participate in a with saves one from being seen as unaccompanied, but exposes one to being judged according to one's companions.

It should be borne in mind that—at one level at least—social settings and social occasions are not organized in terms of individuals but in terms of participation units. Some places disallow unaccompanied guests but welcome the same persons when accompanied; and other places (albeit not many) enforce the reverse. Some dances welcome cross-sexed withs and disallow same-sexed withs. There are bars that exclude solitary women and all-female withs but welcome females in cross-sexed withs.[29] There are

---

[28] Lofland, *op. cit.*, p. 139.

[29] A fact complained of by supporters of female rights. (See, for example, Deborah Harkins, "The City Politic: Sex and the City Council," *New*

streets that disallow adolescent singles during certain hours but permit these unfortunates to be there accompanied by adults; and, as suggested, there are times and places where females find it is not respectable (and certainly not advantageous) to be present as a single.[30] However, since it is often the case that an individual is qualified to participate in either unit, that is, in a single or in a with, we often neglect to appreciate that rules at two different levels are involved, one regarding allowable units and a second regarding who is allowed in the unit.

It seems characteristic of users of a street that ordinarily they get to it, move on it, and leave it without changing their participation unit, excepting only that the unit may form and disband at planned junctures requiring some participation as a single. It is the same with ballroom dancing and theater-going, although in the latter case, seating arrangements tend to process entering withs so that at first glance the hall seems to be filled with seated singles. In many other gatherings, this continuity is not found. By and large, social parties are entered in withs and left in the same ones, but during participation itself, it will be expected that withs will give way to the special participation unit of ongoing sociable occasions, namely, shifting conversational clusters—except at certain junc-

---

York Magazine, April 27, 1970, pp. 10–11.) An argument of management is that to allow women in bars and restaurants unaccompanied by men is to encourage use of the bar as a place of assignation, leading eventually to unsuitable patronage. There is a structural point behind this concern. Since, by conventional standards, women in both their all forms (singles and withs) constitute—especially during the evening—an incomplete participation unit, males are naturally encouraged to perceive the need and to attempt to satisfy it, thereby releasing a flood of gallantry out of keeping with some establishments. Interestingly, in natural language the term "unaccompanied female" is sometimes applied to a woman who enters in the company of other women, a literal error but unambiguous because structurally correct.

30 Indeed, it has been recommended that female spies, especially pretty ones, are occupationally disadvantaged by virtue of being conspicuous when appearing alone in a range of doubtful place. See Oreste Pinto, *Spy Catcher* (New York: Berkeley Publishing Company, 1952; London: Hadder & Stoughton, Omnibus edn., 1962), p. 21.

tures. Note that when one member of a two-person with leaves his partner temporarily to telephone, or to go to the bathroom, or to talk to someone across the room, this may leave the latter looking like a single. But this appearance is correctable; every overture can be answered with a "I'm with someone," and body stance can underscore one's holding oneself in abeyance. Thus, as we might expect, persons alone who do not want to be seen to be a single may give silent and spoken evidence of waiting for an immanent arrival, just as, incidentally, those in an unfavoring with can attempt to conceal their acute discomfort in having to be in it.[31]

There are, of course, social occasions where encouragement is given to changing one's participation status: singles can team up or

---

[31] The full treatment of this latter issue is provided in a military novel by Andrew Sinclair. The occasion is a dance during the London Season in the post-World War II years. I cite Sinclair's description at length:

> The most miserable of all there were those female duets or trios of ugly sweet-seventeens, who stood talking brightly to each other, desperately not noticing that they were not being noticed. Every dance of the sixty in the Season was torture to them; convention demanded that they could not take their lonely taxi home until at least one o'clock in the morning; and, to justify all the expense, they had to appear to be happy, although Bumbo thought that their parents should be prosecuted by the R.S.P.C.A. for deliberate and protracted cruelty to pets. Meanwhile, they stood, in their giggles and gaggles, with their chaste cheeks behind and before tight with the effort of not seeming abandoned. Their eyes, seeking rescue, seeking any old family joke so long as he wore trousers, twitched ceaselessly away from each other round the noisy room, while their lips continued to open and shut, as they let out the conventional adjectives of enjoyment. If a wandering male, met once six months ago, came within five yards of a deserted group, he would be hailed by the castaways as though he were the Admiral of the Home Fleet; if he was green to the game, or moved by compassion, they would suck him into the puddle of their gossip, until he felt a moral obligation to save one of the girls by asking her to dance, anything for partial escape. If, however, he was an old hand at the game, and beyond pity, he would drop his excuses in their laps like a visiting-card, promising to come back later, after a brief call on a waiting partner, a long-unseen friend, or the cloakroom. Bumbo usually carried two full drink-glasses in his hand, so that his excuse for passing on, that he was taking some champagne to another girl, always seemed reasonable. Anyway, he could drink twice as much. But once, caught without glasses, he had had to plead claustrophobia; the girls had offered to accompany him outside to the fresh air; eventually, Bumbo had gone back to the Barracks early in full retreat, although he had been enjoying himself and had wanted to stay.

The Breaking of Bumbo (London: Penguin Books, 1961), pp. 59–60.

join a with, and withs can merge, but this possibility seems to be peculiar enough to determine the characterization given these settings.[32] There are also social occasions where temporary withs are fostered, giving rise, incidentally, to a standard "closing-out" problem.[33] By and large, however, it is socially noteworthy when someone who had come to a party accompanied leaves alone or "with someone different."

---

[32] Recently "singles bars" have sprung up, especially in New York, but while these purport to legitimate pickups (as indeed do a set of bars in San Francisco), individuals nonetheless tend to enter in withs, often single-sexed ones, presumably as a protection against undesired or interminable overtures and being seen as seeking.

[33] Seatmates on an extended airline flight are free to transform incidental conversation into a with, but once this is done, deplaning will require the closing out of the with, yet not provide an easy occasion for doing so; between exit from the plane and entrance to the area where greeters can wait, an indelicate, extended "thinning out" of the with may be attempted so that nothing remains of it by the time awaited loved-ones come into view and take over. Similarly, during dances of the ballroom variety, a dancing couple constitutes a with, and the object of participants will be to manage not only conversation—which, after all, can be allowed to lapse occasionally—but also the closing out of the with when the dance or series of dances is over, and yet produce neither a sense of rejection nor the sense of being "stuck." (Incidentally, dancing is a complex matter in these respects. A woman who has granted a request for a dance, or has allowed her escort to do so, becomes with the grantee a with until he thanks her and returns her to her post. But this dancers' with begins at least a little before the dancing proper does and lasts at least a little longer than the music does. The actual dancing itself has its own ritual brackets enclosed within the ones that mark the beginning and ending of the with. Thus, the flourish of the ending step or the clapping of hands can mark the termination of the particular dance but not the with containing the dancers. The dancing itself has some conversation-like properties, so that we might want to consider it a non-spoken engagement or encounter but one that is not so demanding as to disallow conversational side-involvements by the dancers on matters irrelevant to the dance—a right of dissociation from the current task not usually permitted, for example, in the conversation-like activity of sexual intercourse. Note, the current dancing practice, much bewailed, of no physical contact or close integration of steps during dancing merely undercuts the encounter-like character of the dancing; it does not affect the holding power or sentimental value of the with sustained—as of old—by the dancers.)

It is useful to look at the relation between withs and conversational encounters.[34] As suggested, members of a with—at least in our society—may unceremoniously take up and leave off talking together. Cross-talk—a conversation or conversation-like activity maintained by persons who differentially share other interaction capacities—is also possible where one member of a with momentarily sustains exclusive talk with someone who is not in the with.[35] And, of course, talk is possible between persons who are

---

[34] Perhaps a review might be in order concerning encounters, that is, states of talk, and the gatherings in which they occur. Three people alone in one room or alone together on the street are capable of the basic communication alignments in social situations, that is, the basic arrangements in regard to ratified communication that can be sustained among persons present.

The three can be said to be co-present in a social situation and to comprise a gathering. Here the following possibilities arise.

First, no encounter or face-engagement may be present, the interaction being restricted to the unfocused kind, even though the participants may be bunched into physical touch of one another. (The possibility of nonengagement is independent of whether or not two or all are in a with.) Secondly, it is possible for all three to be in the same encounter, thereby constituting a conversational circle that exhausts the gathering. Thirdly, two of the three may be joined together in a state of talk while the third is a bystander, his presence rendering the encounter an accessible one.

These three possibilities represent the first order of analysis. A second order pertains to collusive communication, namely conversation or conversation-like gestures that are not ratified as an official basis of action. Here there are two basic alignments. First, in a three-person encounter, two participants can engage in collusive byplay, the third participant being excluded. Second, in a two-person encounter, one participant can engage in collusive signs with the bystander, the second participant being excluded. (It is technically possible for one participant in an encounter to sustain two different collusive nets simultaneously, but this perversity seems quite uncommon.)

A third order of analysis pertains to spontaneous involvement. Participants in conversation may enact involvement in it while their prime concern is the bystander; in brief, they can posture an encounter. And a bystander may convey disinterest through civil inattention while all along he is following the talk and suppressing orientation to the speakers.

[35] At such moments, as suggested, the defecting member may attempt to stabilize the with by a holding gesture of some kind, as though to make sure that the other members will not get away. A very pretty example of

not in a with at all, as happens, for example, when one asks a stranger for directions, or maintains a desultory "subordinated" talk with those one is working alongside of, or joins a conversational cluster at a party.[36] Talk in the form of salutations, it may be noted, has special functions for a with, usually marking its formation and termination and the arrival and departure of a member.

Just as the relation between withs and encounters can be considered, so can the relation between singles and encounters, except that this is a topic which has received considerable comment in those etiquette manuals and advice columns that serve to save our polite classes from a fate worse than isolation. The general rule in middle-class society certainly seems to be that unacquainted persons should not strike up talk in public places lest the lesser be deemed forward and the better loose; however, the circumstances that neutralize this reason, and hence this taboo, can be found easily in a natural state and manufactured easily by man. So the fundamental arrangement in public life is that singles and withs are to be treated as though sealed off from their setting, and at the same time the understanding is maintained that these barriers can be breached for good and bad reasons, exposing those in the setting to one another's conversation.[37]

---

this is described by Ray Birdwhistell, namely, the lower limb shift, whereby a member of a two-person with about to engage in cross-talk with a third party shifts his upper trunk to the outsider, thereby providing that encounter with the orientation due it, even while he shifts his lower limbs so that they will be closer to and parallel with those of the other member of the with. A similar transfix (to use Birdwhistell's term) occurs when orientation to the cross-talk is compensated for by the defector shifting his arm or hand so as to more firmly and markedly embrace the other member of the with.

[36] In an unpublished paper on Philadelphia's Skid Row, James F. Rooney suggests that although blacks and whites talk to each other and eat alongside each other in the local cafeteria, still, except for bottle gangs, cross-color withs do not form. ("Negro-White Relations on Skid Row," p. 8.)

[37] Obviously there are great cross-cultural differences here. The French seem much more prone than the British to engage in cross-talk, the breaching of conventional closure seeming in France—especially the south of France—to be more the rule than the exception. A very nice statement

Participation units—singles and withs—tell us about the individual's condition as he moves about during the day. Participation units thus link up directly to three other concepts: the daily round, the service stop, and the expedition, this last involving a non-routine, one-shot foray, typically requiring at least a few hours and the wending of one's way to and back from a place of consummatory experience. It is against the background of an individual's daily round that we can plot the course of the single or with which contains him and the junctures where his participation status changes.

IV *Conclusions*

In this brief statement I have touched on the individual as a vehicular unit and as a participation unit, and by way of contrast have incidentally introduced two other capacities in which the individual may be active: co-participant in an encounter and someone reckoned simply as present in a setting or a social occasion. As suggested, in rough observation and analysis, it is probably enough to conceive of these distinctions—when indeed they are conceived of—as pertaining merely to different roles in which the individual is active. In fine-grain analysis, however, it may be that the notion of the individual as such will prove too imprecise, and instead a need will appear to use a variety of technically defined terms. Thus, if we look closely at the concept of territoriality, especially the "egocentric" forms, the notion of the individual ceases to have an analytically coherent, single meaning, and several different terms have to be employed in its stead.

---

of the circumstances for breaching conversational barriers, and the consequence thereof, is available in an early story by a considerable student of face-to-face interaction, Mary McCarthy, "The Company Is Not Responsible," *The New Yorker*, April 22, 1944, pp. 77–80.

[2]

The Territories of the Self

I *Preserves*

At the center of social organization is the concept of claims, and around this center, properly, the student must consider the vicissitudes of maintaining them.

To speak closely of these matters, a set of related terms is needed. There is the "good," the desired object or state that is in question; the "claim," namely, entitlement to possess, control, use, or dispose of the good; the "claimant," that is, the party on whose behalf the claim is made; the "impediment," meaning here the act, substance, means, or agency through which the claim is threatened; the "author" (or "counter-claimant"), namely, the party—when there is one—on whose behalf the threat to claims is intended; and finally, the "agents," these being the individuals who act for and represent the claimant and counter-claimant in these matters involving claims.

When we restrict our attention to activity that can only occur during face-to-face interaction, the claimant tends to be an individual (or a small set of individuals) and to function as his own agent. The same can be said of the counter-claimant, but in addition the impediment that occurs in his name is likely to involve his own activity or body. Therefore, conventional terms such as "victim" and "offender" will often be adequate. And one type of claim becomes crucial: it is a claim exerted in regard to "territory." This concept from ethology seems apt, because the claim is not so much to a discrete and particular matter but rather to a field of things —to a preserve—and because the boundaries of the field are ordinarily patrolled and defended by the claimant.

Territories vary in terms of their organization. Some are "fixed"; they are staked out geographically and attached to one claimant, his claim being supported often by the law and its courts. Fields, yards, and houses are examples. Some are "situational"; they are part of the fixed equipment in the setting (whether publicly or privately owned), but are made available to the populace in the form of claimed goods while-in-use. Temporary tenancy is perceived to be involved, measured in seconds, minutes, or hours, informally exerted, raising constant questions as to when the claim begins and when it terminates. Park benches and restaurant tables are examples. Finally, there are "egocentric" preserves which move around with the claimant, he being in the center. They are typically (but not necessarily) claimed long term. Purses are an example. This threefold division is, of course, only valid in degree. A hotel room is a situational claim, yet it can function much like a house, a fixed territory. And, of course, houses in the form of trailers can move around.

The prototypical preserve is no doubt spatial and perhaps even fixed. However, to facilitate the study of co-mingling—at least in American society—it is useful to extend the notion of territoriality into claims that function like territories but are not spatial, and it is useful to focus on situational and egocentric territoriality. Starting, then, with the spatial, we shall move by steps to matters that are not.

1. *Personal Space:* The space surrounding an individual, anywhere within which an entering other causes the individual to feel encroached upon, leading him to show displeasure and sometimes

to withdraw.[1] A contour, not a sphere, is involved, the spatial demands directly in front of the face being larger than at back.[2] The fixed layout of seats and other interior equipment may restrictively structure available space around the individual in one dimension, as occurs in line or column organization. When two individuals are alone in a setting, then concern about personal space takes the form of concern over straight-line distance.

Given that individuals can be relied upon to keep away from situations in which they might be contaminated by another or contaminate him, it follows that they can be controlled by him if he is willing to use himself calculatedly to constitute that object that the others will attempt to avoid, and in avoiding, move in a direction desired by him.[3] For example, we read of the engaging action of a pickpocket "stall" who uses his body to "pratt in" a mark, that is to cause the mark to hold himself away from a body that is pressing on him, and incidentally hold himself in a position from which his wallet can be reached; similarly we read of the "pratting out"

---

[1] Sociological versions of this territory of the self are provided by Robert Sommer, "Studies in Personal Space," *Sociometry*, XXII (September 1959): 247–260, and Kenneth B. Little, "Personal Space," *Journal of Experimental Social Psychology*, I (August 1965): 237–247. An ethological source is H. Hediger, *Studies of the Psychology and Behaviour of Captive Animals in Zoos and Circuses* (London: Butterworths Scientific Publications, 1955). A precursive statement is the 1936 paper by Kurt Lewin, "Some Social-Psychological Differences between the United States and Germany," in his *Resolving Social Conflicts* (New York: Harper & Row, Publishers, 1948), pp. 3–33.

[2] This is nicely illustrated in Eastern seaboard parlor cars designed with a wide, longitudinal aisle and single seats at intervals on either side, the seats arranged to swivel. When there is crowding, travelers maximize their "comfort" by turning their seats to exactly that direction that will allow the eyes, when oriented in the direction of the trunk, to gaze upon the least amount of passenger flesh. Standing passengers may crowd right up against the seats but in doing so will find themselves ringed in by two rows of backs. In ordinary railway or bus seating in America, passengers who feel overcrowded may be able to send their eyes out the window, thereby vicariously extending their personal space.

[3] This argument derives from H. Hediger's well-known discussion of "flight distance" and "escape distance" and its bearing on lion taming. See his *Studies of the Psychology and Behaviour of Captive Animals in Zoos and Circuses*, *op. cit.*, pp. 40, 123.

of one bystander whose position prevents theft from another.[4]

It is a central feature of personal space that legitimate claim to it varies greatly according to the accountings available in the setting and that the bases for these will change continuously. Such factors as local population density, purpose of the approacher, fixed seating equipment, character of the social occasion, and so forth, can all influence radically from moment to moment what it is that is seen as an offense. Indeed, in human studies it is often best to consider personal space not as a permanently possessed, egocentric claim but as a temporary, situational preserve into whose center the individual moves.

Take, for example, the social organization of co-waiting. Obviously, to stand or sit next to a stranger when the setting is all but empty is more of an intrusion than the same act would be when the place is packed and all can see that only this niche remains. In theory we might expect also a continuous process of adjustment whereby each arrival and each departure causes alterations throughout.[5] What seems to occur in middle-class society is that arrival creates sequential reallocation but departure leads to somewhat more complex behavior, since an individual who leaves his current niche to take up a freed one produces an open sign that he is disinclined to be as close to his neighbor as he was. (When the two are of opposite sex, there exists the added complication that failure to move away when possible can be taken as a sign of undue interest.) In consequence, a departure may leave an empty place and no change in the remaining allocation, or at least an appropriator may wait for some tactful moment before making use of the newly available resource. In brief, moving in on someone or having oneself moved in on is a less delicate task than removing oneself from proximity to him. In consequence, as say a streetcar empties, there will be a period when two individuals signal by

[4] David W. Maurer, *Whiz Mob* (Publications of the American Dialect Society, No. 24, Gainesville, Florida, 1955), pp. 62–65.

[5] See J. H. Crook, "The Basis of Flock Organization in Birds," and his discussion of arrival distance, settled distance and distance after departure, in W. H. Thorpe and O. L. Zangwill, eds., *Current Problems in Animal Behaviour* (Cambridge: Cambridge University Press, 1961), pp. 140 ff.

proximity a relationship that does not in fact exist.

All of this may be seen in miniature in elevator behavior. Passengers have two problems: to allocate the space equably, and to maintain a defensible position, which in this context means orientation to the door and center with the back up against the wall if possible.[6] The first few individuals can enter without anyone present having to rearrange himself, but very shortly each new entrant—up to a certain number—causes all those present to shift position and reorient themselves in sequence. Leave-taking introduces a tendency to reverse the cycle, but this is tempered by the countervailing resistance to appearing uncomfortable in an established distance from another. Thus, as the car empties, passengers acquire a measure of uneasiness, caught between two opposing inclinations—to obtain maximum distance from others and to inhibit avoidance behavior that might give offense.

2. *The Stall:* The well-bounded space to which individuals can lay temporary claim, possession being on an all-or-none basis.[7] A

---

[6] There are other general features of body behavior in elevators. In a useful unpublished paper ("Behavior in Elevators," 1965), John Gueldner suggests that the general practice is for male riders to be somewhat at attention, with hands to the side and no side involvements, with an equivalent posture for women—as if all activity had halted while individuals were in transit. Gueldner suggests that the seeking of a defensible niche establishes standard priorities: first entrant takes up the corner near the controls or one of the rear corners; the next entrant is likely to take up the corner diagonally across from the taken one. The third and fourth passengers take up the remaining corners, the fifth the middle of the rear wall, the sixth the center of the car. Members of withs, however, tend to stay together, retaining an ecological expression of their status even though eyes are front. Gueldner also suggests that there is a point of crowding when effort to maintain space is rather suddenly given up and something approaching indiscriminate packing occurs.

[7] The term has been used by ethologists who study the daily round of the domestic cow. Note, stalls are to the underlife of bounded regions what personal, fixed territories are to the underlife of local communities. Thus public telephone booths in hotels like the New York Statler-Hilton are sometimes used by ambulatory schizophrenics as places to sit, rest the burden of their all-purpose shopping bag, and have a nice long hallucinatory talk at the world through the open booth door.

scarce good will often be involved, such as a comfortable chair, a table with a view, an empty cot, a telephone booth. In the main, stalls are fixed in the setting, although, for example, at beaches devices such as large towels and mats can be carried along with the claimant and unrolled when convenient, thus providing a portable stall. When seats are built in rows and divided by common armrests (as in theaters), then personal space and stall have the same boundaries. When there is space between seats, then personal space is likely to extend beyond the stall. And, of course, there are stalls such as boxes at the opera which allocate several seats to the exclusive use (on any one social occasion) of a single "party." The availability of stalls in a setting articulates and stabilizes claims to space, sometimes providing more than would have been claimed as personal space, sometimes less—as can be seen, for example, in regard to seats when a class of six-year-olds attends an adult theater or when parents have a meeting in an elementary school room.

It should be noted that a stall can be left temporarily while the leave-taker is sustained in a continuing claim upon it; personal space cannot.[8] Furthermore, often the claimant to a stall will not be an individual but two or more of them who properly share it, as illustrated nicely in public tennis courts and commercial bowling alleys, these being designed to provide a large, well-equipped stall to parties of players for stipulated periods of time. (In our society the most common multi-person stall is the table, there being relatively few too small for more than one person or too large to be claimed by a party of only two.) Personal space, on the other hand, is largely a one-person possession, although in crowded places, such as packed elevators, a small child grasped to a parent

[8] In gentlemen's clubs, mental hospitals, old folks' homes, and domestic living rooms, proprietary claims tend to grow up around chairs and other stalls so that although these start out as part of situationally provided territories available on a first-come basis for any continuous period of use, they soon take on the character of fixed territories possessed by one individual whether or not he is present to claim by use. See Michael A. Woodbury, "Ward Dynamics and the Formation of a Therapeutic Group," *Chestnut Lodge Symposium*, Rockville, Maryland, mimeo (1958), and Alan Lipman, "Chairs as Territory," *New Society*, XX (April 1967): 564–566. Reading carrals in university libraries suffer the same transitional status.

may be treated as part of the latter's personal space, and couples engaged in affectional entwinings may also be treated as claiming a single personal space.

The point about stalls, as suggested, is that they provide external, easily visible, defendable boundaries for a spatial claim. Stalls provide a contrast in this regard to personal space, the latter having ever-shifting dimensions. This points up a problem in the organization of American public places. Here, for practical considerations, equipment such as picnic tables or park benches is often built to a size to suggest that each can be claimed as a stall by a participation unit, a "single" or a "with." However, when crowding is such that this allocation would leave some individuals standing, then a rule is understood to apply that gives unaccommodated participation units the right to enforce a fictional division of a stall into two (and occasionally more than two) stalls. Obviously, then, as crowding increases, those already ensconced will begin to have to give up exclusive claim to a stall. An ambiguity results, because there is no well-established principle to order the sequence in which various claimants, already ensconced, will be obliged to give up their exclusiveness. A field is thus opened for personal enterprise. Hence, on buses, streetcars, and trains, seats designed to hold two persons, and fully recognized to be designed to accommodate two strangers when necessary, nonetheless establish for the first arrival a territory he may attempt to retain for himself by standard ruses: he may leave his own possessions on the empty place, thereby marking it for his own and obliging competitors to move (or ask to have moved) something that symbolizes another; he may deny his eyes to those seeking a seat, thereby preventing them from obtaining the fleeting permission that they tend to seek, failure to receive which can cause them to move on to the next available place; he may expose some contaminating part of himself, such as his feet, or allow part of his body to fall on the disputed place, so that those who would use the place must invite contamination; and so forth.

3. *Use Space:* The territory immediately around or in front of an individual, his claim to which is respected because of apparent

instrumental needs. For example, a gallery goer can expect that when he is close to a picture, other patrons will make some effort to walk around his line of vision or excuse or minimize their momentarily blocking it. Persons holding a conversation over a distance can expect a similar accommodation from non-participants whose bodies might block the giving and receiving of conversation management cues. Sportsmen of all kind expect some consideration will be given to the amount of elbow room they require in order to manipulate their equipment, as do convicts using pickaxes to break stone. Gymnasts using a vaulting horse expect that others will "stay out of their way." A crewman obliged to scrub and polish a designated portion of the surface of his warship expects, especially on the day before weekly inspection, to be able to keep everyone away during and right after the cleaning.[9] Note that circumstances can allow the individual to offer instrumental grounds for demanding limits on the level of noise and sound, especially when the source is physically close by.

4. *The Turn:* The order in which a claimant receives a good of some kind relative to other claimants in the situation. A decision-rule is involved, ordering participants categorically ("women and children first," or "whites before blacks"), or individually ("smallest first, then next smallest"), or some mixture of both.[10] Typically

---

[9] See Philip D. Roos, "Jurisdiction: An Ecological Concept," *Human Relations*, XXI (1968): 75–84. Roos provides a case history argument for making a sharper distinction than I have done between territoriality, involving exclusion and possession, and "jurisdiction," involving only exclusion.

[10] Upon fuller consideration, we are likely to find that the means employed to manage the allocation of a minor good (such as a turn) involve more than one rule. And rules about rules may develop to cover standard problems, determining what should be done when no rule seems to apply, or when one that should apply cannot, or when mutually incompatible rules apply. One rule may be defined as overruling another on all occasions when they both apply, or each may be accorded a sphere where it overrides the other. One rule may serve to rank categories of persons and another to rank members within a category thusly ranked. Note, individuals often identify a social order by a well-known rule that figures in it, but the viability of this rule is often dependent on a complex of associated rules

claimants are required to have been present in order to establish their claim on a turn, but once this has been done and marked in some way, they may be allowed to absent themselves until their turn comes up. In our Western society, perhaps the most important principle in turn organization is "first come, first served," establishing the claim of an individual to come right after the person "ahead" and right before the person "behind."[11] This decision rule creates a dominance ranking but a paradoxical one, since all other forms of preference are thereby excluded.[12]

Turn-taking requires not only an ordering rule but a claiming mechanism as well. This may be formal, for example, number-tickets, names on a receptionist's list, or informal, as when the individual remains close to the place of service and assumes that a tacit

---

covering the natural range of contingencies. The longer and the more widely a given rule is in force, the more developed, presumably, is the complex of rules that buttresses it.

[11] In many cases, a claimant is allowed at will to let the party behind go ahead of him; he may even be allowed to pick any place lower down in the line, presumably on the assumption that those behind his original place and above the place he picks will have gained a turn and those below this point will have lost nothing. And in all cases, the claimant apparently can give up his turn entirely. In brief, turn as here defined is a right but not a duty. This raises the issue of "negative queues," namely, an ordering of persons who are to receive something they do not want, such as a place in a gas chamber. (Similarly, some prisons have seats that cannot be given up for a lady.) A dialectical way of assimilating such organization to the notion of preserves is to describe the good that is involved as a claim to postponement. Naturally, here one would be allowed to take any turn ahead of one's position but disallowed from stepping behind or giving up entirely one's position.

[12] It might be said—with apologies to Simmel—that it is the essential character of everyday turn-taking to be a middle ground, the claims of property and contract being held in check at one end, the claims of social rank at the other. To take one's turn is neither to take one's property nor to take one's social place. Utilitarian goods are involved, but typically ones so minor that it would have been easy to put their allocation into the service of ceremonial expression. Whereas ceremonial expression provides bodily expression of social position when things go right, turns in daily life do so only when things go wrong.

consensus will operate. Sometimes a line or row formation (a queue) will be employed as a collective, mnemonic device, and sometimes this formal device allows the participant to sustain a formally unmarked turn during brief absences.[13] Many queues qualify a with as a claimant, especially where one member can transact all of its business (as in movie queues), and this often leads to permission to join an acquaintance ahead of where one otherwise would have been, since in these cases a single already established in line will be able to act as though he is merely the agent

---

[13] A useful paper on turn-taking in one type of extremity is Leon Mann, "Queue Culture: The Waiting Line as a Social System," *American Journal of Sociology*, LXXV (November 1969): 340–354. Some turn-taking merely involves a decision between two users as to which will use a road or walk first, but in most cases, it appears clear that a service of some kind is the good that must be allocated. Service systems are one of the fundamental organizational devices of public order, and their close study has hardly begun. The complete paradigm involves at least five roles: supervisor, server, served, next-up, member of the line. There are, of course, automated systems without supervisors and servers, and many systems which frequently have neither next-up nor member of the line. A service system is the collective form of which the individual's part is the service stop, this involving one complete cycle whereby a participation unit (a with or a single) moves off from some base of operation, seeks out and obtains some service, and then returns to the base.

It might be added that many services are provided in such a manner that an encounter, a ritually ratified face-to-face contact, occurs only if something out of the ordinary happens and must be managed, providing us with a clear case where server and served can be in contact but not in conversational touch. (Indeed, the server need not even look at the served, but only at, say, the article chosen for purchase, the customer's money, and perhaps his hand.) This sort of deritualization of transactions is sometimes cited as a mark of incivility and urban impersonality, an allegation that is half true and half nonsense. A great deal of consensus and mutual understanding is required to support service transactions executed without the help of social ritual. In some shops a year or so of patronage is required before patron and server know each knows that talk and eye contact can be dispensed with and actions allowed to do all the speaking. (Of course in other service settings, such as better-cashier dealings at race tracks, newcomers quickly learn to sustain "blind" transactions.) On the prevalence of deritualized service transactions, I am indebted to a useful paper by Marilyn Merritt, "On the Service Encounter," unpublished (1968).

for a with that is just now fully arrived. I want only to add that when turns are held by bodies standing in single file, then each participant will be involved both in maintaining his turn and his personal space. However, since the taking of turns provides a clear reading of events, great reductions of personal space can be tolerated along with attendant bodily contact.

5. *The Sheath:* The skin that covers the body and, at a little remove, the clothes that cover the skin. Certainly the body's sheath can function as the least of all possible personal spaces, the minimal configuration in that regard; but it can also function as a preserve in its own right, the purest kind of egocentric territoriality. Of course, different parts of the body are accorded different concern —indeed this differential concern tells us in part how the body will be divided up into segments conceptually. Among the American middle classes, for example, little effort is made to keep the elbow inviolate, whereas orifice areas are of concern. And, of course, across different cultures, the body will be differently segmented ritually.

6. *Possessional Territory:* Any set of objects that can be identified with the self and arrayed around the body wherever it is. The central examples are spoken of as "personal effects"—easily detachable possessions such as jackets, hats, gloves, cigarette packs, matches, handbags and what they contain, and parcels.[14] We must also include a claimant's co-present dependents because, territorially, they function somewhat like his personal possessions. Finally, there are objects that remain tethered to a particular setting but can be temporarily claimed by persons present, much as can stalls: ashtrays, magazines, cushions, and eating utensils are examples. One might also include here regulative command over mechanical creature-comfort devices: control over radio, television sets, temperature, windows, light, and so forth.

7. *Information Preserve:* The set of facts about himself to which

---

[14] In the matter of territoriality, a distinction in law has some relevance. The issue is that of possession, not ownership; the exertion of current, not ultimate control. See also Roos, *op. cit.*

an individual expects to control access while in the presence of others.[15] There are several varieties of information preserve, and there is some question about classing them all together. There is the content of the claimant's mind, control over which is threatened when queries are made that he sees as intrusive, nosy, untactful. There are the contents of pockets, purses, containers, letters, and the like, which the claimant can feel others have no right to ascertain. There are biographical facts about the individual over the divulgence of which he expects to maintain control. And most important for our purposes, there is what can be directly perceived about an individual, his body's sheath and his current behavior, the issue here being his right not to be stared at or examined.[16] Of course, since the individual is also a vehicular unit and since pilots of other such units have a need and a right to track him, he will come to be able to make an exquisite perceptual distinction between being looked at and being stared at, and, God

---

[15] Traditionally treated under the heading of "privacy." See the current review by Alan F. Westin in *Privacy and Freedom* (New York: Atheneum, 1967). See also Oscar M. Ruebhausen and Orville G. Brim, Jr., "Privacy and Behavioral Research," *Columbia Law Review*, LXV (November 1965): 1184–1211.

[16] No doubt there is a link here between having the body touched and having it seen, as in the biblical sense of "knowing" someone or the legal sense of having carnal knowledge. This is not the only ambiguity. Name, both Christian and family, can function like a bit of discretionary information whose divulgence one would like to be able to control but cannot always do so. Here see, for example, A. C. Reich, "Police Questioning of Law-Abiding Citizens," *Yale Law Journal*, LXXV, no. 7 (1966). Name can also function as a self-identified personal possession whose use by others the individual may be prepared to license providing they stand in the right relationship to him. In this regard, note the situation of the English better classes at the turn of the century as described by Harold Nicolson, *Good Behaviour* (London: Constable and Company, 1955), p. 272:

> In my own youth, had I been addressed by my Christian name at my private or even my public school, I should have blushed scarlet, feeling that my privacy had been outraged and that some secret manliness had been purloined from me, as if I had been an Andaman Islander or a Masai.

In general, there is the fact that concern for preserves such as the spatial can be partly based indirectly on a concern for information preserves, the former supporting the latter.

help us, learn to suspect, if not detect, that the latter is being masked by the former; and he will learn to conduct himself so that others come to respond to him in the same way. Incidentally, wherever we find such fine behavioral discriminations, we should suspect that what is at work is the need to keep two different behavioral systems functioning without interference in the same physical area.

8. *Conversational Preserve:* The right of an individual to exert some control over who can summon him into talk and when he can be summoned; and the right of a set of individuals once engaged in talk to have their circle protected from entrance and overhearing by others.

I have touched on eight territories of the self, all of a situational or an egocentric kind: personal space, stalls, use space, turns, sheath, possessional territory, information preserve, and conversational preserve. One general feature of these several forms of territoriality should be noted: their socially determined variability. Given a particular setting and what is available in it, the extensivity of preserves obviously can vary greatly according to power and rank. Patients in a charity hospital may have to wait until dying before being given a privacy screen around their bed; in middle-class private hospitals, the patient may enjoy this privilege at other times, too, for example, when breast feeding a child.[17] Similarly, clinic patients in a hospital may be discussed by physicians by name, while private patients in the same hospital are given the privacy rights of being referred to by room number.[18] In general, the higher the rank, the greater the size of all territories of the

---

[17] David Sudnow, *Passing On* (Englewood Cliffs, N.J.: Prentice-Hall, Inc., 1966). W. Rosengren and S. DeVault report that clinic patients in a studied hospital were obliged to accept having the delivery door open; private patients, however, frequently enjoyed the privacy of a closed door. See W. Rosengren and S. DeVault, "The Sociology of Time and Space in an Obstetrical Hospital," in Eliot Freidson, ed., *The Hospital in Modern Society* (New York: The Free Press, 1965), p. 278.

[18] W. Rosengren and S. DeVault, *op. cit.*, p. 280.

self and the greater the control across the boundaries. (Within a given household, for example, adults tend to have vastly larger territorial claims than do children.) Cutting across these differences, however, there is another—the variation that occurs in the understandings sustained by any one set of individuals as they move from situation to situation. For example, middle-class Americans at Western ski lodges allow their bodies to be stared at and touched-in-passing to a degree that would be considered quite intrusive were this to occur in the public places of their home town.[19] Finally, there are group-cultural differences that crosscut these cross cuttings. For example, there is some evidence that lower-class blacks are more concerned to obtain eyeing avoidance than are lower-class Italians.[20]

II *Markers*

The claim to a preserve by a putative possessor is made visible by a sign of some kind, which, following ethological practice, may be called a "marker." [21]

Markers are of various kinds. There are "central markers," being objects that announce a territorial claim, the territory radiating outward from it, as when sunglasses and lotion claim a beach chair, or a purse a seat in an airliner, or a drink on the bar the

---

[19] Similarly ski lodges tend to allow more license with respect to the initiation of encounters among the unacquainted than is the case in business settings. Here I am indebted to an unpublished paper, "Ski Resort Behavior Patterns" (1965), by Beatrice Farrar.

[20] Gerald D. Suttles, *The Social Order of the Slum* (Chicago: The University of Chicago Press, 1968), p. 67.

[21] An early sociological use in print of this term is Robert Sommer, "Sociofugal Space," *American Journal of Sociology*, LXXII, no. 6 (1967): 654–660.

stool in front of it, or chips on a 21 table the closest "slot" and the attendant exclusive right to make bets from it.

There are "boundary markers," objects that mark the line between two adjacent territories. The bar used in supermarket checkout counters to separate one customer's batch of articles from the next is an example; the common armrest between theater seats is another. Note, when boundary markers are employed either on both sides of an individual or in front and back, they function as "spacers," ensuring the user personal space in a row or column, if not a temporary stall.

There are (if I may use the phrase) "ear markers," that is, signatures embedded in an object to claim it as part of the possessional territory of the signee, as when names are burned into sports equipment, livestock, and slaves, or when numbers are embossed on engine blocks, and so forth.

It is here that the "system of reference" problem becomes acute. Since territory implies a field of contiguous items—especially in the case of possessional preserves—it comes to pass that one means of marking possession of an object is to have clearly possessed things next to it. When, for example, a book is left on a newspaper, individuals will perceive that the newspaper is not to be taken, because the book and the newspaper will be understood to "belong together." Hence an object that is part of a territory can also function as a marker of territory; indeed, signatures of various kinds are of this order. Thus, personal effects, constituting a preserve in their own right, are frequently employed as markers; moving them or even touching them is something like touching their owner's body, and such acts are avoided in many circumstances or performed with suitable circumspection.

The issue of system of reference is especially delicate in connection with the territorial functioning of the body. The very notion of an egocentric territory suggests that the body is not only a preserve but also a central marker of various preserves—personal space, stall, turn, and personal effects. This becomes especially evident when the preserve in question is claimed not merely for the possessor of the body but for a multi-person party of which the possessor is only one member.[22] Words can also be used as markers, as when moves toward a stall are warned away verbally by someone nearby who claims the area. And it is thus that the hand or foot in touch with a person can function as a "relationship marker," that is, a sign that stakes out a relationship claim. (Important among these are "with markers" which establish who is in a with with whom.) In the case of relationship markers, note, bodily contiguity or contact can function as an expression of a relationship from the point of view of those concerned to note this and as a possession marker from the point of view of those concerned to note that.[23]

A final point. When a personal possession is used as a marker of personal space, the possessor will necessarily be on hand to face offenders: he can challenge any displacement of the marker and fight off—or at least bear witness to—its appropriation. He who would retain a stall, however, is less well protected because he may not always be present to guard the means of marking it. The marker itself is likely to be some personal effect that can be stolen and may well be worth stealing, reminding us that effects involve ownership in addition to possession. To hold a stall, then, one may have to expose a personal possession to theft. It follows that in

---

[22] This is but one example of the limitations of the term "individual" as a technical unit. Clearly we use the term individual as an easy equivalent of good, claimant, marker, impediment, and counter-claimant—when the occasion is right. The term is also used to designate a vehicular unit in traffic organization, an interactant in conversational organization, and a member either of a single or a with. In all of these cases, distinctively different systems of reference are involved and hence, ultimately, different units. By allowing the word "individual" to cover all of these meanings, to shift from one to another in the same sentence, and to enter the argument at various levels, great flexibility in discourse is obtained. The price, of course, is rigor.

[23] There are some nice issues here. In doing a "pick up," the male must transform a two-person talk into a with, and if successful in this will come to employ standard with markers. There are ghetto males so oriented to active work of this kind that they have learned to maneuver a girl into not disallowing their employment of these markers even after she feels she has closed out matters conversationally. My sense is that this technique is often effective, the more so since no one can quite say what is happening.

communities in which petty theft is rampant, stall organization may be less found than usually. Recent trends in social organization bear this out. Beaches along the southern coast of France are heavily populated by individuals from a variety of nations, classes, and age-groups. Yet purses and trousers are used as markers by individuals who have disappeared momentarily into the waves. American beaches that draw users from large American cities are less conducive to stall organization. New York itself, as an environment of possible stalls, may be currently something of an extreme in this regard; its citizenry has appreciably foregone the use of this basic form of public social organization.

III *Modalities of Violation*

If territory-like preserves are the central claim in the study of comingling, then the central offense is an incursion, intrusion, encroachment, presumption, transgression, defilement, besmearing, contamination—in short, a violation. Now it seems the case that the chief agencies and authors of this kind of boundary offense are individuals themselves and what can be intimately identified with them.

Turn now to consider human agencies of violation and examine first the different modalities.

1. There is ecological placement of the body relative to a claimed territory. The model here is classical Indian caste relations, with its conception of measurable distances which mark a safe approach between persons of different castes, the ranking person serving as the center of a personal space and the other as a source of contamination, the potency of which depends on the social distance between the castes.[24]

[24] A statement of the traditional conception may be found in J. H. Hutton, *Caste in India*, 2nd edition (Bombay, New York, Indian Branch: Oxford University Press, 1951), esp. p. 79. What indeed took place at various

2. The body, including the hands, as something that can touch and through this defile the sheath or possessions of another. The extreme here in our society is no doubt sexual molestation.

3. The glance, look, penetration of the eyes. Although in our society the offense that can be committed by intrusive looks tends to be slighter than other kinds of offensive incursions, the distance over which the intrusion can occur is considerable, the directions multiple, the occasions of possible intrusion very numerous, and the adjustments required in eye discipline constant and delicate. Note, the need for great eye discipline is reinforced by the fact that glances of the eye also play an important role in a different frame, that of applying to acts internal to an encounter, as in requests for and ratification of talk, the management of turn-taking among speakers, head aversion in support of modesty, shame and tact, the application of sincerity stress, middle-distance looks, and so forth. Within the encounter frame, direct gaze is often not an invasion because it has other jobs to do.[25]

Although concern about various forms of incursion can be thought to increase positively with social class status, and although it certainly seems the case that the more affluent an individual, the larger the preserves he can command, nonetheless, as suggested, the relation is not simple. Eye behavior is an example. In lower-class Mexican-American youth gangs, for example, the notion of a "bad look" seems fairly well-established, involving an infraction of the rule that subordinates are supposed to avert their gaze after

---

times and places in India is, of course, another question. A current statement regarding the issue of contamination can be found in Louis Dumont, *Homo Hierarchicus*, Mark Sainsbury, trans. (Chicago: The University of Chicago Press, 1970), pp. 130–151.

[25] In addition, of course, there are great cross-cultural differences in the rules observed *within* the encounter frame. It has been suggested, for example, that one difficulty Puerto Rican schoolchildren have in American schools is that in casting their eyes down in what they take to be the proper response to being scolded by the teacher, they can give an American adult a sense that they are trying to refuse concern, which can lead to more scolding. (Thomas Kochman, "Cross-Cultural Communication: Contrasting Perspectives, Conflicting Sensibilities," unpublished paper, Department of Linguistics, Northeastern Illinois State College, 1970.)

having returned the superordinate's for a brief time. Turf and the dominance hierarchy can be at issue. Further, at dances, a youth may find it necessary to defend the integrity of his relationship to a girl whom another boy has looked at overlong from across the hall—a gallantry not perhaps as pronounced among those who can protect their relational possessions with the usual privacies that money can buy.[26]

In middle-class society, care in use of the eyes can be readily found in connection with nakedness. In nudist camps, for example, apparently considerable effort is taken to avoid appearing to be looking at the private parts of others.[27] Topless waitresses sometimes obtain the same courtesy from their patrons, especially when engaging them in close serving. A rule in our society: when bodies are naked, glances are clothed.

4. Sound interference, being those noises made by an individual that are felt to intrude disruptively on bystanders, demanding, as it were, too much sound space for him. Also there is the practice of sustaining an encounter over a distance that is longer than proper according to the prevailing norms.

5. The addressing of words, as when subordinates in an encounter speak up, or remarks are addressed by way of cross-talk from an individual to those with whom he is not in a ratified state of talk,[28] or when street hustlers of various sorts initiate importuning encounters with passers-by, this latter, incidentally, being the source of the unpleasantness Western tourists face in begging cultures.

6. Bodily excreta, to be considered in terms of four distinct

---

[26] I draw here on an unpublished paper (1965) by Nick Vaca. See also Lewis Yablonsky, *The Violent Gang* (New York: The Macmillan Company, 1962; London: Collier-Macmillan, 1962), p. 157.

[27] Martin S. Weinberg, "Sexual Modesty and the Nudist Camp," *Social Problems*, XII, no. 3 (1965): 315.

[28] A nice illustration is provided by Tom Wolfe, "The Voices of Village Square," in his *The Kandy-Kolored Tangerine Flake Streamline Baby* (New York: Pocket Books, Inc., 1966; London: Mayflower Books, 1966), pp. 272–278.

agencies of defilement. First, corporeal excreta (or their stains) that contaminate by direct touch: spittle, snot, perspiration, food particles, blood, semen, vomit, urine, and fecal matter. (A germ-theory rationale supports our attitudes to this element, the classical extreme in contamination being the suppurative sores of lepers.)[29] Second, there is odor, including flatus, tainted breath, and body smells.[30] Like looking, odor operates over a distance and in all directions; unlike looking, it cannot be cut off once it violates and may linger in a confined place after the agency has gone. Third, a minor factor, body heat—to be found, for example, on sheets in "bird-cage" hotels, on toilet seats in powder rooms, in jackets and sweaters recently removed by their users and lent to, or mistakenly appropriated by, others.[31] Finally, most ethereal of all, markings left by the body in which some bodily excreta can be imagined to remain; plate leavings are an example. Note that in this matter of markings, knives function in an interesting way (as do other serving implements), since they provide the means of taking without contaminating, as middle-class children learn the first time their mother finds a teeth-marked crater in a cake, a loaf of bread, or a piece of fruit. These craters are defiling, and it is very important to disinfect the object and its setting by cutting away with a clean knife until only a flat surface remains. Note, these understandings are neither recent nor local in Western society. Thus the Florentine, Giovanni Della Casa, in his book of manners published in 1558, suggests:

---

[29] Useful arguments that the germ theory merely rationalizes ritual concerns can be found in Mary Douglas, *Purity and Danger* (London: Routledge and Kegan Paul, 1966).

[30] Commercials regarding measures to be taken so as not to "offend" provide rather risible material in this connection but are not nearly so risible as the facts. The care that some individuals do in fact take so as not to contaminate others by various bodily excreta would surely do credit to a saint. For example, males brushing close to females may say "excuse me" implosively so as to prevent possible contamination by their breath.

[31] The first treatment of the ritual implications of body heat is Edward Hall, "A System for the Notation of Proxemic Behavior," *American Anthropologist*, LXV (October 1963): esp. 1014–1015.

> It is also an unpleasant habit to lift another person's glass of wine or his food to your nose and smell it. I would even advise you not to smell your own food and drink, because drops may fall from your nose, and even the thought that this may happen is disgusting. I must also recommend you not to offer anyone else a glass of wine which you have tasted and touched with your lips, unless he is a very close intimate of yours. Still less should you offer him a pear or any other fruit from which you have already taken a bite.[32]

Here reason is not an immediate basis for understanding. Couples who are sexually intimate may still feel repelled by the notion of using each other's toothbrush. Men will drink from the same bottle (and indeed might feel it unmanly to decline to do so) who would not touch each other's half-eaten food. An individual who feels it improper to use his own knife to take butter from the table's dish may be quite ready, nay eager, to eat in the Chinese style at a Chinese restaurant.[33] An individual who is quick to pick up and use a pair of sunglasses found in the street may decline to retrieve a comb or brush similarly seen, in many cases even when no one sees the seeing. And greasy and creamy foods that are not considered to contaminate the mouth can yet be felt to contaminate the hands should contact have to be made without insulation by utensils.

---

[32] Giovanni Della Casa, *Galateo*, R. S. Pine-Coffin, trans. (London: Penguin Books, 1958), p. 26.

[33] In part, no doubt, because of a sliver of acculturation. In his Autobiography, Malcolm X provides an illustration. On his first being offered food in the Muslim style, he declines: "The trouble was, I have to admit it, at that point I didn't know if I could go for their manner of eating. Everything was in one pot on the dining room rug, and I saw them just all fall right in, using their hands." Some time later, after having been very well received, the following:

> But the Muslim world's customs no longer seemed strange to me. My hands now readily plucked up food from a common dish shared with brother Muslims; I was drinking without hesitation from the same glass as others; I was washing from the same little pitcher of water; and sleeping with eight or ten others on a mat in the open.

The Autobiography of Malcolm X (New York: Grove Press, Inc., 1965; London: Hutchinson, 1966), pp. 330, 343–344.

The intrusive effect of bodily associated matters, whether proximity, touch, or excreta, varies greatly depending on what it is that intrudes. In Western society the elbows and upper back seem to have little capacity to contaminate, the sexual organs a great deal. Interestingly, something of a parallel is found in regard to preserves; as suggested, the elbow is part of the body that is little vulnerable to contamination, the "private parts" more so. It is thus that the elbows can be used in our society for spacers, ensuring the actor some measure of personal space, elbows being a part of the body which can hardly intrude or be intruded on.[34] In spite of this parallel, however, it should be clear that the character of the individual as a territory (or as the center of territories) is not simply an opposing counterpart to his being a source of violations. In the first role he holds others off, in the second, he penetrates; the shapes taken in the two roles are different.

IV *Territorial Offenses*

Discriminating types of territory and types of violation does not provide us with all the framework we need to bring order into the varieties of territorial offense.[35] The complication is that the claimant to a territory and the impediment to the claim are not neces-

---

[34] Since in every society individuals have to somehow get through the day, we can expect that in any society in which some parts of the body are defined as contaminating and contaminatable, other parts of the body will have to be given relatively neutral status. (Of course, as suggested, we are to expect that societies will differ widely in the way they segment the body for ritual purposes.) A comment on the pattern in India is provided by Henry Orenstein, "Toward a Grammar of Defilement in Hindu Sacred Law," in Milton Singer and Bernard S. Cohn, eds., *Structure and Change in Indian Society* (Chicago: Aldine Publishing Company, 1968), p. 123.

[35] A useful classification of territorial offenses is available in Stanford M. Lyman and Marvin B. Scott, "Territoriality: A Neglected Sociological Dimension," *Social Problems*, XV (Fall 1967): 243–244.

sarily seated in different persons, nor are the agency of offense and the author of the offense necessarily located in the same individual.

1. The prototypical territorial offense occurs when one individual encroaches on the preserve claimed by and for another individual, the first thereby functioning as an impediment to the second's claim.

It should be noted that encroachment involves two different kinds of sin. One is suggested by the term "intrusion": this is the obvious case of an individual entering a territory to which he has no right of access, or otherwise contaminating a preserve. Authorship is variable: the act can be perceived to be unintentional, or a knowing by-product of some urgent design, or malicious, that is, performed merely to offend. The extremes are interesting. One is rape. Another, less well known, is defilement of fixed territories by means of defecation.[36] Still another is described by Valachi in his comment on his prep school, the New York Catholic Protectory:

> The roughest one was Brother Abel. He was in charge of the tailor shop, and he would lay into us with his tape stick something awful. It didn't matter whether we did anything wrong or not. The best thing to do was stay out of his way unless you were looking for a beating. Then one day Brother Abel died. They put his body on display in the chapel. I'll never forget it. All the kids from the five yards of the protectory had to line up to view him and pay their last respects. All told, I'd say there were about 300 of us. I was near the end of the line and when it was my turn to view the body, I almost fainted. Brother Abel's chest was all covered with spit, so what could I do? I spit on him, too.[37]

---

[36] See, for example, Albert B. Friedman, "The Scatological Rites of Burglars," *Western Folklore*, XXVII (July 1968): 171–179, and Albert K. Cohen, *Delinquent Boys* (New York: The Free Press, 1955; London: Collier-Macmillan, 1955), p. 28. This sort of defilement is to be distinguished from the routine use by various animals of their urine and feces as a means of territory claiming through marker distribution.

[37] Peter Maas, *The Valachi Papers* (New York: Bantam Books, Inc., 1969), p. 60. During the 1968 difficulties at Columbia University, the then Vice-President, David Truman, received a somewhat similar accolade from some students. See Jerry L. Avorn et al., *Up against the Ivy Wall* (New York: Atheneum Publishers, 1969), p. 200.

To intrude, then, is one way to encroach; a second is to obtrude. I refer here to the capacity of a claimant to press territorial demands into a wider sphere than others feel is his due, causing them to feel that they themselves could be seen as functioning intrusively, even though they feel that this is not the case. The standard example occurs when an individual makes what are taken as overextensive claims to personal space, incidentally encroaching on the personal space of those adjacent to him or on areas felt to be public in the sense of being non-claimable. "Offensive" loudness which sustains an encounter over a long distance is another common case. Thus, the ski slopes of New England are beginning to enjoy patronage by young men of no background, who, having their own understanding of ritual sociability, maintain a running exchange of derisive greetings, banter, and other loud impieties from slope to lift, finding that this sort of separation between friends is a reason for establishing connection, not foregoing it, thereby giving considerable offense to those properly born to the silent sport. Kingsley Amis, explaining why he did not like Cambridge, provides a parallel illustration, but with the class difference reversed:

> However understandable it might be that undergraduate Cambridge is still the resort of the upper classes, the results of this depressed me. To hear all of those young chaps—a small minority, no doubt, but how vocal—braying and baying to one another across the streets or in the interiors of pubs distracted me from thoughts of Donne. At times I became a one-man resistance movement, broadcasting baleful glares, trying to force them to thank me when I stood aside for them in shop doorways, stopping them from hijacking taxis. No good. They were too firmly seated. Early one lunch-time I was enjoying a quiet beer and minding my own business in Miller's Wine Parlour when a voice suddenly bawled:
>
> "Well of course I know that type of acting's been pretty much left behind these days, but I must say that a fellow like Gielgud does seem to *me* to have a certain *presence* and *authority* and at least one does get the feeling that the man's read a *book* occasionally and can come on to the stage without *throwing himself about* like a. . . ."

There was more. What arrested me was not the content of this discourse but its volume. I looked about me in amazement. Nobody else was taking the least notice; even Stanley behind the bar went on calmly polishing glasses. If I had been the father of the orator—he sat surrounded by parents and relatives—I should have laid my finger to my lips or, if that failed, my hand across his mouth. But then, I reflected, I am a child of the lower middle-classes, whose members keep their voices down in public lest others hear and condemn.[38]

In everyday interaction, intrusions and obtrusions may occur simultaneously and, along with the corrective response they call forth, may guide behavior closely. A good example is presented when two individuals are led to have an animated conversation with each other while being required to sit more than comfortably close. A systematic link can then occur between those gestures of the current speaker that figure as the kinesic accompaniment of his talk and the defensive conduct of the current listener as he territorially adjusts to the shifting configuration of the talker. (These roles will switch, of course, as turns at talking are exchanged.) The result provides one basis for what has been called interaction synchrony.[39]

2. There are, then, encroachments, these including intrusions and obtrusions. Consider now the territorial offense that results when an individual violates himself—a possibility implied in what has already been said about the separable ritual roles of the individual.

Self-violations vary in organization. First, there are self-befoulments: the individual as a source of contamination defiles himself as

---

[38] Kingsley Amis, "No More Parades: On Leaving Cambridge," *Encounter*, XXII (February 1964): 25 [stress in the original].

[39] A term introduced by W. S. Condon, of Western Psychiatric Institute and Clinic, Pittsburgh, to refer to the close reciprocity of physical movement between speaker and listener. See W. S. Condon and W. D. Ogston, "Sound Film Analysis of Normal and Pathological Behavior Patterns," *Journal of Nervous and Mental Disorders*, CXLIII (1966): 338–347.

a preserve. The extreme here, at least in our society, is smearing oneself with and eating one's own fecal matter—a type of heroic perversity now becoming rare in our mental hospitals.[40] The cleanliness practices that protect the individual from self-befoulment can everywhere be seen, very nicely, for example, at drugstore counters during lunch time when immaculate typists are to be observed eating messy triple-decker sandwiches while minimizing all contact with what might smear them, affecting this with a finger and mouth dexterity that is awesome, and all the while keeping their elbows and eyes out of the territories of those on either side of them.[41]

It should be noted that bodily excreta that become matters for befoulment or self-contamination typically start out as a part of the body that is not self-defiling, not, as is said, ego-alien. It is shortly after leaving the body that these materials become somehow transformed in character, acquiring the power to befoul—as Allport has described nicely:

> How very intimate (propriate) the bodily sense is can be seen by performing a little experiment in your imagination. Think first of swallowing the saliva in your mouth, or do so. Then imagine expectorating it into a tumbler and drinking it! What seemed natural and "mine" suddenly becomes disgusting and alien. Or picture yourself sucking blood from a prick in your finger; then imagine sucking blood from a bandage around your finger! What I perceive as sepa-

[40] The space program has sponsored research which has incidentally generated a quite contemporary version of these issues. In studies designed to closely measure the human metabolic process, experimental subjects were required to collect (for weighing and analysis) as much of their own bodily wastes as seemed possible, including perspiration. As might be expected, there was strong resistance on the part of the subjects. See Suellen Lanstein, "Human Experiments: Social Structure and Social Control" (Unpublished Master's Thesis, Space Science Laboratory, University of California, Berkeley, n.d.).

[41] In *Portnoy's Complaint* (London: Jonathan Cape, 1969; New York: New American Library, 1970), Philip Roth has recently provided us with a literary treatment of the ritual work associated with bowel movements, which treatment will surely be definitive for a long time, perhaps forever.

rate from my body becomes, in the twinkling of an eye, cold and foreign.[42]

Among self-violations, then, there are self-befoulments. A second variety of self-violations could be described as debasements. An individual can willfully defile himself with contaminants from other persons which would otherwise be routinely avoided. The most eminent example can be cited:

> Pope Paul VI washed and kissed the feet of twelve student priests —most of them nonwhites—at a Holy Thursday Mass yesterday in a gesture symbolizing the church in the service of the poor, the war-torn, and the oppressed.[43]

From a novel, a less ritualized and less exalted instance:

> "Most people have preconceived ideas of how to behave," Harry went on. "Like myself. Renaissance ideas. Not Max. He acts any way he feels like acting. Nothing is either good or bad, dignified or undignified. There is no experience he is not capable of having. He is completely mobile. For example. If when we sat down at this booth there were two half-full glasses of beer left by the previous occupants Max could finish them. He really could. It would not bother him a bit. It would not bother him a bit. . . . That is the real Modern Man." [44]

---

[42] Gordon Allport, *Becoming* (New Haven: Yale University Press, 1955), p. 43. We should not assume, incidentally, that different peoples will have the same conception as to where the shift is to occur between the self-identified and the self-polluting. For example, in the traditional Havik Brahmin ritual idiom, saliva was apparently an intense contaminant, and care was taken to minimize the contact of one's own lips with one's own person—even with one's own drink. (See Mary Douglas, *op. cit.*, p. 33.)

[43] *San Francisco Chronicle*, April 12, 1968.

[44] Chandler Brossard, *Who Walk in Darkness* (New York: New Directions Pub. Corp., 1952), p. 39. The difference here between Max and the Pope is interesting, but has little to do with the fact that one is a fictional character and the other real and that Brossard, to my knowledge, is not a familiar in Vatican circles. Max would be acting for himself in what is called a private capacity; and he would drink the beer not in order to commit an impropriety (in appearances, at least) but in spite of the impropriety. The Pope acted not as a private person but as an agent of the

Jules Henry, in one of the very few reports available on life in an old folks' home, provides some further examples. These, for Henry, were sufficiently telling of the conditions of the aged to render his explicating them unnecessary:

> He [Mike, who works for his keep] went to the women's side room to get their trays. When he came out with them he stopped by Mr. Jacks' bed and offered him some bread that one of the patients had left and Mr. Jacks took it eagerly and put it in his bedside table. Then Mike stopped by Mr. Roberts' bed and offered him the coffee a patient had not drunk. Mr. Roberts thanked him, took it, and quickly drank it so that Mike could take the cup out with the rest of the dishes.
>
> Mike stopped by Mr. Jacks' bedside and held out a partially eaten tray of food. He smiled and asked Mr. Jacks if he wanted the bread from the tray. Mr. Jacks said something, took the bread and placed it on the shelf on his bedside table.[45]

A third class of self-violations, perhaps less important than the other two, involves exposure: an individual with a claim to a particular preserve can act (or be caused to act) so that other persons

---

Church, indeed as its symbol and ritual representative, and his act on the face of it had no utilitarian value, being part of a ceremony. Acts performed as part of a ceremony belong to a different frame than their literal counterpart, and what might be contaminating of self in the former need not be in the latter. (It is thus that the eminent when visiting the poor in a representative capacity are not defiled by the contact.) In spite of these analytical differences, however, Brossard and the Church here drew on the same ritual idiom in formulating acts that are meaningful to others.

[45] Jules Henry, *Culture against Man* (New York: Random House Inc., 1963; London: Tavistock Publications, 1966), p. 416. The notion that half-eaten food is contaminating to second eaters should not be carried too far. In restaurant kitchens, staff will often eat plate-leavings that they would never think of touching when they are themselves guests in a restaurant. (It might be added that in a study directed by Robert Sommer, a student-experimenter who ate leavings from a restaurant clean-up cart in the dining room managed to soon transform the alignment of other guests so that they entered into the spirit of things and jocularly passed him their own leavings.) And, of course, as will shortly be considered, if the leavings are those of a spouse, own-child, or parent, then considerable license may be exercised, almost as if what the food could spread already had been.

exercising only ordinary looks and touches yet find themselves encroaching. Improper attire and posture provide one example; inebriation, crying before strangers, self-revelations are others.[46]

In discriminating between encroachments and self-violations, some notion of the authorship of the violation was relevant, whether the author was or was not the claimant, and whether he was or was not himself the impediment to the claim. Someone's intention and will were thus constitutive features of the resulting description. But it is not sufficient merely to introduce the issue of intention as an initial premise; intention must be further considered. Given these general understandings about intent and offense, we must see that exceptional circumstances are known to occur, calling for a further elaboration of understandings. The difficulty turns on the concept of authorship and, by implication, the concept of responsibility, neither of which can be adequately treated here. Only two complications will be pointed out. First, both of the individuals involved in a territorial offense—the claimant and the counter-claimant—may be seen to have acted innocently and inadvertently, so that in this particular instance no one is held to be the author of the offense. And yet the ritual work that ensues, the accounts and apologies that restore order, will be oriented to what the offense would have been had it been done with the usual, the "thinkable," authorship. That which is shown to be no one's fault is that which would otherwise be seen as someone's fault, and must be so seen if one is to know how to nullify it. Second, under what is seen as extreme constraint, an individual may violate his own preserves or those of others and yet still be seen as not having authored the act. It is thus that a female prisoner, obliged to disrobe in order to be searched, may be forced to expose herself, as may a high school girl who gets an "F" if she refuses to shower nude after gym with eight other girls "and the

---

[46] As here described, exposure has a form that is also found in offenses less interactional in character. Thus, in recent times there has been some effort to impose penalties (or at least disapproval) on those who manage their property so that others can easily be tempted into stealing it or abusing it.

gym teacher standing there watching."[47] Here again those who attend the disrobing may be seen as the ultimate authors of the offense, but the offense that has occurred is one that takes its character from the sort of thing that an individual ordinarily willfully does himself to himself.[48]

3. We have thus far considered the ways in which an individual can intrude and obtrude upon an other or violate himself. A systematic complication must now be introduced. As suggested, it is the case that two or more individuals may together possess the same territory, jointly laying claim to it in the name of their collectivity. Thus when an individual claims a table by sitting at it, he can indeed be claiming the table for his party, a social unit in which he is merely one participant. Every social relationship, both anonymous and personal, implies some joint tenure, and some relationships (such as marital ones) imply a great deal.

It follows, as already suggested, that an act which may intrude or expose when performed by one individual to another can be perfectly appropriate when performed by the same individual to someone else, someone with whom he shares the relevant territory.[49] Thus a policeman who feels it necessary to ask a prostitute in the station to empty her own purse so he can inspect its contents is likely to feel free to dig into his wife's purse for change or cigarettes. Indeed, the very forms of behavior employed to cele-

---

[47] Reported in a letter of complaint to Abigail Van Buren, *San Francisco Chronicle*, October 30, 1964.

[48] Mary Owen Cameron, in *The Booster and the Snitch* (New York: The Free Press, 1964; London: Collier-Macmillan, 1964), p. 161, suggests that by requiring apprehended female shoplifters to strip to be searched, store security personnel hope to humiliate the offender into changing her ways.

[49] That is not to say that an individual who is obliged to give up a preserve because a relationship calls for it will be happy about doing so. A good example is what used to be called (in the last generation when this view was presumably more prevalent) "the repulsive side of marriage." Respectable women of the time elaborately avoided all contamination from men, only to find after the wedding that one of these persons had to be let in. No doubt there was some consolation for these ladies in the fact that although they were obliged to suffer this violation, they were not obliged to enjoy it.

brate and affirm relationships—rituals such as greetings, enquiries after health, and love-making—are very close in character to what would be a violation of preserves if performed between wrongly related individuals. The same can be said for acts performed as a means of signaling the initiation or extension of a personal relationship. And it is hard to see how it could be otherwise. For if an individual is to join someone in some kind of social bond, surely he must do so by giving up some of the boundaries and barriers that ordinarily separate them.[50] Indeed the fact of having given up these separatenesses is a central symbol and substance of relationship—just as the act of *first* giving them up is a central mark of relationship formation. In consequence, an offensive territorial act can usually be seen as a presumption regarding relationship—for there will be some relationship in which the relevant preserve is shared and violation in this connection impossible.

All this leads us to see that in addition to encroachments and self-violations there is a third variety of territorial offense: preclusiveness, namely, the effort of an individual to keep persons at a distance he has no right (in their eyes) to maintain. Refusal to be drawn into talk by kinsmen, or to divulge relevant private information to a legitimate authority, or to disrobe before a physician are cases in point.

V *Conclusions*

I would like to raise three general points in connection with territoriality and face-to-face interaction. First, although there is much here that can be described in traditional Durkheimian terms having

[50] Here the current vogue of "encounter-group therapy" is of interest. Given that the license to enter private preserves is an expression of an intimate relationship, it is possible to closely simulate relationship formation by arranging to encourage violations. During the last war the Chinese attempted something similar with their so-called brainwashing groups. The American version is apparently much more fun.

to do with ritual delicacy and the maintenance and infraction of normative rulings, it is also the case that similarities to animal activity are very marked; indeed, it is from ethology that the basic concepts come. Somehow we must develop a perspective which can closely incorporate these two traditionally alien points of view—at least when studying the small behaviors comprising face-to-face interaction.

Second, the traditional way of thinking about threats to rules focuses on a claimant and a potential offender, and although this certainly has its value, especially when we examine closely all the means available for introducing remedies and corrections, still the role of the situation is usually thereby neglected. A better paradigm in many ways would be to assume a few participants all attempting to avoid outright violation of the rules and all forced to deal with the contingencies introduced by various features of various settings. Here the various aims and desires of the participants are taken as given—as standard and routine—and the active, variable element is seen to be the peculiarities of the current situation. For example, urinals in public toilets in America bring men very close to each other under circumstances where, for a period of time, they must expose themselves. In such places considerable care is taken in regard to eyes lest privacy be violated more than necessary. When two men are urinating next to each other, their eyes will have a very narrow surface territory that will be safe.[51] Similarly, when an individual enters a new region, he may find few places available that are sufficiently far removed from other persons present to allow their being stared at with impunity; and the places that are removed may not provide a cover of occasioned activity for him. Locations that qualify on both counts are thus likely to become resources in the setting, that is, niches that appear to induce staring; the Coke machine in packed bus depots, the coffee machine in busy offices, the checkout counter in supermarkets are examples. Similarly, it is upon entrance to a new region that

[51] A fact which clears the way, of course, for a special use to be made of pointed staring, in which connection see Laud Humphreys, *Tearoom Trade* (Chicago: Aldine Publishing Co., 1970).

the individual will find that orientation scanning is most urgent, and it is there that he will seek a cover for this operation. The slot to which a bus conductor addresses his ticket-taking attentions is a case in point; from here the oncoming passenger will have his first opportunity to check out the people he must ride with, will be far enough away from most of them to allow inoffensive staring, and will have a transaction with the conductor (or change box) to serve as a rationale for pausing. Indeed, settings such as restaurants often give rise to what has been called an "entrance cycle." [52] Just outside the entrance, the incomer may take a last opportunity to perform a grooming check on his personal front; [53] upon entrance, the moment that is given to taking off outside clothes, waiting for other members of the party, addressing himself to the hostess, and so on provides the cover and distance required in order to safely engage in a scanning operation.

The final general point about territoriality. In considering the minor situational and egocentric preserves of the self—the respect shown for them and the defenses employed of them—we are led to deal with what is somehow central to the subjective sense that the individual has concerning his selfhood, his ego, the part of himself with which he identifies his positive feelings. And here the issue is not whether a preserve is exclusively maintained, or shared, or given up entirely, but rather the role the individual is allowed in determining what happens to his claim. An apparently self-determined, active deciding as to how one's preserves will be used allows these preserves to provide the bases of a ritual idiom. Thus, on the issue of will and self-determination turns the whole possibility of using territories of the self in a dual way, with comings-into-touch avoided as a means of maintaining respect and en-

---

[52] Nicely described under that title by Lynette Lofland, in *In the Presence of Strangers: A Study of Behavior in Public Settings* (The University of Michigan: Center for Research in Social Organization, May 1966), p. 100 ff.

[53] In restaurants, opportunity for grooming checks is institutionally provided women by "ladies rooms." At social parties, entering females are often given the same pre-presentational help.

gaged in as a means of establishing regard. And on this duality rests the possibility of according meaning to territorial events and the practicality of so doing.[54] It is no wonder that felt self-determination is crucial to one's sense of what it means to be a full-fledged person. Personal will or volition may be seen, then, not as something which territorial arrangements must come to terms with and make allowances for, but rather as a function which must be inserted into agents to make the dual role of preserves work.

---

[54] Multiple or "overdetermined" use of the same interaction arrangements seems a general feature of public life. In addition to those mentioned, other examples might be cited. Given that a rule exists against seeking out a stranger's eyes, seeking can then be done as a means of making a pickup or as a means of making oneself known to someone one expects to meet but is unacquainted with. Similarly, given that staring is an invasion of informational preserve, a stare can then be used as a warranted negative sanction against someone who has misbehaved—the misbehavior providing and ensuring a special significance to overlong examination. (Thus, if one wants to stare at others with impunity, one need only arrange to cause them to invade a territorial preserve, and then one can properly respond by examining them.) Here see Goffman, *Behavior in Public Places* (New York: The Free Press, 1963; London: Collier-Macmillan, 1963), p. 95.

In general, then, we can say that a rule tends to make possible a meaningful set of non-adherences, only one of which is an infraction, the others being functions made possible by our capacity to discriminate (and to trust others to discriminate) among types of non-adherence.

[3]

Supportive Interchanges

I

Ritual is a perfunctory, conventionalized act through which an individual portrays his respect and regard for some object of ultimate value to that object of ultimate value or to its stand-in.[1]

In his famous analysis of religion, Durkheim divided ritual into two classes: positive and negative.[2] The negative kind involves interdictions, avoidance, staying away. It is what we consider when we look at the preserves of the self and the right to be let alone.

[1] The term "ritualization" is widely used in ethology (following initial work by Julian Huxley) in a derivative sense to refer to a physically adaptive behavior pattern that has become removed somewhat from its original function, rigidified as to form, and given weight as a signal or "releaser" to conspecifics. See, for example, A. D. Best, "The Concept of Ritualization," in W. H. Thorpe and O. L. Zangwill, eds., *Current Problems in Animal Behaviour* (Cambridge: Cambridge University Press, 1961), pp. 102–124. A very useful volume is *A Discussion on Ritualization of Behaviour in Animals and Man*, Philosophical Transactions of the Royal Society of London, series B, Biological Sciences, vol. 251, no. 772 (London: December 1966), pp. 247–526.

[2] Émile Durkheim, *Elementary Forms of the Religious Life*, Joseph Ward Swain, trans. (New York: The Macmillan Co., 1926; London: Allen and Unwin).

Positive ritual consists of the ways in which homage can be paid through offerings of various kinds, these involving the doer coming close in some way to the recipient. The standard argument is that these positive rites affirm and support the social relationship between doer and recipient. Improper performance of positive rites is a slight; of negative rites, a violation.

In contemporary society rituals performed to stand-ins for supernatural entities are everywhere in decay, as are extensive ceremonial agendas involving long strings of obligatory rites. What remains are brief rituals one individual performs for and to another, attesting to civility and good will on the performer's part and to the recipient's possession of a small patrimony of sacredness. What remains, in brief, are interpersonal rituals. These little pieties are a mean version of what anthropologists would look for in their paradise. But they are worth examining. Only our secular view of society prevents us from appreciating the ubiquitousness and strategy of their location, and, in turn, their role in social organization.

Interpersonal ritual in our secular society has a special bearing on Durkheim's distinction between positive and negative rites.

First, as Durkheim could not have expected, current work on territoriality and personal preserves allows us to describe negative rites in very close detail, and not as an occasional restriction, but as a central organizational device of public order.

Second, interpersonal rituals have a dialogistic character, and this differently impinges on positive and negative rites. When a ritual offering occurs, when, that is, one individual provides a sign of involvement in and connectedness to another, it behooves the recipient to show that the message has been received, that its import has been appreciated, that the affirmed relationship actually exists as the performer implies, that the performer himself has worth as a person, and finally, that the recipient has an appreciative, grateful nature. Prestation (to use Mauss' [3] favorite term) thus leads to counter-prestation, and when we focus on minor rituals

[3] Marcel Mauss, *The Gift*, Ian Cunnison, trans. (London: Cohen and West, 1954).

performed between persons who are present to each other, the giving statement tends to be followed immediately by a show of gratitude. Both moves taken together form a little ceremony—a "supportive interchange." Negative ritual leads to dialogue, too, but less directly and through a different route. Ordinary circumspections ordinarily call for no responding comment. When exemplary delicacy is exhibited, signs of gratitude may be returned, although there is a natural limitation here since these displays undercut the very privacy which the initial maintenance of distance ensured. More important, when an infraction occurs, then a dialogue is indicated, the offender having to provide remedial accounts and assurances and the offended a sign that these have been received and are sufficient; in brief, a "remedial interchange" occurs. I might add in passing that these two basic interchanges, the supportive and the remedial, are among the most conventionalized and perfunctory doings we engage in and traditionally have been treated by students of modern society as part of the dust of social activity, empty and trivial. And yet, as we shall see, almost all brief encounters between individuals consist precisely and entirely of one or the other of these two interchanges. In brief, whenever one individual rubs up against another, he is likely to say hello or excuse me. Surely it is time to examine "Hello" or "Excuse me," or their equivalent. Moreover, as we also shall see, conversational encounters of the more extended kind are typically opened and closed by these devices, if not built up in terms of them. Surely, then, in spite of the bad name that etiquette has given to etiquette, it is time to study these performances.

Finally, it is to be noted that when negative and positive rites are examined, it is often found that although one social relationship requires keeping away from a particular personal preserve, another relation will license and even oblige its penetration. All of these penetrative acts through which some persons are shown support are acts, which, if performed to other persons, would violate them. (It is also true, if less generally, that ritually cautious acts that show proper respect in a distant relation can affront a recipient when exhibited for his benefit by someone to whom he is closely related.) Thus every ritual idiom seems to make a double use of behavioral arrangements, as Durkheim, of course, suggested:

> Perhaps some will be surprised that so sacred a food may be eaten by ordinary profane persons. But in the first place, there is no positive cult which does not face this contradiction. Every sacred being is removed from profane touch by this very character with which it is endowed; but, on the other hand, they would serve for nothing and have no reason whatsoever for their existence if they could not come in contact with these same worshippers who, on another ground, must remain respectfully distant from them. At bottom, there is no positive rite which does not constitute a veritable sacrilege, for a man cannot hold commerce with the sacred beings without crossing the barrier which should ordinarily keep them separate.[4]

This essay will be concerned with positive interpersonal ritual, that is, with supportive acts, not avoidant ones. These positive rites are apparently more important for relations between persons who know each other ("personal" relationships, broadly defined) than for anonymous ones. As suggested, these acts have been surprisingly little studied—certainly hardly at all in our Western society, in spite of the fact that it would be hard to imagine a more obvious contemporary application of the analysis recommended by Durkheim and Radcliffe-Brown.

II

One approach to the study of supportive ritual is to bring together phenomenally different acts that seem to have some sort of formal feature in common, some sort of shared interpersonal theme. One example might be cited: the ritualization of identificatory sympathy. The needs, desires, conditions, experiences, in short, the situa-

[4] Durkheim, *op. cit.*, p. 338.

tion of one individual, when seen from his own point of view, provides a second individual with directions for formulating ritual gestures of concern. Here we find the indulgences and solicitousness that hosts provide by way of food, drink, comfort, and lodging; here "grooming talk," [5] as when inquiries are made into another's health, his experience on a recent trip, his feelings about a recent movie, the outcome of his fateful business; here the neighborly act of lending various possessions and providing minor services. And here, incidentally, are positive rites performed between the anonymously related, as when, upon request, an individual gives directions, the time, a match, or some other "free good" to a stranger.[6] Note, the breadth of disinterested concern displayed through these various acts of identificatory sympathy is similar to what a parent exhibits in regard to a child, but the similarity stops there. Courtesies are involved, not substantive care; small offerings are received as though they were large, and large ones, when made, are often made with the expectation that they will be declined.

Other themes suggest themselves. For example, there are those ritual offerings associated with the tactful avoidance of open exclusion, a means of avoiding openly denying the worth of others. Ex-

[5] Discussed in Desmond Morris, *The Naked Ape* (London: Jonathan Cape, 1967; New York: McGraw-Hill Book Co., 1967), pp. 204–206. The phase is attributed to J. A. R. A. M. Van Hoof.

[6] It is interesting that in middle-class Anglo-American society it is often less incursive to ask a stranger for a free good than it is to initiate the offering of one. One reason is that an individual's needs are typically more apparent to him than to others; indeed, when circumstances make it very clear what an individual's need is, help may be volunteered by a stranger, providing the need can be satisfied at little cost to the satisfier. Another reason is that to make a request or accept an offer is to show a need over whose containment or satisfaction one does not have complete self-control; one thereby is subject to a limitation on self-determination and autonomy. When an individual is among strangers, he is usually sustained in the right to decide for himself when he will accept such a limit, this power preserving some of his autonomy in the face even of his losing most of it. Of course, to beg for anything more than a free good is to trade one's autonomy for what can be gotten thereby. The current hippie practice of panhandling is a nice send-up of this whole ritual code.

amples are: the practice of "courtesy" introductions, whereby Harry, when with Mary, introduces her to Dick, who happens to pass their way; the nicety of extending to all those in one's conversational circle an offer to minor comforts and consumables one is about to enjoy oneself; the practice of lightly proffering to all persons in hearing an invitation extended to one.

A second approach to the study of supportive ritual is to try to isolate specialized functions, the assumption being that although all of these rites serve to support social relationships, this can be done at different junctures and in different ways, and these differences provide a means of distinguishing classes of these rituals.[7] One illustration is provided.

There are "rituals of ratification" performed for and to an individual who has altered his status in some way—his relationships, appearance, rank, certification, in short, his prospects and direction in life. Ratificatory rituals express that the performer is alive to the situation of the one who has sustained change, that he will continue his relationship to him, that support will be maintained, that in fact things are what they were in spite of the acknowledged change. In brief, there are "reassurance displays."

Considerable range is shown here. There are the congratulations at marriage, the careful commiserations at divorce, the doleful condolences at deaths; at the other extreme is the ribbing and joking that results when a youth appears among his friends wearing his skiing accident in a cast or when he newly acquires a driver's license.

Ratificatory rituals also present another side. The individual can take many steps that represent self-determined claims to altered and desired status, and when he does, ratificatory rituals may be provided him, not so much to establish a link between the new and the old as to confirm that the new presentation of self is accepted

[7] Here the ethological and the social anthropological approaches employ much the same model and are subject to much the same criticisms. Indeed, to class a handshake as a "mutual appeasement gesture," and to let it go at that, is something both schools could do and could have the same reasons to be leery about doing.

and approved; and this support is the more owed the more the claim is doubtful. Again, a wide range of matters is involved. Marriage congratulations to those who have acquired unattractive spouses are often weighted with this kind of tact, as are the joking remarks made to a male who newly affects a beard. Of special interest, I think, are what the latter illustrates, namely, little strokings called forth by minor, doubtful claims. An example can be cited from a report by a woman who passed as a high school student to relearn about adolescent life, the scene being a shopping expedition by the poseur and a newly acquired girl friend:

> I bought the shoes and made Gretel's day. "Oh, I'm so happy for you," she said. "I know just what you'll go through tomorrow when everybody sees them. Everybody'll say, 'Oh, they're *cute.*' Just you wait. You'll have such fun."
>
> I am obliged to elaborate here. You see, "everybody" knew I was going shoe-hunting because I had said so at lunch. When Gretel got home she would telephone the report on our trip, thereby alerting all eyes to my feet. When I would arrive in school in the morning, if the new shoes were found on me, appropriate comments would be made. Thus did it happen the next morning—and all day long—that everybody did indeed examine my shoes and say, "Oh, they're cute." They also said, "Oh, let's *see* them. Oh, how tough." One girl told me that she loved my shoes without looking at them. She knew just from hearing about them that she loved them.[8]

Occasions for ratificatory rituals are everywhere even humbler. In a conversation, let a participant whom others would rather see silent make a statement, and he will have expressed the belief that he has a full right to talk and is worth listening to, thereby obliging his listeners to give a sign, however begrudging and however mean, that he is qualified to speak. (The complete withholding of these ritual supports is often inclined to but rarely achieved, and understandably. Without such mercies, conversation would want of its fundamental basis of organization—the ritual interchange

---

[8] Lyn Tornabene, *I Passed as a Teenager* (New York: Lancer Books, 1968), p. 144.

—and everywhere unsatisfactory persons would be left to bleed to death from the conversational savageries performed on them.)

It is worth noting that when the situation of one party to a relationship changes, the other party may not be in a position to know it. In such cases the person who is in line to receive ratificatory regard will sometimes provide the information necessary so that the other will see what by way of ritual needs to be done. He "fills in" the other so that the relationship can be updated,[9] and incidentally gives the appearance of inviting compliments or condolences.

An examination of the conduct of individuals who have experienced a sharp change in their social personage throws light on the relativity of "contactability." The greater the change in the self of a person, the further he can be physically from those whom he yet defines as close enough for the telling. And often a careful order of telling will be required, with those "closest" being told first, and so on, so that the flow of information and ratification rituals nicely reflects the relational structure of the individual's social world.[10] Note that in case of deep change, all an individual's close others may have to be allowed to reconfirm their relationship to him before he is able to reestablish some degree of ritual ease. He will have to check his network out, often by engineering contacts that can be given a less delicate apparent purpose.

III

To further consider the themes and functions of supportive rituals, some attention must be given to a concept that is widely used in the study of interaction but rarely defined: "social contact." In the

---

[9] See Goffman, *Stigma* (Englewood Cliffs, N.J.: Prentice-Hall, Inc., 1963; London: Penguin Books, 1968), pp. 78, 95.

[10] A useful treatment of this theme may be found in David Sudnow, *Passing On* (Englewood Cliffs, New Jersey: Prentice-Hall, Inc., 1967), Chapter 5, "On Bad News," pp. 117–152.

fullest sense, contact can be said to occur when individuals simultaneously address themselves to one another, and this is simultaneously known and known to be known.[11] Face-to-face orientation is typically involved.[12] Typically, too, the contact forms part of something more complex, namely, a social encounter involving an exchange of words or other recognition rituals and the ratification of mutual participation in an open state of talk.

There are marginal and derived forms of social contact: "blind" transactions, in which persons come together to accomplish a joint activity but do not bracket this spate of mutual coordination ritu-

---

[11] It is possible and perhaps desirable to define social contact as a unit, the entire period during which a "heightened orientation and relevance of acts" is sustained among a set of individuals. This definition is employed in a useful paper by Suzanne Ripley, "Intertroop Encounters among Ceylon Gray Langurs (*Presbytis entellus*)," in Stuart A. Altmann, ed., *Social Communication among Primates* (Chicago: The University of Chicago Press, 1967), chap. 14, pp. 237–253, esp. 243. The one defect of this use is that it misses a significant sense of the term. The concern is that individuals have come together and are therefore easily open to interactional developments of various kinds, and one's interest is as much in what does not develop as in what does. So the crux, then, is not the *unit* of interaction that results during the period in which contact is sustained, but rather *that* contact has been made, and that one good reason why various dealings did not occur cannot be given.

[12] The term "confrontation" might be better except that this word has recently acquired a special meaning in the reportings of contact between young-minded militants and officials, whether governmental, educational, or domestic. Although the term has not been explicated, it does seem to be used with enough consistency to warrant an effort to state what seems to be involved structurally. It can be argued that all face-to-face dealings are conducted in accordance with ground rules, some of which ordinarily ensure that the participant with superior social power (as assessed by standards and structures external to the business at hand) will be allowed to determine the liberties and license employed by the others in commerce with him. A confrontation occurs when social inferiors are warned that they have begun to encroach, besmear, profanize, and presume, and respond by extending the violation, often in a flagrant way that precludes the superior's responding with defensive inattention. Superiors have always rendered themselves vulnerable to ritual profanization in making contact with their lessers, but somehow in America, it is only recently that this fact has been widely and systematically exploited.

ally, that is, do not sustain a social encounter; "dead-eyeing," where two individuals mutually submit to each other's direct gaze but do not ratify the exchange of lookings with the ritual of "social recognition"; telephone contact, this being very closely patterned on face-to-face encounters; contact through the mails and telegraph where, even when no reply is forthcoming, the sender may tacitly assume that his communication has been received and that contact has been made; one-way contact, where one individual sees or hears another but knows that he is not sensed in return. Note, two individuals may be in bodily contact and not be, by the definition above, in social contact at all. Similarly, if by the phrase "to be in touch" we mean the contact provided in a face-to-face encounter, a telephone conversation, or an exchange of letters, then individuals can be in touch socially without touching.

It is apparent that a precondition for the performance of supportive rituals is that the giver and receiver be in contact, whether face-to-face or mediated. No contact, no interpersonal ritual.

There are three general circumstances in which contact occurs and thereby supportive ritual becomes possible. First, there are sober or non-ceremonial reasons for making contact, namely, business at hand that requires the participants of a relationship to get in touch. At these moments, supportive rituals *can* (although they need not) be performed in passing, as it were, with so very little additional inconvenience that participants may find that it is hard to find reason for not doing so. Second, contact can occur fortuitously when the parties to the relationship make independent but simultaneous use of the same streets, service establishment, public transportation, and the like, or when they find themselves participating in the same social occasion.[13] As is said, the individuals may happen upon, bump into, or come across each other. (Of course, with care, social contact can often be avoided during these various comings together, but not always tactfully.) Finally, contact can occur because the avowed and controlling purpose of one or both

[13] I partly draw on an argument by Emanuel Schegloff, distinguishing telephone conversations from incidental street conversations, the occasion of the former ordinarily being intended openly, the latter not.

of the individuals is to perform a supportive ritual to the other.

These three bases of contact—business, accident, and ceremony—provide not only reasons for being in touch but also rationales, that is, conventionally recognized understandings, each with its own range of appropriate applications. Each basis of contact, then, can provide the given or apparent reason for contact when indeed one of the other two bases actually exists. And, of course, an individual giving one reason may correctly or incorrectly suspect he is suspected of really having another.

If any two individuals at any one time are to arrange to get in touch, costs will be involved in terms of time, money, and effort, whether the contact is face-to-face or mediated, and for whatever purpose.

Related to this, but only partly dependent on it, will be another factor: probability and frequency of contact. Given the business dealings between two individuals, their arranged rituals, and the degree of interpenetration of their daily rounds, what is the probability of no contact during a given interval, or a contact in a given place; and what is the likely frequency of contact during a given period of time?

These measures are an objective feature of the situation of any two related individuals. It is important to note that in the case of many social relationships, participants develop some understanding and presumption concerning the costs and probabilities of contact between them. Ritual support of the relationship will be accommodated to the affirmations that the usual frequency and costs of contact allow. I am arguing then that the folk notion of two individuals living or working "near" or "far" from each other—a kind of straight-line conception—may not be entirely adequate here. It may be better to think of the two as inhabiting an environment or arena anywhere within which much the same cost and probability attaches to contact. Their circumstances in regard to each other can then change either by a shift in the area throughout which a given amount of contact is sustained, or a shift in the probability and economy of contact within a given area, or some combination of both.

One example of arena-related ritual is what might be called "maintenance rites." Given particular presumptions regarding contact, parties to a relationship may engineer a coming together because business, ceremony, or chance has not done so recently enough (it is felt) to guarantee the well-being of the relationship. It is as if the strength of a bond slowly deteriorates if nothing is done to celebrate it, and so at least occasionally a little invigoration is called for. Thus our collectively timed ceremonials of Christmas and New Year's function as a reminder of the need for, and an excuse for the performance of, various supportive expressions. Individually timed ritual occasions, such as birthdays and wedding anniversaries, have a similar function, except that here, especially for the young, a ratificatory element is present.

IV

Given these considerations of relationships and contact, a special focus is possible in examining positive interpersonal rites. We can look at the functionally defined class of supportive rituals of which instances appear to be found in every human society and not a few animal ones: what English speakers call a greeting. Indeed, our own term (along with its Western language equivalents) seems so widely and closely applicable that a technical literature concerning both man and animals is coming to be built upon it.[14]

---

[14] To date, the one paper on human greetings seems to be Irenäus Eibl-Eibesfeldt, "Zur Ethologie des menschlichen Grussverhaltens Beobachtungen an Balinese, Papuas und Samoanern, nebst vergleichenden Bemerkungen," *Z.f. Tierpsychol.*, XXV (1968): 727–744. I believe the first chapter on human greetings is to be found in Hilary Callan, *Ethology and Society* (Oxford: Clarendon Press, 1970), chap. VII, pp. 104–124. See also, for example, Jane Van Lawick-Goodall, "The Behaviour of Free-Living Chimpanzees in the Gombe Stream Reserve," *Animal Behaviour Monographs*, 1, Part 3 (London: Bailliere, Tindall, and Cassell, 1968), p. 284. It might be added that there could hardly be a better argument for there being common ground between animal and human studies than that provided by greeting behavior.

A selection from a set of behavioral displays is involved. Two individuals upon approaching orient frontally to each other. Their glances lock for a moment in communion, eyes glisten, smiling expressions of social recognition are conveyed, and a note of pleasure is briefly sustained. Hand-waving, hat-tipping, and other "appeasement gestures" may be performed. A verbal salutation is likely to be provided along with a term of address. When possible, embracing, hand-shaking, and other bodily contacting may occur.[15]

The interpretation of greeting behavior is more or less standard. When acquainted persons find themselves facing each other after a period of separation, some show of pleasure in the company of the other is obligatory. This display marks the delight an individual takes in finding himself in the presence of a loved and worthy object and provides assurance that the separation just now terminated, not having been malicious, is not an expression of the relationship. Often greetings will also affirm a differential allocation of status, specifically attesting that the subordinate is willing to continue to keep his place. (For example, American military practice obliges the subordinate to salute first and to hold the salute until the superordinate has returned it.) Also, when greetings are performed between strangers, there is an element of guarantee for safe passage. (So that in urban settings, where nods are not ordinarily exchanged between the unacquainted, circumstances can be found, as when marked trust and cooperation are required in a narrow passageway, when a nod exchange is employed, evidence that both individuals are willing to show themselves in the open,

---

[15] One must bear in mind that the rituals available for greeting are not likely to fit precisely the job the user would like to have performed, a condition met with in almost all use persons make of the ritual idiom available to them. At airports, for example, males of the social class whose members do not employ the "social kiss" may feel awkward in kissing *or* not kissing an arriving female family friend. If the former possibility is chosen, there may be an effort to partly guy the act, or to restrict the kiss to a peck that is approached from more than the usual standing distance, thereby ensuring respect for personal space with one part of the body while another part is necessarily abrogating it. Here I draw on an unpublished paper (1965) by B. L. Irving, "Departure and Arrival."

having no evil intent to hide.) And there are less obvious elements. For example, the fact that an individual can return a greeting when one is made to him conveys that he is sufficiently in control of his situation to be free to orient momentarily to the interchange. Thus, parents can use a greeting to test whether or not an angry child has recovered from his sulk. Friends, finding that a greeting has not been returned, can feel that "something is wrong." [16]

The initial description of greeting practices is, then, fairly easy. However, closer analysis exposes a multitude of complicating issues, requiring us to shift from an everyday term to a technical one. Middle-class American practice can serve as a starting point.

1. When two acquaintances pass close by each other on their separate daily rounds in consequence of what is seen as the routine intersecting of their activities, they are likely to exchange "passing greetings," often without otherwise pausing. (In rural areas, something like these social-recognition rituals may be performed between passing strangers.) Often these displays will be relatively muted and fully exhaust the encounter to which they give rise; nonetheless, the spontaneous impulse to perform them is very strong.[17] Note, the apparent structural assumption behind these

---

[16] In an unpublished field study of the Berkeley Police, Walter Clark, describing a cruiser-car officer, records: "Before each liquor store, he stopped and, without leaving the car, waited until the clerk noticed him and waved in a relaxed fashion."

[17] Ordinarily in our society this rule regarding recognition rituals is so ingrained that an individual desiring to avoid the act for strategic reasons (whether on his own by acting as if he has not seen the other, or collusively, by collaborating with the other in acting as if they are not on greeting terms) will nonetheless show some self-conscious inhibition of the inclination. And when an acquaintance of an individual appears right before him and insists on being greeted in spite of having been carefully "not seen," then rather great strength of character is required if the individual is to continue to decline to greet. A nice fictionalized version of this issue is presented in Saul Bellow's *Dangling Man* (New York: Meridian Books, 1960; London: Penguin Books, 1960), pp. 32–36. An instinctive basis for greetings is therefore easy to imagine. And yet there are persons with the disadvantage of youth or color who effectively decline to participate in this circle of civility. Thus, for example, Liebow, reporting on informal social organization among Washington, D.C. blacks, says:

displays is that the probability of contact between the two participants is fixed and that what the passing exchange marks is an ordinary, anticipated instance of the contact ensured thereby. Thus, these greetings have much the character of maintenance rituals.

Passing greetings can be considered in conjunction with "greetings of surprise." Given the understanding two individuals have of the likely place and frequency of contact, occasions can arise of their meeting "unexpectedly." Here the greeting exchanged ("What in the world are you doing here?") is likely to be more expansive than the passing variety and the encounter that carries it likely to require a momentary holding-up of the otherwise independent courses of action. Furthermore, surprise greetings will often involve the participants in a certain amount of fumbling and embarrassment, since the circumstances of their unexpected contact can find them little disposed to orient themselves to the requisite mutual consideration and, by definition, little expectant of having to do so; in fact, often what has come to pass is a breakdown in "audience segregation." Nonetheless, passing greetings and surprise greetings ought, I think, to be classed together; both have primarily a maintenance character.

2. When two individuals who are favorably disposed to each other by virtue of acquaintanceship and/or mutually desired dealings come together in talk, they often mark its beginning with an exchange of salutations; in short, they greet each other.[18] Note

---

> When the father walks into the home, the child may not even look up from what he is doing and the father, for his part, takes no more notice than he receives. If their eyes happen to catch one another's glances, father and child seem to look without seeing until one or the other looks elsewhere.

Elliot Liebow, *Tally's Corner* (Boston: Little, Brown and Company, Inc., 1967), p. 79. I might add, in further argument against the instinct theory, that it is possible to catch middle-class parents in the act of teaching their young to mark passing contact with a recognition ritual.

[18] The individual display during what comes to be the beginning of an encounter is complex, and the role and place of greetings within it are variable. The first mover's first move may function as a "summons"—to use Emanuel Schegloff's apt term—calling the attention of the recipient to the fact that an audience is requested. (This may take the form of a knock at the door, a shuffle outside an office, a word tentatively conveyed, a ring-

that this particular ritual is structurally somewhat different from what was described as a passing greeting. The latter, as it were, looks in only one direction: back from the contact to the relationship of the individuals who have momentarily come into each other's ken. The greeting associated with encounters, however, looks in two directions: back to the relationship of the participant but also forward to the temporary period of increased access that has just now come into being.

---

ing of the telephone.) This opening move can be responded to with a word such as "Hello," which establishes that channels have been opened, or that they soon will be, or that opening them is impossible now. If the first is the case, the summoner may convey a salutation, state his personal and/or social identity, and provide a purpose for the summons and a suggestion as to how long the business will take. The recipient of the summons can then salute the summoner in return and authorize his continuation of talk. These initial moves on the part of the summoner and recipient can then function to ratify mutual orientation and openness for talk, suggest what statuses are to apply, and how long the encounter is to be sustained. If pleasure in the prospect of the engagement is not always conveyed, then at least a willingness to hold back hostilities for the duration of the talk is implied. Note, in circumstances where individuals disposed to one another come into close co-presence quickly, all of these functions can be overlayed on the opening greeting; in other circumstances, these various opening messages may be conveyed through a sequence of gestures and words. "Hello" uttered with proper accent may thus not be a greeting at all, but rather a sign that channels are open and that the summoner can now provide reason, if he has it, for warranting an audience; if he then succeeds in qualifying himself, he will then be greeted, typically, I think, with a contrastive term such as "Hi." All this is borne out by the fact that a functional equivalent for the open-channel hello is a term such as "Yes" (which Emily Post recommends a lady answer a gentleman with when he calls her name preparatory to introducing himself and his legitimate connection), but this term would not qualify as a functional equivalent of "Hi," although phrases such as "How are you?" would.

Sheila Seitel, of the Department of Anthropology, University of Pennsylvania, who has been studying greeting behavior among the Haya of Tanzania, suggests that the first mover's first move may rely on a greeting form to provide unseen others a warning that someone is in their vicinity and a request for permission to enter an area to which they have a territorial claim. Our "Hello" called out with a rising inflection can function in this fashion. As in the case of the summons, if this call is answered, the intruder may then provide a greeting, but with a word that allows easy differentiation from the one employed as the "no-intrusion-intended" sign.

The initiation of an encounter marks the beginning of a period of heightened access among the participants. It is plain, however, that this is not the only way in which two individuals might suddenly find themselves with increased access, and it is interesting that at the initiation of each of these other arrangements, something like a greeting may be found. Thus, when two individuals join each other to form a "with," they obviously expose themselves to increased access and typically, on doing so, greet each other. Similarly, when business or ceremony leads them to attend the same social occasion where they will be in "open contact," that is, destined to happen into contact many times during the hours to come, greetings again occur. Something similar can be said of an individual arriving on the factory floor; or, after work, arriving home; or, in the morning, getting up and once again becoming available to other members of the family.[19] In all of these situations, too, the individual will find himself in sudden increased contactability with a set of others, and again greetings are likely to occur. Finally, when an individual moves to a new neighborhood or region, he will find that he has suddenly increased his accessibility to those already residing there; once again, greetings occur. The conclusion is obvious: in our society, greetings occur between individuals at the point where they find themselves about to enjoy a period of heightened access to each other. This allows us to account, incidentally, for the peculiar fact that when two individuals are introduced by a third, a little dance is likely to occur; faces light up, smiles are exchanged, eyes are addressed, handshakes or hat-doffing may occur, and also inquiries after the other's health —in fact, just the small behaviors we might expect during a greeting. And this is only natural. A similarity of forms bespeaks a similarity of function. A social introduction marks the initial point

[19] As suggested, the military version of the greeting is the salute, and it has the sociological charm of formalization, both with respect to how to perform it and when to perform it. Thus, the rule on board small ships, apparently, is that an enlisted man salutes an officer (other than the captain) the *first* time he sees him on each day. I draw here on an unpublished paper by David L. Cook, "Public Order in the U.S. Navy" (1969).

when two individuals come into a personal relationship, and relationships themselves, apart from matters of geography, increase the ease of access between the persons related. Access, after all, is one of the things that personal relationships are about. An introduction, like a greeting, is an access ceremony.

3. Let us retrace our steps for a moment. Once we have seen that conversational encounters often begin with a greeting, it should not be hard to see that when they come to be terminated, a supportive ritual will again occur, namely, some form of farewell display performed during leave-taking.[20] (The interpretation is standard: the goodbye brings the encounter to an unambiguous close, sums up the consequence of the encounter for the relationship, and bolsters the relationship for the anticipated period of no contact.) And of course a similar argument can be made in connection with the other bases of access—withs, social occasions, neighborhoods, and so forth. In these cases, too, leave-taking is marked by ritual display.

4. Taken together, greetings and farewells provide ritual brackets around a spate of joint activity—punctuation marks as it were—and ought therefore to be considered together. More generally, greetings mark a transition to a condition of increased access and farewells to a state of decreased access. It is possible, then, to employ a single definition to cover both greetings and farewells: they are ritual displays that mark a change in degree of access. I propose to call such behavior "access rituals." Passing greetings here constitute a marginal case; the increased access they represent is one in theory only, for once the contact occurs, it is likely to be lost again as the greeters proceed on their way. A passing greeting is almost like the ritualization of a ritual, a ceremonial acknowledgement of the possibility of access. Hellos are exchanged, but goodbyes are often dispensed with, as if the end of not being in touch was being marked but the beginning of being in

[20] Greetings appear to have a broader base than leave-takings. As suggested, many higher animals clearly engage in greetings similar to ours, both in form and in functional location. An animal version of human goodbye is much more difficult to establish.

touch not realized and therefore its termination unneedful of ritual comment.

Note that ritual bracketing is likely whether the period of increased access was brought about by accident or by design, and if by design, whether for business or ritual purposes. Furthermore, it is plain that mediated access also qualifies. When a conversation is held over the phone, this mediated period of contact will be bracketed by salutations, too, again regardless of the purpose of the contact. Finally, when a letter is written, it, too, will begin and end with a salutation, as though in writing the letter the reading of it can be taken for granted.[21]

V

Having progressed from the lay term "greeting" to the concept "access ritual," let us examine some of the things that can be said about this behavior.

1. As is true of other arrangements within the domain of public order, the expectation that an access ritual will be performed by a certain person at a certain moment establishes a time-person slot such that anything issuing from him at that moment can be very closely and imaginatively read for a functional equivalent of an access ritual. Certainly physical gestures can be used instead of words and a wide range of constraining contingencies will be seen as sufficient reason to allow use of quite atypical equivalents. Indeed, a jokester can suppress all response to a salutation while looking into the faces of those who provide it and know that if he breaks into a smile just at the point when his return salutation

[21] It should be borne in mind that in the case of some encounters, both face-to-face and mediated, and especially among the unacquainted, greetings and farewells may not be the only ritualization of access. As suggested, a request for a hearing or an apology for an intrusion may open an encounter, and a thanks-for-the-audience may terminate it.

should have ended, that the others will display a little laugh to show that they get the point that a friendly joke was being played. The jokester, in brief, can count on those who make the first move retrospectively reading the *absence* of any reply as a joking statement that was going on all the time. Social nature abhors an empty slot. Anything can be dumped in it and read as the anticipated reply. It is in this light that we are to understand the oft-remarked fact that when A asks B how he is feeling, the questioning is not to be taken literally; a question is not being asked, a greeting is being extended.[22] The answer provided is not an answer but an independent greeting, one available to second speakers. If identificatory sympathy alone were involved, then we might expect some reciprocity as in the following sequence:

A: "How are you?"
B: "Fine, thanks."
B: "And how are you?"
A: "Fine, thanks."

But in passing greetings, in fact, we often find *in toto* the following:

A: "How are you?"
B: "Fine."

which denies reciprocity. Or solely the following:

A: "How are you?"
B: "How are you?"

which omits all answering. Indeed, if the context is right, then one

[22] One qualification ought perhaps to be allowed. When the recipient of a greeting is a hopeless invalid with a painful disease or someone who has just sustained an overwhelming personal loss, the greeter may feel a trifle uneasy about using the standard form, "How are you?" Halfway through the offering the greeter might find himself giving feeling to his words, and that, of course, would be disastrous. Emily Post recognizes that the recipient, too, might be uneasy about using the standard return in these circumstances and recommends, "All right, thank you."

individual's statement can be taken as a functional equivalent for the full interchange. Thus, when one individual races past another in order, say, to catch up with some friends, the racer may be thrown a hello whose tone and gesture will suggest that it is understood that no answer will be possible, or he himself may initiate the ritual with a wave of his hand and a half-twist of his upper trunk, a greeting the reply to which his forward movement will obviously prevent him from witnessing. Thus the following:

A: "Helloooo"
B: (gone)

A: "Can't stop"
B: ———

We find these apparently incomplete variants because they are functionally equivalent to the complete form.

2. Although I have classed various greetings together, it is obvious that a significant difference exists among them. The "Hi" one laconically employs when passing a neighbor each day would not be appropriate, indeed would be a sign of trouble in a relationship, if extended to someone known to have been away a long time or known to have been a great distance away and cut off from contact.[23] Instead of "Hi's," "Hello's" would probably be exchanged, followed by a spate of grooming talk. The restoration of one's self to another self would have to be celebrated.

What is said here about greetings can also be said about farewells. If the leave-takers are merely going back into the same felt probability of contact from which they came, and if this probability is high, then a phrase such as "See you" or "So long" may well be employed; on the phone, currently, it is "B'bye." But if the de-

[23] Before the advent of jet airplanes, the time during which an individual was away from his neighborhood and the distance over which he had traveled were nicely correlated; both variables could be managed in the same simple ritual equation. One of the novel aspects of the recent space voyages (it is said there are others) is that men who warranted the biggest goodbye and hello in the world had been gone for only a few days.

parture is to a place which for a time will render contact costly, then something more serious is likely to be said, namely, "Goodbye." [24] And similarly, when one "moves on" from a conversational circle during a party or business occasion, there being an expectation that co-participation in conversation will soon recur, an "excuse me" or a hand gesture may be all that is given.

In considering the appropriate expansiveness of access rituals, I have tacitly kept constant the closeness of the relationship binding the two individuals who perform the display to each other. But obviously, of course, a long-absent neighbor will ordinarily be owed less of a show than a long-absent brother. However, relationships themselves carry an implication of probability of contact, and so the two factors, degree of access and closeness of relationship, are not independent. This is nicely seen in traditional etiquette, which seemed to recognize that the farewell given a stranger should be distinctive, in part, perhaps, because he might never be met with again:

> A lady terminates an interview with a stranger who has come to see her on business, by bidding him "Good afternoon." On like occasions she would say "Good morning" or "Good evening," but not "Good-by" or "Good night"—both of which are said to friends.[25]

In any case, it must be admitted that rituals of greeting and farewell are responsive not merely to the issue of access but also to the kind of ritual license binding the performers; thus, presumably "Hi" would not be appropriate coming from a subordinate to a very sacred official, even though the two parties enjoyed an environment in which contact between them was, and was known to be, frequent.

3. As suggested earlier, the implication is that in many cases an appreciation of the probability and costs of contact is built into a relationship, and, in consequence, any return to a wonted ease of

---

[24] Our term "farewell" connotes a potentially permanent leave-taking, but now has a literary cast; the same can be said of the French "adieu."

[25] Emily Post, *Etiquette*, 3rd ed. (New York: Funk and Wagnalls, 1937; London: new edn. Cassells, 1969), p. 21.

contact upon the termination of distancing circumstances warrants special celebration.[26]

Given the above, we are to see that the following structural problem arises. On reattaining easy contact after an unusual separation, individuals owe each other an expansive greeting. However, the performance of this display will necessarily coincide with an increased likelihood of more frequent subsequent contact. If on each of these following contacts a full display were performed, the participants would soon find activity becoming clogged with ritual. An understanding must be available, then, whereby individuals can progressively leave off their inital obligation; there must be an "attenuation rule." Nowhere can this be seen more prettily than in the conduct of long-separated, closely related friends who newly come together during a social occasion. On first contact, an expansive greeting will occur. A moment later when the next proximity occurs, a reduced version of the initial display will be provided. Each succeeding contact will be managed with an increasingly attenuated greeting until after a time the two will exhibit the standard minimal middle-class social recognition only—a rapid grimace involving little change in eye expression, the two ends of the mouth stretching a little in a cheek flick. (After this point has been reached, the two may cooperate, of course, in seeing to it that one of them can act as though his eyes have not fallen on the other, thereby obviating all display, even the most attenuated.)

It should be noted that although an attenuation rule must be available in order to manage greetings, such a rule is not needed in

---

[26] This argument partly clears up an interesting ritual problem. When persons who are barely acquainted or not quite acquainted happen upon each other as tourists in a foreign land, they are likely to exchange expansive greetings and shows of pleasure and surprise at the prospect of being in each other's company. Why? One reason, I think, is that the two are suddenly forced into the status of persons close enough to know when there has been a marked increase in cost of contact between them—since it is now apparent to each that were he at home he would never be able to make contact with the other. But since at this very moment of discovery it costs nothing at all to groom each other, the opportunity to do so can hardly be forborne.

regard to closing salutations simply because once a farewell occurs, departure is likely, which means that if matters go as expected, contact will be broken and additional ritual for the time becomes impossible.[27]

4. Another issue. When accessibility is about to shift markedly in either direction—typically involving geography—parties to a relationship may make special arrangements to come together for a sociable period just to mark the transition. Thus whenever close friends newly find themselves in the same country, region, city, or neighborhood, they will often make a point of getting in touch, directly or by phone or mail, in order to mark the fact. Similarly, when a friend departs for a job in another state, enters the army, is to leave for an extended trip, or changes neighborhood or place of work, then the departure is likely to receive some ritualization: farewell parties are held and gifts may be given. Note that these ritual occasions are slotted into activity at an opportune time. In case of greetings, there will be an economy of effort in waiting for easy contact before a supportive display is performed (and correspondingly, a heightened affront in not so using the opportunity); similarly, the point of leave-taking is the last moment when getting in touch is possible at reduced rates.

These expansive access ceremonies draw attention to an interesting issue, which linguists call embedding. The ritual recognition that is accorded a significant change in access (especially geographical access) can itself be a period of high access, as in the case of social parties, dinners-out, or telephone calls. But these little periods of open contact, being something in their own right and not merely the functional equivalent, say, of a gift, must themselves be marked and bounded by opening and closing salutations following the rule for handling periods of heightened access, whatsoever their cause. That the reason for being together is to celebrate a felt

[27] Attenuation has also been considered by ethologists in an evolutionary time frame in regard to changes in species performance and use of particular displays. Here see M. Moynihan, "Control, Suppression, Decay, Disappearance and Replacement of Displays," in *Journal of Theoretical Biology*, XXIX (1970): 85–112.

shift in access does not alter matters. Obviously, on first making contact with a friend on the occasion of a farewell dinner for him, one still says hello or its equivalent. One does not initiate the encounter or social occasion with a goodbye. And the final closing salutation will contain within it at least two notes, one attesting to a small period of open access that is about to terminate and a second, no doubt the more significant, attesting to the beginning of a shift downward in the economy and likelihood of such a contact occurring.

5. Access ceremonies of the extended kind exhibit in a marked way what is often found in brief salutations also, namely, a division in ceremonial labor: the division between guest and host. Leave-takers typically leave someone who remains to represent the prior social world, and those newly arriving are typically in a guest or visitor relation to those amongst whom they newly come. The same in fact can often be said about social occasions and the period of open access which they provide: the premises are likely to be under the jurisdiction of someone who is therefore in the host role, and the others who participate are likely to be in a guest role. The complication here is that what is owed an individual in terms of one's relationship to him can be different from what is owed him in his situationally generated role as guest. Indeed these obligations can be in opposition. Thus when a stranger from another city is brought along to a dinner by someone who himself is merely a guest, the host will be under special obligation to make the stranger welcome, and this to the degree that the stranger might doubt the appropriateness of his presence. In any case, we are to see that an opening greeting may take the asymmetrical form of a welcome, just as a closing salutation can take the asymmetrical form of a "well-go," involving a nice-to-have-had-you on one side and a thanks-for-everything on the other.

6. Access ceremonies held in private homes have a relevantly troublesome feature. To greet someone in one's house who has recently come from far away is not to have availed oneself of prior opportunities that necessarily occurred when he came within practical reach. For one's house cannot be gotten to without first com-

ing into one's country and city and neighborhood. Similarly, to say goodbye to a loved-one from one's doorstep when the leave-taker is to become quite inaccessible for a period is to disavail oneself of the opportunity to follow along with him to a somewhat later point in his departure, which is almost inevitably a practical possibility. These greetings and farewells understandably, then, want of something. And it is understandable that courtesy will often require that the arrival be met at the airport or station or dock—this being the first practical contact point—and be said goodbye to in the same setting. Long-distance travel by car solves this problem, particularly when the vehicle can be parked close outside the door.

7. Saying that greetings come at the beginning of increased access and farewells at the end, does not cover all the structural differences between these two rituals. Another is suggested here.

Since a greeting marks the initiation of a period of easier contact, the participants may be concerned to constrain their enthusiasm so that a misleading indication of what is to be expected will not occur. Closing salutations figure differently. Since the participants can assume that they soon will be less available to each other, at least for a time, the way is opened for supportive accesses which otherwise might create burdensome anticipations—a concern which often inhibits individuals from treating their associates too well. High praise and substantial offerings can be accorded since there will be no chance for this level of giving to be established as the norm. Desires for increased closeness and involvement can be expressed safely because there will be no chance to realize them. Reservations the senders-off have about the merit of the leave-taker are erased, because soon close evaluation will not be an issue. At the same time, the participants can demonstrate and affirm with only one down-payment that they are persons who give weight to the feelings and fate of others. The one qualification here, of course, is that favors extended at the beginning of increased access are likely to be easier to reciprocate than those extended at the beginning of decreased access, and this may influence the giver's decision as to when to give.

8. In the context of this difference between greetings and farewells, we can properly see another. In the main, greetings are oriented to the lapsed time of no contact that is now terminated, and once these rituals are performed, their significance cannot be undercut. A second and third recontacting following close on the first can carry a little reflected warmth as a means of preventing embarrassment to the initial greeting. And should anticipated contact fail to occur for extraneous reasons, disappointment can be felt, and there the matter can rest. Farewells, on the other hand, are situated in a fundamentally different way in regard to the management of relationships. A farewell is oriented not to the termination of the social occasion or sociable moment wherein it takes place but to the sharp decrease that is about to occur in the possibility of such comings-together again occurring—at least for a time. And the more lengthy and absolute the predicted separation, the more expansive the ritual. Yet no matter how long and complete the anticipated separation, the fact that the participants are at the moment in easy access situates them favorably for the separation not to occur as planned. Farewells, in short, inevitably expose the participants to unanticipated recontacting. And should this occur, the performers will find that the ritual already performed is improperly profuse for what has turned out to be a short absence; yet there is no way to take it back. And if the actual departure then comes, the need will arise for a performance that has already been completed. Something has been "worked through" which now must be, but cannot be, worked through again. A twinge of anomie results, the kind that comes about when ritual statements are made that undermine the idiom itself. All of this is exacerbated by the fact that when a person is accessible to others to a given degree, the social life that results takes this into consideration. Once he alters this accessibility downward, his social place begins to close up over him. Returning unexpectedly, he finds that there has begun to be no room for him.

Examples of the disordering effect of failed departures are numerous. An individual leaving a social party, having been given a handsome well-go by the host, discovers a block away that he must return to retrieve something left behind; the greeting that is due him on re-establishing easy access must be attempted in the face of a recently performed farewell which now proves to have been performed in vain. Another example often noted occurs in connection with ocean voyages. Shipboard friendships can be enthusiastically established, bringing together persons who would otherwise stay clear of each other, because it is evident that bondedness need not continue after the voyage. Promises to meet soon can be warmly exchanged when the ship docks, it being half-understood that these promises cannot or need not be honored. The activity associated with disembarkation, however, provides an arena where ensured farewelling cannot be accomplished because there is no way to identify in advance the point of last easy contact. Almost inevitably the full farewell is performed and then recontact occurs shortly. Something similar occurs when a friend is taken to a train and followed to the platform. The final farewell is readied and the stage cleared for its performance, but if the train does not pull out on cue, the developmental rhythm held natural for emotions is broken; the stayer and goer must face each other in the wings, the deadness of the wait an embarrassment to the animation which is to occur as the train pulls out.

Another standard example of spoiled ritual is the office departure ceremony. An employee leaving for another job in a different city or about to retire may be treated to some sort of party and a farewell gift collectively paid for. On unexpectedly having to stay, or to return after a very brief absence, the recipient will find that he has caused himself and the givers to participate in an inappropriate statement, yet one that cannot be unsaid. (The final example here, of course, is the Enoch Arden case in which a person returning unexpectedly finds not only that his place is no longer available to him, but that another person has filled it, thereby creating what may be worse than a sociological demise, namely, a sociological double.) [28]

---

[28] Failed departures, greeting obligations, and attenuation rules can together give rise to some jumbled occasions. For example, in the United States in higher academic circles, fast travel, soft money, and expanding oc-

9. There is yet another difference between greetings and farewells that is worth considering. The display owed a close friend at his departure upon a long and perilous voyage is nicely balanced in its way by what is owed him upon his safe return; the same balance is found between the muted greeting of two neighbors when stopping for a back-fence chat and the muted farewells they exchange upon termination of the small talk. Indeed, it might be thought that for every type of greeting there is a corresponding type of farewell. But this is not the case, and the reason is supplied by a very obvious feature of relationships. For relationships must begin and end. They can begin with a social introduction, and when they do, this greeting-like ritual must necessarily be light because there is yet hardly any relationship to warrant something deeper—at least ordinarily. Relationships *can* end through a process of very gradual attenuation, but they can also end violently, either because of bad feelings or because circumstances such as death or geography are about to make the participants totally inaccessible to each other. In these latter cases, a farewell can occur that marks the simultaneous termination of a moment or two of being in touch and the relationship that made being in touch in that way possible. The poignancy of such a ritual hardly has a parallel or opposite expression in what can occur in greetings.[29]

---

cupational choice have led to considerable job mobility over distances, especially between the coasts, under circumstances where once a man has departed with suitable ceremony, he is likely to bob up again very soon on business, and then again and again and again. His first revisit is often marked with considerable social ritual; his ties are still warm, there is a chance he will change his mind and return, and there is an urge to ceremonially reinstate him as a member of the community. On the second revisit considerably less is made of him. By the third and the fourth, the attenuation rule will begin to govern, and his closest local friend may become his only one. Those involved will begin to seek for ritual rules that are in keeping with jet air travel.

[29] The exception occurs when an offspring introduces his new spouse to his parents, or when a parent introduces his new mate to his child by a previous spouse. Here full relationships may be ready to be taken up, awaiting only introductions.

10. A last difference. Preparation for a greeting can be done at one's ease, since the person to be greeted is not then present to examine the preparatory effort and the feelings generated by having to engage in it. Preparation for a farewell can be a much more delicate operation, since one party may be less inclined than the other to get on with the inevitable, thereby obliging the other party to instigate the process in advance by cues that are effective but not blatant.[30]

VI

I would like to add two concluding points about supportive rituals. The first concerns the category in general. Although it was suggested that positive ritual tends to be restricted to individuals in a personal relationship, there are significant exceptions; the possibility of giving and receiving free goods does bind those who are anonymously related. But here we must always expect to find a potential conflict between the provision of minor services to unacquainted others and the obligation to keep one's distance. This is nicely illustrated in the management of eye communion. When, for example, a man holds open a door for a lady, she falls under the obligation to show gratitude, the form available to her being to say, "Thank you." The man in turn, if he is a traditionalist, and if he wants to show the nicest of consideration, can decline to take advantage of this opening, can decline to ratify the encounter by a return of his eyes or words, and can instead make the kind of acknowledging bow that can be read by anyone present (not merely by those in a conversation), while specifically cutting his eyes and himself off from an orientation to her whom he has assisted. Here the "natural" ritualization of a supportive interchange into an encounter is inhibited, and the man in fact acts as though part of him had done nothing at all.

[30] Suggested by William Labov (in correspondence).

It should be apparent that deritualized support-giving introduces the problem of managing an official closure to the event, the usual devices employed for this involving more connectedness than is to be expressed. Here a beautiful practice might be cited, now much in abeyance: the hat-lifting rule. When, according to traditional, official etiquette, a gentleman was thanked by a strange lady for his holding the door open, or offering her a seat in a public conveyance, or picking up a dropped parcel and proffering it to her, or saving her from a runaway horse, he bowed slightly and raised his hat, all the while specifically not returning her gaze.[31] That motion allowed him to imply that the act was but a single expression of the worthiness of the recipient's self based upon her gender attributes, that he acknowledges the obligation of orienting himself to such qualities and to the passing predicaments of their possessor,

---

[31] Emily Post, *op. cit.*, pp. 26 ff, provides a good source of half-analyzed material on the hat as an element in the ritual idiom of a hypothetical class. Taking the hat off (or more accurately, having it off) marked an occasion when a gentleman was at ritual attention, his animal parts in full subjugation, and he himself meekly oriented to the presence of some sacred object, such as a lady, a casket, or the flag, the duration of his bareheadedness being coterminous with the duration of his being in the Presence. Ritual correlates were also found, such as careful posture and cigarette held out of mouth. Note that since a conversational encounter with a lady or head of state was also a period of presence, hat-holding could exactly span such a period.

Hat-lifting (or tipping) in the traditional ritual idiom is, as it were, different phonemically from holding the hat off. As suggested, its central role apparently was to show regard while simultaneously restoring the doer and recipient to a state of mutual civil inattention. Thus it was employed as a means of greeting to a stranger (as distinguished from the bow, which was the functional equivalent for acquaintances), an accompaniment of a please or thank-you to show that no overture was implied, and a response to another's thank-you, as a means of showing that no contact advantage was to be taken. The complication was that hat-tipping was also performed by a man when gaining or leaving face access to female acquaintances (including his own wife) to whom additional rituals were owing or had been performed. What appears to have been involved here is that the gender of the recipient required a vestigial recognition even while personal aspects of the relationship required other forms of ritual recognition.

and that the exchange has been brought to a close. It might be noted that females of the time could (and no doubt still do) draw on functionally similar devices; for example, in response to having a door held open for her, a woman could give a brief, verbal thanks while very carefully maintaining an even, resolute pace that records no orientation to an encounter.[32]

The second point, the final one. From the fact that greetings are found among many of the higher primates, as well as in any number of preliterate societies and all civilized ones, it would be easy to conclude that something like access rituals are universally found in societies. But, of course, universals are exactly what good ethnography brings into doubt. For example, of behavior in Arab villages it is written:

> The norms of modesty apply particularly in public and they apply to men as well as women. In Kufr al-Ma women do not greet men on village paths and men do not greet women. If they are near relations of opposite sex, they may greet one another without exchanging glances or after passing one another.[33]

And there are examples closer to home. American Indians of more than one tribe apparently take social relationships very seriously, not something to be lightly entered into, and at the same time appreciate that absence may induce change. In any case, they may decline to extend introductions within incidentally formed encounters, refrain from assuming that co-participation in the same with demands or even permits the quick initiation of talk between non-acquainteds, engage in silent courtship, and, to the point here, avoid verbal display when first re-establishing easy contact with a loved-one after a long separation.[34] I think it reasonable to con-

---

[32] Suggested by Hilary Callan.

[33] Richard T. Antoun, "On the Modesty of Women in Arab Muslim Villages," *American Anthropologist*, LXX (August 1968): 675.

[34] I draw on the useful paper by Keith H. Basso, " 'To Give Up on Words': Silence in Western Apache Culture," *Southwestern Journal of Anthropology*, XXVI, no. 3 (1970): 213–230.

clude, then, that certain social arrangements, such as the contact of acquainteds after an appreciated period of being out of touch, strongly facilitate the emergence of greeting ritual, and that where this point of renewed access is not ritualized, we are to look for special circumstances—circumstances which might not otherwise have been noticed but which are worth noticing.

[4]

Remedial Interchanges[1]

I *Norms*

A social norm is that kind of guide for action which is supported by social sanctions, negative ones providing penalties for infraction, positive ones providing rewards for exemplary compliance. The significance of these rewards and penalties is not meant to lie in their intrinsic, substantive worth but in what they proclaim about the moral status of the actor. Social sanctions themselves are norms about norms—techniques for ensuring conformance that are themselves approved. It is to be added that sanctions can be organized or diffuse, to use Radcliffe-Brown's terminology, or formal or informal, to use current terms: formal when a specialized agency that has been officially delegated the sanctioning task acts in due response to a schedule of sanctions; informal when the work is done locally, largely by the very person whose concerns have been jeopardized or by those who personally sympathize

[1] This treatment draws on and extends an earlier one, "On Face Work," reprinted in Goffman, *Interaction Ritual* (New York: Anchor Books, 1967), pp. 5–45. I am grateful to William Labov for suggestions incorporated throughout.

with him, the sanction itself taking a rough, ready, and changing form.

Although the notion of social norms is basic to the social sciences, there is not much beyond a few discriminations which can be recommended concerning instances of the class. For example, we can distinguish between prescriptions and proscriptions; supportive ritual typically involves the former and respect for another's territory the latter. We can distinguish between principles and conventions, that is, between norms felt to be desirable intrinsically and those whose only support comes from a current agreement to facilitate mutual dealings by means of them. We can also distinguish between strictures and standards, the first enabling and requiring full compliance, the second supporting an ideal that no one is expected to realize fully and many are known to fall considerably short of. Literacy in Western society is an example of the first, "looks" (in the physiognomic sense) of the second. And we can distinguish between substantive and ritual norms, the first regulating matters of value in their own right, the second displays, ceremonies, expressions, and other bits of conduct whose primary significance lies in the attitude which the actor can therewith take up to objects of ultimate value.

Norms presumably can be classified according to the sort of sanction attaching to them. Formal sanctions sustain regulations, informal sanctions what are sometimes thought of as social pressures. Regulations themselves have been divided into two parts: law, the regulation of behavior that draws upon the power and authority of the state, and rules, namely, norms enforced by an authorized agent, but one whose authority comes from some organization less inclusive than the state—an interesting distinction except that "rules" is too useful a term to define as anything other than synonymous with norms.[2]

It can be argued that norms or rules impinge on the individual in two different ways: as an obligation that requires him to do (or

---

[2] Recommended in Jack P. Gibbs, "Norms: The Problem of Definition and Classification," *American Journal of Sociology*, LXX, no. 5 (1965): 590.

refrain from doing) something in regard to others, and as an expectation that leads him to anticipate righteously that something will be done (or specifically not done) by them in regard to him. These obligations and expectations sometimes are called rights when they are desired by the person who has them and duties when they are not. It might be added that a norm often is assumed to be but one part, an integral one, of a code or system of norms.[3] Informally sanctioned codes are little explicated, whether by those who adhere to the rules or those who study adherents. Even quite formalized codes, such as the one regulating traffic on roads, leave many matters tacit.

Social norms are almost always couched in general terms, as if applying to a particular event because the event is one instance of a class to which the rule applies. Any deviation, then, on any one occasion when the rule is supposed to apply can give the impression that the actor may be delinquent with respect to the whole class of events. And any compliance can carry assurance regarding the actor's handling of all other events that come under the rule. (This is not to say that the individual can formulate the rule in general terms upon request; ordinarily an act of deviance or an act of notable conformance is required before he can demonstrate a competency to make judgments as if geared by a rule.) This tendency of individuals to read acts as symptoms gives an important expressive or indicative quality even to acts of a quite substantive kind, carrying as they do evidence of the actor's general relation to a rule and, by extension, his relation to the system of rules of which the one in question is a part. And, of course, such information often is taken as relevant for an appraisal of the actor's moral character.

---

[3] Simmel makes the interesting suggestion that terms such as "ethics" and "honor" refer to informal codes sustained by individuals acting in special sub-worlds—business, profession, politics—wherein only part of the self becomes subject to judgment, whereas the notion of morals and morality pertains to an informal code involving judgments that cannot be segregated. (Georg Simmel, "Morality, Honor and Law," being a section of his *Soziologie* translated for mimeographing by Everett C. Hughes.)

Rules are effective (insofar as they are) because those to whom they apply believe them to be right and come to conceive of themselves both in terms of who and what it is that compliance allows them to be and in terms of what deviation implies they have become. The sanctioning system associated with a rule is effective (insofar as it is) because it proclaims the individual's success or failure at realizing what he and others feel he should be, and, more abstractly, proclaims the individual's compliance with or deviation from rules in general.

Underlying these bases of efficacy is the fundamental notion of responsibility—in law raising the issue of what is called the mental element.

There are several relevant senses in which the term "responsibility" is employed, and hence there can be several elements that enter any particular use of the term.[4] There is the responsibility of immediate causation, in the sense that Mrs. O'Leary's cow can be said to have caused the Chicago fire. There is responsibility for compensation, in the sense that she whose cow starts a fire might be sued to recover costs even when it appears that an average person could not be expected to manage a cow so as to totally avoid such possibilities—the conception in law of strict liability or "absolute responsibility without fault." There is the responsibility consequent on acting "knowingly," here meant to involve the notion that the actor was aware of the side effects of his act, reasonably able to desist from performing the act, but yet nevertheless went ahead and exercised self-volition or will to complete his act. (The implication is that although the individual's main purpose was other than to bring about the event in question, he was ready to see it occur as a by-product of his actual intent.) Finally, there is the responsibility of controlling intention, in which the consequences in question are the ones the actor predominately had in mind to bring about. When the effects are evil, the term "willful" is sometimes used to describe the intent, and malice is imputed.

[4] I am grateful here and in what follows to some critical comments from Martha Alschuler of the University of Pennsylvania.

The kind of responsibility we will be concerned with might be called moral. Involved are the notions that he who fails to guide himself by a particular rule has done so at best because of momentary lapse, at worst because of faulty character, and that although he has not conformed, he is capable of doing so, should have desired to conform, and, in any case, ought now to conform. Note that this sense of the term responsibility is intrinsically diffuse since it combines into one concept the notion of why the individual acted as he *did*, how he *could* have acted, how he *should* have acted, and how in the future he *ought* to act. It is as though the concept itself somehow were designed to bind users to a belief that a single issue is at stake, when, in fact, essentially disparate elements are involved.

Typically, when moral responsibility is imputed, so are other forms, and when moral responsibility is reduced, it is because some of these other forms of responsibility are felt to be absent; however, this is a complex issue upon which no easy word is possible. Here I want only to stress that the issue of responsibility must be raised when considering the significance an individual's fellows impute to his action, even though students of society typically have left to lawyers and theologians all such consideration, involving as it does the need to deal with utterly dubious matters such as cause, will, and intent. As will be argued, the question of responsibility must be raised in regard to minor acts as well as magisterial ones, for without knowing how those involved in an act attribute responsibility for it, we cannot in the last analysis know what it is that has occurred.[5]

A final point about responsibility. I want to argue that the in-

---

[5] I do not mean to imply here a completely relativistic position. In any imputation of causality, it is apparent that many factors that could have been singled out for consideration are not, and that the particular choice has something arbitrary about it, howsoever valid as a cause. On the other hand, it is just as apparent that when all parties to an action agree as to its cause, they can, in terms of their own culture's selection practices, be wrong. Believing something is true only makes it true (W. I. Thomas not withstanding) if this belief so fits with other practices for assessing fact in the society that no contrary evidence would be possible in that society.

fraction of a rule introduces a dual set of issues for the offender and the offended. He who fails to sustain his obligation is responsible for trying to make amends for his offense *and* for showing proper regard for the process of correction. They whose expectations are not sustained must show that they are not to be delineated by what the offense expresses about them *and* that at whatever cost to themselves they have a proper relation to the sanctioning system, for their failure to commit themselves to this social mechanism can reflect more harshly on them than does the original offense. (This last helps account for the concern offended individuals manifest in regard to "the principle of the thing," as when, for example, a shopper is quite ready to allow someone with only one purchase to go before him in a checkout line upon polite explanation and request, but if this getting out of turn is done blatantly, without a by-your-leave, while the offender looks directly into the eyes of the victim, then violent defense of rights may result.)

In this paper the norms to be considered are those that regulate public life, specifically the co-mingling of individuals, both acquainted and unacquainted. This leads us to a very tricky matter bearing on the issue of communication. Careful consideration is necessary.

A man shoots a deer out of season. One could say that his finger communicated pressure to the trigger and that the rifle expressed a bullet, but this would merely be a manner of speaking. Clearly the offender was engaged in a piece of conduct, a morally relevant intentional act, a physical doing, but not in this case that special kind of doing we call communication.

A game warden is witness to the deed, sees the man aim, the rifle recoil, the deer fall, hears the shot, smells the burnt powder. What he thus obtains is an expression of the misdeed, a basis for assessing what happened. Immediate perception of the offense is involved, and consequently one might want to say that the offense had been communicated to the witness, but that again would be loose talk. The spent shell and the markings on the slug are also expressions of the crime, but ones that are not likely to be described even loosely as communication. Note, any effort by the offender to control these expressions, to conceal them or fabricate them, with an eye to misdirecting those who might attempt to assess his act, is not in any necessary way a communication, at least when narrowly defined, merely an attempt to control assessment. And also note that should no one ever discover that a deer has been shot (except the hunter and, I suppose, the deer), an infraction has still occurred, an undetected one. Indeed, a man can be robbed of a possession without ever discovering that an offense has occurred and that he is the victim, although it has and he is.

Our warden, home for dinner, tells his wife what befell that day; *that* is communication. When the offender, arrested, gets to confer with his lawyer, that will involve communication, too.

Clearly, then, a basic distinction must be made among three matters: the doing of an act, the expression of one's having so done (along with the assessment by others of one's action), and communications about action and assessment.

Two complications must be addressed. First, the report that the warden gives to the court about what he witnessed is called in law "direct testimonial evidence," and the spent shell a piece of "direct physical evidence." This standard distinction reflects the fact that one type of evidence involves communicating about perception and the other involves something that can itself be perceived. To give testimony, after all, is merely to tell about the occurrence of an expression; it might better be called giving indirect evidence except that that phrase has been conventionalized in law to refer to evidence of the circumstantial kind. Of course, in the context here considered, written or spoken communication is also and significantly a form of conduct, very much a "performative utterance," and is judged in such terms, for the warden is under an enforceable obligation to communicate in a normatively regulated way, namely, honestly and fully. Any failure on his part to abide by this rule for communicating constitutes a palpable offense in its own right, a form of misconduct much like the out-of-season shooting of a deer, to be analyzed first off in terms of norms and deviations, not in terms of the concepts of communication engineering.

Second, to say that there is a rule against shooting deer out of season and that the man broke the rule is to speak laconically. The rule in question actually implies that the offender intended to hit the deer and that the shooting was done for motives of sport. If it can be shown that the man shot in self-defense, or that he had good reason to think that all he was doing was checking his new telescopic sights, then a case could be made that although it appeared that out-of-season hunting was involved, actually it was not. In short, law is concerned about the attitude of the offender to the rule he seems to have broken and the conjunction of motive and consequences—not merely with the end result. The *situation* of the offender must therefore be considered, the world he is in, and it is considered, implicitly if not explicitly.[6]

---

[6] Take, for example (with apologies to Austin), an act that is tolerably clear: a man driving through a red light. What is he doing? What has he done? (1) Where he comes from they have signs, not lights. (2) The daylight was bad and he couldn't see. (3) He's lately become color blind. (4) He was late for work. (5) His wife is giving birth in the back seat and he'd like to get to a hospital. (6) The bank robber in the front seat is holding a gun on him and has told him to run the light. (7) He's always done this when no cops are around, figuring that the occasional cost can be distributed across the times when he isn't caught. (8) It's four o'clock in the morning, and no one is ever on the street at this hour, and in addition, he's taken a close look up and down the street to make sure his running the light is completely safe. (9) It's raining, and it's safer not to try to stop on the oil slick. (10) A policeman has waved him through. (11) His brakes gave way. (12) He just plain forgot to look at the light. (13) He's part of a funeral procession. (14) No one is about to challenge him; he's known too well for that. (15) He's an inspector testing the vigilance of the cops on duty. (16) He's driving (he claims) under a posthypnotic trance. (17) He wants to get in a race with the local cop. (18) The cop on the corner is his brother and he is putting him on. (19) Those are diplomatic plates he has. (20) The light was stuck on red, and he and the other motorists finally decided to go through. (21) The light was changing at the time. (22) He was drunk, high. (23) His mother has a lamentable occupation, and he has a psychiatrically certifiable compulsivity in regard to red lights. (24) There was a police ambulance immediately behind, sirening to go through, and the other lane was blocked with a line of cars.

So our man has passed through a red light. But at his hearing when the judge asks him what he was doing running a red light, he will provide an argument as to what was really happening. Obviously, what makes driving

Now it is possible to look more closely at the norms that govern the behavior of the individual during and by virtue of the presence of others—behavior sometimes referred to as demeanor, deportment, and manners.

It is apparent that rules will differ according to how well or how badly nonconformance is incidentally designed to produce telling evidence. Obviously a rule against shooting at deer and a rule against thinking evil thoughts are differently situated in regard to the production of adequate evidence regarding compliance. It is here we must note that rules of public order are such that evidence regarding compliance is often fully available; for these rules govern something that must, by definition, occur under the eyes of the possibly offended. In matters regulated by rules of financial probity or sexual fidelity, it is common for an offense to occur long before it is (if ever) discovered. But in questions of public activity (for example, behavior at social parties), evidence of a failure to abide by the rules derives in the main from catching the culprit red-handed. And the evidence had better be obtained in this way. For here the entities at stake have at best a very brief life, as brief, say, as the life of a conversation or a picnic. The offense itself, then, is likely to be of small duration, and moreover, its ill effects are likely to fade away almost as quickly as do entities of the kind that were damaged. Stealth in nonsituational infractions typically leaves the offended ignorant of the culprit's identity and the date of the offense; stealth in situational delicts typically leaves the offended ignorant of these matters but also raises the issue as to whether in fact any delict was committed. For in regard to the niceties of face-to-face behavior, the absence of the offended party really means the absence of any opportunity to offend. It is not merely, then, that situational norms are of the pragmatic kind, sustained only when witnesses render infraction costly, but, more deeply, that they pertain in the main to the perceptible and therefore do not allow for concealment of infraction in the usual sense

through a red light a discernible, isolable event is that a rule stipulated in regard to the light was broken. The objective "fact," then, must be as variable as is the individual's possible relation to the rule.

of the term. An exception to this argument is based on a special and limited type of concealment—one in which the offense occurs in the immediate presence of the victim and is evident to witnesses even while it is being shielded from him.

There is, then, this issue. I have argued that an individual's conformance to a rule is not the same as his intentionally providing evidence (howsoever valid) that he has conformed, and this, in turn, is not quite the same as his communicating verbally or by any other conventionalized means that he has conformed. And this argument is made even though it is apparent that part of his actual conformance is likely (with his knowledge) to provide others with a "natural" indicator that he has conformed. Now in most realms of activity it is easy to distinguish between an individual's conformance to a rule and his giving mere appearance of conforming. (There is also the notion of "compromising appearances," which recognizes that he may appear not to have conformed when in fact he has.) When, however, this distinction between actual and apparent conformance is carried over into the realm of demeanor, confusion results. For in this expressive domain, it is usually the case that he who would produce a mere show of proper appearances must conform to do so. To say here of someone that he falsely appeared to conform to the norms usually can mean only that the appearances he maintained were not consistently or persistently maintained.

Because face-to-face conduct pertains to quickly changing displays, the main method for collecting evidence of conformance is to watch (and listen to) the actor himself as he engages in these displays in one's presence. Therefore we can easily think that what is being studied is communication. It is not. Language may not be involved, and when language is involved, as when an individual pronounces a word incorrectly, conduct is still at issue, the conduct of speaking. And in general, although the individual's conformance to a rule gives evidence of his moral state, and although he may conform solely for the purpose of giving a good impression, the conformance itself, howsoever motivated, is not an act of communication—not, at least, in the narrow sense of the term. It is simply a bit of conduct, the perception of which incidentally gives evidence of the standards sustained by the actor, who may himself be interested in manipulating this evidence. And even when we must examine communication narrowly defined—say, in studying the organization of encounters—it is primarily as a form of conduct that we do so.

Once we arrive at a critical and circumscribed conception of communication, we can risk a broadened notion of offense. Throughout the discussion, it was held that a rule involves two individuals directly: he whom the rule requires something of and he who can demand that something should occur because of the rule. In the case of infractions, then, there will be an obligated person who offends and an expectant person, a claimant, who is offended. This perspective must be broadened in one particular. Among the norms that the individual is obliged to sustain when amongst others, there is an important set, deviation from which causes little harm or concern to those (other than himself) who witness the offense. Infraction of these norms mainly has the effect of jeopardizing the actor's tacit claim to being a person of normal competence and character. The image that is offended is the offender's own. These self-offenses, as well as the mutually involving kind, must concern us.

II *Social Control*

The traditional view of social control seems to derive from classrooms, courtrooms, and other places where those in charge can foster a parental impression: that the individual has the option of adhering to the rules or concealing violation and that if he does neither, he will be plucked out of his situation and made to pay the consequence, the two perversions of justice envisaged being his escaping apprehension or paying for a crime he did not commit.

If we limit our concern to offenses in the public realm, to people co-mingling, then the traditional view of the social control process can mislead us badly.

First, when individuals come into one another's immediate presence, territories of the self bring to the scene a vast filigree of trip wires which individuals are uniquely equipped to trip over. This ensures that circumstances will constantly produce potentially offensive configurations that were not foreseen or were foreseen but undesired.

Also, strangers will impinge upon each other briefly and wordlessly in passing, the result being that the individual will be witnessed by others in an act whose meaning depends on its place in his unfolding course of action, and the witness will have no opportunity to wait for this unfolding to occur.

Finally, there are the actor's motive and intent. Although the actor himself can know about these directly, others can only infer them, and this they may fail to do or do incorrectly. In turn, motive and intent are significant because often one must understand them in order to discover just what situation the actor was in, and it is essential to know this if one is to piece out his attitudes toward a rule on the occasion of his apparently breaking it. And all these factors must be known in order to specify the kind and degree of responsibility the offender is to be given for his offenses. But as already considered, to determine all of this for an infraction is in part to determine what kind of offense was committed. In brief, issues not revealed often will have to be inferred before it is possible to know what it is that has happened.

Because of these contingencies in face-to-face interaction, the actor will have the task, often the right, of providing clarifying information. He must ensure that his relation to what seems to be occurring is a viable one, and this will require not merely correct action but the provision of corrective information. Note that because the individual does provide help to those who would take readings of his situation, he will be in a position to try to cover improper intent and motive with false explanation. In brief, the individual will make an effort to provide corrective information designed to prevent not only his being misunderstood but also his being understood too well.

In addition to the issue of the meaning of an offense, another factor must be considered. The traditional view of social control seems to divide the world into three distinct parts: in one the crime is committed, in the second the infraction is brought to trial, and in the third (should the actor be found guilty) the punishment is inflicted. Thus, students of social control typically study each of these phases of the corrective process separately. However, most of what is of concern within the realm of public order cannot be divided up in this manner. The scene of the crime, the halls of judgment, and the place of detention are all housed in the same cubicle; furthermore, the complete cycle of crime, apprehension, trial, punishment, and return to society can run its course in two gestures and a glance. Justice is summary.[7] The individual therefore must not only provide clarifying information but when he cannot convince others of his innocence, he also must be prepared to do penance and provide reparations on the spot in exchange for being accepted back into good graces a moment later. Thus, social situations are not to be seen as places where rules are obeyed or secretly broken, but rather as settings for racing through versions in miniature of the entire judicial process. It might be added that since interactional offenses pertain mainly to claims regarding territories of the self, and since these claims amount to expectations regarding forms of respect, remedies will be ritual, that is, designed to portray the remorseful attitude of the offender to an offended object of ultimate value.

There is a final limitation on the traditional social control approach that we must consider. In major crimes the fuss and bother created by apprehension and trial is of less concern to everyone

[7] Recent studies of the police, of course, suggest that even in regard to crimes in the traditional sense (for example, those against property), justice is more summary than had been thought. See, for example, Jerome Skolnick, *Justice without Trial* (New York: John Wiley and Sons, Inc., 1966); Egon Bittner, "The Police in Skid Row: A Study of Peace Keeping," *American Sociological Review*, XXXII, no. 5 (1967): 701–706.

than the crime and its proper attribution; or at least (it is felt) it ought to be. But in interactional matters things are different. Since the guilt is small and the punishment smaller, there often will be less concern—and admittedly so—to achieve proper attribution than to get traffic moving again. When a robbery is committed, no innocent party is likely to volunteer himself as the culprit; when an interactional offense occurs, everyone directly involved may be ready to assume guilt and to offer reparation. The adversary theme that marks negotiations at court is here not strong; rather a tacit collaboration is likely to be sustained even though the participants may be unaware of their coalition.

We start, then, with norms and the process of social control whereby infractions are discouraged. We end by seeing that in the realm of public order it is not obedience and disobedience that are central, but occasions that give rise to remedial work of various kinds, especially the provision of corrective readings calculated to show that a possible offender actually had a right relationship to the rules, or if he seemed not to a moment ago, he can be counted on to have such a relationship henceforth. Obviously, of course, this arrangement introduces flexibility; did it not exist, public life would become hopelessly clogged with the commission of minor territorial offenses and their adjudication—indeed, our present articulation of the territories of the self would become quite unworkable.

III *Remedial Work*

In order to understand remedial work, I think it is useful to assume that the actor and those who witness him can imagine (and have some agreement regarding) one or more "worst possible readings," that is, interpretations of the act that maximize either its offensiveness to others or its defaming implications for the actor himself. This ugliest imaginable significance I shall call the "virtual offense." This name is selected because the remedial activity that follows a possibly offensive act very often can be understood best by assuming that the actor has these worst possible readings in mind as that which he must respond to and manage. Note that the virtual offense has largely a cautionary effect, detailing what everyone concerned must be careful to avoid confirming. It should be added that to speak of a virtual offense requires speaking of a "virtual offender," the individual most likely to be perceived as the party at fault, and a "virtual claimant," the individual who is the most obvious choice for he whose claims have been infringed.

The function of remedial work is to change the meaning that otherwise might be given to an act, transforming what could be seen as offensive into what can be seen as acceptable. This change seems to be accomplished, in our Western society at least, by striking in some way at the moral responsibility otherwise imputed to the offender; and this in turn seems to be accomplished by three main devices: accounts, apologies, and requests.

1. *Accounts:* The nature of accounts has been considered somewhat by students of law in connection with the issue of defenses, pleas, the mitigation of offenses, and the defeasibility of claims. Law, then, provides the beginning of an analysis; its weakness for us is its concern with arguments of an extended verbal kind made considerably after the event and in regard to relatively major offenses.[8]

First, the offender can introduce a "traverse" or "joinder," arguing that the act he is accused of committing did not in fact occur. Or he can grant the occurrence of the offensive act but argue that he himself had nothing to do with its happening, that, indeed, the wrong person has been accused.

Second, there are acts that the individual admits to doing, admits

[8] See John Austin, "A Plea for Excuses," in his *Philosophical Papers* (Oxford: Oxford University Press, 1961), chap. 6, pp. 123–152; H. L. A. Hart, "The Ascription of Responsibility and Rights," chap. 8 in A. G. N. Flew, ed., *Logic and Language* (First Series; Oxford: Basil Blackwell, 1955), pp. 145–166; see also Marvin B. Scott and Stanford M. Lyman, "Accounts," *American Sociological Review*, XXII (February 1968): 46–62.

to foreseeing the adverse consequences of (or agrees that although he didn't foresee the consequences he would have proceeded even if he had), but claims that the circumstances were such as to make the act radically different from what it appears to have been, and that, in fact, he is not really at fault at all. To throw someone to the ground, thereby injuring him, in order to prevent him from stepping on one's clean floor is an offense; to do the same act in order to prevent him from being hit by a sniper's bullet is, in fact, not to do the same act. In the latter case "higher" considerations alter the meaning of the deed. Similarly, there are killings that are claimed to be not murders but acts of self-defense. Indeed, there are many circumstances in which the individual can attempt to redefine what he is accused of doing by shifting some or all of the responsibility for the offense to his accusers, a process described as "counter-denunciation," albeit one whose consequences can hardly be remedial unless the sympathy of a third party is at issue.[9] Note, here again we see that there is no act whose meaning is independent of reasons understood for its occurrence; and there seems to be no act for which radically different reasons cannot be provided, and hence radically different meanings. That the individual routinely imputes intent while forming a perception of the act and then typically finds no reason to change his view should not blind us to the fact that the perception is dependent on an assessment of intent and is necessarily subject to reappraisal, for there is no such assessment that is immune to the possibility that it might have to be altered.

Third, the putative offender can agree that the act occurred and that he did it but present the mitigation that he was ignorant and unforeseeing, excusably so, and could not reasonably be asked to have acted so as to forestall it. He can claim that his was an involuntary motor act whose occurrence he did nothing to facilitate, as when one stranger pushed him into another stranger who was

---

[9] Case study examples are provided in the useful monograph by Robert M. Emerson, *Judging Delinquents* (Chicago: Aldine Publishing Co., 1969), esp. pp. 155–166.

thereby injured. Or he can claim that although his act was self-controlled, its dire outcome in this case was not something he could be expected to foresee or take precautions against, but that certainly he would not have so acted had he known what was to happen.[10] Here is the case of the truck driver who runs over someone who has left a note testifying that this is how he planned to die. Here, too, the individuals whose gossiping becomes destructive because no one participating could be expected to anticipate that the subject might be in the next booth overhearing. And here to be included, too, is the plea more typically heard outside of court but also, in fact, employed in regard to very serious crimes: the argument of unseriousness. In brief, the offender can claim that all along he had been acting unseriously, for a joke, and that certainly had he known of the unhappy consequences that were to result, he would have refrained from his playfulness.

Fourth, there are pleas that claim reduced responsibility by virtue of reduced competence, the understanding often being that although the actor is guilty of something, it is guilt for being incompetent and not guilt for the specific deed resulting therefrom. Here are claims of mitigation based on sleepiness, drunkenness, youthfulness, senility, druggedness, passion, lack of training, subordination to the will of superiors, mental deficiency, and so forth. Reduced states of competency vary, of course, in terms of their power to excuse: sleepwalking can absolve the individual totally; drunkenness, on occasion, can increase the fault instead of diminishing it. Here, too, the context must be considered. To fail to arrive in time for tea is excusable on the grounds that one was

---

[10] The law, of course, is much concerned with the difference between the foreseen and unforeseen, and, within the latter, the difference between the excusably and inexcusably unforeseen. Criminal liability tends to attach only if it can be shown that the offender in some way or other did anticipate the adverse consequences of his act; civil liability, a much broader possibility, applies if it can be shown that the offender either foresaw what was to happen or was inexcusably ignorant and unthinking, that is, unwitting in the way a reasonable man would not be—and there are even some grounds on which "strict liability" can be pressed in civil action, warranted ignorance not being a defense.

geographically unsure of the neighborhood and drove in the wrong direction; an ambulance driver, on the other hand, cannot offer this kind of incompetence in explaining why it was that he failed to pick up a dangerously ill person until forty minutes after the call was placed, this being twenty minutes eternally too late.

Finally, the weakest of pleas, he can admit that he was fully competent at the time to appreciate the consequence of his act, that he was easily able to desist from performing it, that he would have desisted had he known what was to occur, but that he was indefensibly unmindful or ignorant of what was to happen.

Note, the more an actor can argue mitigating circumstances successfully, the more he can establish that the act is not to be taken as an expression of his moral character; contrarily, the more he is held responsible for his act, the more fully it will define him for others.

When individuals speak of a "good" account for an act, they seem to mean an account that succeeds in restructuring the initial response of the offended and appreciably reducing the fault of the actor—at least among the fair-minded. And a "bad" account is one that fails to perform this service. The goodness or badness of an account must, of course, be distinguished from its trueness or falseness. True accounts are often good, but false accounts are sometimes better.

As suggested, the possibility of introducing a false, good account adds flexibility, making it feasible to bypass rules or break them with impunity provided only that proper wit is applied. However, this flexibility is reduced somewhat by the fact that good accounts acquire a bad name, being exactly what quick-witted offenders would come up with were they to offer false ones.

In common usage, the terms for accounts—explanations, excuses, pretexts—tend to be used interchangeably, although some differentiation can be detected.[11] An explanation can be defined as an account that attempts to exonerate the offender fully by pro-

---

[11] A treatment of these differences is suggested in Scott and Lyman, *op. cit.*

viding details concerning what it was he was actually about, this being offered after the virtual offense but before blame has been imputed openly. An excuse is an account provided in response to an overt or implied accusation but presented as only partially diminishing the blame. A pretext is an excuse provided before or during the questionable act.

2. *Apologies:* Although accounts have been treated at considerable length in the literature, especially, as suggested, in the legal literature, apologies have not; yet they are quite central. An apology is a gesture through which an individual splits himself into two parts, the part that is guilty of an offense and the part that dissociates itself from the delict and affirms a belief in the offended rule.

In its fullest form, the apology has several elements: expression of embarrassment and chagrin; clarification that one knows what conduct had been expected and sympathizes with the application of negative sanction; verbal rejection, repudiation, and disavowal of the wrong way of behaving along with vilification of the self that so behaved; espousal of the right way and an avowal henceforth to pursue that course; performance of penance and the volunteering of restitution.

Note that the offender's willingness to initiate and perform his own castigation has certain unapparent values. Were others to do to him what he is willing to do to himself, he might be obliged to feel affronted and to engage in retaliatory action to sustain his moral worth and autonomy. And he can overstate or overplay the case against himself, thereby giving to the others the task of cutting the self-derogation short—this latter, in turn, being a function that is safer to lodge with the offended since they are not likely to abuse it, whereas he, the offender, might.

As suggested, apologies represent a splitting of the self into a blameworthy part and a part that stands back and sympathizes with the blame giving, and, by implication, is worthy of being brought back into the fold. This splitting is but one instance, and often a fairly crude one, of a much more general phenomenon—the tendency for individuals when in the immediate presence of others to project somehow a self that then is cast off or withdrawn from. In the case of apologies, there is usually an admission that the offense was a serious or real act. This provides a contrast to another type of splitting, one that supports an account, not an apology, in which the actor projects the offensive act as something not to be taken literally, that is, seriously, or after the act claims that he was not acting seriously.

3. Two principal forms of remedial work have been considered: accounts and apologies. Although both may occur, as we shall see, before the virtual offense has taken place, they characteristically are seen as occurring after the event. The third main form of ritual work consists of requests; these typically occur before the questionable event or, at the latest, during its initial phases.

A request consists of asking license of a potentially offended person to engage in what could be considered a violation of his rights. The actor shows that he is fully alive to the possible offensiveness of his proposed act and begs sufferance. At the same time he exposes himself to denial and rejection. The recipient of the request thus clearly is presented with the possibility of making an offer, one that would allow the suppliant's needs. An offer, in short, is stimulated. The value to the potential offender of doing this is based, of course, upon the character of offers.

An offer is not a remedial ritual but a supportive one, albeit of a special kind. Although most supportive acts entail some penetration of the recipient's preserves (and can be thought presumptuous for this reason), offers very often involve penetration of the *maker's* preserves, the recipient's territoriality being less at issue. The fact that offers are possible reflects a basic organizational principle in social life. The assumption is that when a violation is invited by he who ordinarily would be its victim, it ceases to be a violation and becomes instead a gesture of regard performed by this person. A single act thus can have related but different symbolic meanings, and behavioral arrangements can be given double use, once as part of "positive" supportive rites and once as part of "negative" avoidant ones. Note, in presenting a request, the actor gives up his autonomy in regard to deciding the matter; the recipient of the request, in granting the request, retains his, it being assumed that he alone was the one to decide the matter.

The value of transforming a virtual violation into a request is recognized so broadly in our society that a whole style is available whereby, for example, all compellings are clothed, howsoever lightly, as requests. (A nice example is the personal search technique employed in precinct stations. Routinely in American practice, the police *ask* the subject to empty purse and pockets instead of doing this themselves.[12] In this way the prisoner can be given a slight sense of the autonomy and self-determination the law presumably guarantees him, and the slight mollification of him this produces be used in managing him.) For every territory of the self, then, there will be a means of requesting permission to intrude. Moreover, there are countless dodges whereby an importuner seeks permission in advance for a violation that has not yet been specified, as in the questions, "Can I ask you something personal?" or "Will you lend me something?"

It has been suggested that there are three basic types of remedial work: accounts, apologies, and requests. A common practice among students is to consider these remedial acts as part of "dis-

[12] See, for example, Donald M. McIntyre and Nicholas D. Chabraja, "The Intensive Search of a Suspect's Body and Clothing," *Journal of Criminal Law, Criminology and Police Science*, LVIII, no. 1 (1967): 18–26. It might be added that whenever an individual's body is to be managed, there is very likely to be some juncture where he is accorded the courtesy of performing the other's will on his own, if for no other reason than the fact that the body is hard to manage nicely without cooperation. Thus, for example, in the early days of drop hanging, the victim apparently was allowed to govern the moment of his own demise by being put in charge of the signal (a handkerchief) for the drop. See Justin Atholl, *Shadow of the Gallows* (London: John Long, 1954), p. 48. Today, apparently, persons being gassed are allowed to signal for the pellet and are encouraged to breathe deeply on their own. Last requests, of course, can be similarly understood; the self-determinism is somewhat displaced in time and content but still attests to the fact that the person going to his death is someone whose will and competency are being respected. How clever, if not obscene, are the workings of society that occasions of ultimate coercion can be used to affirm ritually the respectfulness of the coercers and the free will of the coerced.

tributive justice," a sort of payment or compensation for harm done, the greater the harm the greater the recompense. And of course there is some evidence supporting this actuarial approach. For example, often a brief apology is given for a minor offense and a protracted apology for something bigger. But in fact when corrective behavior is examined closely, it is found that apparently there are two different, independently occurring processes involved. One is ritualistic, whereby the virtual offender portrays his current relationship to rules, which his actions appear to have broken, and to persons present whose territories should have been protected by these rules. The second is restitutive, whereby an offended party receives some compensation, especially of a material kind, for what has been done to him and, by implication, to the rules that otherwise would have protected him.

It is apparent that there is great variation from case to case regarding the weight that is given these two processes. An individual whose vault has been robbed may be little concerned to obtain an expression of remorse from robbers if they have already disposed of the money. He can find their change of heart of little consequence, much preferring to deal with unrepentant criminals who have been caught with the loot still in hand. There are other offenses in which the party offended is concerned principally with the principle of the thing and not with compensation.

The behavior of the offender will also illustrate this split between substantive relations and ritual ones. Thus, when an individual commits crimes deemed to be quite heinous, crimes for which his life is small compensation, he still may feel strongly obliged to ritually disavow his previous self and show that the person he now is sees his offenses from the perspective of a moral-minded man. No matter what is done to the individual by way of punishment for crime, he is likely to have a moment free before the punishment is inflicted to proclaim identity with the powers whose ire is about to be visited upon him and to express separateness from the self upon whom the justice will fall.[13] No matter what a person

[13] A nice example is provided by Albert DeSalvo's testimony regarding himself during the court hearing to determine his competency in connec-

has done, he can express a change of heart at any moment, and although this may not soften appreciably what is done to him, he must either be disbelieved or be allowed to create something of a new self for himself on the spot. The position can be taken that this sort of redemption is but one expression of the "splitting" character of the self during interaction, that is, the general capacity of an individual to handle himself by stepping back from what he seems to have become in order to take up an alignment involving distance from this person; and that, in turn, this capacity results from the inevitable interactional fact that that which comments on what has happened cannot be what has happened. I here attempt to derive a property of interactants from interaction. My claim is that the individual is constituted so that he can split himself in two, the better to allow one part to join the other members of an encounter in any attitude whatsoever to his other part.[14]

A further illustration of the difference between ritual concerns and substantive ones comes from occasions of accident in which the carelessness of one individual is seen as causing injury or death to another. Here there may be no way at all to compensate the offended, and no punishment may be prescribed. All that the offended can do is say he is sorry. And this expression itself may be *relatively* little open to gradation. The fact—at least in our society—is that a very limited set of ritual enactments are available for contrite offenders. Whether one runs over another's sentence, time, dog, or body, one is more or less reduced to saying some variant of "I'm sorry." The variation in degree of anguish ex-

---

tion with the crimes he committed as the "Boston Strangler." Even after strangling a fair number of defenseless women, some very unpleasantly, and terrorizing a city, he still could find a little spot to stand upon in court as he cut himself off from himself. After all, no natural man could have been so beastly, and so there must have been deep-seated psychological reasons for his misbehavior and some value to the world in his helping to find out what they were. See Gerald Frank, *The Boston Strangler* (New York: The New American Library, 1966; London: Jonathan Cape, 1967), especially pages 361–363.

[14] Christian theology has been much concerned with this same divine splitting, but its derivation of this duality is not fully convincing.

pressed by the apologizer seems a poor reflection of the variation in loss possible to the offended. In any case, while the original infraction may be quite substantive in its consequence, the remedial work, however vociferous, is in these cases still largely expressive. And there is a logic in this. After an offense has occurred, the job of the offender is to show that it was not a fair expression of his attitude, or, when it evidently was, to show that he has changed his attitude to the rule that was violated. In the latter case, his job is to show that whatever happened before, he now has a right relationship—a pious attitude—to the rule in question, *and this is a matter of indicating a relationship, not compensating a loss.*[15]

Just as a right relation to the rules must be established in matters so monumental that this seems hopeless, so, too, a right relationship must be established no matter how minute the issue is. This is but another way of saying that regardless of the substantive character of the offense, much the same sort of ritual work must be done. As suggested, a single ritual idiom of remedial moves must be called on whether a toe has been accidentally stepped on or a destroyer accidentally sunk. It therefore follows that in occasions of face-to-face interaction in which many minor, potential delicts arise, ritual performances will be very frequent; and frequent they are, no matter how perfunctory.

IV *Dialogue*

When an individual makes a request, it is plain that he will need a reply of some kind from those to whom his plea is addressed so that he may learn whether or not it has been received, and if so,

[15] The best discussion of these issues is still, I think, the very fine section on ritual in Talcott Parsons, *Structure of Social Action* (New York: McGraw-Hill, Inc., 1937; London: Allen and Unwin, 1949, new edn., 1968), pp. 429–441. I might add that a caution is implied for students who would apply an exchange perspective to all areas of social life.

whether or not it has been granted. Similarly, when the individual provides an account or makes an apology, he becomes needful of the addressee's providing a comment of some kind in return; for only in this way can he be sure that his corrective message has been received and that it has been deemed sufficient to reestablish him as a proper person. (As suggested, in the division of ritual labor, the offender himself would hardly seem to be the person to vest with this power, else the ritual work be foregone entirely or continued too long; in any case, the sender of a message cannot be the one to say that it has been received. In fact, indicating that enough ritual work has been done is vested in the one party safe to invest it in—the offended. If the offended has been satisfied, then surely things have been set to rights.) In brief, a reply allows a request to be granted, an account to be credited, an apology to be proven sufficient, and in all these cases, an acknowledgement to be made that the remedial message has been clearly received.

We find, then, that when a virtual offender performs remedial work in reference to a particular virtual offense, the virtually offended typically replies, whether with silent gesture or words, this reply being directed to the offense and to the remedial work done in connection with it—the directedness being seen as such by all concerned. When a virtual offense occurs, then, we are likely to find that offender and offended each get a chance, a turn at, ritual work, and that an exchange or "round" (to use a term suggested by Harvey Sacks) [16] results.

Activity of this sort has interesting properties. First, although it is convenient to speak of statements and replies (as I shall), and although verbal utterances are often employed, it is not communication in the narrow sense of that term that is at the heart of what is occurring. Stands are being taken, moves are being made, displays are being provided, alignments are being established. Where utter-

[16] Unpublished lectures, University of California, Irvine, 1967. "Round" is the more general term, referring to one turn each by every active participant; an "exchange," then, is a round involving only two participants. Sacks has been an originator in the close study of conversational sequencing, and I am much indebted to him.

ances are involved, they are "performative." Mutually relevant figures are being cut. A ceremony occurs, something closer to a minuet than to a conversation.

Second, if we take as the controlling criterion that close relevance to a particular virtual offense must be involved, then a single exchange is not necessarily all that can figure. The reply to the first move may require or allow the first mover to provide a counter-reply, which itself then becomes the final action that is specifically oriented to the initial virtual offense. Or the counter-reply may call forth a second move from the second mover, it too related to the initial offense, providing us thereby with a ritual containing two rounds. And perhaps more than two rounds are possible. The total set of moves made in connection with a particular virtual offense, I shall call a remedial interchange. It is one kind of naturally bounded ritual dialogue.

Third, in many cases—although by no means all—it can be expected that the termination of the dialogue will mark a state of moral pacification of the parties involved, allowing the troublesome matter at hand to be dropped and other business to be attended to. Or if misgivings remain, at least some sort of show can be sustained that matters have been put to right. A remedial interchange, then, includes all the moves taken in regard to a virtual offense, and these usually, but not inevitably, will leave the participants in a position to act as if the issue can be dropped.

Fourth, the dialogue is complicated structurally by the fact that each participant must address himself not only to the virtual offense, but also to his own role and the role of the other as participants in a system of control through which corrective work can be handled reasonably. And this latter orientation may be phased in time so that it occurs later than the initial ritual activity. (As will be considered, an individual who too flatly declines a minor request may precipitate a reaction aimed at correcting the injury he has done to the means for peacefully handling matters of ritual concern.)

The final point. Although offenses and their dialogic remedies can occur whenever individuals have dealings with each other, they are very likely to occur when these dealings are face-to-face. Furthermore, these concerns are apt to occur in connection with situational and egocentric preserves, although fixed territories can cause trouble, too.[17] As already suggested, these territorial claims are so pervasive that events that could be read as threats to them constantly occur and constantly introduce the need for corrective remedial work. Further, the fact that bodies will be present in a physical context ensures that quite varied configurations and quite fugitive ones will be available to serve as reply and counter-reply. Together these various means of causing offenses and correcting for them establish not merely conditions of co-mingling but the forms and structure of its organization.

I want here to summarize what has been said or implied thus far about the individual as an entity capable of sustaining face-to-face dealings with others. Three orders of functioning are involved, the second built on the first and the third built on the second.

We start with an elementary set of passive capacities: the individual is claimant to a set of territories, and he is a source of contamination of others and of himself.

Next, there is the assumption of intelligent self-control. The individual comes to appreciate the claims of himself and others and exercises his ability to manage his own behavior so as to minimize infraction. Of course animals, in effect, have this capacity, too.

Finally, there is the assumption of ritual license and the relationship an individual must be allowed to have to himself if this license is to be possible. In relation to his claims to territory, he has the

---

[17] For example, it is the special experience of those who live in low rent, urban housing developments that territorial concerns often are activated in regard to fixed settings, namely one's apartment, and often face-to-face, as when the superintendent, janitor, or welfare officer pays a visit, does not like what he sees, and feels within his rights to try to correct matters. (The recurrent "shake-down" of prison cells, school dormitories, and children's domestic quarters by officials is another case in point.) Here see, for example, Paul Jacobs, *Prelude to Riot* (New York: Vintage Books, 1966), pp. 159–164. Middle-class house dwellers are, of course, spared most of these violations; it is in public and semi-public places where such lack of control as they suffer is manifest.

right and duty to call attention to offenses, demanding that something be done to set matters right. He can ratify the apology work of others, grant requests, and make offers, all of which enable him to nullify what otherwise would have to be treated as an offense to him. In relation to himself as a source of contamination, he has a right to make requests, that is, to present himself as someone in search of dispensation who does not mean to give offense, and to offer apologies, the latter implying the capacity and the right to turn upon himself and to cut himself off from what he once was. Note that the individual's exercise of this license in regard to self is itself judged against cultural standards in accordance with rules for the management of rules, and it is this judgment (as Cooley suggested) that informs an important part of the personality and character imputed to him. If he is prone to allow others to intrude and lax in demanding proper treatment of himself, he can be thought easygoing or without honor, depending on the cost to him of taking action. If he is quick to take offense, he can be thought to be over-touchy. If he is guarded and careful in the management of his own territory, he can be thought taciturn, suspicious, or mean.

V *Body Gloss*

What we have considered thus far about remedial work assumes, by and large, that the offender's remedial effort is directed to a particular other, typically the party virtually offended. Something like a dialogue is involved whether the speakers are in each other's immediate presence or negotiating by telephone or mail.

When we come to restrict our interest to public life in which the offended and offender are present together and the offense is something that occurs while they are thusly placed, then the dialogue would seem to occur within an encounter, that is, within a ratified state of talk involving a single focus of visual and cognitive attention. The ritual moves made by one of the parties are directly addressed to the other party much in the manner of statements made within a conversational circle.

However, there are many circumstances in which an individual who offends others or his own standards is not engaged at the time in a "with," let alone an encounter—at least not with the relevant parties. When this sort of thing occurs and the individual finds himself in need of a conforming reply to the remedial work he feels obliged to perform, he often will be allowed some license to initiate an encounter with persons who otherwise would be inaccessible to him, thus enabling him to deposit his little offering. (In fact, if one wanted to engineer a conversational contact across an ordinarily forbidden line, this could be done by unseriously acting out of character and then reaching across for confirmation that the unseriousness had been perceived and accepted.) [18] Further-

[18] Note, here three-person play may be involved, with one individual in a two-person encounter behaving in the unseriously improper manner and the other individual cutting across to the party outside the encounter for cross-talked confirmation:

> Middle-aged man and woman observed at restaurant table. He says out loud, "You going to treat me or am I going to treat you?" She looks around the room, finds the closest strangers, and breaks into a wide collusive smile with them, implying, "He's a cut-up and only kidding."

May I add that if an individual looks at the public life around him as a circle of others conversationally closed to him and wants to break this conspiracy of silence, a number of devices are available to him, in addition to projecting a self others will feel he has a right to dissociate himself from. He can, of course, use the occasion of a stranger's impropriety to enter into collusive remonstrating asides with fellow witnesses. He can seek out someone who is doing something that can be construed as being a little out of character (including circumstances which suggest action under constraint) and then address a remark that initiates the actor's dissociation from this self. (A woman in a supermarket wheeling a cart with but one kind of foodstuff in it, but twenty cans or boxes of it, is fair game, and she is likely to exhibit a deeply buried sense of obligation to take in good spirit her action being cast in a humorous light by a remark from a stranger, whatever her actual feelings in the matter. He who steps into an elevator the lights of which are entirely off has a right to address the strangers already there and to receive a chuckle in return no matter almost what he says.) In sum, although the right to strike up a conversation with a stranger may be circumscribed closely in middle-class society, the right to make a remark or two can be exerted almost always depending only on the wit of

more, in many cases when it appears that no witness can be called on, someone in the vicinity will decently volunteer to provide a truncated but relevant reply. In our own middle-class society, for example, there is a standardized little Scarsdale smile, held overlong, for confirmatory expressions of this kind, "transfixed" so that throughout the whole period of an offender's behavior he will be accorded a sign that no offense is being taken, that no contest is involved, and that sympathy is present for whatever alignment to the situation he chooses to take. These are "no-contest" signals, which form an important part of the system of courtesy which binds unacquainted persons into a common civil order. (No-contest moves also occur, of course, when little choice is available as to who may provide them. For example, when a middle-class white in a lower-class black neighborhood is approached by a native for change for a quarter to feed a meter, the black may feel it necessary to broadly mime the innocence of his intent and the adequacy of his resources by making sure his coin is evident, and the white may find it natural to display a no-contest smile not only throughout the actual transaction but also during the few moments preceding it when it is evident that he is being approached for something.)

There are, then, ways in which an encounter can be coerced from a gathering so that remedial work will have a place to occur in. But when circumstances prevent even these minimal interchanges, the offender may still feel obliged to provide a broad ges-

the initiator in finding a definition of the situation that casts someone present as an offender whom others present will have to be willing to collude about, or that casts someone in a guise from which he will have to allow himself to be dissociated. Further, the individual may clown, through accent and posture, a character obviously not himself and, like a ventriloquist, talk to strangers through this dummy personage, on the assumption that real rules only apply to real people. (A moment later he can make further remarks, this time exercising his right to dissociate himself from the very guise through which he has just finished talking.) Here, I think, in the matter of opening up a closed scene, nightclub comedians are the natural masters. Fortunately for the quiet decorum of our better public places, comedians are not always willing to perform free. Just as whores protect our marriages, so the stage protects our streets.

ture for anyone who cares to receive it, enabling him thus to clarify the character and legitimacy of what it is he is about. He externalizes his inward feelings. He provides a gloss on his situation, a bodily enactment of his alignment to the events at hand, a gesture in the round. Since there is a rule against talking aloud to no one, such broadcast acts mainly involve gesture and posture, although in context words can be muttered to a whole room.

So there are gestures in the round. Of course, these round displays in particular cases may be designed to convey something to a particular other, but again, if this is to be effective, the available-to-anyone style must be sustained. For example, in getting off a crowded bus which has brought someone of inferior social status to sit beside him, a middle-class person sometimes makes sure to present a bustling, purposeful air, so that it is readily readable that he is leaving the setting in order to get off the bus and not merely to change seats. This little dramatic production is designed primarily for his erstwhile seatmate who otherwise might see the leave-taking as a device to avoid contamination, but although the special audience for the show is obvious, the show itself is intrinsically a public one, a portrait in the round, in principle available to whomsoever looks. Or, it should be added, whomsoever can be assumed to overhear:

> An airport waiting room. A toddler leaves his mother's side, walks over to a seated man, touches the pencil in the man's hand, then drops his hand and stares. Mother emits in a loud, clear, adult tone: "Billy, you know you're not supposed to do that."

Here, plainly, the admonition is designed for the offended, not merely for the offender—designed to show that the with is socially responsible even though one of its elements isn't. The degree of verbal understanding of the little culprit is not at issue; a dog, a monkey, or a trained seal in the same slot could well be admonished with the same broadcasted words.

It might be added that there are more of these public-yet-directed displays than one might think, and for a significant reason. As already suggested, public life has the distinctive feature that in it there is a range of offenses against particular individuals which others are ready to perform providing the victim himself is not quite in a position to witness the offense, although others are. Violation of informational preserve through staring is an example. Thus, a noteworthy individual often produces in passers-by a standard "behavior sequence" during which he is stared at until close enough for an exchange of recognition signals, then civil inattention is proffered until he is just beyond the sight line, whereupon the curious turn and stare once again.[19] The implication is that whereas direct staring is to be avoided, one is free to be exposed in one's staring before those whom one is not staring at. Now a stand-

[19] Another example of this standard behavior sequence can occur when a middle-class American approaches the post of a stemmer, pamphleteer, or other street importuner. The threat will be fixed in the oncomer's focus up to the point when a search for a possible escape route still can be maintained tactfully. When this point is passed and no escape route has been discovered, then a phase of studious eye avoidance often occurs until the danger of being accosted is past. If the importuner is seeking alms of some kind and the decision of the pedestrian is to give, the latter may try to get the offering ready in advance (or allow a child to give it if one is in the party) so as to minimize involvement. (Women sometimes stop outside of the immediate range of the importuner to search their purses for an appropriate coin, only then advancing past him.) If the pedestrian accepts a leaflet or contributes a coin, then this seems to provide him with the license to decline the importuner's eyes even though the fiction of not having noticed him has been forborne; refusal of a direct accost, on the other hand, seems to demand a brief eye engagement, although the importuner can find himself treated as someone who has made no overture even then. Of course, once the pedestrian is past the line of fire and has his back to the importuner, the situation is changed dramatically, so much so that the pedestrian now can turn around to stare at the odd doings through which he has just passed. Interestingly, when withs approach an importuner, the members can feel awkward about simulating the unseeing of the latter, since this requires a private act in a collective context, and as a result they can break into a forced conversation, concealing from one another that they feel the conversation is being sustained from without, not from within. Once past the obstacle, whatever the tack employed in passing, members are likely to make editorial-like, self-justifying remarks, providing thus a nice illustration of the fact that apparent noninvolvement in an importunement may be only apparent. (I draw here on two unpublished papers: Eileen Goldwyn, "A Description of the Beggar-Passer-by Relationship" and Sandra Nicholson, "Charitable Donations," both 1965.)

ard defense against being caught staring is to enact a scan that gives the appearance of happening to fall upon the victim the moment he happens to look at the scanner. (This coincidence can, in fact, happen with genuine scans and constitutes a contingency of scanning.) In consequence, the offender's rapid withdrawal of gaze can be presented as a natural movement and not an admission of guilt.[20] The point here is that while a glossed scan is something available to the sight of anyone in the vicinity of the scanner, it is designed primarily for the victim's consumption, and the latter's reaction to the possible delict may be the only one that the offender has any concern about.

Everyone knows, of course, that the individual necessarily provides a reading of himself when he is in the presence of others. Gender, age, class, state of health, ethnicity will all be conveyed, in the main unwittingly. Further, when the individual appears at a social occasion or in a well-established social setting, his attire and manner ordinarily will be in tune with the events at hand.

But the expressive materials involved here are inflexible. A note once struck must more or less be sustained at least for the duration of the social occasion; and certain expressions, such as those associated with the actor's gender, remain more or less fixed for life across most of his occasions and settings. And this is not an embarrassment. These forms of display are by nature a response to something that is slow moving, something that remains constant over appreciable periods of time.

Except, then, for marginal acts, such as removing one's jacket or tie, slipping into ethnic interaction style, and the like, the standard resources mentioned allow little by way of commenting upon cur-

---

[20] Among various species of primates it is not uncommon for dominant animals to be kept in view by subordinates so that the latter will know as soon as possible how it is they might be called on to act, yet when their gaze is returned, turn away to avoid the challenge and incursion that can be implied by staring. In consequence, apparently, animals employ some of the same glosses we use. Suzanne Ripley suggests that macaques in the presence of a dominant will turn their heads away and evidently simulate interest in a distant event even while they maintain bodily and spatial orientation to the activity of the latter.

rently occurring, particular events. Specific happenings that occur within, say, the end phase of a social occasion will not be able to be addressed. Those engaged together in talk, of course, can respond to one another verbally and gesturally in regard to quite fleeting matters, but this still leaves open the issue of how to give evidence about passing events to those who are in easy range but not in the talk.

It is thus midway between relatively fixed guise on one hand and infinitely fluid speech on the other that we find what here is being considered, "body gloss," that is, relatively self-conscious gesticulation an individual can perform with his whole body in order to give pointed evidence concerning some passing issue at hand, the evidence to be obtainable by anyone in the situation who cares to perceive him. Here, then, we have the externalization of evidence, the lack of which might cause the individual to be ill judged; here use of the body to portray in a sort of mime what otherwise might be missed.

Note that bending the body to expressive use constitutes a kind of emergency effort in the face of the usual relation between response and situation. Ordinarily, I think, we might expect that the means of exhibiting a reaction has some natural relation to what is being reacted to, so that slow-moving behaviors would be used to express alignment to a longish-lasting condition or event, and a word or two would be used to take up a position relative to a speaker's sentence. However, behavioral gloss, as here defined, gives the impression that the actor is having to make do. He will use relatively sluggish behaviors to convey something about rapidly changing events or, for example, use a smile—which can be thought to be intrinsically a fleeting thing—as a transfix, sustaining it over the whole course of a lengthy incident so that a single reading can be applied to all of it. Involved also will be the individual's effort to compress into a moment's expression an indication of the course of action, its pace and its direction, which he anticipates engaging in during the oncoming minutes.

It is tempting to say that gestures in the round are employed only when directed, encounter-relevant ones are not manageable, but the decision is probably more complicated than that. For one thing, the individual may, at the same moment and in regard to the same matter, try to make himself readable both by gestures in the round and by directed verbal statements.[21]

It has already been suggested that the individual is concerned to manage not merely the offense he might give to others but also the defamation of himself that his current situation might produce. Now I would like to suggest that a special relation exists between offenses to self and communication in the round. There is a special set of competency norms that applies to bodily behavior; these bear on such matters as physical balance, efficacy in small tasks, neatness, and strength. They expose the individual to judgment on the part of anyone in sight. Ordinarily these norms are sustained fully and unthinkingly. When, therefore, an untoward event occurs that brings these routine accomplishments into question, the individual can feel strongly compelled to try to correct impressions by performing an enactment in the round. Note, the question here is not whether appearances give a warranted or unwarranted view of the individual; as long as the view is unfavorable, he will have reason to correct it.

Body gloss, then, is a means by which the individual can try to free himself from what otherwise would be the undesirable characterological implications of what it is he finds himself doing. We must expect every variety of example. A boy taking his girl into an amusement park picture booth, alive to the fact that the booth is seen as a place where couples go to neck, elaborately goes to the change booth for change and holds the necessary quarter up high by means of two fingers, so anyone present will see that his in-

[21] Example: A man in the A & P holds two quarts of milk in his hands and seeks to make use of, and hence intrude on, the cart ahead of him, since it has only a few things in it and could easily hold his. However, its claimant happens not to be immediately discernible. By way of accounting for the offense he is about to commit, he turns to the stranger behind him in line and says, "It's so cold you can freeze your hands." Then he leans over and places his cold burden in the cart ahead that isn't his. Then, as a gesture that everyone can see, he broadly gives himself a self-hug, saying "Brrr."

tended use of the booth is innocent.[22] A man looking at a girly magazine in a store specializing in this commodity may be careful to leaf through the magazine at a rapid pace, giving the same amount of attention to each page, as if looking for a particular article or wanting to see what in general a magazine like this could be like.[23] A girl in a university dormitory, desiring to receive mail although no one is in correspondence with her, may see that she is observed going to the dormitory mailbox, give the appearance of looking for a specific piece of mail that she presumably has been expecting, and on finding that it isn't there yet, shake her head in puzzled wonderment—none of which she bothers doing when she thinks no one is observing her hopeless quest.[24] A male participant at a get-acquainted dance, who would say (if he could get to talk to everyone) that he had merely dropped in this once, on his way someplace else, to see what it was like, feels it necessary to buy a drink to hold in his hand and to lean against one of the pillars, as if merely stopping by for a quick drink.[25] A girl entering the table area of a ski lodge wanting to see and be seen by boys who might possibly pick her up, but not wanting to be precisely exposed in these aims, gives the appearance of looking for someone in particular, and she does this by grasping and fixing her sun glasses, which, in fact, remain well above her eyes resting on her hair.[26]

Underlying the variety of body glosses, some distinctive themes can be detected, each corresponding to a basic norm of conduct which the individual must sustain lest he be thought wanting in some fundamental way. Three of these themes will be considered here.

1. *Orientation Gloss:* When an individual is present with others,

---

[22] Teresa Levitin, unpublished paper (1965), "Observational Study."

[23] James M. Creager, unpublished paper (1965), "'Contamination' in Bathrooms and in Locations of 'Girly Magazines'."

[24] Unpublished study directed by Robert Sommer.

[25] Richard H. Schroedel, unpublished paper (n.d.), "The Formalized Mixer Party."

[26] Beatrice Farrar, unpublished paper (1965), "Ski Resort Behavior Patterns."

he often feels obliged to be engaged in some recognizable activity patently occasioned by objectives defined as the official ones for that time and place. When the task he is actually performing gives rise to expressions that cast doubt on this commitment to the current situation, then he may try to act out suitable evidence. Thus a person waiting at a bus stop in the middle of a block sometimes will lean over the curb and peer intently down the block presumably to determine when the bus is coming, even though there will be plenty of time to get ready when in fact it does turn the corner. An individual waiting in a hallway for a coffee machine to do its work may, instead of merely standing there as if loitering or "away," set about helping the machine function—realigning the cup, tapping the spout, and checking up on the innards of the machine by banging the outside.[27] A person standing in an occupied elevator will examine the floor signal lights as if this activity were required in order to ensure getting off at the right floor. An adult male, having left his chair in an airline boarding arena in order to obtain a newspaper and returning empty-handed because none is available at the stand, finds, upon sitting down again, that he forgot to mail a letter. If he gets up again and returns with no visible reason, he half fears he will be thought "funny." He therefore takes the letter out of his jacket pocket, looks at it carefully, and then gets up and leaves the compound to mail it. An airline stewardess who is halfway down the aisle from the service kitchen and remembers something that requires her to turn and retrace her tracks, snaps the fingers of her right hand while shaking her head in mock disgust with herself, thus providing easily available evidence that at least right now she is not disoriented and has her senses about her and, moreover, is secure enough to split herself in two in order to allow one part to sit in open judgment of the other.

It is to be noted that orientation gloss not only establishes that its provider is oriented in the situation but also makes it easy for others in the gathering to orient themselves to him, since his mim-

---

[27] Susan Johnson, unpublished paper (n.d.), "A Hand at the Cup."

ing allows them to read him easily for what he is up to. The giving and getting of orientation would seem to be a generally important element in interaction, and we should expect functional equivalents to what has been considered when we change the "frame," that is, the domain of activity under question. When persons are joined together in the close demands of a conversational encounter, evidence of a participant's orientation to the proceedings will come in part from the relevance of his statements to the preceding course of conversation and the synchrony of listening gestures with junctures in the speaker's talk; at the same time his body as a whole may be allowed a lack of tonus. During interaction between radio performers, orientation requirements take a still further turn. What one performer can easily see about another, and easily be seen by this other to be so seeing, may have to be stated explicitly so that the unseeing audience can orient themselves to the activity between the performers; and this will be an explication of what ordinarily would be taken for granted. Televised interaction between two performers provides still another version of orientation work that must be done. Although a performer can take it for granted that what he sees about his fellow performer the audience sees, too, he still must explicate personal matters that he and his co-worker both know and know the other knows—matters, therefore, that would usually be left unsaid—for the audience cannot be expected to have this knowledge. Performers on the silver screen have the biggest orientation job of all to do, since their task is not only to show that they have a suitably occasioned activity in progress but also to externalize those quite personal responses to current happenings which in ordinary interaction would remain concealed or at best revealed only to intimates through small collusive signs.

2. *Circumspection Gloss:* When an individual finds that his action may be construed as an encroachment or threat of some kind, he often provides gestural evidence that his intentions are honorable—illustrated in the use of scanning to cover staring, which has already been mentioned. Further illustrations can be

suggested. On crowded New York subways, where women have had reason to accuse standees of mashing, a man may hold on to a center post with both hands fixed to the pole high up so everyone can see that whatever happens, his hands did not do it. An individual moving someone else's parcel from one seat to another when it is not clear who the owner is may feel he must show he has no designs on the other's personal property and is not overruling maliciously the claims of a possession marker; he handles the article very gingerly and at its edge, thus contaminating it minimally. Similarly, a man finding a newspaper on a waiting-room coffee table, not knowing whether the paper has been left and can therefore be appropriated or is a personal possession serving as a marker, may, in picking it up and holding it to read, do so diffidently, so that at a moment's notice he can relinquish his claim and reconstitute the paper into someone else's property. A man finding that he has tried to unlock the wrong blue VW sedan steps back from the door and takes a look at his key (which he holds far away from him to increase visibility) while shaking his head in a frown of puzzlement. An individual entering a wrong room where a meeting is in progress may screw up his face and upper body into a comment on his act and ever so quietly withdraw and close the door after him, managing to tiptoe with his face and upper trunk; someone leaving the meeting early may perform the behavior sequence of giving an apology signal to the chairman or speaker and then half tiptoe out, all the while wearing the look of someone already half-involved in business vital enough to warrant his leaving early because of it, this purposefulness only disappearing from his appearance when he has shut the door behind himself and can no longer be seen by those whom he has left to listen to the bitter end. So, too, prospective buyers of a house being shown through it by a real estate agent and coming upon the owner immersed in a domestic activity may spend their brief moment in that particular room as though the floor would break if stepped on fully and as though full breathing somehow would use up too much of the owner's air. A driver of a moving van, tieing up traffic as he maneuvers to back the rig into an alley, demonstrates concern for the delay he is producing by providing a show of total exertion as he turns the servo-assisted wheel. And, as what may be the most common example of all, there is the "loller's tuck." When one individual is leaning up against a wall that is flush to the sidewalk, and another individual approaches, the ensconced individual, however subtly, very often will draw himself in and back as this other gets adjacent to him, thus reducing his own personal space and cooperatively easing the other's task, which is neither to encroach nor to become contaminated. Of course, the passer-by, too, may gloss his passage, twisting his body just a little and increasing his pace, thereby displaying a minimizing of interference.[28]

3. *Overplay Gloss:* When in the presence of others, the individual conducts himself so as to appear to be acting under no severe constraint and, consequently, to be more or less in charge of himself. An implication is that he has a part of himself available always to address to the others should the legitimate need arise. Ordinarily, of course, the individual fully and unthinkingly satisfies this obligation to sustain perceivable self-control when with others. However, circumstances can arise which cast some doubt on his being in full control. One tack he may employ at such times is to manage facial expression stiffly as if nothing noteworthy is occurring, or at least nothing that he cannot handle. The gloss to be considered here, however, involves something like the opposite tack. Given the direction his bodily expression would take if the

---

[28] Silent film comedies were, of course, full of circumspection glosses, Chaplin perhaps carrying them further than anyone else. Seeking to encroach on someone's dinner, letter, girl or skull, the hero would find that the victim had turned to look at him, whereby the precarious intent was displaced into a very broad show of going about one's own business. (In contemporary comedy, Peter Sellers has drawn heavily on the same device.) Since the encroacher is turned upon very late in the act of encroachment, the gloss of innocent intent must be assembled very rapidly and under almost hopeless conditions, the humor residing not in the use of this gloss (which everyone employs), but in having no option but to draw on it under circumstances in which there is hardly any chance of bringing it off.

constraint were overpowering, the individual throws himself into what would thus become of him, but he does so in an unserious manner, thereby covering any signs of real constraint by much larger unserious ones of the same kind. Lifting a heavy object which might expose him in naked effort, a man enacts utter strain unseriously. Pushing open a heavy door, a young lady enacts loud sounds of muscular exertion. Running across part of a hotel lobby so as not to miss friends who are leaving, an individual "over-runs," mockingly throwing himself into a gestured race that would carry him considerably faster were it part of actual running.[29] Falling down on a skating rink or ski slope, the overturned performer plays it big, taking the fullest possible fall, ending spread-eagle, and stays longer than necessary in that position. Walking on a narrow plank that requires some balancing effort, the individual guys the balancing act as though he were walking on a slippery wire. A girl having to pass through a knot of party guests to get to the bathroom employs a broad swimming motion to cut her way through, showing with these strokes that she has not been made bashful by her intent. A middle-class, middle-aged man having forgotten a parcel on the counter of a repair store, returns twenty minutes later to retrieve it, breaks into a mock run as he enters the

---

[29] "Doing a run" is part of our ritual idiom and appears in functionally different slots in different behavioral sentences. To show that he is concerned about being late for a meeting with someone, the individual will wait until he is a short distance away and then throw himself into a mock run, this serving as part of the penance. Tearing herself away from a friendly conversation with three of her neighbors in order, as they know, not to miss a TV serial, a little old lady gets clear of the circle with twenty feet of hobbled over-run, makes a self-deprecating little laugh, and then assumes a normal gait. Passing in front of a car that courteously has stopped for him, a grateful pedestrian enacts hurriedness, although in fact his actual rate of movement changes little; anticipating that he is going to miss an elevator, the individual may guy a run so that the person who might come to be visibly frustrated is not a serious person. A teacher, about to leave his office with an armful of books to go to a class, funnies up a run through the door that is being held by the student with whom he had been talking, a nun.

store, and shakes his head, silently broadcasting support of the bad opinion that others present might have of someone like himself who is so forgetful. A sixty-year-old, heavy woman being helped into the back seat of a car by her friends and husband, over-groans a strain display while wedging herself in. Bowling his fifth straight strike, the bowler turns back to those seated behind him and does a mock expression of prideful achievement, blowing on his fingernails, thereby covering what otherwise might have been a naked show of self-congratulation. A young man, seeing that friends across the street have not seen that he is waving at them, throws both arms up in a Y shape and jumps up and down, an exaggerated, soundless scream on his lips, his mouth fully opened. Similarly, one member of the family, finding that another member of the family has turned the home movie camera on her, will wave, shout, and grimace to the lens, completing by bluster her side of the face-to-face challenge that the camera has initiated, her reply to which she can neither inhibit completely nor realize conventionally, since the camera is both more and less than another person. Note that in all of these cases, if the individual is to express some dissociation from the constraints in the situation, he must make sure that his position is made clear. He must graphically enact his predicament in order to make sure it has been seen; only then can he perform unambiguous evidence that his serious self is not constrained by this predicament.

There are, then, standard displays that the individual offers to those in the gathering at large who care to look.[30] The equipment

---

[30] As might be expected, the work an individual does within unfocused situations with body glosses he also on occasion does within an encounter for the more or less exclusive benefit of its participants. Overplay glosses, for example: not being able to thread a needle, a woman goes into a mock rage; pricking herself, she does an unserious cry. A grocery clerk receiving what he takes to be a pre-emptory order from a customer, responds with half a salute, "Yes sir," and a visibly rapid execution of the order. An individual reading a passage in a book aloud to friends finds himself approaching a French phrase he is not confident of pronouncing perfectly (or approaching a long, technical English word that similarly threatens him); he makes an overly clumsy stab at it, as if to use this occasion to mock those

employed is the whole body, and the evidence provided through its posturing serves to establish the alignment of the actor at moments when undesired readings might be made of him. Body gloss thus provides a first move designed so its maker can suffer going unanswered—in a manner of speaking, a displaced involvement in remedial interchange. As will be seen, this sort of behavior has little of the structural charm that characterizes the complex sequencing found in ordinary conversation, and we will have little further concern with it. It does, however, nicely show that persons present together who are not engaged together in talk, nor members of the same with, can still, of course, interact quite significantly with each other. The notion that a person is alone when he is in a crowd, an anonymous atom, has a literary truth, but this is not the truth that actual street scenes are made of. Alone he may be, a silent single, but as ready with displays as a deaf mute at a block party.

Nor because body gloss involves bodies are we to assume that something particularly individualistic is at issue. The behavior in question is merely performed by bodies; it is generated in slots and pertains or applies to *all* those who happen to be in the relevant niche. Two females and one male, all in their early twenties, walking down the main street of a large Eastern city while together carrying by hand a second-hand, medium-sized sink, constrained out of all measure from sustaining the usual poise of downtowners in a with, may, in unison, with much laughter, act out immanent collapse for the whole duration of the trip; just as (I am told), in the early days of World War II, the two men in a British unit assigned to march at the rear of the column in order to lug the machine gun box without entangling the others, extended their forced clumsiness and isolation into the role of buffoon, the role clearly attaching to the duty, not the personalities, of the men stuck with it.

---

who could not pronounce it, or to show that he has not been made bashful by this sort of incapacity, or to illustrate that he can handle the word properly but is too modest to demonstrate this.

VI *The Structure of the Remedial Interchange*

This analysis began on the most magisterial note I can attempt: moral rules and their function as the link between self and society. This led, with little loss of abstractness, to a consideration of deviations from the rules and the ritual dialogue that provides a remedy. But now it has been argued that moral claims are made with respect to a multitude of minor territories of the self, and that correctives for infraction are to be found in body gloss—the indignities of overacted gesticulation. This brings the study of remedial activity into the street, into the little interactions that are forgotten about as soon as they occur, into what serious students of society never collect, into the slop of social life. That is right where I want to continue to consider it, but now the focus will be on activity that occurs within encounters, activity involving statement-like moves directed to particular others who respond in a replying-like fashion so that something clearly like a dialogue results. In what follows, an attempt is made to build up a picture of immediate remedial interaction systematically, one step at a time. Some explication of the obvious is required and some repetition. My excuse for introducing detail really should be an apology for providing so little of it; for phenomenally speaking, remedial interchanges are of enormous importance. Middle-class children in our society are taught to preface every statement to an adult with a request or by-your-leave and to terminate every encounter, if not every interchange, with some version of thank you. They are taught a formal approach to social life; it is impressed upon them that all dealings, important or unimportant, extended or momentary, between the acquainted or unacquainted, mediated or face-to-face, in work or play, are to be treated as similar and isolable in that all are to be transacted from within ritual brackets. Transactions and dealings that share nothing else at all are made to share this; all are to be tied up with the same ribbon. These teachings are reinforced throughout life. Among adults in our society almost every kind of transaction, including every coming together into a moment of talk, is opened and closed by ritual, if not remedial then supportive. This infuses into every area of life—harsh, easy, personal, and impersonal—a constant checking back to, and reminder of, a small number of central beliefs about the rights and character of persons.

Start the analysis, then, with a little street incident:

> One pedestrian trips over another, says "Sorry," as he passes, is answered with "Okay," and each goes on his way.

1. It appears that three different elements are involved in the incident. First, as already suggested, are the virtual considerations: offense, offender, and victim. Here, at worst, the offender can be seen as someone with no control over his body, no reign on his intent, and the victim as someone over whose territoriality no one need concern himself; or, in slightly different circumstances, the offender can give the impression that he might be trying to create a showdown purposely. Second is the ritual work that is performed in the situation. Here the apology and its acceptance. Third is the "deed," the act—real, not virtual—which otherwise might be an offense but for the ritual that is performed in association with it, this work functioning to modify the worst possible implications of what in fact has occurred. A deed, then, is an act whose meaning is addressed by ritual work that is designed to establish what this meaning will be, the work itself being oriented to a worst possible reading of the deed; it is an act claimed as something not to be seen in any light other than the one provided by the remedial activity. In the incident under question, the deed is the striking of one foot by another, and the reading that is pressed is that it was an unintentional act expessing minor clumsiness, for which the actor is sorry.

By according one turn at talking to a line, by letting letters stand for persons, and by allowing the end of the transcription to mark the end of the ritual work that seemed directly oriented to the incident in question, the entire interaction can be recorded as follows:

Deed: A trips over B

A: "Sorry"
B: "S'okay" [31]

2. The ritual work described allows the participants to go on their way, if not with satisfaction that matters are closed, then at least with the right to act as if they feel that matters are closed and that ritual equilibrium has been restored. If any discontent remains within either party, presumably it will have to be expressed or exhibited at some other time. In other words, after the ritual work, the incident can be treated as though it were closed. So the "round" that has occurred is also a complete interchange.

3. It would seem that instead of providing an apology, the virtual offender could play through the sequence by providing an account ("Have to catch that train."), or a request ("May I get through?"), or a combination of two or three ("Sorry, may I get through, I have to catch a train."), and that at some level of analysis, these function in exactly the same way as does an apology. Instead, then, of speaking of an apology (or an account or a request), we might speak of a "remedy," designating by this term what is common to the way in which the three ritual moves function in the remedial dialogue.

Similarly, whereas it might be said that the virtual victim accepted an apology, or granted a request, or saw an account as sufficient, it is plain that here, too, a functional equivalence is found. In fact, if we treat as the same, things that have the same ritual consequences, then still other possibilities must be added. In the

[31] The interchanges in this paper are drawn from notes taken on actual interaction, except where quite stereotyped or apocryphal interplay is cited. I have done this because it is easier to record interactions or cull them than to make them up. In all cases, however, their intended value is not as records of what actually happened, but as illustrations of what would be easily understandable if they had happened and had happened with the interpretive significance I give them.

case of requests, the person asked can give an "acceptable" reason why his granting of it must be postponed or even denied. Such an "accounted denial" need but express that the asker was right in making his request and that the person asked is sympathetic to the plea; thereby the ritual implications of a denial can be held in check even though the asker is literally denied. Here, too, we need a term for referring to the responses to a remedy by what is common functionally to them. For want of a better word, I shall speak here of "relief."

remedy A: "Would you pass the milk?"
relief B: "Gee, I'm sorry. There doesn't seem to be any left in the pitcher."

4. It is apparent that when the victim provides a sign that the remedy offered by the offender is sufficient, then this places the offender under some obligation to show gratitude or thankfulness, this counting as a third basic move in the remedial sequence. In brief, appreciation or thanks can be given:

remedy A: "Would you pass the milk?"
relief B: "Here."
appreciation A: "Thanks."[32]

Note, this appreciation is owed the victim not merely as evidence that the offender is fully alive to the virtual offense and desirous of dissociating himself from the sort of person who would commit it, but also as proof that he is alive to the norms and practices associated with the management of negative sanctions. Appreciation, then, informs the victim that his act as someone who generously handles his role in sanctioning is respected and, incidentally, pro-

[32] It has been argued that in the West historically there were two basic appreciations. One, involving our current terms, expressed that the receiver also could be a giver. The other, using phrases such as "God bless you," expressed gross inequality, namely, that the recipient never would be in a position to reciprocate the relief, at least not to he who had given it to him. Here see the comment by Erika Bourguignon, "On the Dyadic Contract," *American Anthropologist*, LXIV, no. 6 (1962): 1301.

vides evidence that the offender possesses at least one of the traits of character of a worthy person, namely aliveness to favors done him.[33] Again we have a general term covering acts that are phenomenally different but functionally equivalent, that is, they fall into the same slot in the remedial sequence and perform the same work in ritual interchanges. It is understandable, then, that an ac-

---

[33] Signs of thanks or gratitude often function also as a means of closing out an encounter. This leads to some otherwise strange behavior. Employers who draw an employee aside to tell him privately that he is being let go may find that the termination interview is terminated by the employee thanking the employer. Similarly, Walter Clark, a student of the Berkeley police, reports that when an officer gives a traffic ticket to a motorist, the latter often will terminate his dealings with the officer by saying "Thank you," which can puzzle the recipient and make him feel that to respond with "You're welcome" would be awkward. No doubt a factor here is that the motorist may feel he has not been treated as badly as he might, which, indeed, is often the case, since officers routinely understate actual speed on a ticket in order to have a basis of control over those they ticket. In part, however, employees being fired and motorists being fined say thank you because that is a way encounters are closed out. The same seems to be the case in regard to the airline hijacker who pays for the drink he orders and thanks the pilot when the latter, on request, offers a light (*Philadelphia Bulletin*, April 14, 1969). I might add (as previously implied) that since requests provide proper ways of initiating certain encounters and interchanges, we can find politeness at both ends of a transaction in circumstances where this might not be expected. Thus, during the Great Train Robbery when the handcuffed fireman was allowed to smoke, the following apparently took place:

> Then seeing the tempting smoke rising from the fireman's lowly position, the robber [guarding him] said, longingly, "I want one, if you have one to spare." The fireman politely passed up his lighter; and the man who had just robbed a train of millions, having cadged a light and a fag, thanked him courteously for both.

Peta Fordham, *The Robbers' Tale* (London: Hadder and Stoughton, 1965; New York: Popular Library, 1965), p. 88. The close analysis of what robbers *actually* say when they confront their victims hardly has begun. Newspapers print purported records of savageries and marked gallantries, but ordinary details go unreported. How, for example, does a robber ask a victim where the bathroom is? How does he initiate the interchange? How does he terminate it? If a robber chooses to answer a ringing phone, what does he say? And how does he sign off? Where, if anywhere, is ritual bracketing not employed? The point, of course, is that we are not dealing here with "politeness," but rather with rules for opening and closing encounters and interchanges.

counted denial, being ritually equivalent to the granting of a request, should lead the person thus denied to terminate the interchange with an appreciation move, in this case phrases such as "Thanks anyway," "That's all right," or "I understand."

Following this third move is sometimes found a fourth, namely, an act on the part of the victim that repeats in diminished form the relief he provided as the second move, shows appreciation of the appreciation shown him, and rather fully terminates the interchange. In current American speech, examples of this are: "You're welcome," "That's all right," "Think nothing of it," or "It's okay." The effect is that the victim graciously makes light both of what he has foregone or suffered and of the quality of character he must have to make light of this sort of thing. This move I shall call a "minimization." It completes the full expansion of the basic remedial cycle, describable as follows:

Deed:	A virtually offends B
remedy A:	"Can I use your phone to make a local call?"
relief B:	"Sure, go ahead."
appreciation A:	"That's very good of you."
minimization B:	"It's okay."

5. Between the first round in the remedial cycle (remedy and relief), and the second (appreciation and minimization) is a shift in concern from the issue of the norm that was violated to the way the participants handle their management of infractions. Note, too, that between the first and second round there is in effect a rule of attenuation, a rapid diminution of ritual activity associated with the ritually relevant event. Relief creates the need for appreciation; the latter creates the need for a minimization. But by the time this fourth move is made, the participants can let go and go on with the other business at hand. And there is good reason for this. As will be considered later, any ritual move can be seen as putting the mover in some kind of jeopardy and thereby generating a need for a saving response from the other parties. Every second move thus becomes itself a first move requiring its own second move. If each succeeding move were not attenuated quickly, ritual would come

to take all of everyone's time. Each occasion on which a remedy was provided would lock the provider and recipient into an interminable "After you, Alphonse" routine. Understandably then, remedial interchanges often terminate after the second move, that is, after relief is given, and when appreciation *is* provided, the final move in the full sequence, namely, minimization, may not occur (resulting in a three-move interchange) or do so in an almost imperceptible form.

6. Until now, the discussion has tacitly assumed that a turn at talking (what in linguistics is sometimes called, with unclear warrant, an "utterance") and a ritual move are much the same, all of what an individual does and says during his turn at bat constituting one ritual move. But when we examine actual turns at talking, this often proves not to be the case:

A: "I'm taking the rake. Okay? Thanks."
B: "Sure. Nothing at all."

What we appear to have here are turns at talk, each of which involves more than one ritual move of an interchange in progress. (The first turn involves a request and an appreciation, the second, relief and minimization.) In short:

A: request / appreciation
B: relief / minimization

If, instead, B omitted the "Nothing at all," then the interchange would have the following structure:

A: request / appreciation
B: relief / ———

And if B omitted the "Sure," then, as follows:

A: request / appreciation
B: ——— / minimization

7. The remedial interchanges thus far described could be ones that "exhaust" the encounters in which they occur; a state of talk is opened with the first move of the interchange and closed with

the last. (The same could be said for many "supportive interchanges," involving the exchange of greetings and the like; they, too, can exhaust the encounter in which they occur.) Such "encounter interchanges" are extremely common, comprising, it seems, the bulk of the focused interaction that occurs in public places, but, of course, there are encounters that are merely opened by such an interchange, or merely closed, the encounter itself containing many interchanges. If, for purposes of analysis, we can assume that the encounter proceeds by these ritually closed spurts and is compounded entirely from them,[34] then the question arises as to how these interchanges are linked or chained.[35] If we restrict ourselves to two-person talk and to two-move interchanges, that is, ones made up entirely from one exchange or round, and if we use superscripts to designate second and further interchanges, some rough answers can be suggested.

Two linkages seem obvious and basic. First, he who makes the initial move in one interchange can make the initial move in the next interchange:

A^1: "Where have you been?"
B^1: "The bookstore."
A^2: "Get anything?"
B^2: "No."

Second, he who makes the terminal move in one interchange can make the initial move in the next:

A^1 : "Where have you been?"
B^1/B^2: "The bookstore. / Did you fix the tap?"
A^2: "No."

The latter form involves a turn at talking that contains two moves. It suggests a third possibility, one already considered in connection

---

[34] This argument is made in the paper "On Face Work," in *Interaction Ritual*, *op. cit.*, pp. 37–38.

[35] I take the term "chain" and the question it implies from Harvey Sacks. In his unpublished papers he considers, for example, the organization of rounds involving more than two speakers.

with moves within an interchange, namely, an opening turn at talking that itself contains two first moves, leading to a second turn at talking that contains two second moves. This is commonly found in service encounters. Once a customer enters the area or "post"[36] where his presence functions as a summons, the server is likely to provide a greeting and an offer of service, thus combining the beginning of a supportive interchange with the beginning of a remedial one. The same sort of linking is found in encounters between friends:

A^1/A^2: "Hi. / Say, I owe you five bucks. Here."
B^1/B^2: "Hi. / I'd forgotten."

Finally, there is a linkage that corresponds closely with what linguists call "embedding," here meaning the inclusion of one interchange within brackets established by another:[37]

A^1: "What'll ya have?"
B^2: "Ya got those almond things?"
A^2: "Not today, honey."
B^1: "Black coffee and a toasted muffin."

Once some basic linkages are described, we can expand the analysis by including interchanges containing more than two moves and linkages between the linkages, but although it is easy to record and transcribe these lattices, it is less easy to find additional reasons for doing so.

8. Earlier it was suggested that in the fully expanded remedial cycle—remedy, relief, appreciation, minimization—the second pair of moves involves a shift in concern from the instigating virtual offense to the manner employed in dealing with it, and that these two moves (appreciation and minimization) are likely to be attenuated. Given these differences between the first and second

[36] This term is taken from an unpublished paper (1968) by Marilyn Merritt, "On the Service Encounter."

[37] Here I draw on the very nice treatment by Emanuel Schegloff of Columbia University in a forthcoming paper. His term for it is "insertion sequence."

round of the full remedial cycle, we can anticipate a degree of organizational looseness between them. At least at certain levels of determination, it appears that the participants in a remedial interchange have a choice as to whether they will terminate matters with one round or go on to introduce a second.

This looseness suggests a parallel in the linkage of interchanges in an encounter. For it seems to be the case that when one or both of the participants in a conversation are not particularly primed for its maintenance, the talk will proceed by two-move couplets, each fairly closed ritually, with considerable choice as to whether any current round will be followed by a next. Consider, for example, one student (A) borrowing a pen from another student (B), the pen turning out to be one with a nib, and consider the apparent arbitrariness of the length of the chain:

A^1: "Pen?"
B^1: "Here."
A^2: "I like that nib."
B^2: "I always use that kind."
A^3: "Me, I always lose them."
B^3: "That's the trouble."
A^4: "Still."
B^4: "Ya."
A^5: "It's very light."
B^5: "It's light."

The same could be said about standard interrogation-type encounters not directly remedial in character in which a chain of three-move interchanges can be expanded or contracted almost at the interrogator's will, he being the one to take two-move turns at talking:

A^1:	"Did you read *Red Harvest?*"
B^1:	"No, I missed that one."
A^1/A^2:	"Terrific./Did you read *The Glass Key?*"
B^2:	"No, but I saw the picture. I liked it."
A^2/A^3:	"Was better than the book./You see 'The Maltese Falcon'?"

B^3: "Ya, it was swell."
A^3/A^4: "It was better than the book, too./You like Ambler?"
B^4: "I've read him all, but I don't know. I don't think I like him much."
A^4/etc. "I like him./etc."

Here again we can see the thrust of naturalistic analysis. Although the sentence is the traditional unit of linguistic study, it is apparent that a turn at talking may contain more than one of them; and yet a turn at talking is a natural unit in some respects. This unit itself may operate as one functionally differentiated move (such as a remedy or an appreciation) within the sequence of moves that comprise an interchange so that move and turn can be the same; but a single turn can also contain two such moves. Moreover, a single turn at talking can, as illustrated, contain the terminating move of one interchange and the opening move of another. Any technique, then, of quantitative analysis that takes the sentence as its codable unit, or even the turn at talking, is likely to average out some of the significant realities of the interaction.

VII *Variations on Structural Themes*

The basic remedial sequence in either its one- or two-round form is a literal and constant part of our public life. But even more important, perhaps, it provides a background of understanding against which deviations are understood by the citizenry. It is the basic schema that makes variations possible; it is a ground that allows for figures. This is a difficult matter to deal with analytically simply because its allowance reduces control—exceptions become grounds for confirming the value of the argument, and that is always bad. Nonetheless, some such argument must be made. Perhaps the best that can be done at this stage is to try to be clear about the kinds of variations that take their meaning from the basic form, that is, the kinds of transformation of the basic remedial cycle that are possible.

1. It is certainly the case that remedies and relief can be conveyed by gestures or actions as well as by words, whether because the context makes a gesture eloquent, or renders speech difficult, or both. After all, we are dealing not with statements but with moves or stands or alignments that individuals take in regard to moral judgments that can be made in the situation. An act or event that can be read as coming "from" an individual and indicating the position he takes up in response to a virtual offense or to an immediately prior move is what is under consideration. We deal with the sequencing of action in which the move of one participant is followed by that of another, the first move establishing the environment for the second and the second confirming the meaning of the first. Until ritual equilibrium or some other form of recognized termination is restored, any one move creates a slot in place and time such that almost anything occurring immediately thereafter can be seen to derive from the person whose turn it is, and will be carefully inspected to discover some way in which it can be read as a reply.[38] The apparent exception here gives its own weight to the analysis. As Harvey Sacks has argued, in conversations with more than two participants, a first speaker's move directed to a particular other (the "addressed recipient") provides an environment in which an unaddressed participant can interject an elaboration or echo of the first move, providing only that the anticipated

[38] Thus, when the purpose is to simulate conversational interaction with a toy, animal, ventriloquist dummy or puppet, a lively sense of its participation can be generated simply by establishing something like a conversational definition of the situation, and then pointedly according the object a next turn at talking and the task of furnishing a reply for an interchange that will be left dangling without it. Any movement sensed as coming from the thing will then be readable as a reply, as will human words spoken off-key and formulated as if issuing from it. Indeed, the interaction so vividly perceived to occur between puppets during a performance is due less, I think, to human-like figures than to human-like slots. Interaction sequences establish slots, and slots can effectively be filled with whatever is available: if you haven't got a sentence, a grunt will serve nicely; and if you can't grunt, a twitch will do.

timing and content of the reply is not thrown off.[39] These interjections will be inspected for a reading as the one thing that the sequential ordering of moves can best use them as, namely, a recompletion of the first move. The capacity of interactants to interpret the words of a current speaker as a continuation of the move initiated by the prior speaker and not as a reply in their own right is itself what makes interjections possible. All in all, then, we are to see that the interpretive sensitivity and discriminatory power of interactants is uncanny. (This seems especially the case in regard to the various paralinguistic and kinesic devices by which a listener can manage during a speaker's turn at talking to distinguish between two moves of an interchange or the terminal move of one interchange and the opening move of another.) In consequence, the linguistically oriented literature on conversational encounters which leans on transcribable sentences provides a hopelessly bookish view of this kind of interaction.

2. In illustrating the basic remedial cycle, it was suggested that the deed that necessitates the remedial work occurs first, before the ritual activity itself. But in fact, that arrangement largely characterizes what are called "accidents." The place where the deed occurs can vary, and its coming first is more the exception than the rule. (In the case of requests, the deed hardly can come first, although something like simultaneous occurrence with the request is observable in minor incursions.) Since the individual knows how his act might be construed, that is, knows the worst possible readings that can be placed upon it, he usually performs the ritual work first and then, when he has obtained relief, executes the act, but now in a style and manner that reinforces the agreement which has been reached as to how the act should be interpreted. Thus, when an individual asks for and receives permission to remove another's coat from a chair and then does so, the act is likely to be styled with care, the coat held in such a way as not to crease it or soil it. The virtual offense here is what is implied by roughly

---

[39] Mimeographed lecture notes, 1967.

throwing another's coat to the floor; the deed, when it comes to be performed, not only has been ritually authorized, but also has incorporated apology and gratitude through the physical style of the act itself. Further still, in the case of requests such as "Please pass the butter," the deed is performed routinely by the virtually offended, not the virtual offender, becoming styled thereby as an offering.

3. When actual ritual activity is observed closely, it is often found that the individual who provides a remedy may not, in fact, receive a reply that provides relief, yet he will take for granted that this relief has been provided in effect. He need but be sure that the context is right, that the contingencies of the moment provide him and the other with the common understanding that no reply is really necessary. Thus in providing an apology while moving quickly, the offender can allow himself to be gone before he can receive official relief, knowing that the others appreciate that here his waiting for the full sequence is impractical and unnecessary. It should be added that positive ritual provides a parallel case: many greetings are made under circumstances in which the act of one party must be taken as supplying an act for both of them. Again it must be remarked that while these one-move interchanges could be read as arguments against the dialogic character of supportive and remedial activity and even an argument against the term interchange itself, this, I think, would be unwise. The single act here stands for the completed interchange; that is its meaning. If it were not obvious to both parties that the reply would be taken for granted, then it is likely that these one-move ceremonies would not be employed.

4. As already suggested, it is often the case in social situations that when a virtual offense occurs between two parties, both may simultaneously take on the role of offender and simultaneously supply remedies. The gain in quickly getting through the incident can override all fine issues of justice. This can, as suggested, lead to a multiple "after you" sequence, but ordinarily a single statement from each party is taken by both to be enough; indeed, a rapid

moving on may be encouraged further by the slight embarrassment of being faced with two first moves for the same interchange instead of a first and second move.

5. It already has been argued that in all remedial ritual two issues are involved: the offense itself and the character sustained by the participants as persons who properly manage the sanctioning system. This, of course, exposes the participants to "run-ins," that is, to direct challenges.[40] By pointedly refusing to provide a remedy or to give relief, an individual occasionally can force the other to take strong action or to stalk openly out of the encounter in a huff. This disruptive possibility is endemic to the ritual organization of encounters, created by the very frame of reference whose purpose seems to be to protect occasions from such discord. But here, perhaps, we come to the limits of speaking of the transformations to which the basic remedial cycle is subject.

6. Between interchanges that terminate equably and those that lead directly into run-ins, there is a midway possibility that must be considered. When one individual finds that others are conducting themselves offensively in their current dealings with him (whether because no ritual work has been performed, or insufficient work, or too much), he can wait until they have closed out the interchange with him and turned from the encounter, and *then* he can express what he "really" feels about them. Here several possibilities are open to him. He may employ a body gloss, enacting his indignation in-the-round for all but the offenders to see and perhaps add some *sotto voce* complaints, thus illustrating the structural design behind what are called "mutterings"; he may turn to a member of his encounter or with and flood into directed expression; he may engage in cross-play, bringing in a mere bystander for the purpose of sharing expression. Whatever his choice from among these directions of expression, the individual here employs a fundamental adaptive device. Although he openly gives up the possibility of receiving what he considers to be appropriate reme-

[40] Run-ins are considered in "Where the Action Is," in *Interaction Ritual, op. cit.*, pp. 239 ff.

dial action from the offenders (and in a manner, gives them up, too), he nonetheless conveys to others around him that he still believes the offenders' conduct was unacceptable. He engages in what might be called an "afterburn," a remonstrance conveyed collusively by virtue of the fact that its targets are in the process of leaving the field.[41] It should be added that the timing of these ritual moves is not so much aimed at preventing the targets from discovering the alignment that is being taken to them, as it is designed to give the targets the right and duty to act as if they were out of range. Note, whether the individual appears to everyone to accept the treatment given him, or responds with a run-in, or engages in an afterburn, we deal with stands that are taken, not feelings that are necessarily felt. An individual may find it strategically desirable to stage a run-in even though his feelings have not been much aroused; he can do an afterburn because he feels obliged to; he certainly can sustain the impression that the interchange has gone off satisfactorily although within he is furious at what he has had to countenance.

Expansive, dramatic afterburns are not numerous, but this should not blind us to the fact that brief, minor ones involving only a flicker of expression conveyed collusively to bystanders are a constant feature of public activity:

---

[41] The central example in Anglo-American society, practiced primarily by children, consists of sticking out the tongue or putting thumb to nose after someone whose authority has had to be accepted turns from the encounter in which the authority was expressed. I believe these two conventionalized acts give children not merely a device by which to vent their feelings against authorities, but also, and perhaps mainly, an opportunity to practice what will be a life-long circumstance of social activity—an ecological division between what can be seen about oneself and must therefore embody certain standards of propriety, respect, etc., and what is shielded and therefore relatively free. I might add that in modern times, the automobile has introduced a wonderfully well-designed arrangement for afterburning. By keeping his windows up and doors locked, a motorist can become involved in all kinds of run-ins, express himself to fellow passengers very vociferously, and yet, in effect, be out of range of the enemy before him. Another standard locus for afterburning, already mentioned, occurs at the moment a with passes a street importuner.

> Woman shopper in little Italian grocery story. She holds up a green pepper in one hand and addresses the owner.
>
> Shopper: "How much are the peppers?"
> Owner: "Seventy-five cents a pound." (He turns away.)
>
> The shopper puts back the green pepper, purses her lips in brief dismay, then, being alone, seeks out the eyes of two shoppers not with her and gesturally expresses that the owner must have optimistic notions about the possibility of selling peppers. Returning a pepper now has become something she is prepared to be quite unashamed about doing.

The point here bears repeating: when an individual is in a public place, he is not merely moving from point to point silently and mechanically managing traffic problems; he is also involved in taking constant care to sustain a viable position relative to what has come to happen around him, and he will initiate gestural interchanges with acquainted and unacquainted others in order to establish what this position is. In a public place, the individual appears to be indifferent to the strangers in his presence; but actually he is sufficiently oriented to them so that, among other things, should he feel the need to perform corrective rituals, he can transform the strangers around him into an audience to receive his show.

7. In describing the basic remedial cycle, it was assumed that by and large the virtual offender makes the first move, namely, the provision of a remedy. Now it must be suggested that the ordinary cycle sometimes can be prefaced by a "priming" move. When a claimant or victim finds that expected remedial work is not forthcoming, he can act so as to call attention to the work that needs to be done. The query or "interrogative challenge" thereby conveyed is not quite a first move in its own right because the response it seeks is for the party that should have made a first move to make that kind of effort.[42] "You want to look at my newspa-

---

[42] Issuing a challenge can set up the situation so that the *challenger* can accept defeat. Thus, in an unpublished study (1969), Roberta Kass suggests that when individuals maneuver for priority in entering a bus, he who complains to another about that other's conduct and receives an apology in

per?" said after one's paper has been expropriated is not a request for information but a last opportunity for the expropriator to set things right and do quickly now what he should have done before taking liberties.

Apparently priming actions can occur at all points in the basic remedial cycle and can be performed by either party. When, in the ordinary course of events, a virtual offender provides a remedy, the recipient can hesitate in providing relief, or even mildly dispute the adequacy of what is offered, and by doing so induce a replay of the remedy.[43] Similarly, by giving relief in an ironic

---

response to this priming action is likely then to feel obliged to let the offender enter first unhampered. Similarly, when the offender himself initiates an apology for pressing forward, acceptance of this apology is often acceptance of his precedence. It might be added that in losing place, the loser may come in for ritual compensation not merely so the books can be balanced, but also so that the advantage which has been taken of him will not be read as what may always be done to him. Correspondingly, in gaining place, the gainer may provide apologies not merely as recompense but also as a means of allaying feelings that he might always demand more than his due.

[43] The inducing of a remedy replay is a widely available minor aggression that only seems to have been taken up seriously by lower-class, urban blacks. When a virtual offender does his little dance of disaffiliating himself from his just completed action, the witness looks directly at the dancer's eyes and checks back all facial expression. The consequence, usually, is that the apologizer does another apology and feels uncomfortable:

> A, seeing hotel elevator about to close, rushes to make it in time and manages to squeeze in before the door shuts. Looking at the one passenger already there, he initiates the following:
>
> A: (Shakes his head as if to comment on the risks involved in urban living)
> B: (Makes no sign, just looks at A)
> A: "Ya can lose an arm in these things."
> B: (Still no smile)
> A: "Sometimes I get to it and it closes."
> B: (Gives a little smile and shakes his head sympathetically)

Tom Wolfe has a version:

> Then Chaser would say, "Now when we get there, I want you to come down front and stare at the man and don't say nothing. You just glare. No matter what he says. He'll try to get you to agree with him. He'll say, 'Ain't that right?' And 'You know what I mean?' And he wants you to say yes or nod your

tone, the giver can remind the offender that he should have provided a remedy or can inform him that the one he provided was not quite enough. So, too, there are ironic deliveries of minimization that induce an appreciation move that had been omitted. (In these cases we once again see that the environment within which a very minor gesture can take on a clear, firm meaning is the one generated by the prior moves in a ritual sequence.)

Note the performance of a priming move inevitably opens up the possibility that instead of this act inducing the occurrence or reoccurrence of the standard remedial cycle, a run-in may occur, the recipient taking the position that improper demands are being placed upon him. For this reason, priming moves tend to be made in various disguises. Thus, instead of an outright challenge, we are likely to find devices such as a "set-up question": should the asker receive the expected answer, he will be in a clear position to challenge or to negatively sanction the respondent, but at the same time he leaves a little room open for an unanticipated answer that might adequately account for the apparent infraction and even show that it is the asker who is at fault. Common, too, are the sort of bodily statements whose implication can be denied, if necessary:

> At lunchtime in a busy cafeteria a man brings his tray of food to a four-person table that has dirty dishes on it, apparently assuming that no one "has" the table. He clears a place for his own dishes, takes them off the tray, and sits down. At this point two young men come up carrying dishes of dessert and coffee:
>
> Youths: (They place themselves directly in front of the table, both leaning into it a little, and, dishes in hand, look at the man in the eye as if to give him the first move.)
>
> Man: (Gathers up his plates, puts them on his tray, rises, and says), "Sorry, I thought no one was here."
>
> Youths: "Sorry, it's our table." (They sit down.)

---

head . . . see . . . It's part of his psychological jiveass. But you don't say nothing. You just glare . . . see . . ."

Tom Wolfe, *Radical Chic and Mau-Mauing the Flak Catchers* (New York: Farrar, Straus and Giroux, Inc., 1970), pp. 101–102.

It might be added that in the process through which children acquire ritual competence—perhaps the most fundamental socialization of all since they thereby learn about the nature they are to have as actors—priming occurs openly, without the cover of irony or sarcasm or question-asking, and in regard to every move in the remedial cycle. A child's failure to properly complete the remedial cycle can lead to a halt in the proceedings, this accomplished by an adult interjecting a phrase such as "What do you say?" Children thus are constantly required to rerun their actions under corrective demands. Socialization into the military and other such pervasive, post-adolescent systems also relies on explicit priming.

8. Remedial work often gives rise to "recycling." An accounted denial of a request may lead to coaxing, wheedling, "pretty please," to second and third tries until the plea is granted or seems assuredly hopeless.[44] The provision of relief similarly can lead to recycling, the recipient (the initial offender) replaying his remedy once or twice to make sure that the relief is being given without reservation. And, of course, the appreciation move can be replayed, too, in order to establish gratitude more certainly. Any of this recycling activity can become conventionalized and expected, but nonetheless, the possibility of engaging in ritual work of this kind adds to the flexibility of the standard process.

9. It has been argued that a virtual offense brings forth remedy from the virtual offender and relief from the virtually offended, and that when this has been done to everyone's satisfaction, the potential incident can be dropped and the participants, whether together or separately, can get on with the business at hand. During incidental contacts in public places between unacquainted individuals, these remedial interchanges may fully exhaust the encoun-

---

[44] Wheedlers often seem to be involved in a special kind of exchange. They accept being seen as not quite self-respecting and in return need not be stopped by the first no. Our stereotype is that although it may be all right for children, women, and blacks to wheedle, full-fledged adults should decline to do so, setting their dignity and independence above what could be gained by such entreaties.

ter that contains them. In the protracted movement of withs moving about, remedial interchanges may involve merely brief distractions from the ongoing conversation.

Now we must see that this perspective allows us to deal with supportive rituals as well as remedial ones. If two individuals are bound by obligation to accord each other face-to-face displays of supportive ritual concern, then their coming into each other's immediate presence establishes conditions such that if no supportive work is performed, virtual offense will occur, requiring a remedy. Thus, when someone forgets another's name or face, a little apologetic flurry results much as if an offense had occurred. In short, greetings can be analyzed as a correction, a remedy, for what otherwise would become an offense. The same is true with an offer. If the setting is such that omission of a particular offer conveys disregard, then provision of the offer functions as a remedy for which thanks are owed. The same can be said about commiserations, compliments, and other members of the class of ratificatory rituals. In general, then, the presumption of support creates much the same circumstances as does the presumption of distance keeping. Remedial interchanges correct failures to *not* do certain things, and supportive interchanges—in effect—correct failures to *do* certain things; the first corrects for incursive violations, the second for slights.

One further argument can be made concerning the connections and parallels between supportive and remedial ritual. As suggested, when a request is made, a recipient who is about to refuse it is likely to respond with an accounted denial, thus providing the asker with ritual relief even though he gets nothing more for his plea. The point here is that if an individual initiates an offer without the recipient actually having made a request, and the recipient chooses to decline the offer, then the latter is in a position to show that the giver's favors are little regarded or improperly given. This the recipient typically avoids by giving an account of why he is refusing the invitation and giving thanks for its having been offered. Interestingly, an accounted declination may be followed by a minimization such as "Perhaps next time" or, "I'll ask again sometime." In any case, a clear parallel can be seen between an accounted denial that a refused request calls forth and an accounted declining that a refused offer calls forth; each serves to control for virtual offense, and in each case this is a second-order offense pertaining not to an initial virtual offense but to the offense that can arise from the way in which supportive and remedial work is managed. It might be added that like remedial ritual, supportive ritual can be recycled; when offers are declined it is not only possible to repeat them, but in some circumstances it will be understood that unless they are repeated they ought not to be accepted.[45]

10. Supportive rituals, then, lead to situations that can be understood in terms of the remedial form. This should be seen as but one instance of a much more general rule, namely, that the stand a particular individual takes before others is likely to have some defensive function for him, allowing a reading that accords him a defendable position in the face of discreditable interpretations that could be made. This being generally the case, it will be generally true that those who witness the individual will be under obligation to provide him with assurances of some kind that his message has been received and the viability of his line granted.

One example of this reply dependency is found in the already cited cases of overplay gloss—the little shows that individuals put on when they mock-zealously grab for a newly vacated chair

---

[45] He who has what others want and gives them it not appears as a person of small sympathy, bent and constrained by his possessings, owned by what he owns. Therefore, he needs must make an offer. But just as much, he needs this offer declined lest his goods diminish as a consequence of entering the company of others. Happily they who receive a first offer have their reasons to decline it. A quick acceptance could demonstrate a lack of concern for the situation of the giver, and show the recipients to be overgoverned by their needs and wants and passions. Re-offerings, when they come, will allow recipients to keep their character *and* eat a second helping. Thus, giver and receiver conspire to empty the first offer, ritualizing a ritual. Note, if selves were not constructed in this way—constructed so that each man maintains that he likes what he has and little desires the goods of his neighbor—public life would falter, for he with the more could ill afford to find himself in the close company of those with the less. All civility in social intercourse would give way to clamorous beseechings.

or unseriously perform a run to miss being a little later in a ticket line. These momentary splittings of the self render the actor needful of confirmation as to the efficacy of his maneuver. Therefore, he is typically given a reply by strangers, very often a little sympathy grimace, that is, a smile, sometimes accompanied by a slight shaking of the head.[46] May I repeat, although these little acts of

[46] Smiles, I think, have important functions in public order and are to be examined in terms of the slot in which they occur in the streaming sequence of behavior. Smiles serve as silent "thank you's" and "your welcome's." Smiles allow the individual to announce no contest even before he has discovered what the contest will be about. When an individual in the close quarters of an elevator, hall passageway, or party gathering finds a stranger's eyes touch his, he may attempt to show social grace by allowing a smile to flick across his face as if giving recognition to the common social situation of the two of them but without going quite as far as full-scale social recognition.

Smiles are also to be examined in terms of their role as transfix markers, that is, devices for bracketing a period of time and activity as something to be given a single reading. When a tennis player returns a ball to a neighboring court on request, he may attach a smile to the period during which he is out of his own game and engaged in assisting the other court, this serving both to mark a time-out period in his own court and to override any tendency for his courtesy to be used by the recipient as a wedge for conversation. Passing a parent and infant, an individual holds a smile, suggesting that as a member of the league of child lovers he is to be trusted fully, and furthermore, whatsoever the child happens to be doing now or is about to begin to do and whatsoever the parent must do to control this, it will be understood that the parent is doing a good job. A waitress approaching a table newly taken may keep a fixed smile on her face as she cleans off its surface with a rag and places the requisite number of glasses of water on it, the smile serving to neutralize the minor territorial invasion that this work entails and to hold off order-placing until this work is done. When parents stay clear of their house for an evening so that their adult son and daughter-in-law can have a party in a place that is big enough and they return after midnight to a social occasion still in progress, they may thread their way to the kitchen, then back to the dining room for some party fare, then upstairs to bed—all the while wonderfully holding a no-contest you-have-every-right-to-be-here smile. Similarly, a wife can hold a smile of amused patience on her face over the entire period during which her husband nearby flirts with another woman, the smile proclaiming that his actions are not to be taken seriously. Indeed, when in doubt, play a smile.

No doubt a baby is the sort of actor who can break into a momentary

sympathy seem meaningless, they are not, for by offering one, the giver foregoes exploiting the position he is in to keep the initiator dangling, caught with the possibility that what he projected as a little act may be seen as a hopeless performance or, still worse, no performance at all.

When, then, the individual splits himself in two, he becomes very needful of evidence from others that the disassociation is perceived and accepted as he defines it. We now should go on to see that this dependency on a reply is also found when the individual plays himself straight. For any configuration of events with which he can be associated closely carries a worst possible meaning which could serve to reflect unfavorably on him. So he must continuously supply remedies and his witnesses relief.

The remedial cycle thus will be present as an organizing influence in what participants take to be uneventful talk. Look, for example, at two basic conversational forms. One of these is the question-answer couplet—the interrogative interchange. One person asks a question pertaining to fact or opinion, a second person provides an answer. If we assume that when the question is asked (especially among non-familiars) the asker exposes himself to worst possible readings, to the committing of a virtual offense (in this case that he is unworthy of being spoken to, that his speaking up is uncalled for, and that his question is obtuse and presumptuous), then we can see that any more or less straight answer, however dutiful, however mechanical, however vague, however incomplete or beside the point, can provide relief and let the asker off the hook. Once an asker creates a slot for an answer, he will be ready to see a properly timed microsecond shrug as filling it. For

smile spontaneously, and no doubt a physiological-psychological model fits here. But adults, it can be argued, don't break into anything; they take up alignments in situations and use their animal equipment to mark the period, however long, to which their expression is meant to apply. Little smiles are made by everyone all day long, but we never think to study them syntactically. Suggestive ethological comments on smiles and similar "appeasement gestures" are provided by Konrad Lorenz, *On Aggression* (London: Methuen, 1966; New York: Bantam Books, Inc., 1967), pp. 171–173.

although the asker will have a variable concern to obtain the information he asks for, he will have, distinct from that, a constant concern to obtain acceptance of his asking. A question, after all, is one form of request—a request for information—and as such is to be analyzed as a ritual move, not an inquiry—a move that can be as satisfyingly answered by an accounted denial of information as by the full facts. At least, that is the way it seems to be in our own society.[47]

A second basic couplet found in ordinary talk is the declarative interchange. First speaker propounds an argument, enunciates an opinion, draws a moral, provides a little editorial, muses aloud, vents his feelings, and so on, all in the guise of saying something that should have some relevance and even validity for all who can hear; second speaker, in return, provides an affirming reply at the proper conversational juncture—a grunt, a nod, a verbal agreement, a counter-argument—any of which confirms first speaker's claim to being the sort of person who has a right to express opinions and who is worth attending when he does. To make a declaration, after all, is but to establish a line that might not be viable, and, as such, commits the declarer to obtaining support from hearers—support not so much for what he says as for the propriety of saying it.

Questions and statements, then, can be seen as a claim to a kind of status, and replies will be examined for, and ordinarily engineered to provide, affirmation that this claim is not a presumption. Once again we see that, in regard to required ritual work, the line between some supportive interchanges and some remedial ones can become so thin as to deny the necessity for drawing it.

11. The position is being taken, then, that the individual constantly acts to provide information that he is of sound character

[47] It would be easy to read these organizational devices as prerequisites for conversational interaction in any society, but this should not be done. Apparently other kinds of conversational organization are possible, as suggested, for example, in regard to West Indian interaction, by Carl Reisman in a forthcoming paper, "Contrapuntal Conversations in an Antiguan Village."

and reasonable competency. When, for whatever reason, the scene around him ceases to provide this information about him, he is likely to feel compelled to act to control the undesired impression of himself he may have made. It is here that a further variation on the remedial theme can be found: the concern of others for the offender can cause them to intercede on his behalf before he does. They provide him a line to take. They make a pre-emptive move. He is then put in the position of providing a reply that conveys that the work of his well-wishers is not a presumption and in addition is effective. He thus provides relief for the remedy provided for his own offense. Note, offenses that call forth this tactfulness may be very minor indeed—merely a hint that the actor has presented himself in a possibly awkward light:

> At a checkout line in a supermarket the carts have begun to pile up. After unloading his groceries on the checkout counter, a man finds there is no place to put his cart. He steps back out of line and puts it into another located between the checkout lines. But to do this, he must put two others together, and he ends up pushing four out of the traffic area. Consequently, he is taken out of his own course of action and involved considerably in a task that might be seen as falling outside his proper role. On his return to his place in line, a large, working-class, black woman, not an acquaintance, initiates the following interchange:
>
> She: "That's a good job."
> He: "If we won't do it, it won't get done."
> She: "That's the truth."

12. Pre-emptive supportive moves may be made not only by the offended for the offender but also by third parties, and when this occurs we can see anew how deeply the remedial form cuts:

> Middle-aged woman in crowded downtown sandwich cafeteria at lunchtime. She brushes against a youth in his twenties as she takes cutlery from the bin on her way to the service line. He says: "Sorry." She, instead of doing the same, keeps on going, without acknowledging him, but muttering to herself: "Some people." He watches her move on with no expression, apparently ready to let the matter drop. A second male standing nearby, unacquainted with the

victim, having seen the incident, says to him, "Gracious, isn't she." First male, with feeling, "I'll say."

The point is this: When an offended party responds with neither an interrogative challenge nor an afterburn, this need not mean that somehow the remedial formula has ceased to apply. Even when the victim chooses to do nothing, it is still likely to be the case that he has opened himself up to the understanding that he has been offended; because of this, unacquainted third parties, initiating a supportive remark, can be sure that he will sympathetically understand when they do his afterburning for him. More than it spreads damage, a virtual offense spreads interpretability; and this it does utterly, rendering all next acts in the vicinity subject to a reading that everyone present can be counted on to entertain, if not to give.

When the individual offends but is not present to remedy matters himself, then obviously others will have to be relied upon if any excuse-making is to get done; less obvious is the fact that these others may find themselves involved in remedial ritual because this seems the only natural way of behaving. When A makes a business phone call to B, who should have been there to answer but wasn't (or personally appears at B's post when B should be there but isn't), and C must answer the query, it will hardly be possible for C to reply to A without transforming this reply, if only paralinguistically, into a ritual move, whether to show sympathetic support for the frustration that A is facing, or, by a slight, conspiratorial lightness in tone, to direct A into momentarily setting aside the serious frame of the work world and, hence, B's apparent lapse from it.

13. In suggesting that remedial ritual is employed in regard to everything from major offenses to minuscule ones, and that its formulae can be applied in a variety of transformations, I am suggesting that interpersonal ritual is a powerful device for ordering events accommodatively. Indeed, the warrant for a formalistic approach to social activity, one that treats encounters as comparable regardless of difference in content, is partly to be found in the or-

ganizing effect of ritual. One weakness of this commitment to interpersonal ritual was also mentioned: the possibility that the pointed use of affronts or the escalation of righteously indignant response could lead to run-ins. Now brief mention will be made of a second weakness inherent in ritual organization.

It seems to be a fundamental feature of remedial ritual that it provides an obligatory way of dealing with one-shot deviations from ordinary rules, a means of sustaining routine understandings in the face of guileless infractions. Accounts, apologies, requests all mark an effort on the part of a virtual offender to show that what he seeks is not a change in his apportionment of rights but rather a single exception to restrictions and standards he is ready to continue to accept. And what is asked of the virtually offended is a generosity of spirit, a flexibility, a willingness to treat as out of frame an otherwise unsupportable occurrence, for the assumption is that the victim is being asked to accept a single exception, not a permanent reduction of his rights. When, therefore, a remedial interchange has been played through, the one who has supplied the remedy has a deeply imbued expectation that that will be the end of it. Indeed, that it will be the end of it is the basis for allowing that particular ending.

However, circumstances can, of course, arise when a virtual offender, having just provided a remedy and having just received relief, happens then to immediately create again the same offense involving the same victim. And this may occur a third time and in some special cases a fourth. It is then that the pair will find that no ritual work is really available to deal accommodatively and routinely with what has happened. Accounts, apologies, and requests cannot be made, at least not with any grace or niceness; after all, remedial work is designed to show that he who asks indulgence is now very much alive to what it was that produced the need for indulgence in the first place, but such a person is exactly what the offender disproves himself to be by virtue of repeating his offense. The victim finds that what he gave on the grounds that his giving would be exceptional is now asked of him again. (Something similar is found in connection with "spoiled" farewells, ones that are done on the anticipation of a departure which then does not occur.) It is here we find that the patience and good will of the victim are likely to be meager and fitful, for no pattern exists in this particular structural nexus to provide a mold for accommodative response; and it is here that the embarrassment of the offender is itself embarrassed, for it has already done the work allowed it and cannot effectively serve again. This disorganization is found even in regard to the management of what must be our most frequent "repeat offense"—repeatedly getting the same wrong number.

Just as remedial ritual management can be effectively applied to substantial infractions as well as minuscule ones, so here it appears that the good will of the victim can quickly break down whether in the face of minuscule offenses or substantial ones; howsoever inconsequential the boon he has asked for, it can be too much. And so when we assess for any particular group the capability of its remedial ritual, we must consider not only the range of one-shot events that can be organized accommodatively, but also what, if any, forebearance in depth is provided for repeat offense.

VIII *Overlays*

The occurrence of virtual offenses and the consequent provision of remedies and relief provide a close model for some interaction. The transformations to which the basic remedial sequence is subject provide a design for still further behavior. Now we must examine another extension of the remedial sequence as a determinant of behavior. But now matters become considerably more complex.

Whatever is the case with ritual addressed to supernatural entities, secular interpersonal ritual is anything but merely single layered. It seems that once well-understood forms become available for easy use among individuals, conditions are established for slightly modifying set responses in such a way that additional lay-ers of meaning become manageable. By judicious minor modification in timing and tone, in stress and gesture, overlays are possible, that is, tacit meanings to be understood as contained in other meanings. Just as a move creates a slot for a replying move, and just as this slot renders all participants in the interaction extremely discriminating in regard to minor events occurring at that moment and place, so the replies that usually are given to fill a slot provide a base—a virtual framework—against which minor variations stand out. What results is something that is very difficult to reduce to a pattern, although, of course, the competence to employ and to read these superimpositions is no doubt as standard a consequence of ordinary socialization as is the capacity to play things straight. Apparently, these overlayed meanings are almost as conventionalized as the ones that serve as a vehicle for them.

All of this has been implicit in considering the variations on the basic remedial cycle, especially in the discussion of priming moves and their reliance on irony. Here I want only to examine some interchanges selected so as to allow us to explicitly consider overlays.

For example, the conditions which establish the suitability of an appreciation move provide the basis for a multitude of overlays. A woman who finds a door held open for her can play it straight and reply to this move with a "Thank you." If the door is not held open, she is in a position to use the virtual sequence as a basis for sarcasm with a thank you said at the moment ordinarily appropriate, thus admonishing someone's failure to provide a courtesy. If the door is held open by someone who must pause considerably in his own course of action to do so, she can provide through the phrasing and tonal color of her thanks, two thanks, one for the traditional act and an extra measure for the extra effort. (Similarly, a man holding parcels who finds a door opened for him by a woman can give proper notice of the switch in role by saying thank you with a special emphasis.) Here, of course, a shift occurs from deed to doer, from thanks for an act to thanks for the exemplary conduct of the actor. Finally, finding a door held open by someone who is very considerably ahead of her, a woman may say thank you in a tone of puzzlement, again using a virtual base as a contrast to what in fact she conveys.

Overlays can occur in other ways. For example, when an individual is asked a favor which he sees as a little demanding, he can comment on the propriety of the request even while he complies with it. His granting of the request provides the environment within which the negative sanction can be administered safely:

> Citizen off the street, needing change for a meter, enters an apartment hotel and asks the lady at the desk to change a dollar.
>
> Lady: (Giving change) "We ordinarily don't have change at the desk, but I happen to have some for the postman I can give you."
>
> Citizen: "That's *very* good of you." [48]

Similarly, when a request is pre-emptory and borders on being a naked command, the act of compliance can be styled to convey resentment, or at least reservation concerning the propriety of the demand, this degree of resistance being allowed the subordinate because his physical obedience assures that the other's immediate control of the situation is not being threatened. So, too, overlaying is possible in terms of the usual anticipations that attenuation will occur between the remedy-relief round and the appreciation-minimization round of the remedial sequence. By giving his appreciation move more stress than his remedy move, the individual can make a special point of his gratitude.

It is obvious, then, that any close and realistic view of the functioning of remedial sequences will have to consider overlays upon this ritual base. It should be just as obvious that remedial sequences can be superimposed on talk that appears to have quite other purposes. To make sense of the give and take in ordinary conversation, we must appreciate its laconicity, that is, the tendency of the participants to assume, and correctly so, that allusions to items of common experience will serve effectively as full refer-

---

[48] Here again, incidentally, we see that the standard appreciation in the standard slot for appreciation provides the virtual environment for understanding the appreciation that does occur.

ence.[49] (Indeed, an obligation of speakers is to pitch their references so that the fullest understanding shared by the participants will be depended upon.) This should lead us to see that any neutral comment uttered at a particular juncture in the interaction clearly may be meant to be taken as a tactfully presented ritual move in the remedial cycle; similarly, an ostensible ritual move can function as the vehicle for a quite different ritual action. In these cases it is likely that the response that results will be understandable only if it is assumed that the implied move is in fact being made. Two interrogative challenges presented as requests for information can serve as illustrations:

Father: (To daughter who stands before him on the phone) "You on the phone?"
Daughter: "Oh! I'm sorry, I forgot you wanted it."

Father: (To son whom he sees entering the house empty-handed) "Did you get the paper?"
Son: "I'll try to remember next time."

Interestingly, such indirect moves are read so naturally for their tacit meaning that it can become difficult to see that in fact an overlay has been made and attended to:

A: "I see you have your house for sale."
B: "We got tired of looking after a big house. We're going to get a nice small one."

or

A: "I thought you were going to phone me right back."
B: "I'm sorry, I just couldn't get near a phone."

In these cases A's statement functions as a priming action to induce an account; that, literally speaking, he actually introduced a different move—a statement of information—requires special attention to appreciate. It is thus that playful teasing can occur in conversation, especially by the young; the standard dodge is to

---

[49] A useful explication of this point is provided by Harold Garfinkel, *Studies in Ethnomethodology* (Englewood Cliffs, N.J.: Prentice-Hall, Inc., 1967), pp. 38–42.

redirect an interchange by replying to the literal meaning of a statement and not to the implied move that everyone appreciates is involved: [50]

A: "Do you know the time?"
B: "Yes, do you?"

A: "Do you have the time?"
B: "Yes. Do you have the inclination?" [51]

And when the literal meaning of a statement is addressed *seriously* without reference to the implied ritual move, this is likely to be read as a purposeful obstruction of the course of the remedial cycle—a strategic move in its own right.

Wife: "I dented the fender again coming into the garage."
Husband: "You what!"
Wife: (With inflection and volume rising above her husband's) "You heard what I said."

Even here, where two moves literally involve reference to hearing, it is understood that questions of unclear speaking and faulty hearing are in no way at issue.[52]

---

[50] Alan Dundes of the University of California, Berkeley, has made a collection of these utterances, and the two examples are taken from a report on his work published in the *San Francisco Chronicle*, May 9, 1966.

[51] Again note how fully one takes the tacit meaning as the sole one. "Do you have the time?" is not seen as any different from "Would you tell me the time, please?" although, in fact, the first is the more tactful since it easily allows for an accounted denial, "Sorry, I don't have a watch on me."

[52] Requests (or commands) for repetition need not, of course, be negative sanctions uttered by someone who has no desire to hear the statement again in its original form. Often the recipient will be correct in thinking that the asker actually wants a rerun. But even here, *actual* failure to hear need not have occurred, indeed may not even be likely. As is considered later, the asker really may want a moment to orient himself to the encounter, a moment to bend his attention to what is to come, which he obtains by arranging to sit through the opening move a second time. He may also want to introduce the nicest of reminders that perhaps he has been brought into an encounter on insufficient grounds and without quite enough ceremonial preparation. Thus, if really pressed, he who asks for a rerun usually can say what it is that was said the first time.

IX *Structural Speculations*

Given these speculative observations on the transformations to which the basic remedial cycle is subject, I would like to speculate about these speculations and try to sketch in the framework that might be necessary if we are to begin to deal with the complexities of ordinary verbal give and take. I take direction from "utterance play," such as cracks, comebacks, and squelches, and—odd as it may appear—from discoverable uses of rhetorical statements, these latter turning out to provide leads concerning the structure of interaction.[53]

A statement that constitutes the first move of a ritual interchange (be it supportive or remedial) appears to establish two crucial boundaries for the play of conversational interaction: first, it establishes limits regarding offensiveness, the assumption being that a run-in is not the intent; second, it establishes an expectation—a prefigurement—of how the interchange will unfold, including

---

[53] Rhetorical questions have many different roles to play in talk, and only a few are considered in this analysis. The following additional roles might be mentioned.

A rhetorical question can serve as a greeting that initiates an encounter, as when a man coming out of the lake is addressed with the question: "Been in swimming?" It can be used as a means of "setting up the interaction," that is, providing the initiator with an opportunity to ask permission to open a state of talk, while at the same time giving the participants a moment to orient themselves to the involvement to come, as in: "Hello, Cindy. Is that you? Are you up?"

Since the purpose of all such rhetorical statements will be to provide first moves to which a replying move is as automatic as possible, it is understandable that little value will be placed on the literal content of the phrase, providing only that an answer to it is obvious; and it is further understandable that use of these devices will expose the user to what *Mad Magazine* calls *Snappy Answers to Stupid Questions* (New York: Signet Comic Books, 1968; London: New English Library, 1968), a useful source book brought to my attention by William Labov.

how many moves away the terminal move is likely to be.[54] (Whenever a particular interchange exhausts the encounter in which it occurs, the issue of anticipated sequence will be especially marked.) It is within this doubly bounded framework that much of the lively goings on in conversation can be analyzed.

As a text, I cite at length an early statement by Paul Goodman:

"Do you always say the teacher sent you to buy stamps?"

"Only on that corner where I know who's who. Sometimes I say that my family had a moider. If it's an old woman, I say I'm just gettin' over polio; that's great. Other times I tell 'em my mother—who's really post-mort'm—is a schoolteacher an' won't send me 'cause it stinks. A good one is: when a lady asks you say, I'm ashamed to tell, it's dirty, and burst out laughing or crying, depending. Or the Boy Scouts are goin' to call on the Mayor. I can make these up by the million—I'm good at it. You tell tramps you're playin' hooky an' they say, That's the right spirit! an' give you a roll-your-own cigarette that you can stick up a pig's ass."

Best of all was to say—nothing. But it was better to tell a flat lie than an ambiguity such as Don't have school today, because this led to *more* questions. You must plan a conversation like a game of checkers with the object that the other person should have no next move. Thus, the following was wrong:

A: "Why aren't you in school?"
B: "Teacher sent me for stamps."
A: "She's got her crust, on the taxpayer's money! Does she always send *you* out. . . . You must be teacher's pet. . . .
I'll walk you back that way, etc."

But the following was right:

A: (A lady) "Why, etc."
B: "I'm shamed to tell, it's dirty" with a wild laugh. Then, either she stops or she's safe. A two-move game. But even so,

[54] There are, of course, other indications available for prefiguring endings. Hello's and farewells typically lead (and even oblige) participants to come close together. An individual who is greeted on another's doorsteps and kept in close distance by him is likely to sense that he must move on soon; inside a house, a guest may acquire the same feeling when he finds that his host has suddenly moved up close and begun a chain of compliments.

> the more definite the stop, the more curiosity, resentment, inquiry, later. She tells her neighbor, grills her little boy; this leads to a general investigation and all the unsolved misdemeanors are attributed to you. You get a bad reputation. Therefore, this gambit was absolutely only for transient neighborhoods; yet how could one tell which neighborhood is transient, for the interesting and the desirable always live round the strange corner? Therefore—never. It's great, but the time to use it is—never.[55]

Two lessons can be drawn from this text. First, a technique of analysis: to get at the significance of a move, play through the interchange not only as it actually (or purportedly) happened, but also as it would have happened had all the participants acted in the most routine, mechanical fashion imaginable or, contrariwise, the most cuttingly; then compare. Second, to appreciate the significance of a move, look for the effects it has on anticipations as to how the interchange in which it occurs was to unfold. Using the Goodman technique, then, look at some ways in which anticipated sequences can figure actively in the significance of a move.

1. *Set-ups:* The individual wanting to make a move of a particular kind makes an earlier move such that the other's likely response will be one to which the desired move can be a reply. Thus, for example, the sympathy set-up:

A: "What happened to your leg?"
B: "I had polio when I was young."
A: "Oh, you poor thing, I'm so sorry to hear that."

2. *Cut-offs:* Here we have the foreclosure of a set-up. For example, the asking for a "free good" can be seen to be a way of establishing an interchange that allows for a thanks as a third move. Thus, snappy answers to requests for the time leave the asker with his thanks dangling. Similarly, there is the widely found move, the

---

[55] Paul Goodman, *The Empire City* (New York: Bobbs-Merrill, Inc., 1959; London: Collier-Macmillan, 1964), pp. 16–17, first appearing in *Grand Piano* (1942).

"cripple's rejoinder," this being a means of cutting off a set-up of sympathy.

A: "What happened to your leg?"
B: "I guess I must have left it at the store."

There is also the cut-off to be used against those who would mix negative sanction with sympathy:

A: "Why did you get into this business?"
B: "Just lucky, I guess."

And there are moves that cut off a priming cycle aimed at inducing an apology:

Customer: "Hey, you've got your finger in my soup."
Waitress: "That's okay, the soup's cold."

The obvious device in these sallies, of course, is for their maker to direct his reply to a part of the literal content of the other speaker's words that was meant to be irrelevant, while he shows himself to be composed and unrepentant; the less obvious factor, however, is that in so directing his reply, the anticipated reply to his reply can be immobilized. Thus we can understand the mechanics of the following story reported by a columnist:

> . . . the case of a man charged with driving 110 mph on an E. Bay Freeway (the arresting officer testified he had to go 130 to nail him). "And why were you doing 110?" the judge inquired. "Because," replied the driver, "my car won't go any faster." This so infuriated the magistrate that he bopped the defendant on the head with his gavel—so hard that the wize guy went to the hospital.[56]

3. *Decoupling:* In actual interaction, something like a cut-off can occur under subtle structural circumstances bearing on the linkage between two interchanges. For example, in restaurants offering a limited fare, a routine opening interchange in the service transaction between waitress and customer can go as follows:

Waitress: (Wiping table and placing glass of water) "What'll ya have?"

---

[56] Herb Caen, *San Francisco Chronicle*, April 26, 1966.

Customer: "Black coffee and a toasted muffin please."
Waitress: (Turns from customer and shouts to cook) "Toast a muffin."

Now it would be easy to imagine that interchanges could be linked to the one cited. For example, before the order, there could be an exchange of greetings; indeed, very often there is. Similarly, as described previously, a way will be available to embed an additional interchange within the given one. So, too, a

$$\begin{array}{l} A^1 \\ B^1/B^2 \\ \quad\; A^2 \end{array}$$

linkage is possible, as follows:

Waitress: "What'll ya have?"
Customer: "Geeze (pauses to think). / Ya got a menu?"
Waitress: "Sure, I'll get it."

However, if the customer strictly responds to a tacitly precluded implication of the literal significance of the waitress's question and talks flatly enough so that his turn at talking pointedly contains only this move, then he can decouple the sequence from any to which the waitress can tie her next move:

Waitress: "What'll ya have?"
Customer: "The menu, please."
Waitress: (Turns to fellow waitresses and says, *sotto voce*, as an afterburn) "God, it's going to be one of those days."

Note, again, the basis of the difficulty caused the waitress is a result not merely of the customer's responding to a literal meaning that was meant to be disattended. The disorder is deeper than that. The customer reply she has anticipated is one that retrospectively demonstrates that her first move had a function, or if not, then at least that its not having a function in this particular case is something for which she is owed some consideration. A flat request for a menu makes her opening move useless and necessitates her making it again after the menu is read.

A second example. This time what is decoupled is the first and second round within an interchange. A boy on the phone is trying to hustle newspaper subscriptions. The anticipated routine would be:

Boy:	"Would you be interested in taking the *Oakland Tribune* for six weeks to help me out?"
Respondent:	"Gee, I'd like to help you but I can't. I already get the *Chronicle*."
Boy:	"Thanks anyway."

The respondent's turn at talking here shows the significance of an accounted denial. A query is answered in the negative and at the same time an account is provided that allows the asker to treat his request as an offer that the recipient is grateful for but can't accept. It is this part of the reply that allows the initiator of the interchange to close the interchange and the encounter with the device available for this, namely, an appreciation move. Now look at what can (and did) happen:

Boy:	"Would you be interested in taking the *Oakland Tribune* for six weeks to help me out?"
Respondent:	(Flatly) "No, I wouldn't."
Boy:	(Pauses in confusion, finally stammers) "Thanks." [57]

[57] Charles Schulz does a four-frame version (*San Francisco Chronicle*, November 29, 1967) that is structurally very sound.

First frame:	Schroeder is playing his piano and Lucy, elbow on other end, says, "You don't like me, do you?"
Second frame:	Schroeder says directly into Lucy's face, "No, I never have liked you, and I doubt very much if I ever will like you!"
Third frame:	Schroeder is back to playing the piano and Lucy to leaning on it, but no word is spoken.
Fourth frame:	Lucy says, "I can tell you don't like me." Schroeder looks up nonplussed.

Lucy's fourth-frame response is what she would have said in the third frame had Schroeder said what was expected of him in the second, namely, some sort of denial of Lucy's self-disparagement. So necessary was it that the second frame be filled in this prefigured way that Lucy, after a moment's pause to gather her resources, must stubbornly act as if Schroeder had in fact done what the sequence demanded of him—for there is really nothing else she can do. The nice point about the strip is that the timing and duration of a ritual move in the sequencing of an interchange is given

Incidentally, it is when decoupling is tactfully avoided that we can see anew the capacity of individuals to read small events as moves—a capacity that seems to derive in part from the desperate need to find something that will allow participants to sustain the anticipated sequencing in order:

A man has his head in his arms on the table in a coffee shop so that his eyes are covered.

Waitress: "Ya must of had a bad night./What will you have?"
Customer: "God./Give me a cup of coffee."
Waitress: "Sure."

Obviously, here the customer's double reply lets the waitress off the hook, that is, acknowledges that she was not out of line in addressing a personal move of sympathy to a customer. Between "God" and "Give" there is a pause that links God to the bad night comment and the coffee to "What will you have?" in a standard interchange coupling:

$$A^1/A^2$$
$$B^1/B^2$$

Instead of saying "God," almost any little gesture will do, as long as it is made in such a fashion that something like a period can be put after it and a new orientation taken in issuing the order. The customer will find that he gently coerces himself into providing this double move; he properly couples the two interchanges concealing this structural labor from himself by an admission, if asked, that he is merely being friendly. May I add that instead of thinking of persons as subtle devils who can use the slightest gesture to say a great deal, it might be better to think of sequences as subtle frameworks which allow any wisp of behavior to serve in the moment as a means of taking a stand.

---

an exact spatial representation, in this case by means of a frame that contains no words and apparently no action. Indeed, the time taken to look at a third frame when the total sequence contains four fits with the time a Lucy would be obliged to allow in order to give a move that was not to be made a chance for it not to be made, and then to decline to let it pass for what it is.

4. *One-liners:* Sometimes called "cracks" or "remarks," [58] there are two varieties. First, given that a move can be an anticipatedly final one in an interchange, it is possible for the maker to use this opportunity strategically to introduce statements that cast him in a good light and/or the other in a bad one, the assumption being that the structure of the sequence prevents the victim from continuing on with the introduction of a rejoinder. Indeed, when one individual uses a last move to ask a question rhetorically, the other is left with an interchange that has closed but that does not quite let him go.[59] One-liners that close out an encounter along with an interchange seem particularly effective:

A: "Goodbye, it was nice seeing you."
B: "Goodbye, it wasn't."

Second, given the presence of a two-move interchange that calls for the second speaker to provide a perfunctory reply to the first speaker, the first can introduce disparagements of the second to which only a nominal reply is necessary or practical. In consequence, there are standard half-rejoinders: "Oh yeah?" "Says who?" "That's what you say," "Wait and see," and so forth. Here the second speaker makes a vain effort to demonstrate that he is still on his feet, is in there fighting. But he really uses a turn to effect nothing more than a terminal crumble. A move has been forced on him, the assumption being that this is safe because he won't be able to do anything with it.

5. *Comebacks:* He who does a one-liner has closely established what the last move in an interchange will be. A comeback occurs when the other person acts so that the interchange (and often the encounter) is neatly kept open for another move or round of moves. Thus a crack or remark sets up the possibility of a coun-

---

[58] In popular use, the term "remark" has additional meanings. It is used to refer to a *sotto voce* comment, one meant not to be a ratified part of an encounter, an afterburn; and it is used to refer to the initiation of an interchange encounter, typically an unserious one, with someone not anticipating this connection.

[59] Alan Dundes (*op. cit.*) calls these moves "tag-lines."

ter-riposte, topper, or squelch, that is, a comeback.[60] And the more the initial move seems destined to leave the victim with no recourse, the more effective will be the move that does keep the interchange open. One example may be cited: [61]

Boy and girl at dance in school gym.

A one-liner:	Boy:	"Care to dance?"
	Girl:	"No, I came here to play basketball."
	Boy:	(Crumbles)
A comeback:	Boy:	"Care to dance?"
	Girl:	"No, I came here to play basketball."
	Boy:	"Sorry, I should have guessed by the way you're dressed."

The implication is that to perform a one-liner is to establish a contest, and it is best to make sure that no effective shot is available to the other player. One safety device is to make one's remarks on the run so that distance helps to close out answering. Safer still is the politician's game of inserting one-liners in the body of a speech, thereby precluding all possibility of comebacks.[62]

---

[60] William Labov has recently made a structural analysis of "sounds" as employed in utterance play among lower-class, urban black youth. The structure of these devices establishes a move that is designed to serve as a comparison base for another's effort, his object being to exceed the prior effort in elegance or wit. This is topping, too, but not the kind that relies on active use of the interchange structure. A comeback in sounding is established aforehand as the anticipated procedure. Comments on sounding also may be found in Thomas Kochman, "Toward an Ethnography of Black American Speech Behavior," in Norman E. Whitten, Jr., and John F. Szwed, eds., *Afro-American Anthropology* (New York: The Free Press, 1970), pp. 145–162. Kochman provides a pretty example of a comeback involving a full rejoinder taking the place of a terminal crumble (p. 145): "Thus, when someone indifferently said 'fuck you' to Concho, his retort was immediate and devastating: 'Man, you haven't even kissed me yet.' "

[61] From *Mad*, *op. cit.*, pp. 160–161.

[62] When a remark is made across a communication line, as when a member of the audience heckles a performer, the latter's comeback, if he is to make one, must take the form of ratifying the remark as a move to be openly recognized, part of the official proceedings, and this can easily endanger the line between performer and audience. Heckling, then, is rarely

6. *Post-terminals:* An individual can set up what is taken as a final move, one to occur following his own, and then when this is induced, make another move, showing that the other individual, without suspecting it, had been set up.

First comedian:	"But I do want everyone here to know what a fine trouper you are and a fine comedian."
Second comedian:	"Why thanks, that's awful nice of you."
First comedian:	"Of course, you can't go by me. I'm drunk." [63]

I have suggested various ways in which one participant in an interchange can discomfit the other; in some cases standard jokebook illustrations were provided. This is hardly something worth doing in its own right. However, there is a double warrant. First, each of these devices seems to allow its user to interfere in some way with the anticipated structure and sequence of the interaction or exploit these anticipations, and so in learning how the device works, we can learn how interaction is structured. Second, in seeing what can be put to work against an interactant, we can begin to appreciate the protective care that is often provided him (and tacitly de-

---

answered directly and therefore usually succeeds in retaining last-move status. Performers who leave their place even while maintaining it, who ratify a breach even while they close it, acquire reputations for stage competence, as a report (*Time*, April 1, 1966) on a British politician suggests:

> Heckling is an honored British tradition, and Wilson, for one, thrives on quick parries with dissenters. At a recent rally, when a heckler shouted "Rubbish!" Wilson shot back: "We'll take up your special interest in a moment, sir."

[63] Post-terminal ploys can involve a two-man team. On Telegraph Avenue I once observed the following routine performed by two hippies sitting on the sidewalk, their feet out, their backs against a store wall. As a passer-by came abreast of one, a hand would go out along with a request for a few pennies. Some pedestrians would say an equivalent of "Sorry, I haven't got any," and use their normal rate of movement past the asker as the means for effectively terminating the encounter. Just as this termination seemed to have been achieved—by which time the pedestrian would be alongside the second hippie—the latter would shoot his hand out, in which there were a few pennies, and ask the pedestrian if *he* would like a few pennies. Many pedestrians were put quite out of countenance with this rather elegant structural design.

manded from him) by those with whom he interacts. In a manner of speaking, we have here surface considerateness based on deep structure. In closing, I would like to provide some examples bearing on three different aspects of this structure.

First, on remarks and the jeopardy into which they put their maker.

> A drugstore in Philadelphia sells *The New York Times* for only a dime at a time when most other vendors charge twelve cents. Some customers come to the drugstore just for the saving. Some of these patrons feel that this is a questionable practice and employ various dodges to show that they are not abashed. For example:
>
> Customer: (Taking and paying for paper) "Best bargain in town."

Here the customer opens himself up for the following:

> Customer: "Best bargain in town."
> Clerk: (Flatly). "Here's your change."
>
> Customer: "Best bargain in town."
> Clerk: "You might buy something else sometime."
>
> Customer: "Best bargain in town."
> Clerk: "And I see you found it."

What (on one occasion) he received was this:

> Customer: "Best bargain in town."
> Clerk: "Ain't it lovely."

In brief, if the recipient of the remark is to protect the maker, he may have to enter quite sympathetically into the definition of the situation the maker has attempted to introduce. Indeed, the recipient may even have to cast himself in a guise he had not been in, if only to provide a self that makes sense out of the other's remark:

> A man next in line behind a woman who has paid for her groceries (and is now putting them in her shopping bag) notices that a carton of eggs remains on the counter:
>
> Man: "The eggs are yours?"

Here the man opens himself up for the following:

Man: "The eggs are yours?"
Woman: "Who asked you?"

What occurred was:

Man: "The eggs are yours?"
Woman: (Self-mockingly) "I always leave them for the last so they can fall out."

Second, on joking openers. An individual can initiate an encounter-interchange with a stranger by raising an issue that casts the stranger in a role from which he will be ready to dissociate himself. By making the opening remark unserious, the initiator can attempt to make sure that the recipient will follow along and enter the play in a dissociable capacity. But nonetheless he exposes himself to the possibility of being taken seriously, which, among other things, transforms his initial remark into something that was not merely ineffective but also forward, for in their serious roles the two strangers may have no easy basis for an encounter. He who makes a joking opener, then, is likely to anticipate a three-move interchange: his remark is the first move; the other's assurances that the sally is accepted is the second; and he himself provides the terminal move, this being an open laugh of appreciation at the statement just made. What the initiator desires, then, is to get to the position where he can make his laugh, for if he does, then he has ceased to be in jeopardy. To prefigure this desired outcome, he is likely to start laughing rather early, almost as soon as the other begins to reply to the opening remark, thereby sympathetically directing it. And he is likely to read almost any response from the other as evidence that the sally is accepted and that the third and terminal move, the laugh, can be made. Tact comes from providing the initiator a remark that really will warrant the laugh he is going to provide:

B in elevator pushes button for the thirteenth floor.

A: "You ain't superstitious, are you?"

B: "Not enough to change my floor."

A: (Big laugh)

Finally, the question of transfixes. When an individual finds that his action may affront another and his aim is to avoid doing so, he can try, as suggested, to address his act to that self of the virtually offended from which the latter can dissociate himself. To accomplish this, the individual may make a special effort to touch the other and to hold the touch throughout the virtually offensive act, as if to guide and fix the held one in his taking of the act in the right spirit. Lawrence Durrell provides an example:

> It was one of these dreadful remarks which once uttered seem not only inexcusable but also impossible to repair. Nessim, however, appeared delighted rather than offended, and with his usual tact, did not permit himself to laugh aloud without touching his friend's wrist with his hand, lest by chance Mountolive might think the laughter directed at him rather than at his mistake.[64]

The delicacy here is that the hand of one person should neatly guide the mental alignment of another, that the timing and touch of one interactant should be blended perfectly into the situation of another. Durrell is wrong in only one particular. We don't have to go to Alexandria for this sort of thing; it happens all the time in the most alien parts of America.

X *Conclusions*

When persons are present together, many contingencies arise that could reflect discreditably on them. The individual finds that he has acted (or is about to act) so as to give the appearance of encroaching on another's various territories and preserves; or he finds himself about to give a bad impression of himself; or both. In these circumstances he is likely to engage in remedial activity in order to reinforce a definition of himself that is satisfactory to him.

---

[64] Lawrence Durrell, *Mountolive* (London: Faber and Faber, Ltd., 1958), p. 40.

He engages in gestures in the round, bodily enacting information for anyone who can witness his antics. And he directs ritual moves to particular others, typically those he has virtually offended, in anticipation of receiving a ritual reply. So, too, as someone who bears witness to the remedial work initiated by others, he stands ready when called on to provide relief of various sorts.

I have argued that this remedial activity is a constant feature of ordinary interaction and that, indeed, through ritually closed interchanges, it provides the organizational framework for encounters. Ritual interchanges, especially remedial ones, articulate behavior, resulting in functionally unified cuts in the behavioral stream. Here, however, in conclusion, another theme might be stressed.

Throughout the history of Western civilization there has been a continuity in official moral ideology establishing the personal attributes that proper males and females should manifest during face-to-face dealings with others. The literature on the gentleman, beginning to be marked from the sixteenth century, is but one example. The classical virtues of good character are involved: honesty, gratefulness, justness, generosity. Also there are the values associated with bodily behavior, some special to each sex, some common: cleanliness, fair appearance, constraint on appetitive passions, strength and physical courage, dexterity, grace and poise. So, too, the interactant's virtues: candor, respectfulness, modesty, and the like. And finally the schooling virtues associated with knowledge, language, and cultivation. In all of this, of course, Christian doctrine has played an important role.

This common core of beliefs which links Western societies has been slighted by students of behavior. We have been quick to see that these conceptions of virtue are the province of mothers and schoolmasters, that these notions have never been a good guide to actual conduct, and that, in any case, they are less preached these days than they used to be.

However, this skepticism has a blindness of its own. If we examine what it is one participant is ready to see that other participants might read into a situation and what it is that will cause him to provide ritual remedies of various sorts (followed by relief for these efforts), then we find ourselves directed back again to the core moral traditions of Western culture. And since remedial ritual is a constant feature of public life, occurring among all the citizenry in all social situations, we must see that the historical center and the contemporary periphery are linked more closely than anyone these days seems to want to credit. These core values establish for everyone in the society an understanding of how he might be judged wanting. Furthermore, these understandings do not refer only to specific demands but also to principles that can be applied to every face-to-face social situation. Given this primal lore, the individual finds himself not so much with a guide for action (although presumably on occasion there is that), but a guide as to what to be alive to, a guide that tells him what is seeable in a particular situation and therefore what it is to which he might be well advised to take a stand—whether to offer an account, an apology, an excuse, whether to mock or guy, whether to bluster through uncaringly. The clear fact is that although there is great variation in the way individuals sustain the common values concerning desirable qualities, there is incredibly little variation in the need they seem to have to remark in some way, through words or gestures, upon the discrepancy an other might see between their practice and these values.[65] The central values do but itch a little, but everyone scratches.

To repeat: the individual does not go about merely going about his business. He goes about constrained to sustain a viable image of himself in the eyes of others. Since local circumstances always will reflect upon him, and since these circumstances will vary unexpectedly and constantly, footwork, or rather self work, will be continuously necessary. Each lurching of whatever the individual is standing on will have to be offset, often by his leading into the fall with a self that has been projected as unserious, the real person thereby made free to tacitly take up a counterbalancing position.

---

[65] A well-known statement along these lines can be found in Gresham M. Sykes and David Matza, "Techniques of Neutralization: A Theory of Delinquency," *American Sociological Review*, XXII (1957): 664–670.

Thus, the individual constantly employs little *schticks* to keep himself in some sort of defensible posture. He engages in little performances to actively portray a relationship to such rules as might be taken to be binding on him.

Of course, an individual can carry around his own cause for defensive action, namely a visible stigma, a sign that he has failed to embody one of our standard expectations. With it he will always be in a position to play himself off against himself and often will feel obliged to do so. A lower-class restaurant worker, middle-aged, plain-looking, with a serious tremor, braves out her table-waiting without admitting to customers that she knows quite well what they are thinking, and waits until a decent familiarity has arisen before sadly avowing, as she jiggles their food, "I godda be the only waitress in Philly with the shakes," thereby linking her neighborhood station to the ways and values of the Western world.[66]

These norms to which the individual is concerned to demonstrate a relationship of his own choosing are norms about personal qualities, norms at the center of our official religious beliefs, which designate the virtues and qualifications the individual ought not to deny through his behavior. The individual can mark his freedom and his alienation by demonstrating an unaccepting relation to these expectations regarding conduct or by showing concern for some at the obvious cost to others; but however skittish he might be about behaving properly, he nonetheless takes care to have some behavioral reply ready in any situation where circumstances suddenly have called him into question. He need not honor a rule of conduct that applies to him. He need not even provide virtual accounts, apologies, and excuses for his deviations. But at least he must be at pains to portray an advocable relationship to the negative judgment of him which results.

---

66 Recently the Women's Liberation Movement has begun to affect the largest source of these bits, the "I'm only a female" response. The second largest source remains intact, however: the tag interjections of ironic self-praise that those over fifty give themselves in a thousand situations on the basis of their age.

No doubt self-determination is involved, at least at one level. An adult tripping on the pavement has the option, for example, of jokingly overplaying his fall, or, with a slight frown of intelligent interest, turning and examining the sidewalk for something that is surely as strange and noteworthy as is his seeming lapse of control. But the corpus of quick displays for establishing a viable alignment to the untoward event is by and large a given of the culture—a given that opens up the possibility of choosing even while it closes the range of choices. And even more deterministic is the need, the obligation, the compulsion, to take some kind of stand relative to the perceivable deficiency in question.

It is strange, and more Durkheimian than it should be, that today, at a time when the individual can get almost everything else off his back, there remains the cross of personal character—the one he bears, albeit lightly, when he is in the presence of others.

[5]

Tie-Signs

I *Social Relationships*

The individual is linked to society through two principal social bonds: to collectivities through membership and to other individuals through social relationships. He in turn helps make a network of society by linking through himself the social units linked to him.

The two individuals tied to each other by a social relationship can be called its "ends." Presumably what they are tied by are prescriptions regarding mutual treatment, the obligations of one end being the expectations of the other.

This is an anthropological view. Sociology comes to relationships by way of role. It is seen that the individual is obliged to engage in specific activity in established situations, a bundle of obligatory dealings in each type of situation. Those whom he deals with in one type of situation have a role relationship to him. When he deals with the same individual in more than one type of situation, he has more than one role relationship to him, resulting in an "over-all" relationship that is "multi-bonded."

My concern, however, is to stress that mutual treatment occurs within a framework of identification—a fact that early social anthropology could easily take for granted and neglect, and modern students have not handled nicely in their efforts to characterize "personal" and "impersonal" dealings.[1] By "social identity," I mean the broad social categories (and the organizations and groups that function like categories) to which an individual can belong and be seen as belonging: age-grade, sex, class, regiment, and so forth. By "personal identity," I mean the unique organic continuity imputed to each individual, this established through distinguishing marks such as name and appearance, and elaborated by means of knowledge about his biography and social attributes—knowledge which comes to be organized around his distinguishing marks.[2]

In all societies there are "anchored relations" (or "pegged" ones) such that each end identifies the other personally, knows the other does likewise, and openly acknowledges to the other that an irrevocable starting has been made between them—the establishment of a framework of mutual knowing, which retains, organizes, and applies the experience the ends have of one another. In our society there is the curious understanding that once two individuals have been thusly bonded, their relationship can change drastically but never revert to non-acquaintanceship; forgetting another's name or face can be excusable but calls for an excuse.

Most societies also have "anonymous relations," that is, patterned, mutual treatment between two individuals who know each other solely on the basis of instantly perceived social identity, as when an individual courteously passes a stranger on the street.[3]

---

[1] Recently Thomas Scheff has considered this point. See his "On the Concepts of Identity and Social Relationships," in Tamotsu Shibutani, ed., *Human Nature and Collective Behavior: Papers in Honor of Herbert Blumer* (Englewood Cliffs, N.J.: Prentice-Hall, Inc., 1970).

[2] The concepts of social and personal identity are developed at greater length in Goffman, *Stigma* (Englewood Cliffs, N.J.: Prentice-Hall, Inc., 1963; London: Penguin Books, 1968), Chaps. 1 and 2.

[3] The anchored-anonymous contrast is in part a version of Parsons' particularistic-universalistic distinction. See also the distinction between "personal" and "group" relations in Robert Paine, "In Search of Friendship: An Exploratory Analysis of 'Middle-Class' Culture," *Man*, IV (December 1969): esp. 512–513.

Between anonymous relations and anchored ones there are some minor intermediate forms: when one end personally identifies the other but is not, and knows he is not, personally identified in return, this being the commonly lamented fate of first-year college students in regard to their teachers; when each end personally identifies the other, but this mutual identification has not been ratified through an exchange of acknowledging looks, introductions, and so forth, in consequence of which contact tends to be limited to cognitive recognition without social recognition.

Every anchored relationship has a history of its own and a career or natural development;[4] like a person, it is a structure-building entity. Anonymous relations do not have a career, although the relations between two categories of persons can have a social history, even a natural history of sorts,[5] as can the relation of an individual to members in general of a particular category of others. Also, anonymous relations can but establish how two particular individuals will treat each other *should* they have occasion for mutual dealings; anchored relations, on the other hand, are likely to have built right into them an understanding of the circumstances in which dealings are anticipated and even obligatory.

The difference between anonymous relations and anchored ones could be viewed in terms of the standard dichotomies, distance-intimacy and impersonal-personal, a particular relationship being described in terms of degree. That would be quite unsatisfactory. An individual who knows another long and well can still treat him in substantive matters much as he would someone he did not know personally; the difference could be restricted to ceremonial matters and even there not be extensive. And obviously, quite pleasant interaction is possible between passing strangers, and acrimony of

---

[4] Recall, for example, the early statement by Park and Burgess (*Introduction to the Science of Sociology*) regarding the natural cycle of dealings between two categories: competition, conflict, accommodation, and assimilation.

[5] Schematically considered in George J. McCall and J. L. Simmons, *Identities and Interactions* (New York: The Free Press, 1966; London: Collier-Macmillan), pp. 167–201.

the fiercest kind can characterize relationships of great intimacy.

Although students have long been concerned with the distinction that is here phrased as that between anonymous and anchored relations, little attention has been given to the descriptive details. For example, the readiness exhibited by two individuals to transform an incidental social encounter into the beginning of an anchored relationship can depend upon the memory each has of having seen the other before in a context that implies for each a relevant social identity for the other. And yet if the second contact does not occur, there may well never be an awareness on either side that the other is someone who has been seen. Thus it can be said that incidental, fleeting, anonymous contacts lay a base for later anchorings but do so without our awareness. Also, it seems that this readiness of memory decays over time so that after a while the first meeting will not be called to mind at the second, but how rapidly this decay occurs or under what circumstances it is delayed, no one appears to have considered.

Unless otherwise specified, the term "relationship" here implies the anchored kind. Three of its properties will be relevant. First, there is the "name" of the relationship, that is, the publicly standardized means of referring to the two ends (brothers, kin, colleagues, friends, married couple) or a means by which one end can address or refer to the other end (husband, mother, employer). Now plainly there are problems with this idea; for example, what seems to be the same relationship can be referred to by terms of varying inclusiveness (kinsman, nephew, mother's brother's boy) and by alternate and different terms (kin, neighbor), raising the tricky issue as to whether different relationships are being invoked or different standards being stressed and whether or not there are rules determining choice of alternatives.[6] Furthermore, names such as aggressor and subordi-

[6] This issue is especially acute in regard to momentary dealings in public places between the anonymously related. Here see James M. Sebring, "Caste Indicators and Caste Identification of Strangers," *Human Organization*, XXVIII (September 1969): 199–207, and Gerald D. Berreman, "Social Categories and Social Interaction in a North Indian City," forthcoming. Sebring's paper also has very useful material on deference behavior.

nate are used for designating situationally generated roles, and these roles refer more to the manner in which a personal relationship is conducted than to the identity of the relationship itself. Nonetheless, whatever the ambiguities, persons do title their relationship conventionally, and it is to this identifying tendency that I refer.

Second are the "terms" of the relationship, meaning here such of its conditions as would cause it to be rated in various ways by those who had reason to pass judgments on it. Thus of one pair of siblings, one might say that they had "fallen out," were on very bad terms; of another, that they were "very close," could not stand to be separated. Note, the notion of terms helps clarify some of the everyday meanings given the words "personal relationship." Sometimes that designation refers to a relationship that is anchored when others like it are anonymous, sometimes to a relationship in which the ends are on "better" or more "intimate" terms than is usual for an anchored relationship of that kind.

Behind the common-sense words for characterizing the terms of a relationship some elements can be discerned, although not adequately enough to be strongly recommended as alternatives.

First is restraint versus license. Given that one end claims various territories and preserves, what liberty—what license—does the other have to penetrate these circles of the self at will? And given these liberties, are they actually exercised? That is, in addition to license, is there familiarity? (Persons in an anonymous relation can be on ritually licensed terms, but only those in an anchored relation can be familiar.) An important component of familiarity is confidentiality, namely, exercise of the license to penetrate another's informational preserve, especially in regard to secret information about self, the extreme here being found in the patient-analyst relationship. Another element turns on the psychological sense of "identification," or, more simply, "sympathy." To what degree are the private interests and concerns of one end treated by the other as his concerns also, thereby creating a source of appeal and support for the first should the need arise? Finally, there is the matter of "company": to what degree do the ends perform activities "together" whether jointly or merely adjacently.[7] Note, "company" is intrinsically a symmetrical arrangement, since one end must be in the other's company if the other is in the first's—although the right to arrange for being together may be one-sided. Familiarity and sympathy, on the other hand, are often one-sided, reflecting rights and duties that are asymmetrical.

Two general features of relationships have been touched on: name and terms. The third derives from the fact that a relationship has, and can be seen as having, a natural history; it starts, develops, has turning points, attenuations, and one of a small set of available terminations. Relationships are not born and they do not die; however, like social persons they must have a beginning and must come to an end. The term "stage" will be used to refer to the phase a relationship has reached in its natural history. Obviously there is a connection between the terms of a relationship and its stage, especially in regard to certain terminations, but the connection is not a simple one.

In the social sciences, consideration of anchored relations has been structural, as when friendship circles and old-boy nets are examined as a basis for class endogamy or monopoly of occupational opportunities. Links between relationships have recently been considered in their own right in work on social networks, both of the egocentric and net-centered kind.[8] However, this essay is concerned with public order, and that leads us to turn from social structures to displays, alignments, and expressions.

---

[7] The original source here is Elizabeth Bott's *Family and Social Network* (London: Tavistock Publications, 1957).

[8] For a recent example, Adrian C. Mayer, "The Significance of Quasi-Groups in the Study of Complex Societies," in Michael Banton, ed., *The Social Anthropology of Complex Societies* (London: Tavistock Publications of A. S. A. Monographs, 1968), pp. 97–122. No doubt most students of relationships have had clinical, not sociological, interests, as when an individual's management of relationships is analyzed as a projection of his personality psychodynamics.

II *Tie-Signs*

When persons theretofore unacquainted come into each other's immediate presence, the fact that their relationship is anonymous, or at best has just begun not to be, is made evident for them and others by means of many signs. Similarly, when those with an anchored relation come into unobstructed range for effecting social contact, the fact that theirs is not an anonymous relation is made evident. Indeed, in both cases the participants are under subtle obligation to treat each other in such a manner that these bits of intelligence incidentally become available. All such evidence about relationships, that is, about ties between persons, whether involving objects, acts, expressions, and only excluding the literal aspects of explicit documentary statements, I shall call "tie-signs."

Except in some special strategic situations, information regarding the anonymity of a relationship fully establishes whether it is or not. Ordinarily, then, the tie-signs provided by an anonymous relationship cannot be of much concern to the student. It is when we consider anchored relations that tie-signs become complex and important, because these signs will not only inform that the relation is anchored, but will also provide some information about its name, its terms, and its stage. And one is dependent on these signs. Because anchored relationships subsist and govern over time, involving a likelihood and often an obligation that certain kinds of dealings will occur and be managed in a certain manner, there is no way at any one moment in time to see directly the whole of the bond. Only indications are directly available—events having symbolic or symptomatic value. In what follows, then, unless otherwise stated, I will restrict the discussion to anchored relationships and (incidentally) to middle-class American practice.

Tie-signs can be found where neither end of the relationship is present, as in family photographs stored in the attic; or where only one end is present, as when a man carries pictures of the wife and kiddies in his wallet or a tattoo of their names on his arm. (These one-ended signs have the special character that they may last long after the relationship they signify has passed into a "past" stage, becoming then a memento, an embarrassment, or even a source of blackmail.) However, I will be concerned only with those tie-signs whose composition requires the ends of the relationship to be currently present together and to figure through body placement, posture, gesture, and vocal expression in the substance of the sign.[9] These signs alone provide evidence of the *current* character of the relationship, pertaining as they do to a present state, not to one that possibly no longer obtains. These indicators are "tied" tie-signs, although it would be cumbersome to continue to say so.

I want to make clear that my interest here is not in how ends communicate facts about their relationship (although that is involved), but rather in how their conduct while in each other's presence can contain evidence about their relationship. Whether the ends are unaware or aware of the information they are exuding, and if aware, whether they are concerned to reveal, conceal, or falsify this information (or are unconcerned about its availability) is not the first issue; nor do tie-signs refer only to evidence that someone gathers. All of these factors merely introduce issues concerning the validity and reliability of the signs. As here defined, tie-signs *contain evidence;* they do not *communicate messages.*

Two sorts of persons can be informed by a tie-sign: the ends of the relationship or third parties. And signs may be specialized in this regard. For example, hand-holding is (among other things) an open declaration to third parties that they are in the presence of a certain kind of relationship; squeezing a held hand and declining to let one's hand be found for holding (or once released to be re-

---

[9] This does not mean that the two ends must literally be within eyesight of each other or simultaneously visible to third parties, but only effectively so. "Experiential" co-presence is involved. As Dean MacCannell has suggested to me, individuals coming out of a swimming pool at different times to use the same skin lotion can be seen as being "together" although not literally seen together.

grasped) are signs ordinarily designed for the ends' private consumption. The "arm-lock," the device whereby an adult female "takes the arm" of an adult male and thereby signifies that she is in a "with" that provides her male protection, seems to be done for the information it provides third parties—except, of course, when a curb or rough road is to be negotiated, or when one end uses the public character of the hold to prove a point to the other end. On the other hand, during sexual intercourse, expressions of involvement are tie-signs of appreciable significance in some circles, effectively attesting to the state of the relationship, but perforce only for the two individuals directly involved, and even they may use darkness to ensure strategic ambiguity.[10]

In Western society tie-signs tend to be inherently ambiguous in the sense that any one sign can designate relationships of different name, different terms, and different stage—or can entirely and intentionally mislead. Ultimately I think this reflects the fact that there is no one-to-one fit between the elements and units of public life and the elements of social structure. (For example, a chaperone is someone who lends her physical presence to a social occasion to prevent maidens from being carried away by the excitement generated in conversation and dance. She is entirely a creature of public order, her whole existence directed to gatherings and contained within them. Although aging females of assured respectability are especially qualified for the job, holding it need not be habitual, and no one-to-one relation exists between the various social statuses of the holder and the interactional role she performs while holding it.) Only on such social occasions as wedding ceremonies and honeymoons are we likely to have a neat fit between the two realms. The implication is that the reading of relationships will almost always be subject to restrictions and even error, whether the ends have induced this or not, and this fallibility seems understood.

Individuals, knowing this fallibility, make an effort to reduce ambiguity by cross-checking their reading of one tie-sign with a

[10] The considerable informational delicacy of this form of interaction is considered in John L. Schimel, "The Psychopathology of Equalitarian Sexual Relations," *Psychiatry*, XXV (1962): 182–186.

reading of others—just as ends make an effort to facilitate or frustrate this examination. And indeed, so many opportunities for cross-checking are likely to become available that any particular tie-sign is usually redundant and dispensable.

Associated with the process of cross-checking is the conceptually troublesome fact that in order to read the relationship of two or more persons who are present, the reader will typically make use of information diffusely located in the social setting. A tie-sign is in fact dependent on the context for its meaning, even though it is seen as intimately associated with the actions and bodies of the persons in the relationship.[11] Moreover, the idea of context itself cannot be restricted to the *currently* available situation. One's biographical information about the ends of an observed relationship may have been largely acquired outside of the current situation and yet will closely influence the reading put upon the behavior that the two manifest in regard to each other. Similarly, the reading one places upon their current orientation to each other can be greatly affected by one's having seen them in the same orientation a few hours earlier and in a somewhat different setting. Indeed, a first seeing together of two individuals who might be related may tell us little; it is the second or third seeing of them together that carries weight, but only because there has been a first or second seeing.

In general, one tends to cross-check tie-signs against what one can read about the social and personal statuses of the ends of the relationship. This, of course, adds to the redundancy of the whole operation. But we should be ready to see that ties may be read so that the reader can inform himself about the social and personal identities of the ends of the tie, and he may even read them on occasion to inform himself about the social setting. Thus the interesting thing about an old man and a youngish woman holding hands

[11] The contextual nature of tie-signs is seen in the extreme in the case of fixed personal territories such as the interior of domestic establishments. Almost any use of the equipment and facilities by a non-resident will, in the manner of use, provide information about his relation to the householder.

is the suggested tie that links them; their social identities as such may be of little interest. On the other hand, the interesting thing about two men holding hands is not that they have a stigmatized relationship, but rather that each has a stigmatized identity. So, too, often the concern one has on a Saturday night is not so much *who* one is seen with but *that* one is not seen alone—a contingency that explains why dating couples can contain two persons, both of whom would rather be out with almost anyone else, for she conceals from the public that he has no one he likes, and he her similar plight.

What we have thus far considered regarding the informing capacity of two-person behavior can be put in another way. It can be argued that in Western society, as probably in all others, there is the "right and duty of partial display." Two or more individuals present together have the right and duty to make some information generally available concerning their relationship and the right and duty to leave unsignaled other information about their relationship. (Similarly it is possible to speak of the social regulation of information about social and personal identity.) This holds true not only for tie-signs but for tie statements, as when one senses a slight obligation to inform one's with as to one's relationship to a third person one has greeted in passing. Note that this general rule regarding partial display specifically links two disparate domains, social relationships and public order.

A second point to note is that one expects some degree of fit among three factors: identity (both social and personal), choice in relationships, and rectitude of conduct. There is a tendency to assume that information about any one of these items allows the individual to anticipate a range of possibilities regarding the other two, and that it will be possible to read from one of the three to the other two. As suggested, a redundancy of signs will be available.

It should be plain that in a small, isolated, stable community (where each person knows from birth all those younger than himself and is so known from birth by all those older than himself), the general stock of biographical knowledge in the community, occasionally updated to note changes in relationships, usually will render the current reading of tie-signs uninformative. (Of course, in every community there are fallings-out between solidary ends of relationships, and in most communities there is some personal choice exercised regarding mate selection with consequent periods of gradual disclosure; hence there will always be some interest in tie-signs.) Similarly, as suggested, in the most anonymous streets of urban life where mutual impingement is brief and no biographical lore is available to anyone present concerning the others present, a concern about tie-signs may be very weak if it exists at all. An interest in tie-signs seems most evident in situations that fall between these extremes—situations where some biographical knowledge is available but is quite incomplete—or where strangers are brought together for more than momentary co-participation in some social gathering.

III *Function Types*

Acts and events that are tie-signs appear to have some general social functions, and indeed these functions provide us with one means of dividing tie-signs into classes for purposes of description. Three such function-classes will be considered: rituals, markers, and change signals.

1. *Rituals:* Interpersonal rituals are, by definition, tie-signs, for whatever else, they attest to a relationship. This is obvious in the case of positive, supportive rites which can involve a direct reference to the name of the relationship; it should be just as obvious in regard to negative, avoidant rituals. Whenever two persons are physically close, their handling of restrictive rules of co-mingling will provide a reading of their relationship, whether or not anyone

looks at the page. Thus, given usual eye-to-eye distance for comfortable conversation,[12] a boy and girl at a train station conducting a conversation over what seems to be an over-long distance imply that their mutual orientation is something that may be abandoned at any moment and that little commitment to a relationship has been made. Similarly when, to free his hands, an individual passes something to a companion for a moment and does not bracket this act with a please and thank-you, assuming rather that common understandings and interests will be sufficient to explain and warrant his presumption, the implication is that a long-standing relationship is present.[13] So, too, when a couple waiting in a line finds something to say and stands apart in order to address each other facially instead of merely orienting with half-turns, one can assume that the relationship is new enough to warrant attentiveness—a courtesy that will later be foregone should the relationship develop. Something of the same conclusion can be drawn in observing a couple at a restaurant table: he addresses himself fully to her statements and responds quickly and with pleasure, as if discovering unanticipated commonalities, and she speaks introspectively, as though inwardly held beliefs could now be disclosed but haven't yet been; or both draw upon biographical lore, showing that it hasn't been shared yet.

The nicest example of these fugitive informings comes from Henry James and his depiction of how a young lady learns that the woman who introduced her to her husband had not always been innocently related to him. It is worth quoting at length:

> Isabel passed into the drawing-room, the one she herself usually occupied, the second in order from the large antechamber which was

---

[12] In the sense considered by Robert Sommer, "The Distance for Comfortable Conversation: A Further Study," *Sociometry*, XXV, no. 1 (1962): 111–116.

[13] Suggested by Dean MacCannell, who adds in an unpublished paper: "A woman does not pass her purse to the man she is with so that he can hold it for her while she 'adjusts herself' until after they have reached a certain understanding."

entered from the staircase and in which even Gilbert Osmond's rich devices had not been able to correct a look of rather grand nudity. Just beyond the threshold of the drawing-room she stopped short, the reason for her doing so being that she had received an impression. The impression had, in strictness, nothing unprecedented; but she felt it as something new, and the soundlessness of her step gave her time to take in the scene before she interrupted it. Madame Merle was there in her bonnet, and Gilbert Osmond was talking to her; for a minute they were unaware she had come in. Isabel had often seen that before, certainly; but what she had not seen, or at least had not noticed, was that their colloquy had for the moment converted itself into a sort of familiar silence, from which she instantly perceived that her entrance would startle them. Madame Merle was standing on the rug, a little way from the fire; Osmond was in a deep chair, leaning back and looking at her. Her head was erect, as usual, but her eyes were bent on his. What struck Isabel first was that he was sitting while Madame Merle stood; there was an anomaly in this that arrested her. Then she perceived that they had arrived at a desultory pause in their exchange of ideas and were musing, face to face, with the freedom of old friends who sometimes exchange ideas without uttering them. There was nothing to shock in this; they were old friends in fact. But the thing made an image, lasting only a moment, like a sudden flicker of light. Their relative positions, their absorbed mutual gaze, struck her as something detected. But it was all over by the time she had fairly seen it. Madame Merle had seen her and had welcomed her without moving; her husband, on the other hand, had instantly jumped up. He presently murmured something about wanting a walk and, after having asked their visitor to excuse him, left the room.[14]

The availability of such signs should not be taken merely as evidence that public life can be treacherous for those who would conceal relationships. More important, I think, these signs make it possible for individuals in public to engage in encounters without too

---

[14] Henry James, *The Portrait of a Lady* (New York: Modern Library Edition, 1951; London: Penguin, 1969), pp. 164–165.

much fear that their innocence will be misunderstood and that compromising will occur.[15]

2. *Markers:* Acts or arrangements that function to exhibit and establish a party's claim to territory can be called markers. One type of territory comprises possessions an individual carries around with him, such as his clothing, books, purse, packages, dog, and so forth. One such personal possession is any person with whom the individual has a close relationship, especially when this other person is subordinate and subject to attention from third parties. Here markers take the form of tie-signs, often ones that allow the dominant end to direct and control the movement of the other and otherwise patrol claims to the relationship. Indeed, any sign that tells one about a relationship has some role as a marker, for there is no anchored relationship which does not have some exclusivity about it that can be threatened by third persons.

The markers of most significance in providing one with information about relationships seem to be those that designate a with among a subset of the co-present. Co-membership in a with, *per se*, tells us little about the name or terms or stage of the social relationship of the participants, only that an anchored relationship of some kind exists, but experience with the associational practices of various categories of persons allows one—of course, fallibly—to make specific appraisals. Thus an adult male and female together eating dinner at a restaurant of an evening might be merely friends, siblings, colleagues, in-laws, or even only neighbors, but one tends to assume that there is a dating, marital, or extra-marital relationship between them; whereas two men at the next table ordinarily give the sense that whatever their relationship, it is not

[15] In an airline waiting room, I once saw a young, Southern, upper middle-class man engage in a twenty-minute conversation with a drunken, working-class, middle-aged woman, which she initiated with him after having failed to embroil three prior targets. He maintained a considerate show of interest in her stories but all the while held a slight twinkle in his eye and a focus of attention that included more of her than might be accorded someone not in the performer role. Without these gentle means of establishing his distance from her for others, his gallantry might not have been possible.

that. The bases for these readings, of course, rest upon the general social rule in middle-class society that participants in cross-sexed withs are not merely friends; in general that is not where friendship is found—it is found between pairs of males (or pairs of females). One perceives that the information derives from the with in such cases, but it can so derive because one has general expectations regarding association.

Relation markers are best seen in our society, I think, when persons whose with is displayed through mere ecological proximity find that this will be insufficient to ensure its integrity. Thus when couples first enter a social occasion during which they will have to leave each other's side, they may employ special signs of intimacy, such as a hand squeeze and an endearing private smile, this display functioning in part to brace their relationship against temporary separation, but also serving to provide the gathering with initial evidence of the relationship and what it is that will have to be respected.

The behavioral arrangements thus far considered are ones that are conventionally employed as markers. They provide open and direct means for staking a claim, the claim being to a relationship with the marked individual. But, as suggested, if the context is favorable, any tie-sign can take on a marking function. Thus the minor incursions that one member of a sexually intimate pair can take into the territorial preserves of the other may have the special quality of serving to claim the penetrated person, yet in a way that would probably be denied as such were the function to be questioned.

3. *Change Signals:* Acts and events that function to establish and signify a change in a relationship, that is, change signals, constitute a special set of tie-signs. Rituals of birth, marriage, and death form one set of examples. Another comprises occasions when minor liberties are *first* taken—use of the other's personal possessions without a by-your-leave, penetration into the other's personal space, initial use of familiar forms of address, and so forth. And most important, perhaps, are acts of affection on the first occasion of their performance, including here everything from hand-hold-

ing through to copulation. Note, these initial moves always seem to involve the taking of a liberty, the amount (and its weighting in the act) varying from act to act and situation to situation. The first occurrence either of minor liberties or of acts of affection between two individuals is likely to be in private, and perforce the resulting tie-signs are only meaningful for the two participants themselves; the first occurrence of such an act in the presence of third-party acquaintances generates a tie-sign, too, but one that carries different significance from the first, since it tells us not about the intimacy attained in a relationship but about the ratificatory policy which the ends have instituted regarding their intimacy.

It should be apparent that many change signals will be ritualized. Thus the sign that re-establishes a relation to someone coming home from war, prison, or a long trip may take the form of a homecoming celebration. Similarly, and more important, many minor supportive interchanges have significance as change signals. The greeting that acquainted individuals owe each other when terminating a period of separation is likely to contain important information regarding the state of the relationship, often intendedly, and this can have a crucial directive effect even while on the face of it the ritual maintains a standard affirmative cast. An end, by judging closely, can separate out what is owed him by convention from what can be (and may have been designed to be) taken as a portent of how matters henceforth are to go between himself and the other. When a relationship is in its initial phases, this kind of information can be especially significant, allowing the more desirous of relating to know just how close he should try to get and how rapidly, and this without providing third parties any information. In quite settled relations this sort of thing may not be overly important, except at special times to discover when hard feelings are over or sudden good feelings have waned; but in many friendship relations where it can be expected that some decay may well have occurred since the last meeting, hints about where the relationship stands may be necessary at every occasion of contact.

Of all the change signals that could be studied, the one type I want to focus on is that which marks the beginning of a "close" relationship where no relationship existed before or where one of distance existed. The concern, then, will be with relationship formation.

All anchored relationships presuppose "acquaintanceship," namely a state of mutually admitted mutual knowing expressed ritually in the exchange of greetings between the two ends when they enter each other's immediate presence. Acquaintanceship occurs in two ways: by introduction (whether through a third person or through one of the ends approaching the other) and crescively, as when a new member of a community or a firm is slowly brought into the acquaintanceship fold. When acquaintanceship does occur, it is usual that the parties will also become initiated into a relationship of a particular identity. ("This is your new brother"; "This is your cousin from Pomona"; "I'm your neighbor"; "John here will work with you," etc.) The minimal relationship here is the "nodding" or "mere" acquaintanceship, this title recognizing the fact that introductions may be exchanged as a courtesy between persons who are not really expected to acquire much of a relationship thereby—a ritualization of a ritual, as it were.

Most anchored relationships seem to come into being for reasons outside themselves, a direct and immediate result of institutional arrangements. (Sibling, customer, co-worker, neighbor, are examples.) There are other relationships, however, that are intrinsically discretionary in character. Some of these are initiated at the option of the participants because of what comes about during face-to-face interaction. Others antedate a particular coming together, but are given a radical shift in direction and development because of what transpires during it. In either case we can learn how a particular discretionary relationship came about by tracing it backward in time to its starting point, to the circumstances in which something was made out of an occasion of being in touch that need not have led to anything. Incidentally, in Western society it is these discretionary relationships, whether new or redirected, that most immediately involve consideration of public order as expressed in rules of co-mingling, since these rules facilitate and inhibit the occurrence of encounters where relationship work can occur. And, of course, these periods of contact themselves point to the social organizations that provide the wider setting and occasion of their occurrence—neighborhoods, schools and colleges, places of work, social parties, resorts, and so forth.

Of those relationships in our society that can originate or develop because of what can be managed during occasions of contact, three might be given special attention. The first is the "couple" (or "pair") relation, implying here a sexually oriented bond, whether sustaining one date only, steady dating, an adulterous affair, a domestic liaison, or a marriage. Second, the "buddy" relation, a non-sexual friendship bond whose ends are available to each other for various forms of mutual aid and who together form a two-person with for various kinds of social participation. Buddies are typically, but not necessarily, recruited from the same sex. Third, there are "circles," two or more couples (along with an occasional uncoupled individual) who constitute a relatively closed set for inter-dining, ventures in commercial recreation, and small parties. Note, these three units—couples, buddies, and circles—provide much of the non-familial bases of "social life," namely, off-the-job recreational activity.

Of the three relationships considered here, the couple would seem the most important. In modern Western society there is an intense interest in couple formation, both when this involves ends not otherwise paired and ends who are already paired and are therefore betraying a relationship in forming the new tie; the novel, for example, survives on it. Reasons are apparent. Who happens to become one's spouse is of very considerable moment, both to oneself and to the spouse, and yet there is a certain amount of hap-or-chance in the process in spite of tendencies in some social classes toward arranged marriage. Indeed, potential pairing and re-pairing constitute one of the chief hazards and pleasures of public life, at least of the many places in public life where co-mingling of the sexes occurs. This is so not because relationship formation is the only interest or even a main one but because it is this interest that can be incidentally and accidentally realized during all cross-sexed contacts outside of the immediate family.

Obviously it is social situations which provide the opportunity for relationship formation, this being especially true of parties and other such "open" occasions, occasions, that is, where participation itself confers the right to initiate talk with anyone present and to be received in a friendly manner. We can therefore anticipate a basic strategic design. The initiator exposes himself to rejection and to the judgment that he is undesirable, which judgment anyone who keeps his distance is allowed to avoid; the recipient exposes herself to providing personal evidence of another's desirability without obtaining the relationship that is the usual safeguard of this admission. The solution is strategic tact. The initiator undertakes to be tentative enough and discourageable enough so that if he is to be rejected, this can be done delicately, by indirection as it were, allowing him to maintain the line that no overture had been intended. And the recipient when desiring to encourage an overture does so in a manner that can be seen as mere friendliness should the need arise to fall back on that interpretation. What might be an overture is effectively put off with what might be a declination or effectively encouraged with what might be a show of interest.[16] The initiator will not know for sure that his message has been received and that what the recipient did then was the answer; and the recipient will not know for sure that an overture has been made. An ambiguity thus results, but this derives not from some lack of consensus, failure of communication, or breakdown in social organization, but from competent participation in the relationship game. Thus instead of abruptly drawing away from an effort to hold her hand, a woman can tactfully wait for the earliest

[16] Behind these possibilities is something more tentative and constrained still, namely, readiness on the part of an individual to engage in pairing with a particular other, this not necessarily having led to any show of interest at all—a state of checked desire sometimes called "having eyes for." An individual can also give the impression that he is more than ordinarily open to pairing, sometimes called "being on the make."

occasion when it can appear that there is something she needs doing with it and then afterward return it to a less available place.

These circumstances of action give rise, of course, to certain complications. Individuals who would be friendly and gracious must check their impulses lest they seem to be encouraging an overture or making one, and those who would be fully tactful in the face of an undesired show of interest from an other must be concerned lest they allow him to commit himself still further. And toying with an other becomes possible, as does the keeping of some hope alive in him so that he will be available as a reserve resource should matters come to that. And Sartre can describe for us how a woman, out with a new man and sustaining the fiction that his interest is entirely innocent, might deal with developments:

> But then suppose he takes her hand. This act of her companion risks changing the situation by calling for an immediate decision. To leave the hand there is to consent in herself to flirt, to engage herself. To withdraw it is to break the troubled and unstable harmony which gives the hour its charm. The aim is to postpone the moment of decision as long as possible. We know what happens next; the young woman leaves her hand there, but she does not notice that she is leaving it. She does not notice because it happens by chance that she is at this moment all intellect . . . ; the hand rests inert between the warm hands of her companion—neither consenting nor resisting—a thing.[17]

We could, following Sartre, moralistically call this "bad faith," or could follow Bateson and call it something darker; but bad engineering it is not.

This traditional picture of the role of signals in relationship formation must be complicated in one regard, at least when considering traditional middle-class society. The establishing of mere acquaintanceship in public places is approved as such, apart, that is, from the question of who can suitably become acquainted with whom; when properly done it is felt there should be no shame in

---

[17] Jean-Paul Sartre, *Being and Nothingness*, Hazel E. Barnes, trans. (New York: Philosophical Library, 1956; London: Methuen, new edn., 1969), pp. 55–56.

committing this act before the eyes of strangers. But it is expected that a range of other facts will be concealed: the formation of pair relationships, the breaking up of relationships through quarrels and betrayals, and bad terms in general. It is as though related individuals were obliged to present themselves as unchangingly related as far as third persons were concerned. True, to be rejected before others merely adds to a chagrin that is already felt; but a publicly made overture that is accepted can also cause shame, and this both for initiator and recipient, since each will thereby provide evidence of being in the market for relationships.

To this basis for using discretion another must be added. The couple relation is exclusive and when new relations of this kind are formed by persons already paired, concealment of relationship formation is likely lest the betrayal be betrayed.[18]

All things considered, it is no wonder that relationship formation is something that is often attempted through change signals that are ambiguous to the recipient and imperceptible to third parties.

It is here that we can see the bearing of tie-signs on the very structure of public order: for parties and other "social" occasions are not alone as scenes where overtures and shows of interest can occur. It seems a rule of sidewalk traffic and the incidental close co-presence occurring in service establishments and offices that when men and women cross each other's path at fairly close quarters, the male will exercise the right to look for a second or two at the female as she approaches, and the female will often drop her gaze or at least take care not to return the gaze or examine the male—a pair of practices that modify the looks that passers-by ordinarily give each other in order to confirm a workable allocation of lanes.[19] (With this arrangement it is possible for males to

[18] In an unpublished paper (1965), Sue Branscomb has considered "covert withs," namely, the expression through collusive or ambiguous tie-signs of a pair bond between two individuals in the very presence of their unknowing, respective spouses. Displaced gestures of affection, acts performed in parallel, held or avoided glances, innuendo, and the like are involved.

[19] Civil inattention, then, can here involve a degree of role differentiations regarding obligations. There are other circumstances when this is

demonstrate to themselves and their friends that they are in the sexual game and yet undergo very little risk of having actually to play it.) Now given this arrangement, a female can subtly show interest by catching the male's gaze for a moment or by looking at him after he has looked at her or (it seems) after he would have looked at her had he done so. Once this show of interest has been given, other moves can be made (for example, the old-fashioned one of both parties feigning interest in a common store display) in order that the two might bring each other into discrete conversation. Indeed, then, it is structurally possible for a pickup to occur in a public street without third persons knowing that relationship formation has occurred, and furthermore, without either end too much jeopardizing his (or her) own capacity to withdraw at any juncture. No doubt this sort of thing rarely occurs, at least within the respectable classes. But the point is that pedestrian traffic incidentally is organized so that this potentiality exists. And since these openings exist, there must be countervailing norms to prevent the populace from falling through them.

IV *Information Control*

The argument has been that those who are in a relationship to each other exude signs to this effect, especially when in each other's immediate physical presence. Rules of co-mingling are such as to generate at least three major sources of this information: participation in a with, the management of minor territorial prerogatives, and the obligation to extend greetings to incidentally encountered acquaintances. Beyond these central sources of relationship infor-

---

true. Thus when an individual pushes his way to a drugstore counter to sit at a stool that is hemmed in by the two individuals on adjacent stools, the persons already, as it were, in possession will often examine the newcomer openly while he takes care to keep his eyes front. Civil inattention is mutually exhibited but more by the arrival than by those already ensconced.

mation, there is the whole context itself, for it will leak information. Furthermore if evidence is to be concealed concerning a relationship, it will take both ends to do it, which would seem to reduce by at least half the likelihood of doing so. In any case, ends not only give off relationship information, but also are required to do so, although there are limits here, especially, as suggested, in regard to conveying information about changes in stage.[20]

It was also argued that one's expectations of individuals is that their personal and social identity, their moral character, and their relationships will all fit together into a consistent and reinforcing whole. But of course this congruence will not always be found. Furthermore the signs of a relationship are merely that; they can occur in the absence of their referent, just as their referent can occur in the absence of them. Concealment, fabrication, and pointed display are possible on one side; correct and incorrect discoveries are possible on the other. Two ends who make no attempt to conceal information from a third party can become concerned as to whether or not the third party believes in their ingenuousness, for if he does not, they may feel it necessary to take this into consideration; and he who is ready to accept at face value

---

[20] This is not meant in any way to deny that from one society to another great differences exist regarding proper forms for manifesting various relationships in public. For example, Sudanese Arabs are reported to regulate wifely comportment thusly:

> A wife is expected to be circumspect in the presence of her husband and especially so in public. Deferring to him, as expressed in the practice of teknonymy, the wife further should not argue with or contradict her husband, nor should she sit beside him on the same angareb, particularly if guests are present. When they walk in the street, the wife should remain a few steps behind her husband. A wife should not eat with her husband, and any demonstration of affection between a married couple before others is a most shameful act. The taboo includes even touching each other in public. Ideally, then, a husband and wife are expected to act in the most formal manner toward each other except in the privacy of their home. It is true, however, that relations may be relaxed when in the presence of close relatives of the same or descending generations, but the public view of man and wife presents a rigid and formal relationship.

Harold B. Barclay, *Buurri al Lamaab* (Ithaca: Cornell University Press, 1964), pp. 114–115. These tie-sign rules are obviously quite different from our own; but just as obviously, tie-sign rules are involved.

the display that two ends provide may be concerned as to whether or not this is believed of him, for if it is not, then he may feel it advisable to provide assurances. Further, they must see that his show of accepting what they think they are letting him learn might be a strategic cover for doubts, just as he must see that their show of accepting his apparent acceptance of the picture they present may be a strategic cover for their anxiousness about him. In brief, there is created in connection with relationships what is true of any event that can support or undermine the image of an individual, namely, a game of expression.

The most apparent example of these issues of strategy is found in pointed display. It is an old story already alluded to that given that one's own character and worth will be partly read from the relations that one keeps, a desirable relationship may be displayed in proper and populous places for the purpose of establishing one's own value. As used to be said, it is a question of "showing off one's date," except that often what one shows off is one's with, and this is as likely to contain a prestigious business connection as a sexual one.

Given the assumptions about fit between attributes and relationships, we can expect to find individuals whose unconventional status as a couple leads to a stream of misimputations when they participate together throughout their social round as a two-person with. Thus a young wife and her considerably older husband, appearing together in public among persons who are unacquainted with them, must face misidentifications of various sorts.[21] So, too, a British war bride married to a black man and living in Chicago faces, among other contingencies, the following:

> When I go to a show or tavern I find that men seem to take it for granted that a white girl in a Negro place is for sale. It's not a nice way to put it, but that's what they have in mind. They will come

[21] From a *Life* interview, December 1, 1967, p. 48, with Mrs. Justice Douglas: "Sometimes people stare at us when we're shopping, and you know they're thinking, 'Well, I wonder where his wife is.' "

up and stand in front of us, pulling out all their money and talking loudly about all they have. Then they look at me as if they expect some response.[22]

You will note that behind these misimputations is a disinclination to make a correct appraisal that itself might have some implications felt to be disparaging. The misimputation is, then, in effect, a cover created by those from whom it conceals the facts.[23] But, of course, someone with an unconventional relationship can himself create a cover to hide his tie behind. Thus we learn of the child singer with mature sexual tastes who traveled around the country on tour picking up with a different girl in each city, but all handled in public as though they were his mother, this being an easier

---

[22] Hazel Byrne Simpkins, "A Negro's British War Bride," in *Marriage Across the Color Line*, Cloyte M. Larsson, ed. (Chicago: Johnson Publishing Company, 1965), p. 97. (It is possible that part of this response is indirectly caused by cultural differences in rules and understandings. Males in black ghetto communities may generally possess the license to openly address remarks to passing female strangers, somewhat like the Argentinian *piripos* pattern, and white brides in black communities may be attributing to discriminatory treatment what is in fact a general practice.) There are other examples of withs causing bystanders to draw wrong conclusions. For example, a woman at night in an area known to be frequented by prostitutes can have special problems in regard to the police:

> If the woman is accompanied by or is talking to men, she is likely to be arrested unless the men are relatives. . . . A woman who stops to talk to men in a car will usually be suspect. Association of a woman with men of another race usually results in an immediate conclusion that she is a prostitute. If a Negro woman is found in the company of a white man, she is usually confronted by the police and taken to the station unless it is clear that the association is legitimate.

Wayne R. LaFave, *Arrest* (Boston: Little, Brown and Company, 1965), p. 455.

[23] There is a danger here. When a third person offers a favorable misidentification of a relationship, he shows his hand, shows what he takes as normal, and thus is not in a position to act tactfully as if he considers the disclosed relationship a normal one. To forestall such embarrassment, those with a peculiar relationship may set matters straight early on in the encounter before anyone has a chance to get off on the wrong foot—a standard tactic in the management of stigma and special here only in that a relationship, not a personal attribute, is the object of concern.

reading on the relationship than the true facts.[24] There is, of course, the standard extra-marital affair and the covers devised for it. And from Los Angeles comes the term "beard" to refer to a male friend brought along to public occasions by an illicit couple so that he may be considered the coupled male and the other the friend.[25] Most common of all is the mother who allows her daughter to pass as a sister—or at least allows observers to extend the courtesy of acting as if they have momentarily misidentified the relationship.

It is apparent that often the concern of an individual will not be primarily to obtain regard for having desirable relations or to avoid disapproval for having peculiar ones. Rather his concern can be to govern the imputations that are made regarding his identity and hence his intent.

We can consider this issue by beginning with the primal image of innocence in our society and many others—the with containing a foraging family unit. This image is strong enough to be trusted as a shield. Thus there is the smuggler's classic device of appearing at the border with a full family, the assumption being that families are likely to be engaged in travel, not illicit business. Professional shoplifters sometimes employ the same technique, using the true flag of our nation to wrap their unbought bundles in.[26] During World War II, resistance leaders about to be caught in a sweep employed a "make-up" family, also, the assumption being that a family strolling along an alley in a suspect neighborhood would be less subject to suspicion than a man alone.[27] The courting couple dodge has also been employed:

---

[24] See Art Peters, "Comeback of a Child Star," *Ebony*, XXII, no. 3 (January 1967): 44, 46.

[25] The fullest beards of all were those members of royal entourages who married the King's current favorites to provide these ladies with a presentable reason to be at court. Such men—institutionalized beards—had a special patriotism, for they were willing to lay down their wives for their country.

[26] See, for example, Maury Levy, "Don't Wrap It, I'll Steal It Here," *Philadelphia Magazine*, December 1970, pp. 100–102.

[27] E. H. Cookridge, *Inside S.O.E.* (London: Arthur Barker, Ltd., 1966),

> One day Sofie Rorvig arrived with the news that the Germans had staged a manhunt, and had circulated his [Starheim's] description as a "wanted terrorist." While she was telling this an SS patrol arrived. It was a moonlit evening. Starheim and Sofie left the farmhouse, their arms intertwined in a tender embrace—just a couple of youngsters making for the lovers' lane. The SS men let them pass and went on searching houses, barns, and haystacks.[28]

And sabotage has been undertaken in chancy areas by having male and female agents employ a standard tie-sign:

> Jules was assigned the task of cutting the line. And to cover his disguise he decided to take "Denise" with him. Jules decided that "Denise" and he should masquerade as sweethearts and while on a picnic—blow up three of the pylons carrying the main grid to the railways.
>
> Taking a train to Orléans they set out on bicycles for the site of the sabotage operation. In their rucksacks they carried explosives and fuses sufficient for the job. It did not take them long to reach the long row of pylons stretching towards Orléans and parking their bicycles by the roadside, they walked hand-in-hand towards three pylons which were conveniently in one field.
>
> Round the base of each of the pylons they hid sufficient explosives for the job and attached the detonators—pencil fuses which detonated by eating through a thin metal wall in the propelling pencil-like cylinder. The fuses took a certain time to operate but the "loving pair" did not tarry. Still hand-in-hand the "sweethearts" recrossed the field, picked up their bicycles and headed for Orléans.[29]

---

p. 339. In a footnote (p. 340) Cookridge cites what must be the extreme of the family dodge, something very close to a Fanny Brice routine:

> SS General von Brodowsky did not escape justice. On 16 September men of the French 1st Tank Division near Jussey in Haute-Saône saw a German prisoner pushing a child's perambulator. Inside, under a blanket, they found Colonel von Alweyeden, Brodowsky's chief of staff. A search in the vicinity yielded the SS general; he was found asleep in a barn.

[28] *Ibid.*, p. 512.

[29] Charles Wighton, *Pin-Striped Saboteur* (London: Odhams Press, Ltd., 1959), p. 158.

Agents have also posed as brother and sister while traveling together.[30] Similarly, a policeman writes of the following help given him:

> Sometimes silence informs louder than words. One of us was in Richmond, Virginia, in an undercover capacity. To his consternation he ran head-on into a little trafficker, whom he had arrested and prosecuted. Pretense of a mistaken identity was of no avail. "I know you, Cross, from the time you arrested me at Roanoke. Because you treated me like a gentleman, I won't advertise you." To the proposition that he cooperate with an introduction to some peddlers, the prospective informer demurred. Finally we compromised. He said, "I won't introduce you to anybody, but I'll tell you what I will do—I will be seen walking up and down the streets with you." That did it! The informer left town and soon we were approached by peddlers who, having seen us in such good company, figured that we had just one business—"dope." [31]

Note that the impression that is carefully cultivated through momentary association may be a valid one, yet impression management may nonetheless be necessary.[32]

When tie-signs—and, by implication, relationships—are used as a cover, one end of the relationship may not know that covering information is being manufactured. This is the case in Runyon's treatment, "Butch Minds the Baby," in which a safecracker, having to baby-sit his infant, takes it along to the job and later, walking home from work, is able to convince the police that he is out to get something for colic. Another example comes from a

---

[30] Cookridge, *op. cit.*, p. 209.

[31] Malachi L. Harney and John C. Cross, *The Informer in Law Enforcement*, 2nd ed. (Springfield, Ill.: Charles C Thomas, 1968), p. 58.

[32] During the Revolutionary War, a tailor in New York apparently encouraged trade with British officers in order to acquire and pass on strategic information. This trade affronted his neighbors and undermined his reputation. As a correction, Washington was at pains to stop by the tailor's house for breakfast on first visiting the city after victory, thereby encouraging a reassessment of the tailor's loyalty. See Allen Dulles, *The Craft of Intelligence* (London: Weidenfeld and Nicolson, 1964; New York: Signet Books, 1965), p. 31.

sometime participant in English crime, describing how a daytime house thief can create a cover:

> He'd select a district that could be easily reached by public transport. A car, he explained, was a potential danger and an encumbrance. Once on the manor, he'd saunter along the High Street and begin what he called his "building-up campaign." He looked out for an elderly couple and, as he passed them, raised his hat. In almost every case, the couple would acknowledge his greeting. They'd met so many people during their lifetime that they surely knew this pleasant young man. Then he'd stop at the door of a crowded shop and wave his hand to one of the assistants, who'd automatically respond. All this was to allay the suspicions of any bobby who might be taking an unhealthy interest.[33]

Similarly, what appears to be a family party of one man and two women leaving a station may actually be an escapee and two ladies strange to him whose bags he has been at pains to volunteer to help with, thereby providing himself a cover.[34] A Danish member of the Resistance, detained at the SD headquarters for the possession of incriminating evidence, apparently escaped thusly:

> Edith Bonnessen denied that she was the wanted "terrorist" but knew that her chances were very slight. She was left in the room with another *Gestapo* man who was slightly drunk. He tried to become intimate and "Lotte" kept him in a good humour for awhile. Then she asked for permission to go to the lavatory. The man wanted to accompany her, but in his alcoholic state, mistook the door, and, for an instant, "Lotte" found herself alone in the corridor.
>
> She calmly trotted down the stairs, passed several guards and officers, and reached the main hall at ground level. There she saw that to get out of the building one had to show a pass. So she calmly began a solitary tour of the Shellhus. In one *Gestapo* office she equipped herself with a few files which she took under her arm to lend strength to her role as a "secretary." In one of the corridors she saw two high SS officers heading downstairs. She marched firmly

---

[33] Eric Parr, *Grafters All* (London: Max Reinhardt, 1964), p. 37.

[34] R. R. Suskind, "The Man Who Outwitted a Nation," in *Spy and Counterspy*, Phil Hirsch, ed. (New York: Pyramid Books, 1963), p. 153.

one step behind them, and passed the guards at the front door who snapped to attention in deference to "Lotte's" companions. For the benefit of the sentries, as the two SS officers dived into their car, she called out: "*Auf Wiedersehen, Herr Hauptsturm-Führer*, I shall see you in the afternoon!" and walked briskly down the road to freedom.[35]

Still another variation occurs when an end is aware of the deceit and is used against his wishes, as when a desperado takes a woman and child as hostage, forcing them to create a visual appearance for him as head of household in the car in which he is trying to escape. In the Hitchcock twist (the hero, trying to be other than he has been wrongly taken to be, rushes up to the heroine, a stranger, and embraces her roundly as though they were a couple) one end of the masquerade is unwilling and unknowing but is filled in and becomes willing even while false appearances are being maintained —this being the Cary Grant–James Stewart contribution to the lore of tie-signs.

A final cover must be considered. Individuals may act together in a social situation so as to sustain the false impression that they have *no* anchored relationship. This may take the form of their being in easy access and not availing themselves of the opportunity to acknowledge their relationship, as in the so-called "silent-meet" of agents who exchange information without opening a conversation,[36] or the standard strategy whereby two escaping prisoners

[35] Cookridge, *op. cit.*, pp. 588–589.

[36] A good description is provided by Alexander Orlov, *Handbook of Intelligence and Guerrilla Warfare* (Ann Arbor: University of Michigan, 1963; London: Cresset Press, 1963), pp. 119–120:

> The so-called silent meetings are designed to eliminate the obviousness of communication between the two participants and to deceive the surveillants. Such meetings are usually held in parks, museums, libraries, and similar places. For instance, the operative and the "source" pretend to be studying some reference material at the library. Both, independently of each other, make notes while sitting or standing side by side or opposite each other; then one of the two departs and, instead of taking his own notebook or folder, picks up that of his neighbor. Or while perusing a number of books, one of them slips an envelope into a certain volume, which his neighbor retrieves a little later. Only an experienced detective who knows who the two "researchers" are could detect such a sleight-of-hand trick. There are other variations of the same technique:

act on a train and station as if they are strangers to each other. Within the same design is the practice of two related individuals striking up the sort of brief conversation that is permissible between strangers and that, incidentally, provides cover for the secret delivery of messages. In all of these cases individuals act "as if they did not know each other." These covers, of course, are the stock in trade of undercover workers. To be considered here, too, is the act of one or more individuals keeping an other under observation unbeknownst to him. Again the form adhered to is that of non-acquainteds offering each other civil inattention; but underneath is a one-sided, concealed relationship.

Concealing is routinely found in connection with the turning points of a relationship. Thus honeymooning couples often feel some desire to conceal their situation, even though they may also at moments want to reveal it. Hints for honeymooners have been published advising on disguise.[37]

The concealing of a relationship and the inevitable possibility of discovery by others lead to some interesting, strategic issues.[38] The precise identity, terms, and stage of a relationship may be covered, fairly effectively, but it is much more difficult to conceal that something is being concealed. Once the discovery is made that

---

> two persons separately enter a movie theater and take adjacent seats. There, under the cover of darkness, one passes the material to the other. Or the two find themselves together on the same bench in the park. One of them has brought a magazine or newspaper which he puts on the bench between himself and the other person. When nobody is around to notice, the other picks up the magazine (with the envelope inside it) and walks away.

Silent meetings have passed into popular culture via the spy novel and have become the subject of good comic routines. This should not blind us to their interactional significance, namely, that participation in public life routinely brings strangers so close together that civil inattention is relied on to avoid conversational entanglements, and since this means that well-structured rules of conduct are being observed, there will everywhere be occasions when actual connectedness could exist and yet be concealed.

[37] Don't wear outfits that are entirely new, don't fluster or bluster when signing the hotel register, don't engage in the display of too many endearments and courtesies, and don't stay too much together.

[38] I have considered some of these in *Strategic Interaction* (Philadelphia: University of Pennsylvania Press, 1969), pp. 138–139.

something is being hidden—that something is "unnatural"—the discovered persons are subject to the contingency of being thought to be thoroughly suspect; they lose all control over what it is that is suspected of them, and this may be worse for them than their revealing the true facts.

Here it is worth looking at the strategic issues created by the telephone as a communication system. Ordinary face-to-face conversation is organized on the principle that persons who could monitor the talk but are not ratified participants respectfully disattend and that persons who are ratified participants of the talk openly and equally sustain a devotion of involvement to it. The first rule is commonly breached by bystanders who show intrusive concern for what is going on in the talk, the second by participants who display alienation.

The second breach concerns us. One standard form of alienation is an individual's expression of boredom, impatience, or preoccupation. Another is collusive communication within or across the conversational circle, entailing a furtive exchange that excludes some members of the official conversation and indeed betrays them. This collusive betrayal is kept in check—albeit not as much as one would imagine—by the fact that the individuals who would be excluded can scan and monitor the conversational circle for evidence of the loyalty of the participants.

Telephone talk has the special feature that a talker can engage easily in displays of alienation in regard both to the conversation as a whole and to any development within it, because these the other party will not be able to see.[39] Persons on the phone are thus vulnerable to each other to an inordinate degree. When a bystander is

[39] One structurally similar situation is found in hospitals in connection with the glass-walled nursing station often arranged to provide those inside a view of patients in the hallway and dayroom. From within this soundproof observation box, medical staff and orderlies can make candid and flippant remarks to one another about the patients passing before them. Another structurally similar situation is found in small shops where two servers who share an ethnic language face a customer who is assumed to have only the local one. Communication about him to his face is possible and not infrequently occurs.

together with one of the talkers, then the latter—the man in the middle—has a concealed audience before whom it will be easy to play out collusive gestures of impatience, derogation, and exasperation. Furthermore, since the call is likely to have interrupted in some way what the co-present two had been doing, with possible affront to the relationship upon which this doing was based, the middleman may feel a special need to deprecate the telephone encounter in favor of the immediate one. In any case, he owes his present companion signs of how long the interruption will be and what he feels about its being as long as it is turning out to be. In consequence, some kind of collusion between talker and bystanding companion is likely.

Now a complication must be introduced. It seems to be a principle of social relationships that when related persons talk to each other (directly or by phone), they express in some way or other just how intimate and close the relationship is and how pleased they both are to have this opportunity to be in touch. A "sympathy rule" applies. Indeed there is a tendency to display more concern and involvement than might be the case, any error usually being in the direction of effusiveness. When other persons are known to be present, it will be understood by the two that this evidence of closeness will have to be curtailed and muted, at least a little. But when only the two are present, then a stream of "grooming talk" is expected.

Return now to the plight of the person in the middle—the one who has a bystander at his own end of the line and a party at the other.

If the telephone talk is brief and its burden purely utilitarian or official, then the presence of an overhearer may be of concern to no one, and the person in the middle may feel that both his others will be indifferent to whether he expresses the fact that someone in addition to himself is physically present or not. In some circumstances the person in the middle can openly inform the party on the other phone that time and privacy cannot be given to the talk because he is currently engaged with someone present, and he can do this so that both his others receive the same version of what is occurring and neither feels offended. But these two solutions are not by any means always possible. The sympathy rule for conversation between related persons ensures this. Basically the man in the middle will find that if he is as open and warm to the party on the other end of the line as his relationship to this person warrants, then he must improperly withdraw from the bystander and also nakedly expose what is meant to be private; yet if he treats the party on the phone coolly, the latter may take offense and even the bystander may sense that something is being concealed.

There are three standard tacks the person in the middle can take to resolve his dilemma. First, he can try to "fake it," that is, treat the party on the phone as if no bystander were present, while collusively using gestures to bring the bystander into the act. Second, he can code his talk so that the other party will catch on that the conversation is unnatural and that he is supposed to see that it is unnatural, even while an effort is sustained to give the bystander the impression that this is the kind of call that can be conducted openly, his presence a matter of indifference to all concerned. Third, and most delicate of all, the person in the middle can try to select his words so that the party on the other phone feels that the relationship is properly expressed in the talk, while at the same time the bystander feels that this is the sort of conversation that renders the presence of a bystander a matter of indifference. In these circumstances, a tortuous kind of self-control is in fact exerted by the man in the middle; his apparent easy involvement in the phone conversation belies a very close discipline. Yet given the situation and the fact that the manner of conducting talk leaks information about relationships, this precarious line is structurally encouraged and often managed.[40]

---

[40] Of course, insecure calls have a variety of complexities. We have the phrase, "Can you talk?" meaning, might there be exposure—exposure due to a tap on the line, a second open phone on the premises, or a bystander who must be kept in the dark. The answer can warn about the insecurity of the line at the price of disclosing that the parties have something to conceal, or can license statements that are open at the speaker's end but unanswerable with innocent (typically truncated) replies at the recipient's ("Not really, but go ahead."), or can authorize open talk. The tricky problem is to establish how the channel

One further issue remains to be considered in regard to tie-signs and information control. If we set aside dramatic cases of persons who have a peculiar relationship to hide and the special case of talking to one person on the phone while another person is present, we are still left with something important. In the ordinary course of events, the make-up of various "participation units" in a gathering and the rules regulating these units, in short, the structure of the situation, provide relationship information that is sufficient and acceptable to everyone present. That, in a way, is the normal state of affairs. However, minor, ungoverned events will constantly produce configurations of persons in context that produce, relative to relationships, issues about impressions, in short, compromising appearances. The response to this troublesome feature of everyday events is that those who are potentially compromised will not merely have accounts ready in order to set matters straight but will also conduct themselves calculatedly so that the environment around them will give off correct information. However, there is also the belief that a valid expression of relationships is natural and normal, that it is the office of reality to provide adequate information in these respects. Therefore, to a degree, the normality and naturalness of situations (as Garfinkel has argued) are conditions that are accomplished.

One particular instance of this accomplishment occurs in regard to participation units, namely, parties of one (singles) and withs. It is assumed that the natural situation will correctly inform as to who in the setting is a "single" and who is in a with with whom. Ordinarily little conscious intent is required to act so that this assumption will be borne up by what occurs. Occasionally, however, one or both of two socially unrelated persons will consciously have to modify the wonted rate and direction of their movement in order to dispel the appearance of their being in a with. Contrariwise, those in a with who have abandoned their

---

is to be used without giving potential or actual third parties any evidence that this determination is being made. Much better worked out is the technique of using monosyllabic replies which can be overheard without disclosing what is going on or even that something questionable is going on.

ecological tie-sign in the face of the contingencies of riding an escalator, crossing an intersection, or passing through any other displacing or attention-demanding transition pathway, are likely to make a conscious effort to reconstitute visual evidence of the with as soon as ordinary conditions are re-established.[41] One further instance of creating normal appearances might be cited. One can ordinarily read from the setting who it is that is addressing whom (and by implication, that their relationship is such as to sustain this address), because the orientation of the speaker's face and trunk points to the recipient. Indeed, one can accurately assess a line of orientation even when one is at an angle to it. However, when a third person is in the direct line of vision between speaker and intended recipient and happens to be looking at the speaker, then he may incorrectly assume he is being addressed. In these circumstances, we often find that the speaker will grossly exaggerate the narrowness of his orientation and sometimes lean out of his prior position in order to re-establish a direct, clear line between himself and the intended recipient; and the interceptor, who might have found himself improperly responding (or incorrectly assuming that he had been improperly addressed), may duck or otherwise change his position so that indeed the "normal" conditions for contact are re-established. Thus the setting can be made to once again reflect the facts of the relationships.

I have been arguing that one always draws relationship conclusions from what one sees in social gatherings, and that these conclusions may be in error, either because of one's own misimputation or because an effort has been made to cover the facts. That is hardly news, but two less obvious points can be made.

First, social arrangements for the most part are inherently ambiguous, meaning here that the interactional facts are only loosely geared to structural ones. A scene, not uncommon in our society, where a man with a "civilized divorce" dines with his child and former wife at a restaurant—the child having finished the weekend with one parent and about to begin the weekdays with the other—may give little information about the character of the re-

---

[41] Here I draw on an unpublished paper by Virginia Ayers (1965).

lationship between the parents, all with little conscious effort on either side to conceal the facts. The point is that the pattern available for man-woman-child dining does not discriminate with sufficient detail to do this job, unless, of course, microscopic observation is made by the viewer. And so it is no wonder that public patterns can lead to misreadings and be used to misinform.

Second, and more important, although tie-signs are everywhere around the persons tied, the principal sources derive from the very structure of social gatherings: singles and withs; conversational circles; civil inattention between separate participation units; rules for recognition between the acquainted; rules for permissible engagement with strangers. Reference to the stealthy and daring acts of spies is relevant, because these acts point out that when one wants to meddle with the natural arrangements, it is the above-mentioned units and conventions that must be meddled with. By learning how extraordinary relationships are concealed, we are provided with a forcible reminder of the informing capacity of configurations which would otherwise have occurred; and from this, in turn, we learn about the structure of ordinary social gatherings.

V *The Analysis of Ritual Idiom*

Tie-signs could be said to form a language of relationships, but only if we accept a loose and popularistic manner of speaking. Often the ends will not be intent on communicating in the narrow sense of that term, and often the most telling tie-sign is the one that the makers are entirely unaware of. Furthermore, the tie-signs of any particular community do not, it seems, form a grammar that can generate an infinite number of different sentences all on the basis of restrictive permutation of a relatively small number of elements, although certainly users early acquire the competence to read an infinite number of slightly different scenes they have not seen before. In any case, tie-signs, like other elements in a ritual idiom, are not events to which justice can be done by calling them communications or expressions; they are means of taking up a position or alignment in a situation and simultaneously giving evidence that this has been done. What we find, then, is not a language but a ritual idiom, a mixed bag of behavioral arrangements including acts seen as issuing from one person and ecological positionings involving two or more persons. These events, taken together, may not constitute a system, although they certainly constitute a resource.

What then are we to take as the "meaning" of a particular tie-sign, or rather, the meaning of this meaning? Where do we go in analyzing one particular bit of a ritual idiom? In this closing section, I would like to try to make some speculative suggestions in this regard, taking as an example for analytical free association a minor little practice—hand-holding in American society.

Two strategies suggest themselves for analyzing ritual idiom. One is to start with a particular practice, in this case hand-holding, and move from there to a consideration of a class of practices of which it is an example, a class that can be defined naturalistically in terms, say, of function or role and accorded the status of a concept. Thus, hand-holding can come to be seen as a "tie-sign," and interest can then shift to a general consideration of this broad class of events. By and large that is what I have attempted so far, except instead of beginning with hand-holding, I have ended with it. The other strategy is to try to assemble all of the environments in which the particular practice is found and then attempt to uncover what these various contexts have in common. Here the "meaning" of the practice is whatever co-occurs with it. (In rough analysis it will also help to assemble environments in which the practice would seem least likely to occur although other members of its natural class do, the assumption being that we can learn what a thing is by learning what it relevantly isn't.) It is this second mode of analysis that I want to try to illustrate now in concluding this essay.

In American society, individuals below the age of adolescence do not hold hands, at least not in the sense that will here come to be meant, nor, at least with any frequency, do persons beyond their sixties. And those of appropriate age to employ the practice by and large will do it only with a person of the opposite sex. This suggests that the sign implies that the makers of it are within the age for sexual relations and that the relationship that is signified is a sexually potential one. In brief, the party of two is a pair or a couple. Thus, a person who simultaneously and openly holds hands with two individuals of the other sex is seen as not holding hands in the sense here developed.

Also, it seems that the two-person relationship that is signified by hand-holding has a "one-only" character in the sense of being the only one of its kind either end is supposed to possess at the time. Deviations tend to confirm this. A person perceived by the same set of others to be holding hands with two different individuals within an interval too short for the proper termination of one relationship and the initiation of another is likely to evoke quizzical looks from them and manifest sheepish looks himself. Ordinarily he will treat one of these relationships as legitimate and hold its hand (if he must) where he and she can be recognized personally; he will arrange to be in a place where he can't be recognized before holding the other woman's hand but then do so avidly—the poignant act of bravely and openly broadcasting the illicit relationship to the world at large but when no acquaintances are in it.

Those most likely to hold hands seem to be of high school and college age and college-going social status—persons, especially urban and non-Catholic, of the middle- and upper middle-class. Where somewhat older persons are found engaging in the act, they seem (in the degree of their age) to be especially of this world that cultivates higher education. Now it is a feature of these persons that they exhibit a relatively high degree of equality between the sexes and relatively little differentiation in sexual subculture. This is supported by the fact that those who actively disdain to hold hands represent the opposite proclivities. Thus Gerald Suttles, writing of the Chicago Italian slums:

> At the same time, however, they [the Italian youths] perpetuate the old system by automatically assuming that the slightest sign of interest by a girl makes her fair game, even when she may be assuming his good intentions. Out of self-defense, then, the girls are compelled to keep their distance. On private occasions, of course, there are many Italian boys and girls who sneak off to enjoy what others might consider an entirely conventional boy-girl relationship (pet-

> ting, necking). In public, however, they studiously ignore one another. Throughout my time in the area I never saw a young Italian couple hold hands or walk together on the sidewalk.[42]

Sexual equality is borne out by the nature of the practice itself, since practically alone among pair tie-signs this sign is almost symmetrical: except for details, the posture assumed by the male is assumed by the female, too.[43] (The contrast here is with the more general pair tie-sign, the arm lock.)

Having begun to learn about the meaning of hand-holding by looking at those who do it and those who don't, we can go forward. Given the people who do it, we can ask when it is they do it, and when it is they don't (when they might).

First, not doing it. There is a rule in formal etiquette that it is improper for couples to walk down the fashionable shopping streets of a city holding hands. There is another rule that married couples at social parties are supposed to "mix," that is, to lay aside their excluding relationship temporarily so that they can be active simply in their capacity as members of the party. A corollary of this rule is that they are not supposed to hold hands. (They may hold hands on the way to the party and back from the party but not during the party.) It is also the case that although college students can walk on the campus holding hands—in fact that seems to be one of the special places for this sort of activity—they ought not to listen to lectures thusly encumbered. Furthermore, in some social establishments holding hands even outdoors is forbidden. In industrial schools for persons with a court charge, hand-holding may be prohibited within the gates, as it may be to nurse-physician pairs on the hospital grounds. In these latter cases, of

---

42 Gerald D. Suttles, *The Social Order of the Slum* (Chicago: The University of Chicago Press, 1968), p. 113.

43 The details, however, neatly allow an expression of the traditional ideal. The insides of the two hands are pressed together, in mutual embrace as it were, but the outside of the male's hand typically faces the oncoming world, whereas the outside of the female's hand merely follows in the wake of protection. Further, as hand-holding is typically done, he can let go at will, since he is the grasper, allowing him to deal with the enemy; she, however, must wriggle out to be free, which in the traditional view is but meet, for what reason could she have for needing to free her hand?

course, whether for penal or professional reasons, the members must be so strictly disciplined that even when walking between buildings, a high orientation to the purposes of the establishment must be maintained. (As may be expected, other self-involving side-involvements such as smoking may also be prohibited.) It appears, then, that when much of an individual's orientation and involvement is necessary, hand-holding may have to be foreborne —along with other acts through which the mutual involvement of the closely related might be thrust upon the public at large.

The significance of this discipline will be emphasized if we look at situations where hand-holding seems to be approved and even idealized. In our pictorial world of advertising and movies—if not in the real world—vacationing couples are featured walking down crooked little streets in foreign places holding hands. At issue here is the fact that tourists often feel they do not owe the business streets of foreign societies the deference these places often demand from locals; tourists can therefore withdraw, just as they can wear informal clothing. Further, the very foreignness of the place suggests a slight exposure, if not fear, and, for the woman at least, holding the hand of the one she is paired with is a pictured source of support. Magazine couples are also featured holding hands while walking barefooted (shoes in other hand) on the seashore. Here, obviously, the absence of civil society allows a greater withdrawal than might otherwise be tolerated, an undisguised mooning as it were, and the very empty reaches of the ocean might cause an anomic flutter nicely checked by the confirmation of a held hand.

A final possibility is to be considered. It is plain that the involvement denoted by hand-holding is a joint involvement, an openly shared thing, and this common ground may in some situations be something that the ends have a special reason and a special right to demonstrate. For example, the newly engaged at parties given in their honor are prone to hold hands and stay rather close together, but now this mutual involvement is a duty as well as a privilege, since it is this engrossment that the occasion is designed to celebrate. When the two walk down the aisle after marriage, they will be allowed to hold hands, too, and this at a time when the wedding guests feel obliged to mute their own dyadic involvements.[44]

On certain other occasions hand-holding can be thrust upon the assemblage, and moreover under what at first might be considered unfelicitous circumstances. Thus, at court hearings when a middle-class man is arraigned for an act that might be thought to render him unfit for pairing, his spouse may specifically hold his hand to show that she still considers him worthy of the relationship. So, too, a man bringing his wife to a hearing regarding her plot with two other men to have him killed may also hold her hand, again to show that he stands behind her, upholding her as a woman able to be in a pair. Finally, note that when a politician is present to receive news of having been elected (or an astronaut to receive a medal), there is likely to be a hand there to be held, his wife's, to show that at this moment he has not become overfilled with pride and ambition and has not placed himself above the reach of ordinary men: he shifts some of his personal delight into a delight for the couple, a side-involvement to assure that he has not been overswayed. In a similar way in the other circumstance, a politician shows he has not been capsized by defeat.

In general, then, we can say that hand-holding is not merely a way of informing that a particular kind of relationship exists; it is also a way of openly giving a small portion of oneself at the time to the relating, while at the same time affirming the validity and value of the relationship.

But note that tie-signs involving physical acts of love, such as kissing and embracing, also tell us that two ends are engaged in their relationship and in a relationship quite like the one under consideration. The difference, however, should be apparent. Love-making is properly engrossing; it is not only a main involvement, but can itself brook little by way of simultaneous side-involvements. Hand-holding, on the contrary, is in its very nature a side-involvement—an involvement subordinated to some other

[44] In fact, so rightfully involved in their relationship is a marrying couple in our middle-class society that for a brief period after they step out of the church they allow themselves to be forced to employ tie-signs of formidable broadcasting power—rice showers on the sidewalk, cans tied to the car, horns tooting, and so forth.

activity or sustainable along with other side-involvements, such as smoking and walking, without threat to itself. To elevate hand-holding into a main focus of attention would be to utterly spoil it. (Many men have traveled distances to make love, but few presumably have done so to hold hands.)

Hand-holding, then, in the sense here implied, signifies an open side-involvement of two ends in an exclusive, sexually potential, equalitarian relationship. This is the "meaning" of the act as derived from a speculative consideration of the persons and situations associated with its occurrence and its prohibition.

It is possible, then, to explore informally the meaning of a bit of ritual idiom by roughly applying a distributional form of analysis. If this is to be done, there is no reason not to extend what we thereby learn about the practice by introducing the battery of questions and issues that can be raised in regard to any socially patterned activity.

First, there is the history of the sign. What groups were first to start using it? Into what groups is the sign passing now? What is the future of the sign? Thus, whereas lower-class Italians do not much hold hands, the practice apparently is passing into use among blacks. Where these historic shifts can be shown to follow an explicable pattern, we can, of course, speak of the natural history of the sign.

Next, there is the issue of homonyms. What looks like hand-holding of the kind we have been considering may not be hand-holding at all. Some of these possibilities are obvious. A manicurist holds the hand of a client but does not engage in hand-holding, although that she is not doing so may require the assurance of a joke. A police clerk who, in taking fingerprints, must hold the hand of the imprinted is also not holding hands in our sense, and this time no joke may be permissible. A fortune teller also holds a hand but does not engage in hand-holding. Clearly in these cases, a different "frame" is operative, a different scheme of interpretation for the meaning of an act.

But this issue is not so easily settled. Children in our society below the age of puberty will hold hands across and within sex, and this is not quite hand-holding in our sense, although certainly more so than were the earlier examples. The same is true for an adult holding the hand of a child. What we have here is certainly a tie-sign, a signal that the persons holding hands are in a with, are together; but the cross-sexed, pairing implication is not present. In Soviet society, as in many Eastern societies incidentally, hand-holding may occur between male adults, and does so without the implications such an act would have in our society. Again a with is here marked: the buddy relationship, no doubt, but not pairing.

You will note in connection with the non-sexual form of hand-holding that in our society females apparently can employ this tie-sign longer than can males; indeed post-adolescent girls may hold hands in public places. Perhaps this attests to a belief that girls are more needful than boys of support and that in partially withdrawing from the public while being in public, they are merely withdrawing to a point where one feels members of the gentler sex ought to be; they should be less thrust than are men into any kind of public participation. Perhaps in our society hand-holding—especially the non-sexual kind—implies that one or both of the participants are receiving psychic support, and perhaps males of almost any age are disinclined (in our society) to advertise receiving such support, although perfectly ready to advertise giving it. (Two persons who define themselves as proper recipients of protection can through holding hands give some of this to each other; two persons who define themselves as givers of support cannot use each other in this reciprocal capacity.) This would mean that youths would refrain from holding hands with their parents or elder siblings, or would be restive when forced to do so.

The question of homonymous forms leads directly into that of idiom acquisition. How does a holder learn to hold hands? Does he learn by watching others, by watching pictures of others, or is he led into it by those with whom he ends up holding hands? When, where, and how does he learn to discriminate the homonymous forms, and does one of these forms (here presumably the child-parent type) provide the base for the others? I might add that hand-holding belongs to that part of our repertoire of doings for which no description is available and none is thought necessary; holders are likely to find it difficult and pointless to provide a detailed physical account of how they go about doing it. (During the time, once-for-each-relationship, when hand-holding functions as a change signal and ratifies an increase in intimacy, hand-holding can be something that someone, presumably the male, sets about to do. But once hand-holding becomes established between two ends, it will be sensed to be something that one simply finds oneself doing, not something that one sets about to do. On each particular occasion of its occurrence, the move of one hand to the other and the welcoming response of the other will be so subtle and circular, so simultaneously managed, that the sense can be maintained that although a configuration has occurred, no one has engineered its occurrence.)

Having seen that there is hand-holding that is not hand-holding, we can go on to see that there are twos who hold hands but ought not to, yet whose doing is done, as it were, in relation to what they should not be doing, and no homonymous usage is involved. Rebellious grade-school children will sometimes thrust their pairing onto the classroom by walking into class hand-in-hand. Homosexuals, especially at the places or seasons where license is found, will hold hands, an open affront to sexually civil society. And militant, cross-color couples, walking through a questionable neighborhood, may hold hands just to make it evident that alternative viewings of their with are not possible. Those engaged in experimental commune living, I am told, press matters a little further sometimes and hold hands in the presence of others they hold hands with, thus making what would ordinarily be an ungrammatical behavioral statement.

In the same vein we are to anticipate another pair of possibilities. First, given that hand-holding between particular ends or on particular occasions will be prohibited, we can expect that devious or furtive means will be found for doing so safely—"footsie" being an example. Second, since hand-holding provides a standard meaning to events and establishes in part the character of the ends, the practice can provide a cover under which prohibited activities can be sustained—of which examples from espionage have already been given.

Another double issue. Given a practice, in this case hand-holding, we can anticipate that certain functions can be performed that could not be conveniently performed otherwise. Thus in order to manage cross-talk in which one member of a cross-sexed with talks to a third person, the talking member can compensate the with by holding the hand of the other member, even while he sustains the talk by directing his body to it.[45] Contrariwise, we can expect that a price will be paid for the practice and that what otherwise might be easily accomplished, cannot now be so easily done. Thus given the pair-character of hand-holding in our society, two males have to disavail themselves of a perfectly good device for staying together during passage through a dense, rapidly moving crowd.

Finally, there is the issue that if hand-holding is to be seen as an instance of a class, such as "tie-signs," then it will be desirable to consider the functional relationships between the instance in question—hand-holding—and the various other members of the class. Are there well-defined tie-signs that can be used (a) whether or not hand-holding occurs; (b) if and only if hand-holding is called for but for incidental reasons is not possible; (c) if and only if hand-holding is not appropriate? In brief, we could apply the general notion of "substitution rules" and look for rules which function to ensure that no confusion will arise because of the various uses of the practice, and that, in consequence, varieties of use will be possible. For example, it might be argued that the desexed form of hand-holding requires at least one of the holders to be excluded by age or whatever from sexuality status, this automatically ensuring that no ambiguity could arise. Thus, it may be rare but it is not odd to see (as I have) a nun walking on a downtown street holding the hand of her mother. Also, the context itself may so clearly ensure a special balance among the elements involved in hand-holding that the cross-sexed character of a pair can be en-

[45] There is a prettier version. A courting couple may walk down the street merely side by side, relying on ecology to attest to the with, and the two-person with to attest to the pair relationship. However, just as the couple is joined by a friend, hand-holding may begin, the loss of an ecological sign simultaneously compensated by the gain of a physical one, and a continuity of expression maintained of the pair bond.

tirely discounted, thereby generating the conditions required for exploitation of the alternate use. At the funeral of her husband, a young woman can have her hand openly held by her late husband's best male friend, and this will be read as a means simply of giving emotional support, the tightness of the holding itself perhaps differentiating the sign. Similarly, a woman about to slip on the ice can have her hand held firmly by almost anyone, since almost anyone can be defined as a source of helpful steadying. Contrariwise, we can understand why it is that in those prisons where homosexuality is rife, hand-holding between adolescent girls may be prohibited by the authorities and abjured by straight prisoners; for here the very special context introduces an ambiguity regarding the meaning of the practice which can only be resolved by rearranging the rules of use.

We have so far looked at the categories of persons who employ hand-holding, the contexts in which they are likely and unlikely to do so, some examples of acts that look like hand-holding but are not, the history of the act, its role as a cover, the provocative use of the act, the fact that because there is hand-holding as a practice certain other social arrangements are prohibited in consequence (while still others made possible), and finally the possibility of substitution rules. I want to repeat that these questions could, of course, be asked of any social practice and any social rule.

And when we put this set of questions and find answers of some kind or other, what we are getting at is the meaning of the practice. But this is meaning in the structural sense. What we are getting at really is the location or place of the act in the stream of behavior.

A final comment. What has been here said about hand-holding is based on offhandedly collecting and analyzing data, a hit-or-miss license I was encouraged to exercise because few are likely to think the bit of idiom in question is important enough to protect by serious study. And certainly there are some questions about it that are hardly urgent. For example, howsoever hand-holding is learned, it is likely that a wide range of other items in our ritual idiom is learned in the same way, and it is the connection between socialization techniques and this total range of items that is interesting, not in particular how hand-holding itself is learned. Nonetheless, I think something significant about social life can be illustrated through what was attempted here—the piecing out of the meaning of a particular bit of ritual idiom.

Across the face of all the social situations in our society, innumerable combinations occur of persons who find themselves adjacent to each other. In the face of all these easy opportunities, it is yet the case that when hands are held no confusion of meaning ordinarily results; a single understanding effectively orients the various holders and the various witnesses to the holdings. And withall in any gathering, those who hold hands and those who don't are likely to sense no explicit ruling as a guide for action. This is the sphere of life where personal feelings and personal choice seem determinative, where ordinarily the ends themselves are left in charge of what they do, and even between themselves, each can usually find a way to avoid the other's hold with impunity. And yet when the two are in company, they find that no misunderstanding of their act occurs, just as the company finds no immediate need to question the meaning it usually imputes to the ritual now being performed before it. And further, more even than is the case with traffic rules and language rules, this agreement about ritual idiom seems surprisingly uniform across the usual social boundaries of age, class, ethnicity, region, and nation—within the West. Those whose social place leads them to feel that they would not fancy holding hands with anyone and those whose place causes them to lead in performance of the act are bound together in a single universe of discourse, a single ritual frame of reference. They behave differently but understand the same.

Hand-holding is a resource provided in our society for being in a certain state—a legitimate side-involvement in an equalitarian pair relationship—and if one is going to be in that state, one is likely to come to use that indication of it. Our society is loose enough to allow some freedom to choose among various states of being and various settings to be that way in. But there the looseness ends. To be free to be in a particular state is to be constrained to properly employ the standard indicators of it and to be constrained to refrain from misemploying them when otherwise committed. Note again, what is involved is not simply "expression." Nor can we simply say that a message is being sent. What is involved is an alignment taken up, a commitment made to a position, and incidentally the production of conventional evidence that this investment of self has occurred. And so it is when any other bit of ritual idiom is employed.

It would be impossible to read effectively the social scene around oneself or to provide others a reading of it if one were not constrained by the same rules as the other participants regarding ritualized indications of alignment. For just as one cannot learn a new language every time one makes or hears a different statement, so one cannot acquire a new ritual idiom every time one wants to change alignments in a gathering or discover what alignments others present have taken up. It is a technical not an ethical argument to say that freedom to express is contingent on constraint in regard to the idiom of expression. Of course it is possible to break the ground rules for a particular mode of social intercourse, as when individuals attack institutional authority by publicly performing obscene gestures. But even here conventions reign. A particular set of understandings is violated, but the means of violation are themselves necessarily drawn from a wider vocabulary of ritual that is common to all. Revolutionaries of decorum must rely on the same idiom as do those who would gently tiptoe through all their social occasions. Understanding must be shared if any but secret alignments are to be established; it is only the issue of who should perform the ritual with whom and who should merely bear witness that marks the difference.

[6]

Normal Appearances

PART ONE

I *Alarms*

Individuals, whether in human or animal form, exhibit two basic modes of activity. They go about their business grazing, gazing, mothering, digesting, building, resting, playing, placidly attending to easily managed matters at hand. Or, fully mobilized, a fury of intent, alarmed, they get ready to attack or to stalk or to flee. Physiology itself is patterned to coincide with this duality.

The individual mediates between these two tendencies with a very pretty capacity for dissociated vigilance. Smells, sounds, sights, touches, pressures—in various combinations, depending on the species—provide a running reading of the situation, a constant monitoring of what surrounds. But by a wonder of adaptation these readings can be done out of the furthest corner of whatever is serving for an eye, leaving the individual himself free to focus his main attention on the non-emergencies around him. Matters that the actor has become accustomed to will receive a flick or a shadow of concern, one that decays as soon as he obtains a microsecond of confirmation that everything is in order; should something really prove to be "up," prior activity can be dropped and full orientation mobilized, followed by coping behavior. Note, the central thesis here is Darwinian. If individuals were not highly responsive to hints of danger or opportunity, they would not be responsive enough; if they carried this response far on every occasion of its occurrence, they would spend all their time in a dither and have no time for all the other things required for survival.

When the world immediately around the individual portends nothing out of the ordinary, when the world appears to allow him to continue his routines (being indifferent to his designs and neither a major help nor a major hindrance), we can say that he will sense that appearances are "natural" or "normal." For the individual, then, normal appearances mean that it is safe and sound to continue on with the activity at hand with only peripheral attention given to checking up on the stability of the environment. Wariness is handled as a side-involvement; the human animal might say that he can "take things at face value," the unstated implication being that he can predict from what he sees what it is that is likely to come about, and this is not alarming. And when special attentiveness is required, as when humans cross a busy intersection or unpack eggs, it will be understood that this special effort is restricted to a brief period of time.

When the human or animal senses that something is unnatural or wrong, that something is up, he is sensing a sudden opportunity or threat in his current situation.

With these definitions I exercise a double license. Only in the case of man can we say for sure that normalcy is "sensed." Furthermore, what here is called unnatural or abnormal is perfectly natural as naturalists would use the term.

Normal appearances as here defined have only an indirect relation to the notion of expectation, whether in the statistical or normative sense of that term. I am assuming that whatever range of risk and opportunity an environment contains, the individual exposed to these considerations typically comes to terms with them, making what adjustments are necessary in order to routinely withdraw his main attention from them and get on with other matters. (Indeed, when this cannot be done because of threat one sometimes speaks of the individual as being "terrorized"—a term which nicely suggests the rarity of the condition.) Among the individuals we will hereafter be concerned with and will restrict the term to—human ones—this coming to terms is often assured normatively; the individual not only anticipates uneventfulness but also feels that he has a moral right to count on it. Similarly, very rare events can occur in the individual's immediate environment without his feeling that he must be concerned for what they might portend for his survival, in which case he can as easily withdraw his attention from them as he can from what is entirely typical. Also, someone in his presence may behave in a quite improper manner without this necessarily causing him alarm, as is routinely the case, for example, in some police work [1] and in the many mental hospital wards in which attendants infrequently feel alarmed, frequently feeling secure enough to sleep. With persons, then, it is *usually* the case that normal appearances, typical appearances, and proper appearances are much the same, but this agreement conceals the adaptive social processes that produced it and the inevitable possibility that the three appearances will not coincide.

The relation suggested between normal appearances and proper appearances must be qualified. In many situations there are agents of social control such as store managers, school teachers, and the like, whose job in part is to protect the setting and its users and to maintain the proprieties—at least certain proprieties. Suggestions that misconduct is occurring are what constitute for them signs that readiness is required, if not sudden effort, that is, that there is cause for alarm. Police, for example, must be on the lookout for motorists who are untrained, unlicensed, or unsober, and they have a special concern with anyone who by appearance "does not fit in," since they can feel that such a person must be checked out if

---

[1] For example, see James Q. Wilson, *Varieties of Police Behavior* (Cambridge: Harvard University Press, 1968), p. 34.

theft and other troubles are to be prevented before they occur.[2]

Here, then, is one way in which normal appearances link up with the issue of social control. There is another. When an individual finds persons in his presence acting improperly or appearing out of place, he can read this as evidence that although the peculiarity itself may not be a threat to him, still, those who are peculiar in one regard may well be peculiar in other ways, too, some of which may be threatening. For the individual, then, impropriety on the part of others may function as an alarming sign. Thus, the minor civilities of everyday life can function as an early warning system; conventional courtesies are seen as mere convention, but non-performance can cause alarm.

Note that although one ordinarily thinks of alarming signs as occurrences, the absence of an expected sign can serve the same function. A parent who fails to receive a telephone call from a child can be alarmed by the non-ringing of the bell. A little party held by the members of an espionage net can be undermined in much the same way:

> Jack and I were booked to sail in May. A few nights before we left, the Sobles invited Jack's brother and me to their apartment for

---

[2] See, for example, Susan Black, "Burglary: II," *New Yorker*, December 14, 1963, pp. 95–96:

> "It's hard to explain to the layman what the ability to recognize a burglar on sight is," Chief Walsh [a New York assistant chief inspector] says. . . . "The burglary-squad detective will see a guy on the street who has an air or a mannerism that arouses his suspicion and makes him want to take a second look. He usually spots something that most people wouldn't notice. Maybe the fellow's in an area where he doesn't seem to have any business. Maybe he keeps turning his head, looking from one side of the street to another for a likely place to burglarize. Maybe he appears to be very nervous; burglars are as full of adrenalin as the rest of us would be if we were doing what we shouldn't be doing, and it shows. Anyway, the knack can't be explained scientifically, though it has often been called 'radar' by the D.A. when he's telling a jury what made a detective follow a suspect who was subsequently arrested for committing a burglary."

A useful general statement of the involvement of police in normal appearances is Harvey Sacks' "Notes on Police Assessment of Moral Character," in David Sudnow, ed., *Social Interaction*, forthcoming. I have drawn also on the full treatment of police cruising by Jonathan Rubinstein, forthcoming.

dinner. His brother warned Jack against going to Moscow, but Jack merely laughed at the idea that this might prove dangerous. "I'm all right," he said. "I'm in high favor at Home."

Nevertheless for Jack and Myra the evening resembled a nightmare because another invited guest, the son of the owner of one of Paris' best-known cafés, failed to appear. In the underground world of the spy, such an unexplained absence can mean catastrophe—or nothing. And, as always when such things happen, they sat waiting, tense and nervous, for the footsteps on the stairs, for the knock on the door that could mean the end.[3]

Thus far appearances, not actualities, have been considered. But clearly, something can seem to be up when in fact, from the point of view of attention actually needed, nothing is up. Contrariwise, something indeed can be up that soon will sharply affect the welfare of the individual, and yet be so unapparent that it escapes his immediate concern. Of course, as has been suggested, over the long run no person is likely to survive or to pass his incapacity on to many descendants if he is constantly in error in monitoring the environment; even within a protective institution he will need to be right about apparent dangers and opportunities. Yet a capacity for error is necessary in any warning system; if the individual is to pick up early signs or furtive ones, then apparently he must be ready to be triggered by false ones.

Individuals seem to recognize that in some environments wariness is particularly important, constant monitoring and scanning must be sustained, and any untoward event calls forth a quick and full reaction. Casinos, for those employed in them, are an example, the concern being the ever-present possibility of theft by players and dealers. Similarly, individuals seem to feel that some of their situations require little guardedness because nothing warranting alarm seems remotely possible. We will see that this conventional continuum can lead to erroneous conceptions.

In considering the tendency for individuals to oscillate between being off guard and being on guard, it is easy to find some who are

[3] Boris Morros, *My Ten Years as a Counterspy* (New York: The Viking Press, Inc., 1959), pp. 92–93.

deer-like, ever ready to be startled, whereas others are either cow-like, slow to be mobilized,[4] or lion-like, unconcerned about predators and wary chiefly when stalking prey.[5] However, a slightly different difference seems more relevant: a difference in capacity to respond to alarming signs effectively with a minimum of disturbance to routine. This can involve more than a capacity to handle emergencies with composure and skill. Also involved: the quick discounting of false alarms; the capacity to deal effectively with events after having allowed them to develop a little further than others safely can; a nose for minute cues that others miss, leading to an earlier than usual awareness of something being up, thus allowing a longer than usual time to cope before it is too late. What we have here is the cool efficacy that is supposed to come from experience and is, in fact, sometimes called "experience." What will then be one man's alarm will be another's opportunity to show experience. Here, of course, is the mark of the professional—the *machismo* of the expert classes. Here the fur thieves who wait routinely until they hear the police siren before ceasing to strip the racks; the policeman who can read signs invisible to civilians which make a car worth stopping and its driver worth approaching with certain contingencies of response adjusted for; the prostitute who is good at distinguishing genuine johns from entrappers before legally compromising acts have occurred;

---

[4] Presumably animals that sleep and lie down a great deal will not be as alive to their surroundings as are those that are constantly on the move. The notable extreme here in imagery and fact is that stately species bred to have nothing immediate to worry about—the cow. See E. S. E. Hafez et al., "The Behavior of Cattle," p. 282, in E. S. E. Hafez, ed., *The Behavior of Domestic Animals* (Baltimore: William and Wilkins Company, 1969; London: Baillière, Tindall and Cassell, 1969), who cites a study that estimates "that Hereford bullocks spend roughly 50 percent of the daylight hours lying down, during most of which time the animals are ruminating."

[5] Ethologists report that when lions in their home range are not stalking or resting, they will move with an appearance of prideful unconcern. See, for example, Rudolf Schenkel, "Play, Exploration and Territoriality in the Wild Lion," p. 21, in P. A. Jewell and Caroline Loizos, eds., *Play, Exploration and Territoriality in Mammals* (London: Zoological Society of London by Academic Press, 1966).

the pit boss who can tell that a player is going to try to "move on the game" before the move is made—this detection being achieved, for example, by checking to make sure that the player maintains the usual cycle of involvement during each play. A student of British truckers provides other examples:

> "I was on my way to work and I could see this bloke on a minicycle wanted to turn but he didn't make a sign, so just in case, I slowed down. Sure enough, he turned straight in front of me. Well, I didn't hit him because I knew what he was going to do, like, but I was annoyed and I slammed the window down and told him, I said: 'You ought to be more careful, mate; if I'd been in a bit more of a hurry, I'd have hit you.' Well, he picked himself up and said: 'I was driving all right. I've passed my test.' So I told him: 'If you drive like that much more, mate, you'll be passing in a fucking hearse.' "
>
> "The next incident occurred at about half-past three in the morning running towards the end of the shift. It was on the return journey of a long run, the straight clearness of the road suddenly turned into bends, hills and high hedges. A man came out of a telephone box on the side of the road, and my driver slowed down considerably. Immediately round the next bend was a lorry with a flat tire, which he just managed to avoid. 'I thought that fella might be a driver ringing for a fitter, so I reckoned his wagon would not be far away.' "[6]

Another point. It can be expected that in human gatherings (as in congregations of other species) some specialization of function will occur in discovering whether or not anything is up. This specialization has two sides.

When one individual emits a distress cry or shows sudden alert in consequence of becoming alarmed, his sound and appearance are likely to serve as powerful evidence to the others that something might be wrong.[7] An individual, then, seems to have a special abil-

[6] Peter G. Hollowell, *The Lorry Driver* (London: Routledge and Kegan Paul, 1968), pp. 16–17.

[7] When considering animals other than man, warning signs can take additional forms. Death cries, visible injuries, and (among fish) chemicals released into the water all can function as alarms. See, for example, Irenäus Eibl-Eibesfeldt, *Ethology: The Biology of Behavior* (New York: Holt, Rinehart and Winston, Inc., 1970), pp. 135–136.

ity to serve as proxy for an alarm, being more effective in this regard than many other parts of the environment. In fact, animals can serve as specialized alarms for species other than their own, including man, and through this a single alarm system can incorporate the special competencies of more than one species.

Second is the special role or slot that gives an individual a collective duty in regard to standing guard and giving alarm: the role of lookout, sentinel, police, and scout. The specialization that enables an individual to split himself into the part that is keeping its eye cocked and the part that is engaged in the routine business at hand is achieved here by using different individuals, the result presumably being an increase in efficiency. The guarded can give their time to routines freely; the guard who makes this possible can be selected for his special competency and his readiness to forsake his own interests in favor of those of the group. The one, then, can do the job of the many, for the many, and do it better. Overlayed on this social device may be another: the use of "watches," ensuring that before one guard becomes tired and ineffective another can take his place.[8]

Just as the individual can use some items from the behavior of his fellows as proxy signs for alarm, so apparently he can use others as "all clear" signals, that is, as evidence that an expressed alarm is over or false.[9] This function, like that of alarm, can become a specialized part of a specialized role.[10]

---

[8] A possibility reported also in the lesser kingdoms. See F. Fraser Darling, *A Herd of Red Deer* (London: Oxford University Press, 1937; New York: Anchor Natural History Library, 1964), p. 204.

[9] In this, of course, humans are like animals, and indeed it is from the ethologist W. John Smith and his forthcoming paper on display behavior among prairie dogs that I take the notion in the first place. John Smith, may I add, has provided me a great deal of help throughout this paper.

[10] An example is provided in the ethology of the chicken:

> When moving into open ground from scrubby patch, one would hear the group approach and then become quiet while the dominant male appeared, usually standing motionless on a fallen log for a few minutes. His posture was erect, tail erect and spread and his wing-diamond . . . pointed almost vertically downwards (the wing-down alert). Eventually he would crow, whereupon the hens would all cross the log and resume their movement and location calls. The

Once it is seen that an individual can function as an alarm relay, finding reason for alarm in one direction and passing this reason on in another, a distinction obviously becomes necessary: that between a sign or an immediate cause for alarm and an ultimate source of it. Grouse that have been frightened into flight are an immediate cause of alarm for a deer, although an ultimate source neither of danger nor of opportunity for it. The man who has flushed the grouse is the ultimate source of alarm, and should he himself be spotted, sniffed, or heard by the deer, he will also be the immediate cause of it. As here described, an immediate cause for alarm is a source of alarming signs; and this source of signs usually is, but need not be, coterminous with the ultimate source of alarm itself.

The simplicity of these distinctions should not blind us to the intricacies of the alarm process. As mentioned, we can take as a general fact that the individual gives a moment's orientation to any event that might prove to be a source of alarm, and that should its innocence not immediately become established, orientation will persist until matters are resolved. Now it seems to be generally true also that others use this patterning of response as a source of information, the assumption being that what one individual has had to give overlong attention to is likely to be something that they ought to check out, too. Thus, first persons to be alarmed can serve as proxy for whatever is alarming. The complication is that overlong glances and looks can then come to be used by their maker as a means for more or less intentionally warning others that there is something about which to be alarmed. And this practice is especially employed, apparently, when the source of alarm is the very person for whom this sign is intended. Thus, an individual who is about to do something that might endanger him—such as turning wrong-way onto a one-way street, or failing to

---

crow was described as an "all clear" signal, and the whole behaviour was similar to that of a broody hen with chicks crossing open ground.

G. McBride, I. P. Parer, and F. Foenander, "The Social Organization and Behaviour of the Feral Domestic Fowl," *Animal Behaviour Monographs*, II (Part 3, 1969), 136–137.

see an obstruction on the sidewalk—can be warned by someone who looks overlong at him—overlong, that is, in terms of the usual scan of attention given to things in the environment. Similarly, when an individual unwittingly encroaches on another's preserves, he may be given an overlong look, this serving as a warning that corrective behavior is required. It is thus that the basic process of scanning the surroundings comes to be ritualized, in the ethological sense of that term, and thrust into the adjustments that those who are mutually present make to one another.

Now, in conclusion, a definitional note about alarms, required in part because the term is an example of that troublesome class of words that refers in common usage both to that which produces a state in the perceiver and the state itself.

It was suggested that an individual who was alarmed could become the proxy of an alarming sign for his conspecifics. He exhibits signs of being alarmed, that is signs *of* alarm, and these in turn become alarming signs—signs *for* alarm for the others. In the case of human specialists in the matter of standing guard, a qualification is necessary. When they detect signs for alarm they may, like their animal counterparts, give alarm by virtue of appearing alarmed. But if they are well trained, they themselves need not become alarmed, need not become in fact the alarming sign for those for whom they stand watch; instead they calmly transmit a "signal," a conventional sign, which, by prearrangement, has been arbitrarily established for this purpose—the purpose of announcing that there is something about which to be alarmed. And this signal is what often is meant by "*the* (or *an*) alarm." (Thus, an alarm can be mechanical, issuing from a signaling machine, not a person.) Taken all together, these various discriminations can put considerable weight on language: an individual's signs of being alarmed (or signs *of* alarm) are not always, but may be, signs *for* alarm (or alarming signs) for others. An alarm signal is an alarming sign for someone, sometimes the person who gives it, but it is not a sign *of* alarm. And, of course, all of these signs and signals must be distinguished from what it is they portend, namely, the basis or source of alarm.

II *The* Umwelt

It has been suggested thus far that the individual's immediate world can be one of two places for him: where easy control is maintained or where he is fully involved in self-preserving action. (The transition between the two places is produced by the justification or dissolution of alarm.) That there are these two possibilities is the first thing to say about the structure of his world. Now we must attempt to get at some of its other characteristics.

A start can be made by returning to the notion of an individual's acquired experience or skill as a factor in determining what he would sense as alarming. When we examine the activity of a practiced pilot, sword swallower, skier, snake-handler, or bomb defuser, it is perfectly plain that his capacity to be at ease with his activity now was preceded by a period, often quite long, when catastrophe seemed everywhere and his attention had to be completely given over to saving his skin. It should be nearly as evident that almost every activity that any individual easily performs now was at some time for him something that required anxious mobilization of effort. To walk, to cross a road, to utter a complete sentence, to wear long pants, to tie one's own shoes, to add a column of figures—all these routines that allow the individual unthinking, competent performance were attained through an acquisition process whose early stages were negotiated in a cold sweat. A series of formal tests is likely to have been involved and solo trials, that is, distantly supervised practice under real, and hence fateful, conditions.[11] To speak here of the individual learning a skill, a pro-

[11] In fact, acquisition is likely to involve intense alarm on the part of two individuals, he who is learning and (during one phase of learning) he who has the job of supervising the learner's experience under "live" conditions. An illustration of this theme is provided by a popular novel that must stand as the only appreciable ethnography we currently have of its

cedure, or a mode of perception entirely intellectualizes the acquisition process. The individual's ease in a situation presumes that he has built up experience in coping with the threats and opportunities occurring within the situation. He acquires a survivably short reaction time—the period needed to sense alarm, to decide on a correct response, and to respond. And as a result, he has not so much come to know the world around him as he has become experienced and practiced in coping with it.

Once it is seen that the situation around the individual is something in which he is routinely exercising a wide range of necessary competencies, some special to his trade, some special to his sex and his social class, and some common to all the adults in his community, we can appreciate that this world is likely to be vulnerable to moments of stress when acquired competence breaks down and the individual is thrown back momentarily on inadequate mastery.

---

topic, Arthur Hailey's *Airport* (New York: Bantam Books, Inc., 1968; London: Michael Joseph and Sauvenir Press, 1968):

> Deliberately, Keith [an air traffic radar controller informally supervising a trainee] allowed the spacing between an American Airlines BAC-400 and a National 727 to become less than it should be; he was ready to transmit quick instructions if the closure became critical. George Wallace [the trainee] spotted the condition at once, and warned Keith, who corrected it.
>
> That kind of firsthand exercise was the only sure way the ability of a new controller could be gauged. Similarly, when a trainee was at the scope himself, and got into difficulties, he had to be given the chance to show resourcefulness and sort the situation out unaided. At such moments, the instructing controller was obliged to sit back, with clenched hands, and sweat. Someone had once described it as "hanging on a brick wall by your fingernails." When to intervene or take over was a critical decision, not to be made too early or too late. If the instructor did take over, the trainee's confidence might be permanently undermined, and a potentially good controller lost. On the other hand, if an instructor failed to take over when he should, a ghastly mid-air collision could result (pp. 148–149).

I have witnessed many times the same agony on the part of Las Vegas pit bosses who had as one of their jobs the breaking in of 21 dealers. Every break-in eventually has to deal to "live action" under circumstances where players almost without exception will delight in exploiting to the hilt any mistake he makes, and no matter how extensive his training on dead tables, he inevitably will make a great number of mistakes. The pit boss knows these mistakes are going to occur, knows they are going to cost the house money, and must watch them happen. As my pit boss once said to me: "Every time I get a new man, I go through hell."

Nor with adults need we wait for occasions when physical skills must be learned at a new job or old competencies reobtained after crippling illnesses. It will always be possible for the practiced individual to find suddenly that he can no longer mobilize himself effectively to cope with what he is used to handling easily. He can become rattled, "shook up."

Not all of the individual's easefulness is based, of course, on long-perfected skills. He has also learned to avoid times, places, activities, and objects that could not be mastered in this way or at least not mastered without more effort than he is willing to make. (If you don't climb mountains, you don't need piton techniques.) Further, controls are institutionalized: fixed alarms tell the individual what bottle has poison, what road is slippery, what slopes are for experts, what parts of the roof are not fenced in, what stairs are unsafe. More important, safety codes are embodied variously in building practices, factory equipment, means of transportation, and consumer goods, all obviating the need for certain forms of care and attentiveness. (The fact that most houses in the United States have a sufficient supply of gas and electricity to accommodate any executioner is something which residents almost never concern themselves about; the techniques of control are well enough established to permit unconcern about anybody but a child or a suicidal.) And most important of all is the individual's acquired understanding of the motives and intent of others around him, this allowing him in many circumstances to treat bystanders as safely disattendable. However, in these different ways, too, the individual may suddenly find that he has unanticipated bases for alarm.

It is to be seen, then, that the world around the individual is highly social in character. Its features are there by virtue of the socially organized training the individual has obtained and by virtue of some kind of collective guarantee regarding the material and human elements in the situation. But in thus being social, the individual's immediate world is neither subjective nor fundamentally different from that of lesser species. Men and animals both live in immediate worlds that they can take for granted while getting on with the business at hand. Both need and both have a capacity for picking up signs for alarm. For both, what makes a precipice a precipice is the physical limits of sure-footedness and the tendency for organisms to splatter when they fall from heights; and what makes a precipice *merely* a precipice is the adaptive competency of animals and men in dealing with paths and footings—whether this competency comes from natural selection, learning, or various mixtures of both.

The role of adaptive competency can be seen nicely by looking at the situation of prey and predator. Between them there is what might be called a "critical distance." It is that maximal distance across which a predator whose intent is known can still catch his prey, an "open strike distance," as it were; or, more conventionally put, it is the minimal distance across which a prey under attack from a predator can easily escape his attentions. A predator that approaches closer than this critical distance to prey is likely to cause it to take defensive action, hence the phrase "flight distance." [12] Now the point is that it is common for prey to graze or play when a predator is well within their range of sight, providing only that orientation to him can be sustained free of intervening blocks to perception and that flight distance is not violated. Flight distance, then, is usually well within "orientation distance," although admittedly some exceptions occur. (An unpleasant feature of poisonous snakes and spiders is that we are often unaware of their presence until it is too late to avoid flight—in short, too late.) Even more to the point, the margin between these two distances is subject to the effects of experience and a large number of other influences.[13] In any case, we are left with the need to con-

---

[12] H. Hediger, *Studies of the Psychology and Behaviour of Captive Animals in Zoos and Circuses* (London: Butterworths Scientific Publications, 1955), pp. 40–42.

[13] As W. John Smith has suggested to me, of relevance can be the apparent state of the predator, the availability of cover, and even the temperature of the surround:

> [There is] an inverse relationship between body temperature and flight distance: the lower the lizard's temperature, the greater the flight distance. . . .
> A cool *Anolis* approached by a predator probably cannot react as quickly nor move as rapidly as if it were warm, but it appears to compensate for this

sider those events within the orientation range of the individual that can and might become a source of immediate concern to him, even though at the time they may be beyond critical distance. The sphere around the individual within which these *potential* sources of alarm are found, I shall call his surround or *Umwelt*, to use a version of Jacob von Uexküll's term.[14] Since sources of alarm typically will provide signs for alarm, the individual's *Umwelt* can be defined as the region around him from within which signs for alarm can come.

The size of *Umwelten* varies considerably according to the species. For animals some sources of alarm are physically distant by human measures such as miles: floods, volcanoes, forest fires, and perhaps stampedes.[15] Some animals can orient to scents, sounds,

---

> by starting to react when the predator is farther away. That *Anolis* are as difficult to catch when they are cold as when warm is evidence that this compensation is effective.

A. Stanley Rand, "Inverse Relationship between Temperature and Shyness in the Lizard *Anolis Lineatopus*," *Ecology*, XLV (Autumn 1964): 864.

[14] The classic statement is his 1934 paper, "A Stroll Through the Worlds of Animals and Men," trans. by Claire H. Schiller as Part One of her *Instinctive Behavior* (New York: International Universities Press, 1957), pp. 5–80.

[15] Terms for referring to distance involve problems. It is easy to employ an established human scale such as the metric to give an "etic" measure of the distance between two points. But when we try to provide such a measure of what one means by "close" and "distant" (in the literal sense), no single scale really works; what one has in mind is close or distant in terms of some consequence for self, such as escaping, catching, catching up to, seeing, talking to, visiting, and so forth, and each of these doings introduces its own (emic) scale, its own variations according to the particular business at hand. When discussing animals, it is treacherous to say of one that something is close or far from it but not much more treacherous than making the same statement about ourselves.

A rough emic measure, employed in some sports, is body lengths, but this is only rough. One is reduced, then, to using distance terms loosely:

> As a rule, small species of animals have a short escape distance, large animals a long one. The wall lizard can be approached to within a couple of yards before it takes to flight, but a crocodile makes off at fifty. The sparrow hops about unconcerned almost under our feet, thus like the mouse, having a very short flight distance, while crows and eagles, deer and chamois, for instance, have much longer ones.

Hediger, *op. cit.*, p. 41.

and configurations of movement from a very considerable distance.[16] But by and large these distances are exceptional. Typically events that are distal in terms, say, of hundreds of yards, are neither actual nor potential sources of immediate alarm. In the case of man, there is, of course, one important complication. For although he can hardly spot a moth the way a bat can or catch a warning whiff from the distance a deer can, still man can use artificial receptors of various kinds, such as the telephone, telegraph, radar screens, and the like; and these can bring to his attention, through relays of signs, sources of alarm that are many miles away, or, indeed (as in the case of warnings about bombs placed in buildings), sources that are right at hand but totally hidden. The point, of course, about these windows in the individual's surround or *Umwelt* is that although they bring him in touch with very distant matters, these matters are not commonly ones that must be addressed immediately lest opportunity be lost or danger result. Air traffic controllers work in small rooms, yet are involved in uncomfortably large *Umwelten;* others of us, however, in spite of having routine access to artificial extensions of perception, are not (with certain exceptions) likely to have our *Umwelten* extended thereby, since we do not ordinarily obtain cause for immediate action through these channels.

Another general point. The signs the individual obtains can be seen not merely as indicators of objects but also as indications of courses of developing action, whether blind and unintended as in the case of undirected, natural events, or planned and aimed, as in the case of projects of action undertaken by intelligent actors. Note, in the latter case, reliable indicators can be found easily because they are provided purposely, and they can be provided purposely because the provider usually accepts the responsibility of adhering to his indicated plan of action.

In general, then, we can define the individual's surround or *Um-*

---

[16] For example: "Individuals or groups of persons moving about must keep at least one-half mile from condor nests in order to avoid disturbance of the parent birds." See Carl B. Koford, *The California Condor* (New York: Dover Publications, Inc., 1966; London: Constable, 1966), p. 109.

welt as that region around him within which such signs for alarm as he is alive to can originate and within which the sources of this alarm are also located. And for the individual person, this is likely to be measured by means of a radius that is only yards long. His body is what he mainly can become immediately concerned about, and it is principally vulnerable to hits, falls, shots, crushings, poisonings, burning, drowning, and smothering. If these assaults are to occur, they will have to originate where he cannot readily avoid them, and this is *usually* no more than a few yards away. As we shall have to see, the upsetting thing about snipers with telescopic sights is not the general fact that they constitute a danger but that they extend markedly the area over which a human target must show active concern. The interesting thing about a police force whose members are in close intercommunication is that a hunted person's age-old act of bodily escaping the approach of one such predator may bring him to the attention of an ever-extending network of them. Atomic weaponry, of course, is coming to transform the world into one *Umwelt* which includes us all, and perhaps therefore ceases to be something to which one can respond in a manner that is evolutionarily rooted, there being no place out of range.

In human communities, sentinels and agents of social control are often the same person; often he who has the job of detecting alarm will also have the job of dealing with its source. With specialized resources for picking up alarms and specialized means of doing something about the trouble, these individuals can find themselves, like air traffic controllers, in *Umwelten* that have larger than ordinary dimensions and that are more independent than usual of standard boundaries. A humble domestic example might be cited:

> In preliminary tests residents in Brownsville homes have been found to be very conscious of noises and activity taking place in the stair halls. Because their children play and gather in stairwells and halls, adults seem to be unconsciously alert for loud noises or even interruptions of the din of children at play. A sudden silence in the

stair hall was found to bring mothers to the door as readily as a loud yell or crash.[17]

The extreme is found in national defense systems that link early warning designs to strategic air commands, resulting in something like hemispheric *Umwelten*, these being another first for man.

The *Umwelt* or surround is an egocentric area fixed around a claimant, typically an individual. However, individuals do not stay put, so the surround moves, too. As the individual moves, some potential signs for alarm move out of effective range (as their sources move out of relevance) while others, which a moment ago were out of range, now come into it. A bubble or capsule of events thus seems to follow the individual around, but actually, of course, what is changing is not the position of events but their at-handedness; what looks like an envelope of events is really something like a moving wave front of relevance.

This notion of a moving bubble is only approximate. As suggested, from the perspective of any individual, different sources of alarm will involve different critical (and orientation) distances. For example, on the sidewalk the individual will have a vehicular concern to avoid collisions, and this ordinarily will involve attention to the immediate layer of persons encircling him; those one or more persons removed will not greatly concern him. (Of course, this moving sphere itself will expand and contract depending on traffic density.) However, on an otherwise empty street at night the individual can find that the appearance of a pedestrian a half a block away can be a matter of concern. Also, wherever smallish rooms or ritually well-bounded, small, open places are found, his *Umwelt* will not move as the individual does, since almost any place he takes up in such fully bounded places is likely to expose him to the same potential sources of alarms. Walking along the street, the individual's surround follows him; walking around a room, it does not, or does so only to a small degree. Note, the in-

[17] Columbia University Project for Security Design (now of New York University), special publication: *Questionnaire Design for the Improvement of Security in Urban Residential Areas* (n.d.), p. 8.

dividual is likely to concentrate his scanning for signs for alarm at the moment and place of his entering a bounded area. For often it will be at the doorway that he will have to notice alarming things if he is to notice them in time. Coincidentally, it is at the entrance that he will be far enough away from others present to allow his examining them with minimal incursive offense. Moreover, at the entrance, his legitimate need to adjust clothing, receive a welcome, obtain information, inform as to his objective, etc., will provide him a ready cover for the pause to scan. As will be argued, for those already in the room, the entrance and the individual just appearing at it will be worth keeping an eye on, too.

III *The Overdetermination of Normalcy*

Until now we have taken as our point of reference the individual (our subject) who looks around himself for alarming signs, the assumption being that for him there are normal appearances, namely ones whose source he can disattend for the time. The cast that events are to take if he is to be allowed to disattend them will therefore play an important role, but we have considered only half the reasons why.

Of the many matters in the individual's *Umwelt* that can be a source of alarm for him, one requires special attention from us: other individuals. I take it as a central fact of life that they who might, through their doings, alarm an individual, very often will be concerned about this fact themselves. And to consider this we will have to introduce an entirely new point of view, although perhaps not many new facts.

The concern of those who might give alarm has standard forms. They may feel that they constitute no real basis for alarm but that their own interests will be furthered if they can convince the subject that he should be alarmed, should think something is up when it isn't. (This is the situation, in effect, with defensive mimicry in the lower animal orders.) They may be concerned to accentuate a real basis of alarm. More commonly, however, they may feel that alarm is really ill-founded or false and, in addition, wish to avoid giving it. Or they will be concerned to prevent a real basis for alarm from being discovered: as predators they are likely to want to get close enough to pounce; as prey, they are likely to want to stay out of the line of untender attention.

Whichever of these various motives the others have, they will have to address themselves to normal appearances. And with the exception of the case in which they want to cause false alarm or ensure the taking of warranted alarm, their concern will be to find a way to cover or disguise themselves and their doings so as to give the victim the correct or incorrect impression that nothing remarkable is afoot. Among lower animals these tricks are acquired by natural selection; among men, intelligence and learning play greater roles, often with loss of elegance in design. In any case, what is a normal appearance for the subject becomes the cloak that his others must discern, tailor, and wear. (When their concern is to give false alarm or ensure warranted alarm, then what the subject sees as normal must be addressed, too, although not, as it were, dressed.) To disappear from sight, to melt from view, is not, then, to hide or to sneak away; it is to be present but of no concern.

Note that when others address themselves to a subject's view of what is normal, different components of his *Umwelt* will be involved at different times. Sometimes they will be concerned about particular points in his physical scene, for example, places where monitoring devices might be concealed or might be thought to be concealed. Often they will be concerned about his view of how they themselves would appear if they were to be unalarming for him, as when a team of thieves breaks up immediately after a crime, the members attempting to saunter away in different directions without drawing attention to themselves from the citizenry.[18]

---

[18] A note is required concerning the broad class of desperate actions such as crimes and sabotage whose doing can damage their doers should potential victims become alarmed. Three distinct phases are possible in such actions: a "clandestine" phase, in which the alarming action is executed en-

The unit to be normalized may be a "with," as when a vacationing family turns out to be a troupe put together to try to smuggle dope across the face of customs agents or when a loving couple turns out to be two saboteurs using the only cover available to them. In the "big con" it is the whole of a social establishment over the course of an hour or so that is staged. In a bank robbery we will consider later, the unit involved is a ten-hour strip of three blocks of the life of a community. Any such unit within the *Umwelt* of a suspicious person can give him concern and therefore become a structure which potential suspects will be obliged to manipulate.

Initially it was said that normal appearances are what the

---

tirely out of the vicinity of those who would be most alarmed by it; a "covert" phase, in which matters for alarm are concealed in a guise of some kind right under the eyes of the subjects; an "exposed" phase, in which the alarming action is performed openly before those who will be alarmed by what they see and in which some sort of coercive control is usually necessary. It is, of course, the covert phase that involves the maintenance of normal appearances.

It is hard to imagine an action that is all exposure, although if the target is entirely isolated, then it might be possible to have an entirely clandestine action. However, there are crimes, such as check forging, which are entirely covert, this being one of the qualities of this sort of work that practitioners find attractive. Most actions, however, involve two or three different kinds of phases in variable sequence. Thus, a successful bank job presumably involves clandestine planning, covert casing, a covert approach, exposure during the actual robbery and immediate getaway, return to a covert phase as soon as the team is clear of any chasers, and finally a clandestine divvying up of the take. Over-all, these variations tend to exhibit a single basic sequence: normal appearance, then exposure, then normal appearance.

These distinctions involve complications. When a team engages in an activity that would cause a subject alarm and arranges to avoid alarming him by engaging in it someplace that is hidden and distant from him, the members are, in effect, maintaining the normal appearances of those occasions and places under his view in which they otherwise would pursue their activity. Further, the same act can qualify differently depending on the point of reference—a fact that turns out to inform us about the structure of the activity. For example, once inside the bank, the robbers will adhere to normal appearances until strategically placed and then must select one of two strategies: either they try to manage the operation in the

individual has come with time and practice to learn that he can cope with easefully. As his competencies mature, what he expects of his surround will become decreasingly available to his conscious mind; less and less will he be able to tell us what these normal appearances are. We also have seen that others—now in the role of predator or prey trying to avoid causing him alarm—will also have to be concerned about normal appearances. However, the normal appearances that they are concerned with are not normal appearances *for them* but normal appearances *of them* for the enemy. This means that they will have to have some conscious conception of what is natural for the subject so that they might set the scene in accordance with it. They are forced to become phenomenologists, close students of everyday life, not, of course, their own but

---

main covertly so that the patrons and most workers in the bank do not know a robbery is taking place, the teller alone being addressed; or they do the job openly, exposed to all as wrongdoers, control being maintained by firearms and perhaps some anonymity achieved with masks. In either case, the team will pin its plan and its hopes on keeping the operation covert as far as persons outside the bank are concerned. House robbery has the same structure, except that if no one is home or everyone asleep then no one need be directly controlled inside, and the chief points of vulnerability are the moments of entrance and departure. The same could be said of the device of tunneling into the bank from a neighboring building, except that here there is the added advantage that entrance and departure are made at a point removed from the scene of the theft and are therefore considerably less risky than usual. Note, most hideouts in which clandestine activity occurs are themselves not hidden totally; those in them are maintaining normal appearances before someone.

I might add that in the planning of operations there is often an effort to minimize the period of exposure in favor of the other two. (Involved here can be an effort to maximize the safe abort period, that is, postpone as long as possible in the operation the act from which no covert withdrawal is possible.) The choice between covert and clandestine, when there is a choice, can itself be complex. Here see Christopher Felix, *The Spy and His Masters* (London: Secker and Warburg, 1963), pp. 26–27. Note, too, that in the overt phase of an action, the performers have the subtle social-psychological problem of showing enough savagery of resolve to be taken quite seriously at their word but not so much as to produce a plight that male captives might feel impelled to heroically resist. (In the matter of the dynamics of desperate acts I draw on conversations with John Irwin, of the Department of Sociology, San Francisco State College.)

what the subject takes to be everyday life. Whereas experience leads him to become decreasingly aware of what he is taking for granted, experience leads them to become increasingly aware of what he is taking for granted, and so it can be wise to study him by studying them.

It is here, then, that nefarious undertakings become especially useful for the student; for these undertakings constantly require the production of normal appearances under freshly difficult circumstances, thereby drawing attention to structures and competencies that everyone takes for granted:

> Gold smuggling calls for a great deal of stamina and costs a great deal of sweat. The favorite smuggling technique is to use a thin canvas or nylon corset, bearing thirty or more one-kilo bars of gold slotted neatly into rows all around the garment, strapped to the torso. . . . The weight of this golden corset is crippling: it grips you like a vise; the knees buckle slightly. Sitting down is not much relief; trying to stand up again while maintaining a casual air becomes a feat of strength. Walking becomes a deliberate effort with careful strides to maintain equilibrium. "Remember," says the man handing out the jacket, "that you can easily be knocked off balance if you are bumped or jostled in a crowd." . . . ; it is all too easy to collapse ungracefully. Which could be most embarrassing in the midst of a busy airport under the eyes of the authorities.[19]

[19] Timothy Green, *The Smuggler* (New York: Walker and Company, 1969; London: Michael Joseph, 1969), p. 211. I would like to note here that the study of criminals has been influenced and supported by every fashion in academic social analysis: abnormal psychology, social work, urban ecology, occupational sociology, national policy. Throughout this essay still another concern is advocated. The argument is that the important thing about criminals—and other social desperadoes such as children, comics, saboteurs, and the certified insane—is not what they do or why they do it. Nor is it necessary to look into the darkness of their souls in order to learn about the darkness of our own. (Darkness isn't any longer news; it is now known that here we are all an equal match for one another.) The importance of these strays is not in the cue they provide as to what, in our heart of hearts, we do also, but rather in the contrastive light their situation throws on what, in doing what we do, we are doing. A radical ethnography must take ordinary persons doing ordinary things as the central issue. What is accomplished during such acts? What do these doings actively presuppose? If new and gen-

I have argued that the subject scanning his surround for alarming signs and falling back into ease when he finds that everything seems normal has produced in his expectations the cover that those who might be threatened, or might threaten (or who might be seen wrongly as threatening and not want to) must attend. But they must concern themselves with something else, too. When those who would go unnoticed are concerned about the success of their venture, their anxiety over discovery may show in what is called furtiveness. They attend the subject closely but try to conceal this attentiveness by studiously keeping their eyes or face pointed elsewhere, occasionally stealing a glance. They manifest "orientation disjunction," whereby the usual alignment among trunk, shoulders, face and eyes is breached, and one part of the person points in the direction of the subject while the other parts, under greater control, point in an innocent direction. They nicely maintain the proprieties, or breach them in minor ways, but the impression is given that propriety has become a matter of conscious concern, as it very often is, for example, for the innocent motorist when a cruiser car happens to draw up alongside or behind him. Moreover, in appreciating that the subject has (or might think he has) cause for alarm concerning them (an appreciation deriving ultimately from the tendency of individuals to take the role of the other), they initiate the response that his discovery would produce in them and then must choke back this beginning, covering their concern with a tightly held cloak of unconcern. The subject, in turn, may read these various nervous gestures, these furtive behaviors, as alarming signs. Understandably, furtive appearances are among the most important signs the individual looks for; the slightest breath of them has the power of stopping him short, causing him to look again at what otherwise might be the most innocuous others in his surround. Critical distance thus can be extended to orientation distance.[20] And those who conceal matters under

---

eral answers cannot be found for these questions, then we should admit failure and see ourselves more as bad engineers than as bad naturalists.

[20] Apparently sensitivity to furtiveness is not something invented by man. Darling, for example, writes:

what is normal appearances for another will have two different things to conceal: the facts of the matter and the fact that they are making an effort to conceal them. In Ekman's terms, they will be concerned both with leakage and deception cues.[21]

It was suggested that when the subject senses that something is up, his attention and concern are mobilized; adaptive behavior occurs if the alarm proves "real," but if reassuring information is acquired, the alarm proving false, his concentration will decay quickly. This notion of reassuring information has a special role, however, when it is other persons who are the reason for alarm. For individuals who cause alarm can, in the face of this reaction, provide evidence that the alarm is false. They provide an account, underlined by a request or apology, suggesting that although things look strange, they are really explicable, and, furthermore, are explicable in a way that will remove cause for concern. In thus accounting for their act, the alarming individuals need not show that they are acting properly or from ordinary concerns—only that they have a reason for their action and that once this reason is understood by the subject, he will see the act as one that need not disturb him further. That is what is meant when it is said that those who have caused alarm have a good explanation—

> Let us note the reactions of deer at a distance of two hundred and fifty yards watching an observer walking along a footpath. At the first glimpse their heads are raised and the two forefeet come together. These two movements are synchronous. They stand motionless in whatever position they are and watch the person walking. As long as he keeps on walking all is well. They are not frightened and they do not move. But if the observer stops, probably they will go. If he makes any stealthy movements within their sight, such as crawling in the heather or getting behind a rock, they will certainly run away. Human beings in certain places, in certain postures, and gently moving on their way, are harmless creatures, it seems, but highly dangerous under other sets of conditions.

(Darling, *op. cit.*, p. 203.) I would like to suggest the human capacity to detect orientation disjunction in others is everything an animal could ask for.

[21] Paul Ekman and Wallace V. Friesen, "Nonverbal Leakage and Clues to Deception," *Psychiatry*, XXXII (1969): 88–108, esp. p. 89. It is understandable, then, that syndicates that organize smuggling may issue their couriers tranquilizers to take at border crossings, allowing them better to conceal their concern about concealing. (See Green, *op. cit.*, p. 223.)

something, note, they can have even though they may not have a good excuse for causing anxiousness in the first place.

Accounts, then, may be provided the individual when his *Umwelt* suddenly ceases to maintain normal appearances for him, and the explanation given him need not assimilate the alarming event to *these* particular appearances, but to any ones that, were they to appear and be understood, would be seen as no real cause for alarm. Here, then, is a standard for measuring presence of mind, one involving the ability to come up quickly with the kind of accountings that allow a disturbing event to be assimilated to the normal;[22] and we have a base against which to perceive bad accounts, namely, ones that do not dispel the observer's suspicions. (Note, this distinction between effective and ineffective accounts should not be confused with another, that between true and false ones.) Thieves, of course, have a special need to construct false, good accounts at strategic moments and have a word, "con," to cover ability in this sort of covering. Possessing this quality, thieves are blessed and thus speak of having the "gift" of it. As suggested, there is much cause for its practice. For example, when burglars are caught in an apartment, their job is to provide an accounting that will dispel the notion that they might be what in fact they are. Among the possibilities, they can feign drunkenness, claim that the manager let them into the wrong apartment, or, best of all, approach the resident as he enters and, before the latter has a chance to ask the trespassers for an account, say that they are the house security officers and demand an explanation of why the occupant left the door unlocked.[23] A good example of con can be cited from the other side—the near side—of the law, the occasion being the bugging of a loan shark's office on the New York

[22] Wit of this kind is a utilitarian branch of one of the great central qualities of situational life, namely, composure, a less instrumental component being *sang-froid*, the ability to face embarrassing events without becoming visibly embarrassed. Other branches of the family are considered in Goffman, *Interaction Ritual* (New York: Anchor Books, 1967), pp. 222–228.

[23] Susan Black, "Burglary-I," *New Yorker*, December 7, 1963, pp. 116–117.

waterfront at midnight by two agents from the District Attorney's office:

> We had just installed the microphone and dropped the wire out the window when the door swung open and all the lights were switched on. Three tough-looking hoods stood in the doorway. One, who seemed to be the spokesman, said, "What the hell are you doing?"
>
> I would like to say that it was my quick thinking that saved the day but actually it was Bill O'Sullivan's agile mind. In a voice full of indignation he said angrily, "Don't you people have any consideration?"
>
> The trio seemed to have been taken off balance for a moment. One of the gorillas said, "What do you mean, Mac? This happens to be our joint."
>
> Bill dramatically pointed to the electric clock on the wall. "Do you see that Western Union clock?"
>
> One of the fellows said, "So what?"
>
> "That clock of yours was out of order," Bill said, "and because you people didn't have the consideration to call us, every clock on the West Side is out of order."
>
> The three tough-looking gentlemen actually looked surprised. Bill went on to describe very graphically how all over the city from 14th Street to the Staten Island Ferry hundreds of clocks were stopped and had to be reset.
>
> "Do you know it has taken us an hour and a half to fix this one clock?" he demanded.
>
> "Hell, Mac," the spokesman said, "I'm sorry. We didn't know the clock was broken."
>
> "Well, make it a habit to look at it once in a while," Bill said. "Let's gather up the tools," he said to me. I threw everything in our bag.
>
> As we went out Bill turned and said, "Will you boys lock up?"
>
> The three hoods, just staring at the clock, nodded dumbly.[24]

---

[24] Harold R. Danforth and James D. Horan, *The D.A.'s Man* (New York: Crown Publishers, Inc., 1957), pp. 158–159, cited in Samuel Dash et al., *The Eavesdroppers* (New Brunswick, N.J.: Rutgers University Press, 1959), pp. 75–76.

What has been said about the provision of accounts also can be said about the provision of other types of remedial work, such as apology and restitution. If, for example, pedestrians see a motorist drive into a parked car, ruin a fender, and drive off without looking back, they can feel that their *Umwelt* suddenly has contained action so improper that, even though they themselves are not directly involved, alarm is sensed along with a desire to take some action against the offender. If, however, the motorist stops, gets out, surveys the damage he has done, and then writes a note which he leaves under the damaged car's windshield wiper, witnesses can go on about their business, sensing that there is no further need of action on their part. It then becomes not so much normal appearances as the appearances of being restitution-minded that the offender will want to adopt:

> SHAMOKIN, PA. (AP) A hit-and-run driver fooled several witnesses who saw him hit another automobile.
>
> The driver got out of his car after an accident, went to the damaged car and left this note:
>
> "I have just hit your car. People are watching me. They think I'm leaving my name. But I'm not."
>
> The note was signed, "the wrecker." [25]

Here, then, a necessary modification in perspective. From the point of view of a particular individual, there will be a limited, and perhaps relatively small, number of appearances that can strike him immediately as being normal and worthy of no more than a glance. Other appearances will cause alarm. However, when that alarm is produced by human agencies, the subject often exhibits a tendency to hold off responding until the agent has a chance to offer an account and possibly an apology for the odd and alarming thing that has happened. A woman walking down a city street can be at ease when a strange man accosts her and asks for her stockings, providing that he then explains that hers have a run, that he needs the nylon to strain the paint he is using on the neighboring half-painted building, and that he will, of course, pay her for new

---

[25] *The New York Times*, May 10, 1970.

ones.[26] Another example. Those who guard anchored ships during wartime are likely to oblige any small boat that tries to approach to keep its distance. Nonetheless, it has proven possible to deliver an explosive device to a rudder in that manner simply by appearances that provide an accounting that transforms a small approaching boat into a boat that is (apparently) not *really* approaching at all:

> A short time later a lone man in a motor-boat in New York harbour appeared to be having engine trouble. He drifted closer to a ship so heavily loaded with munitions that her Primsoll mark was just awash. Lookouts aboard watched him drift under the counter, hammering on his engine the while. They lost interest. If they recalled the incident later, when far at sea a powerful explosion ripped the rudder and nearly lost them their ship, there is nothing to show it.[27]

Furthermore, the same pacification can be provided by a bystander who attempts to offer an account for an alarming non-human event or one produced by a third party. And it seems that no matter how bizarre and threatening an alarming sight may be, an effective accounting can be discovered for it, that is, an account, true or false, that will allay alarm. This means that normal appearances will have an open character to them. What is normal on first sight may be highly restricted, sufficiently so to provide a practical simulation task for those who want to be sure to escape a subject's attention; but there is no way to describe in detail the number of abnormalities that can be rendered unalarming by creative accounting. The accounter has the world of meanings to draw on; his con alone need be his guide.

Another matter is involved. Once we see that those who would conceal in order to avoid creating alarm must address themselves to the subject's notion of normal appearances, it is apparent that different others with different matters that would be alarming for him will be obliged nonetheless to employ the same cover. For ex-

---

[26] A purported occurrence reported by Herb Caen, *San Francisco Chronicle*, October 31, 1965.

[27] Allison Ind, *A History of Modern Espionage* (London: Hodder and Stoughton, 1965), p. 93.

ample, if a pickpocket is to approach close enough to the subject to pick his pocket, he will want to give an impression of being "like anyone else"; in fact, ideal competence demands that when the victim discovers the loss, he should not even be able to remember who had been near enough to commit the act. This same guise may be employed by he who has a different intent:

> Another method of knife attack or assassination, not uncommon in some areas of the world, may be encountered. It is as old as history and was a method taught to certain groups for use in assassination in German-occupied areas during World War II.
>
> The assassin spies his victim in a crowd and approaches him from the front. His knife is held in his hand with the hilt down and the blade lying flat along the inside of the forearm, or concealed up the sleeve. The handle, of course, is concealed by the fingers. The assassin, with the knife in this position, faces the intended victim, walking toward him. As he reaches a point directly opposite the victim, a simple movement of his wrist frees the blade, and a short arm movement, as he passes, plunges it into the kidney area of the victim. The knife is either left sticking in the wound or may be pulled out while the assassin walks on through the crowd, his movement generally undetected.[28]

And if instead of intending to pick pockets or stick kidneys, the task were to maintain close protective surveillance over the subject without his knowing it, then again the same appearance of being an anyone, the same civil inattention, the same unfurtiveness, the same show of properly going about one's own separate business would have to be maintained. Indeed, those who are predators and want to conceal a threat to the subject and those who are prey and want to conceal from the subject the opportunity presented by their vulnerability must needs address the same design—what the subject will define as normal appearances. And, as suggested, the question as to which side of the law the subject is on need not be relevant. A man covertly carrying $20,000 in a brown paper bag will try to appear before others to be someone who has been

[28] Rex Applegate, *Crowd and Riot Control* (Harrisburg, Pennsylvania: The Stackpole Company, 1964), pp. 460–461.

shopping, and dramaturgically it does not seem to matter whether he has forcibly taken the funds from a bank and wants to avoid the attentions of the police, or whether he is taking the funds to the bank for deposit and wants to avoid the attention of robbers.

IV *Acting Natural*

Consider now some further burdens sustained by normal appearances—ones that strike at the very notions of the subject and his others. It was argued that in order to preserve the subject's sense that nothing was up, others might have to address themselves to what he considered to be normal, including his version of what they would be like if they were to be the sorts of others who could be overlooked. It is this business of the others making themselves look like what the subject will see as ordinary that I want to consider here in detail.

As already implied, the subject's others can have two dramaturgic tasks. First, they can try to play out roles that are alien to them, as when a policeman acts like a graduate student in order to penetrate a radical organization, or a thief wears a telephone company uniform in order to get into a house. It is this sort of subterfuge that fits easiest with the distinction I have employed between subject and others. In fact, however, there are strict, practical limits to disguise; an actor who takes on a part that is too far removed from what might be a "real" possibility for him is not likely to survive detection very long.

The second task of others is to conceal their own concern about giving themselves away, lest this concern itself give them away. They might say that in addition to acting out identities that are unalarming and uninteresting to the subject, they must also "act natural," that is, conduct these identities as though the issue of inadvertently giving alarm, or the issue of becoming alarmed, were not present. But this manner of acting out an alien identity is not itself very alien to these actors, being similar to the manner in which they would act out their own selves were they to have no great concern about the response of the subject. When others make an effort to conceal deception cues, then, what they must do is consciously act out a style of behaving that is in fact their own. A "self-enactment" is required, a simulation of the self, a calculated bit of acting, an impersonation of oneself.[29]

A consideration of this self-enactment leads to complications that I want to examine at length. It is plain that the need to act natural, to act as though there were no reason to be apprehensive, is not restricted to the subject's others; he has it, too. And with

---

[29] Problems of "frame" need not confuse us here. In everyday speech, the phrase "acting natural" is used to refer both to someone who seems indeed to be unalarmed and unconcerned about giving alarm (what might be called "behaving natural") *and* to someone who merely seems to be trying to assure this judgment of his behavior, thereby "enacting behaving natural." Both manners of behavior can be distinguished easily from what a stage actor does. When we say the latter is adept at acting natural, we mean he is good at staging behaving natural, a different kind of art (for example, it is legitimate) from enacting behaving natural. Of course, good actors can also stage enacting behaving natural. And off the stage an individual may sometimes find it in his interests to enact enacting behaving natural, with what chance of success I do not know. I will continue to use the term "acting natural" in multiple ways, allowing the context to establish particular meaning, because explications here can create more difficulty than they resolve, indeed may well have already.

I must add that in opposing "behaving natural" to the staging or to the enacting of this pattern, I do not mean to fall back upon the common-sense distinction between the genuine and the false. An individual may perform a role with genuine spontaneity, unfurtiveness, unself-consciousness and forthrightness. Often this open style comes from his having performed the role a long time, and with consistent support and approval from audiences. Often, in turn, this tenure and support means his role is legitimate; he is socially authorized to perform and can defend his right to perform against all doubters. But facility and legitimacy need only be distinguished, and it becomes clear that one may be found without the other. Moreover, when the individual acts in a genuinely forthright manner (often because of the support he has obtained in his role and the legitimacy of his claim to it), he is still doing that which he has had to learn to do (often when he felt unnatural in what he was doing), that which is culturally prescribed, that which functions as a display to convince audiences, and that which, when something goes wrong, he can become self-conscious about.

him, as we shall see, the enactment of own self will not stop with the matter of inhibiting or covering signs of furtiveness.

Here is the argument. When a subject senses that things are normal, he is likely to exude signs of calmness and ease. His manner will show that he feels that nothing is up and that those in his presence are no cause for alarm. Now if indeed he comes to sense that something is (or might be) up, he may feel it best to advertise that he is suspicious so as to forestall action from those he suspects—a growing practice, incidentally, in connection with closed-circuit monitoring devices that are conspicuously deployed to discourage shoplifters and larcenous employees. But more often, I think, he may feel that the best way to cope is to give those who are a cause for alarm (whether because they constitute a threat or an opportunity) a sense that he has not yet come to suspect matters. If they do not know that he suspects, they will continue in a tack that is, after all, partly being dealt with by him; but if he lets them know that he knows things are not as they seem, then they are likely to change their tack, which could worsen his situation. His signs of suspicion could make them suspicious.[30] So after he has discovered that something is up, he must model his conduct and actions according to how someone like himself would act, were he to feel that the situation was normal. The routines that over time have become automatic for him, inaccessible to consciousness, must then suddenly be managed consciously, and in consequence the individual will come to feel that he is putting on a show, a performance, an enactment. (This will be, of course, an act for which he already has all the props, knows all the lines, and has been well cast; this will also be an act performed to players who are unwittingly giv-

[30] The term "suspicious" is used in everyday speech, interestingly, to refer both to *events* that give rise to suspicion and to the *feeling* or sense that something is suspect. This dual usage could be taken as evidence of how deeply embedded the interactive character of these signs is, the more so since both usages imply that there may be alarming intent behind innocent appearances. (On the other hand, to speak of a "strange" or "peculiar" sound is to refer to something that might give alarm but that need not involve intentional concealment of something portentous.) As already suggested, the term "alarm" has a similar ambiguity.

ing him exactly the right cues at exactly the right times and are helping in ways they know not to gentle him into a good performance.) Not only must he suppress his signs of anxiety, he must also continue on with what he would be doing were he to suspect nothing. But at that point he has begun to enact himself and is no longer merely the subject; he is an other staging an extensive show for other subjects.

Treating together the subject and his others for the purpose of looking at self-enactment, we find three contexts in which to examine this phenomenon. The first has already been illustrated: it is the situation in which the individual finds himself when he discovers that the way he behaves when everything is normal is a design that he himself may want to employ consciously on his own behalf. Note that his reliance on this guise in this situation can be great, indeed, sometimes pathetic. Witness the vain and painful effort of someone sitting beside an obstreperous drunk on public transportation; witness the effort of the individual to act as if the drunk were either not there or not a special point of concern, in either case not something to cause his seatmate to appear to be anything but a person in a situation in which all appearances are normal and nothing is up. Or, even more desperate, is the following reported behavior:

> NEW YORK (AP)—It lasted only 45 minutes, but to 14 year-old Jill Parker it seemed like hours that she lay on her bed wondering when he would kill her.
>
> It all began early yesterday morning when the pretty young high school freshman heard the shuffling of feet and saw a man come into her darkened bedroom.
>
> She pretended she was asleep and pulled the sheet over her face. The man lay down on the bed beside her, fully clothed, and pulled the sheet from her face.
>
> He didn't touch her, she told police. He just stared into her face.
>
> "I was so nervous that even though I tried to keep my eyelids closed, the lids were fluttering," she recalled. "My heart pounded so hard, I was afraid he'd hear the heart-beats."
>
> "I tried to pull the sheet over my head, again pretending I was

> tossing in my sleep," she said. "I didn't want him to see how nervous I was."
>
> "But he kept pulling the sheet down so that he could look at me. I was sure he was going to kill me."
>
> And so it went on—for 45 tormenting minutes.
>
> Suddenly, the family poodle, Gigi, sensed a stranger in the house and broke the silence in the large, 15-room house with a shrill bark.
>
> "I knew the barking would awaken my parents," Jill explained later. "It was then that I started screaming, 'Mommy, there's somebody in my bed'." [31]

Ordinary walking may have to be put on, too, especially, presumably, by the half of our population whose appearance is, and is designed to be, appreciated by all and savored by some:

> A young woman is walking down a city street. She is excruciatingly aware of her appearance and of the reaction to it (imagined or real) of every person she meets. She walks through a group of construction workers who are eating lunch in a line along the pavement. Her stomach tightens with terror and revulsion; her face becomes contorted into a grimace of self-control and fake unawareness; her walk and carriage become stiff and dehumanized. No matter what they say to her, it will be unbearable. She knows that they will not physically assault her or hurt her. They will only do so metaphorically. What they will do is impinge on her. They will use her body with their eyes. They will evaluate her market price. They will comment on her defects or compare them to those of other passers-by. They will make her a participant in their fantasies without asking if she is willing. They will make her feel ridiculous, or grotesquely sexual, or hideously ugly. Above all, they will make her feel like a thing.[32]

Nor is the conscious performance of the self restricted to the basic positions—sitting, lying, and walking. Circumstances can cause the individual to feel that a whole flow of his complex activity is put on even though it is the same activity that was once "genuine." Dramaturgically, that is what lying is about. Telling an un-

---

[31] *San Francisco Sunday Examiner and Chronicle*, May 15, 1966.

[32] Meredith Tax, "The Woman and Her Mind: The Story of Everyday Life," *Women's Liberation: Notes from the Second Year* (1970), p. 12, cited in Norman Mailer, "The Prisoner of Sex," *Harper's*, March 1971, p. 48.

truth allows and obliges the teller to continue on in some role and guise which no longer would be viable were the truth known—a condition especially pronounced in small-scale, intimate social organizations in which he who lies remains in the immediate and continued presence of those to whom he has lied. To continue to be an apparently loyal employee knowing that one quietly has made an agreement to leave shortly for another firm is to transform ordinary work and ordinary collegial relations into something of a game. To continue to cohabit with one's spouse while secretly having an affair or to continue with domestic routines, secretly knowing that one's spouse secretly is having an affair, or to begin planning for the divorce before one's spouse knows that joint consideration of the possibility of separation is slated to be given, is to transform humdrum household activity into an ironic and perhaps nasty show. Ordinarily, then, what makes performances false is not the creation of a new, false routine but the continuation of an old, valid one under altered circumstances, at least, so it seems, in contemporary society.[33] I believe that under these circumstances ordinary people feel moral qualms and also feel doubts about their stage abilities. Further, in finding themselves "on," they tend to experience a special kind of self-consciousness.[34] Yet it seems they soon discover that they can do a better job than they had thought of acting as if nothing were up.

---

[33] It might be noted that in the world of Shakespeare's plays, self-enactment was a basis of falsity but apparently not the central one. In the comedies the main source was temporary impersonation of another in a good cause; in the tragedies, official acquisition of a position by immoral means, leading the usurper to a posturing of the role. Here see Anne Righter's suggestive book, *Shakespeare and the Idea of the Play* (London: Chatto and Windus, 1964).

[34] On "on" see Sheldon L. Messinger et al., "Life as Theater: Some Notes on the Dramaturgic Approach to Social Reality," *Sociometry*, XXV (1962). An illustration might be cited from the novel *Seconds*, by David Ely (New York: Signet Books, 1963; London: André Deutsch, 1964), pp. 7–8. The hero is about to disappear from his own life:

> In the outer office, he paused beside his secretary's desk.
>
> "I'll probably be a little late getting back from lunch. It's such a fine day, I may take a walk."

There, then, when the individual serves his own interests, is one context for self-enactment. The second environment for self-enactment involves a set-up. An individual about to be conned or shaken-down, or sold drugs, contraband, or stolen goods, or recruited as the inside man for a job consults with the authorities and is induced to continue being himself until sufficient evidence is obtained. Or a member of a team engaged in planning an illicit action sells out his mates and is obliged to set them up as part of his trade-off with the law—a dramaturgic position that can also be achieved should he learn before the crime that he is going to be eliminated by his mates after it and decide to betray them before they him. In all of these cases of "playing along," the individual is helped not only by the fact that it is he himself he is enacting, but also by the fact that his required performance may be brief, coaching will be given, and legitimate protection will be waiting behind the scenes, presumably ready to stop the charade should matters become precarious.

The third context involves forced enacting, usually at the point of a gun. Here, often, the object of the coercer is to use the coerced to convince third parties (from whom the coercer may be hidden) that everything is normal. Here, of course, the performance is likely to be very brief, else the coercer be intentionally or

---

"Yes, sir."

He turned and proceeded toward the great glass wall that marked the Broadway side of the bank. Be casual, he told himself. Be ordinary. Remember, you're just going out to lunch. But it occurred to him that he did not have the vaguest notion of how to counterfeit the act of going out to lunch. Was there a special way of walking? Did one saunter or rush out hungrily or what? He had gone out to lunch every working day for more than twenty-five years, and yet now, when he had to pretend to do it, he was baffled.

On Broadway, he paused deliberately to sniff the air and eye the crowds. He supposed this was the kind of thing he usually did on these days when he was going out alone to eat. Something to show how unhurried he was, and that he was of sufficient rank not to worry about the precise time of his return. . . . It did not seem quite possible that he was really never going back. . . . Surely, if he were in earnest, then his demeanor would have been visibly agitated during the past few days. His associates would have divined his intentions, and at any moment they would come rushing out to seize him, with cries of: "Good Lord, man—you can't be thinking of doing *that!*"

even inadvertently given away, and here acting normal is the only possible show, since this is the only one the coerced performer is likely to be able to produce under such nervous conditions.[35] This sort of thing is extremely common in thrillers but uncommon in life; a shielded gun in his back ought to effectively force a subject to enact being a member of a with on the way to entering a car or a building, but public places, I think, provide more protection from kidnappers than this standard episode in fiction implies. But I cite at length excerpts from a newspaper account of a well-planned bank job:

> The desperate hours preceding the robbery began at 10:50 P.M. Tuesday when David Aldridge, 20, a student at Santa Rosa Junior College, arrived home—a pink, frame house at 6885 Covey Road.
>
> The place was dark, nobody was at home. As David stepped onto the small porch, three men emerged from the shadows. Once inside, they ordered silence.
>
> Twenty minutes later, David's mother, Marda, 49, blonde and high-strung, let herself in. She had been visiting a sister.
>
> She was handcuffed to her son, and both held under guard in the bedroom.
>
> A few lights were not switched on—the gunmen wanted everything to seem normal to Robert Aldridge, 51, the bank manager, who was playing poker with the boys at the Odd Fellows club.
>
> Aldridge came home at 11:30.
>
> In a town of this size—population 500—everyone knows everyone, and the car he drives. If a big four-door 1966 Buick, light

[35] If the circumstances and time allow the conditions for blackmailing to be established, then coerced shows can become more elaborate, the victim compelled to follow directions in the physical absence of the coercers; that, in fact, is the point about blackmail. Note, when bank clerks, research and development scientists, and defense agency clerks are blackmailed into betraying their employer, they must for a time sustain normal appearances on the job under very treacherous circumstances. Some of these forced performers do not fail in this terrible task even though they were not selected to make the attempt on the basis of their capacity as performers. A reasonable conclusion is that if these poor fools can successfully enact themselves under such ticklish conditions, everyone else could also, almost any place, almost any time.

blue, had been parked out front, David might have wondered—the others, too.

It wasn't. It was parked a few doors down the road, in front of the Floyd F. Arnett, Sr. place. Matter of fact, the Arnetts had returned about 9 P.M. from a weekend trip and Arnett had remarked to his wife, "Wonder who parked that there?"

. . .

The gunmen were not only aware of the bank operations—they had studied the place well and knew even the work habits of the janitor, Tom Fish.

They wanted to get there before he did, so they could surprise him, not he them. They also wanted to get in the bank with their hostages before daybreak, just in case someone might be up and around at that hour.

They left the Aldridge home, quietly, about 4 A.M. and drove the three blocks to the bank, . . .

The bandit car which was later recovered and identified as stolen in San Francisco pulled up at the rear of the bank, and they all went silently in the back door.

. . .

At 6:35 Tom Fish, the janitor, let himself in by the rear door. He too was locked in the ladies room and also bound.

The robbers had to wait now for the time lock on the vault to open, at 7:30 A.M., but they were careful not to rupture routine.

At 7:20 Joe Pearson, owner of the El Molino market across Main from the bank, happened to glance that way. He saw Tom Fish step out of the bank and shake a foot mat—right on his morning schedule—then go back in.

Once the time lock allowed Aldridge to open the vault, the gunmen scooped up all the currency in sight and dumped it in a big squarish can. . . .

A woman living across First Street saw them come out, so casually she thought nothing of it.

"I thought they were simply taking something out of the bank, like a janitor," she said.

Oscar Ludolff, who lives in a cottage next to the bank's rear parking lot, sat at his breakfast table and looked out at the four-door blue Buick and wondered about it. Then he saw the men come out, but he too suspected nothing.

"They came out sort of leisurely and drove off in no hurry at all," he said.[36]

Here we see the maintenance of normal appearances over an extended period of time by means of concealing most of the operation and coercing small but crucial performances from persons for whom these acts are usually not merely acts. As each victim enters the held place, he ceases to be the subject for the show and becomes a forced performer until the only subjects left are townspeople who dwell in other houses. We also see that a forced performance of one's own "natural" behavior may require very little actual action, and, in that sense, the performer may find that success is as easy as it is repugnant. For there are circumstances, as in the current illustration, in which merely desisting from crying out a warning can generate a perfect show of normalcy.

V *Subjects/Others*

We have looked at three constraining frameworks in which an individual enacts himself, circumstances in which he continues on with what is usual for him but does so, he feels, as though performing on a stage—although that is not how he would feel were he really on a stage. And we have seen that both the subject and his others will have in part the same task, albeit in different degrees, that of enacting one's own self. A further argument must be made concerning the blurring of difference between the subject and his others.

---

[36] J. Campbell Bruce, *San Francisco Chronicle*, September 7, 1967. It is interesting that criminals are said to be "unsocialized" or "sociopathic," even though one or more phases of their criminal action can well involve not only a slavish concern for what others would expect them to be if they are to go unnoticed, but also the staking of a great deal on their being correct in these appraisals. Perhaps it is meant that although they can be very good at taking the point of view of others, they are not very good at identifying their interests with this point of view.

Earlier it was suggested that normal appearances and proper appearances were not the same but were nonetheless connected in various ways. Now another connection presents itself. The subject will have a version of himself that he wants to sustain in the eyes of persons present, and partly this will involve what he conveys by his current conduct, a fact that is true in a special way perhaps for females, attractive dress and looks being more an obligation of that sex than the other. Now if the individual should find himself appearing in a bad light, in a guise or act that he considers appreciably beneath him or otherwise discrediting to him, he may find himself suddenly alarmed by the situation—even though those before whom he believes he is misconducting himself may have no great concern about his appearances, whatever judgment they may make on ideal grounds. His own unseemly behavior or appearance, seen by him to be perceived by others, can cause him alarm. Again, note that the ease he attains in his *Umwelt* presumes that he constantly sustain certain "personal" standards of conduct, for example, aliveness to the scene around him, mental agility, access to memory, sightedness, locomotor competency, literacy, cleanliness, rein on passions, appropriate age and sex behavior. And local contingencies and occurrences can suddenly bring his embodiment of these standards into question. Persons with concealable stigmas are likely, of course, to have still further cause for alarm within themselves; [37] and persons engaged, say, in smuggling or in laying low after a successful crime have more cause still. In any case, it is clear that for the individual the maintenance of these personal standards is important not only as a means of carefully coping with routine difficulties, but also as a means of sustaining an image of himself to which he is attached. Sudden failure to sustain these

---

[37] A general treatment is given in Goffman, *Stigma* (Englewood Cliffs, N.J.: Prentice-Hall, Inc., 1963; London: Penguin Books, 1968). A useful case study is Harold Garfinkel's paper, "Passing and the Managed Achievement of Sex Status in an Intersexed Person," Chapter 5 (and the appendix) in his *Studies in Ethnomethodology* (Englewood Cliffs, N.J.: Prentice-Hall, Inc., 1967).

competencies is, then, a double cause for alarm. In some situations, he will be mainly concerned about the stability of his environment, at other times, primarily about the stability of the impression he gives of himself in coping with it, and at still other times he will be appreciably concerned about both matters. The latter is the case in the precarious romantic trades, in which the individual simultaneously is concerned to conceal what could give others alarm and to discover hidden bases of alarm in his *Umwelt.* Incidentally, note that he will see a self-acceptable level of competency and propriety as "natural" for him, or "normal," thereby applying to himself the same special reading of these terms that he employs in reference to surrounds that are unalarming.

The close involvement of the individual for personal as well as expediential reasons in how he must appear if others are to treat him with no special attention should not surprise us, provided only that we are willing to fall back upon basic principles. George Herbert Mead must be our guide. What the individual is for himself is not something that he invented. It is what his significant others have come to see he should be, what they have come to treat him as being, and what, in consequence, he must treat himself as being if he is to deal with their dealings with him. Mead was wrong only in thinking that the only relevant others are ones who are concerned to give sustained and pointed attention to the individual. There are other others, namely, those who are concerned to find in him someone unalarming whom they can disattend in order to be free to get on with other matters. So what the individual in part must come to be *for himself* is someone whose appearances are ones his others can see as normal. His show of being safely disattendable is deeply him; he has no self that is deeper, although he has some that are as deep.

When we examine the task of sustaining an acceptable image of oneself, we are led once more to see that subjects and their others have a like concern—to appear normal—although perhaps for different reasons. A further basis of similarity between the subject and his others can now be considered: the convergence of innocence and treachery.[38] A subject who appreciates that others present will be trying to conceal what might threaten or entice him may come to see that the most innocent-looking situation may be for this very reason the best one for such others to create, and so what should make for ease can make for its opposite. Similarly, given that it is often in the interests of the subject to conceal that he suspects his surround, including the people in it, they, in turn, may often find it wise to assume that the appearance he gives of finding everything normal is just what he would produce were he suspicious. Thus, just as he may come to feel that normal appearances are the most suspect appearances of all, so they may come to feel that his appearance of being unsuspecting is the least reliable of all appearances. Interestingly, the more the subject has to lose, the more worthwhile it probably will be for the others to execute complex, costly designs that allow them to conceal their intent behind a show of normalcy; so it is then, understandably, that the subject will feel that he ought to be the most suspecting. Similarly, when they have the most to gain by covertly concealing what should alarm him, he is likely to have the most reason for concealing his suspicions. Normal appearances, then, will come to be suspected just at the time when those involved are the most dependent on them.

As mentioned earlier, one usually assumes that there will be a continuum of concern about the situation: at one end there will be persons at ease with themselves and each other, and at the other, a situation in which everyone finds many signs for alarm. Midway, presumably, there would be situations in which some participants will find a few signs for alarm. But, in fact, if the individual and those who might be a source of alarm for him appreciate the strategic value of a show of normalcy, there will be a tendency either for complete ease or complete uneasiness, and when neither, then a tendency toward oscillation between the two. If it is the case that the subject is attempting to conceal all signs of being alarmed

---

[38] See "The Degeneration of Expression," in Goffman, *Strategic Interaction* (Philadelphia: University of Pennsylvania Press, 1969), pp. 58–70.

and the others are attempting to conceal all signs that would give alarm, then any minor sign can be taken as evidence that these shows are being strenuously attempted but have not been totally effective. This means that one sign can be as upsetting as a thousand and warrantably so. Worse still, although a situation cannot always generate even a few outright signs for alarm for the subject or for those who are (or might be) a concern to him, any situation can generate normal appearances; and since these appearances can qualify as reason for alarm, alarming signs will ever by available.[39]

---

[39] Here is to be found a central vulnerability of illegality, a vulnerability unexamined in detail by its students. He who employs a criminal design of any degree of complexity must disclose parts of it in advance of its final realization to teammates, including sometimes an inside man, to buyers when a product of some kind is involved, and to victims when a shakedown is employed. Vital information which can be sold, bartered, coercively extracted, inadvertently disclosed and of course discovered will therefore be available. (There is, in fact, an argument that any kind of organized crime could be stopped merely by increasing the reward to informers beyond what they could earn as performers.) A criminal action also requires the performer to come into some kind of contact with those who are not supposed to be in on the know and to accept the appearances these persons will give of not knowing. And yet the performer must realize that should the law buy, discover, or be given inside information, no immediate legal action is likely, but rather care will be taken by the law to allow him to commit himself further to his project in order to produce enough evidence to ensure conviction, or disclose all the guilty, or maneuver an unrisky arrest. So by the very nature of the criminal enterprise, the participant must doubt the apparent discretion of those properly in on the know and the apparent unsuspectingness of those who should not know; and yet he must thrust himself fully into assuming that those who appear to be properly going about their business really are. During some phases of an operation, a criminal must maintain an appearance of being like anyone else; but during almost all phases he must stake his freedom on the normal appearances maintained by others, including his teammates themselves. He must, for example, entertain the possibility of being subject to one of the great, mythic inversions of public order, the lethal ambush: being led into a place (or allowed to arrive at one) whose normal appearance utterly conceals immanent, close-range crossfire. (A good example is the Firestone Plot, the attempt by two men—one of whom turned informer because he feared the other planned eventually to eliminate him—to kidnap the tire magnate. By the time the desperados presented themselves as deliverymen at the door of the Firestone house, unmarked police cars were staked out around

The subject and his other, then, are similar not only in their concern about acting natural, but also in their suspicions of innocence—the subject being concerned lest what appears to be normal isn't and the others being concerned lest the subject's appearance of unconcern be really a show, and that, by implication, he is the other and they are the subjects. There is still a further link between the two sides, whatever we call them. Both are concerned about concealing something and both are vulnerable to the concealer's circular problem: the more desirous one is of concealing something, the more evident one's anxiety and furtiveness; the more evident these deception cues, the more precarious one's efforts to conceal; the harder to conceal, the more worry and furtiveness about exposure, etc. And the final link. If the individual is to be unconcerned about the others present, in the sense of accepting them as no threat or startling opportunity, then it will be useful if they have the same feeling about him, else he may feel that even though they have no cause for alarm they may think they have and themselves take threatening action in consequence. So the individual (he can feel) might best be concerned. For the individual, then, what is perceived as a normal situation is likely to be one in which he is unconcerned about the other's concerns, including their concern about him.

In this paper, then, we deal with a normalcy show, with one individual seeking for warnings while concealing his suspicions and the others concealing the threat and opportunity they constitute for him while searching for signs that they are suspected. These two shows converge on what is seen as normal appearances, making of normal appearances a normalcy show, a show in which all participants have the task of acting unfurtively.

---

the establishment, three armed police were waiting in the house, and the maid who answered the door was an armed policewoman in disguise. Both kidnappers died on the doorstep from the police barrage. See *San Francisco Chronicle*, January 4, 1966.) And he must face the unsettling fact that if he is being set up, some of those who are doing it will only have to enact themselves to be effective. With ambushes and self-enactments to worry about, how sweetly tempered, how mature, a criminal must be to avoid becoming a suspicious person. And how ill used he is by normal appearances.

PART TWO

I *The Design of Vulnerability*

The treatment so far has been formalistic. It tells us that the individual's *Umwelt* will contain possible sources of alarm, and that for many purposes it is not initially necessary to distinguish his situation from that of others around him who might be cause for his alarm, since both sides must take the same possibilities into consideration. And it has been argued that by learning how normal appearances can be disturbed or faked, we can learn how *Umwelten* are built up—learn, in one sense, what their structure is. And this we must try to do. To say there are background features of his surround that the individual takes for granted that, when breached, cause alarm, and then to give a scattering of examples, is not to say much, even were these examples to be experimentally created as an exercise in intentionally produced alarm. An ordering of these examples must be provided, a glimpse of structure. And for this mere description is not enough, let alone what has thus far been done here, mere analytical discussion.

Examine now some of the things that have correctly meant for an individual that something was up. We need not concern ourselves with anxieties about the not possibly real. Recent bedevilments of the environment have introduced enough real issues, and each real possibility breeds its own set of unjustly suspected appearances. I will, however, consider the assumptions the subject makes "in effect" in regard to his *Umwelt*—in effect because he need not make them mentally but only be vulnerable to a sharp reminder that in the circumstances he had been making these assumptions. In pointing out how alarming circumstances have arisen, I cannot, of course, say that any one person's easefulness *will* be upset in this way ever—only that the surrounds of others have been made alarming in this way and his *could* be.

We will examine sources and signs of alarm—primarily those associated with threat, not opportunity—insofar as these determine the articulations of the individual's surround. One central factor will be the vulnerability of a subject's body; a second will be "critical distance."

One final point about sources of alarm. It seems that the surround is constructed out of elements easily seen as members of classes, and the tendency is to generalize from one member of a class to the other members. If one chair breaks under the individual, he begins to suspect the others. If one wooden step proves safe, he tends to assume the others might be, too. The point here is not whether or not there is warrant for this generalizing process (although for various reasons there is), but rather its consequence for the way the individual is in his world. In this manner we are to understand that acts of sabotage tend to have two effects upon the enemy: one substantive, in terms of the essentials destroyed, and the other "psychological," in terms of the effect on morale when the sabotage is discovered and suspicion is generalized to a whole class of familiar objects, now to be seen as no longer disattendable, with consequent generalization of alarm.[40]

II *The Elements*

1. *The Furnished Frame:* Unlike his feathered friends, the individual must commit himself to walking on a flooring, whether this be the ground or a man-made surface of some kind. Almost always he

[40] A classic case is manufacture by the British S.O.E. of inviscerated rats stuffed with explosives to be left along with their innocent fellows in boiler rooms. The plane flying a batch to Belgium crashed and the Gestapo found them. "They were taken to Gestapo headquarters and from there, after expert examination, they were immediately distributed to counter-sabotage schools. At once, the whole of the German Intelligence was alerted, and the villagers and townsfolk were commanded by the Gestapo to bring in

will be close to walls of some kind—none, of course, in a park or on a country road, but one or two on city streets, and four in rooms, as well as a roof. Typically, there will be material items of various kinds in these semi or full enclosures: mailboxes, parked cars, and the like in streets; furniture, furnishings, and food in domestic places. In brief, the individual spends his time in a furnished or physical frame.

This physical background has certain properties consequent on convention and practice. Walls, ceiling, and floor tend to establish outside limits to a surround, the assumption being that these barriers are stout enough to keep out potential matters for alarm. They establish an "inside" and an "outside."

Further, it is assumed that the materials on the inside will themselves have certain tranquilizing properties. Some explication is required here.

For one, it is assumed that for users possessing the expected range of competencies, these materials will be free of hazard, that is, free of appreciable risk of bodily harm caused by unintentional and unplanned faults, these resulting, say, from bad or incomplete construction, seepage of gas, exposed electric lines, rats, naturally poisoned food, fire, and so forth. Indeed, so customary is this lack of hazard in the domestic settings of our population that we must look to studies of slum housing developments to learn what it is most of us do not have to be wary about.[41]

For another, it is assumed that the frame itself will be innocent, free of concealed and secret ill intent. The assumption is that everything not properly concealed in cabinets, closets, etc., will be visible, as implied also, for example, in the various laws requiring knives and handguns to be worn revealed. Two fundamental mat-

---

to headquarters every dead rat found." Leslie Bell, *Sabotage!* (London: T. Werner Laurie, 1957), p. 35. What resulted was considerably burdensome to the Gestapo.

41 See, for example, Lee Rainwater, "Fear and the House-as-Haven in the Lower Class," *AIP Journal* (January 1966), pp. 23–31. Natural disasters, such as earthquakes and fires, produce very special awareness about the vulnerability of the furnished frame, but such occurrences are, of course, rare and therefore rare, too, the resulting awareness.

ters can be concealed. One is devices designed to do bodily harm: bombs, mines, poisons, and other weaponry. (A nice example, still in considerable use, is the bomb wired to the starting motor of a car.) The other is means of bearing witness to what occurs within the frame—means such as microphones, cameras, one-way windows, and the like. Here a more extended comment is required. A working assumption in everyday life is that one's surround will be "dead," that is, contain no recording and transmission devices. The subject, therefore, assumes that he can scan his *Umwelt* and correctly determine how he is being witnessed and by whom, for at worst there will only be a hearsay link between what happens inside the frame and allegations made about this outside the frame. Orientation segregation is thus taken for granted, and otherwise vulnerable activity predicated on it. In the extreme, as already considered in regard to crimes, plans that the individual concocts and projects of action he initiates can be utterly frustrated if unanticipated others bear witness. And of course relationships that an individual extends to one audience tend to be undercut when other audiences secretly witness the performance.

I have suggested that the individual is likely at any moment to find himself in a furnished frame of some kind and that he tends to assume that it is probably unhazardous and innocent but might not be. Now another alarming feature of physical frame must be considered. Given the fact that boundedness protectively cuts off those in physical frames from the outside, it is to be expected that this sometimes will be turned against an individual in it; for anything that can cut an individual off from sources of alarm can cut him off *with* sources of alarm. Thus, as documented earlier, when bank robbers plan to have the manager open up the vault, they may also plan to spend the night in his house in order to get an early start with him and to hold members of his family hostage while he is being forced to help them help themselves. This is a possible strategy because of the manner in which houses cut off their residents from the street world. Hallways in public housing units can function in a similar way:

> The interior hallways of high-rise apartment projects which are double-loaded are particularly devoid of surveillance opportunity. In addition, the corridors are usually territorially undefined, and common household noises prevent auditory monitoring. Although these corridors are public in nature, they have none of the attributes of public space; i.e., they are not heavily trafficked, they are not under continuous casual surveillance, and they are not easily patrolled by authorities.[42]

An even clearer example is found in elevator attacks:

> Police yesterday arrested a 29-year-old ex-convict and charged him with assaulting four women over the past ten days—all in downtown office buildings.
>
> Inspectors John Mino and George Murray of the department's Sex Detail said that John Duncan operated in elevators.
>
> He would enter an elevator after a girl. And as the door closed, would extinguish the lights and stop the machine between floors.
>
> Specifically, Duncan, who lives at 1906 Ocean Avenue, is charged with suspicion of rape, suspicion of assault to commit rape, and committing crimes against nature.[43]

The great vulnerability of planes to hijacking and bomb scares provides another case in point.

The perspective that has been taken in this paper is that of the individual in any of his possible surrounds. This leaves unconsidered some special circumstances in which he might find himself.

First, the physical frame may be his possession, part of his "fixed territory," and any damage to it can be a damage to him. This makes him vulnerable to others in ways additional to those outlined. He becomes subject to the capacity of others as thieves, as vandals, and as persons of unacceptable standards of care and care-

---

[42] Columbia Project, *op. cit.*, p. 10. Rainwater, *op. cit.*, p. 30, suggests that laundry rooms in slum public housing projects may be avoided by tenants because of the closed-off exposure to robbery, rape, and minor molestations that must be faced in them.

[43] *San Francisco Chronicle*, December 2, 1967.

fulness.[44] Note that the possessor of a physical frame is vulnerable in these ways whether or not he is present at the time of the damage, and, in fact, may be more vulnerable when absent, because no one may be as concerned as he is to protect his domain. (The term "absent" has special meaning here. However far away an individual is at a given moment from his house or privately owned place of business, should he have one, or from his next of kin, these are effectively part of his *Umwelt*. Modern means of communication place him "on call" in regard to them. Should they suffer damage, word is likely to be gotten to him, and immediate action is likely to be required of him.) Nor will concern over one's *Umwelt* be limited to property damage. The individual's sense of privacy, control, and self-respect is tied to the dominion he exerts over his fixed territories, and these expectations can be threatened easily—the extreme is expropriation—with consequent alarm.[45] Those

---

[44] The great modern case is President Grayson Kirk's office during the 1968 unpleasantness at Columbia:

> One and a half hours after the President's suite had been cleared of student demonstrators, Grayson Kirk stood in the center of his private office looking at the blankets, cigarette butts and orange peels that covered his rug. Turning to A. M. Rosenthal of *The New York Times* and several other reporters who had come into the office with him he murmured, "My God, how could human beings do a thing like this?" It was the only time, Truman recalled later, that he had ever seen the President break down. Kirk's windows were crisscrossed with tape and on one hung a large sign reading, "Join Us." His lampshades were torn, his carpet was spotted, his furniture was displaced and scratched. But the most evident and disturbing aspect of the scene was not the minor damage inflicted by the students. The everything-in-its-place decor to which Kirk had grown accustomed was now in disarray—disarray that was the result of the transformation of an office into the living quarters of 150 students during the past six days.

Jerry L. Avorn et al., *Up Against the Ivy Wall* (New York: Atheneum Publishers, 1969), p. 200. The great sociological question, of course, is not how could it be that human beings would do a thing like this, but rather how is it that human beings do this sort of thing so rarely. How come persons in authority have been so overwhelmingly successful in conning those beneath them into keeping the hell out of their offices?

[45] As a reminder of the variety of threats involved and the variety of ways the individual can be made to feel that something is up, I cite an episode from a novel, wherein the heroine is about to confide about her husband to a psychiatrist for whom she works:

> "What is it?" he asked quietly, after allowing a minute's interval. "Tell me."

who feel a proprietary claim on public establishments such as stores, libraries, and museums are even more vulnerable to these sources of alarm, in part because access is broad and some of the social control must begin after offenders have entered, whereas in domestic establishments, those who get by the door are likely to be tractable.[46]

"It's. Uhh. It's Paul, I suppose," Katherine sobbed. The realization came over her that she was about to tell Dr. Einsam everything. She wanted to get up and run away; but she was so sick, so cold, so confused, she simply didn't have the energy. "It's just that he's deceiving me. And I found out last night. I'll get over it."

"Ahh. How did you find out?"

"Well, when I came home from work." Katherine swallowed. "When I walked into the house I knew, really. I mean I knew he must have been there with somebody, because everything was all wrong. The towels for instance: they were hung up the wrong way in the bathroom." Her voice trembled. "I always fold them into thirds, and Paul just kind of throws them over the pole; but last night they were folded in half, and the wash-cloth was next to them, instead of over the tub. And the bed was all made up wrong, with the quilt—"

Alison Lurie, *The Nowhere City* (London: Heinemann, 1965; New York: Avon Books, 1967), p. 188.

[46] In the last decade interesting things have happened to assumptions about the moral order within and around establishments. Ordinary policing, along with the mortification presumably consequent on public arrest, was thought to be all that was necessary in order to keep users of public and semi-public establishments effectively respectful of the property and persons within these places, and of the frame itself. But, of course, other factors were at work, such as actual respect and informal segregation by class, race, and age; and these factors seem to be much less effective in cities today. Many libraries have had to institute checkout search procedures that would have been considered highly intrusive a generation ago. Some stores in some areas of New York have been robbed blind so brazenly that dispirited owners have moved on. Streetcars and buses employ exact-change coin boxes and cashless drivers. Cabbies have experimented with protective dividers between front and back seat. Some banks have introduced remote-control television tellers; others videotaping. Strict security measures have made their appearance at public meetings, political conventions, and presidential appearances. Spray paint defacement of buildings has becomes a problem. Iron mesh and bars for doors and windows have begun to spread from prisons and inner-city jewelry stores to the best commercial (and residential) districts. Doormen have re-acquired essential functions in apartment houses. And a new garrison architecture has developed, involving orientation to an inner court, and street sides that are nearly windowless. In these matters, I might add, building maintenance managers of urban public housing have acquired an experience of our times that is deep, dumb, and

So possession of a furnished frame subjects the possessor to a special basis of alarm. A second special basis occurs in connection with the work required of agents of social control, such as policemen, narcotics agents, or customs inspectors—work which creates for others the alarming possibility of their being suspected of concealing contraband. The assumption apparently made of an individual's furnished frame and his person is that he will have the right to conceal certain things in certain places, and that these safe-keepings are not to be violated, but that he himself is not to use them for concealing contraband, namely, what he is forbidden to have.[47] Drugs and stolen articles are the principal objects hidden. The notion of concealing on one's premises something that the police might be actively interested in finding is a fantasy for middle-class, middle-aged Americans, one kept active perhaps only by virtue of the constant presence of this practice in adventure stories. The younger generation, however, has had very widespread, firsthand experience in this regard; almost all youths who have stashed pot have suffered brief moments of alarm in connection with possible discovery, and by now this includes a considerable number, perhaps surpassing the total membership of the Boy Scouts of America, and even overlapping with that group in a small degree. The moral of the story is that although some basic frameworks of alarm may seem outside the realistic concern of whole classes of persons, their *Umwelten* are nonetheless potentially vulnerable in these connections, and circumstances can always occur to demonstrate this forcibly. It should be added that for those control agents who are judged by their capacity to pre-

---

terrifying. And citizens at large have learned the sociological lesson that their easefulness had been dependent all along on the self-restraint sustained by potential offenders who have never had many reasons for being respectful.

[47] In intelligence work there is the notion of a "safe house," meaning here that the whole building can be established as one in which improper things are contained, namely, agents openly doing their illegal work. It also should be added that contraband can, of course, be persons, the smuggling of these commodities across borders being a very old and still quite active business.

vent the successful concealment of contraband, he who might be concealing something can be as much a source of alarm for them as they are for him.

There has never been a want of interest in the furnished frame as a possible locus of alarm, merely a lack of academic interest. In Western society, folk tales and commercially available fantasy are and have been full of imagery concerning the kinds of things that can happen in and to the physical framework of the *Umwelt:* secret hiding places, slots in bedroom walls through which Speckled Bands can be released upon the sleeper, trap doors, panels that open to reveal stairways into caves, permanently locked rooms, hidden entranceways, bars on the windows and doors, sudden failure of the lights, eerie sounds, concealed machines of destruction that spring out at the strategic moment. Adults read James Bond thrillers to watch an ultimate contest between the worst that can be concealed in the innocent trappings of a room and the best possible reaction time. Youths visit circus fun houses to enjoy firsthand a mocking up of the same room alarms. And children can be found who construct a secret hiding place and then look for something that can be appropriately hidden. (It is as if it takes much effort to induce a child to accept the physical frame around him as innocuous, something to be taken for granted as the background for activity.) In any case these sources of unserious, scary experiences can instruct us in the structure of the furnished frame.

Nor are these the only materials to which we can appeal. There is the instructive lore regarding undercover warfare. The arts of sabotage, but rudimentarily developed in World War I, received considerable attention in World War II [48] and probably attention

---

[48] In the early days of World War II, the British and American efforts along these lines involved plans and devices that were zany beyond belief, and, given the social origins of the individuals first recruited for this work, provide evidence of the imaginativeness of persons who have benefited from a good upbringing and a decent education; for they were able to retain their infantilism late enough in life to put it at the service of their country. They also exhibited a notable capacity to refrain from sympathy for the plight of prospective victims, another advantage perhaps of an early training for leadership.

has not declined since then.[49] In any case, the study of sabotage and the study of normal appearances seem to form a natural whole. Sabotage and some elements of psychological warfare depend largely on agents making drastically tricky use of the surround, specifically elements usually taken for granted as something that never would be a source of alarm and therefore can be unattended and untended.[50] Students of social situations apparently

---

[49] Except for passing comments in the espionage literature, there is very little publicly available on sabotage. I draw most of my examples from one specialized (and popular) book, Leslie Bell, *op. cit.*

[50] The marked tendency of the individual to take his physical frame for granted provided the basis of the development, for example, of anti-personnel mines or booby traps, this development being one of the imaginative high points of military design, the leaders here probably being the British through the Scientific Research Section of the S.O.E.

The choice of objects to mine is instructive. One favorite consisted of objects such as flashlights, which could be seen as things that could be innocently lost and therefore could plausibly be found. A second consisted of small articles in daily use such as bottles of milk, loaves of bread, pens, lumps of coal, and the like. A nice sentimental touch, employed against the Japanese troops because of their known pleasure in the beauties of nature, was the booby trapping of flowers, so that upon being picked, their base exploded (*ibid.*, pp. 120–121). A third, surely sound, was to mine parts of the flooring that tended to be seen as merely there and not worth attending to. Thus the S.O.E.'s decision to manufacture plastic turds, exact replicas of whatever the local animal dropped, which exploded when driven or marched over. To deal with habitat differences in theaters of war, use as models was made of the excreta "of horses, donkeys, goats, mules, elephants, camels, and water buffalo"; the source was the London Zoo (*ibid.*, pp. 116–117). An even more invisible choice was what appeared to be rusty heads of bolts; these, made of papier-mâché, filled with explosives, attached magnetically to ships, were equipped with time fuses. Such devices were so undetectable that even were the enemy to know that some bolts were not innocent, care hardly could be exerted in this regard (*ibid.*, p. 41).

And, of course, just as background items could be used to conceal explosive charges, so also any kind of ordinary article, such as fruit, fire logs, vegetables, could be used, and was, as a cover to transport the materials to make explosives and to keep their makers in touch by wireless with the home supply (*ibid.*, p. 24). Indeed, the American Army in Vietnam apparently used simulated dog turds as homing devices which, when moved in any way, would transmit traceable short-wave signals usable for directing

have not given help yet to those engaged in this kind of mayhem, but this should not deter us from getting help from them—help in sustaining awareness that the easy use of physical frames rests on multiple assumptions that need not be maintained. In point of fact, hostile actions between two opponents always have been limited severely as to techniques.[51] It has always been the case that the orderly life of a group contained many more points of weakness than its opponents ever exploited.

2. *Lurk Lines:* Human perceptual equipment is such that howsoever an individual stands, sits, or lies, there will be a zone that is behind his line of sight, that is, "behind his back." And this zone begins right where his back leaves off. The habit and the convention of ordinarily not turning around increase this area of the proximal unseen considerably. Of course those who are definitely behind the individual's sight line may definitely have *him* well and easily in view.

In addition to this kind of blind spot, the subject has another: partitions that block his view of what is behind them but, being small and at least partly free-standing, allow him to inspect what is

---

long-range artillery. (Reported in *San Francisco Chronicle*, March 17, 1971.)

The point, to repeat, is not so much the actual contraband deliveries and actual injuries effected through these devices, but rather the effect on enemy morale. To orient oneself, one must discount the material frame of one's actions. To feel that innocent elements in the situation might be anything but innocent can have the effect of altering one's relation to the whole physical frame that one is in, rendering usual direction and focus of attention difficult to maintain.

It might be added as a final point that anti-personnel mines often required in their construction a knowledge of the natural world only obtainable from zoologists, botanists, geographers, and other naturalists. After all, to construct a convincing camel turd one needs to consult a student of the form. In the literature detailing the efforts of these consultants to the military, lots of evidence is provided of great devotion to the national interest, a great willingness to pitch in. There is little suggestion that science might be better employed.

51 A useful treatment of these self-imposed limitations can be found in Thomas C. Schelling, *Arms and Influence* (New Haven: Yale University Press, 1966).

behind them. Examples are everywhere: the area behind doors when these are open; inside unlocked closets, and around sharp bends in passageways; the floor of a car's back seat for those who enter the front door; the small space between individuals who are tightly packed, as subway users know who have been improperly addressed sexually by individuals whose improper address is hidden from everyone's angle of vision, the victim and offender alone being in a position to sense what is happening. These "blind" places can even be manufactured on the spur of the moment:

> The dip [pickpocket] may use one of several methods. If the victim keeps his money in a wallet in his breast-pocket, he's tackled from the front. The dip walks towards him with a newspaper held out open in front of him and, when he confronts his victim, his right hand goes sideways and under the paper into the breast-pocket. All the victim is aware of is that someone has nearly run into him walking along reading a paper. He's busy avoiding a collision.[52]

Note, I exclude here the inside of pockets and purses, alarming though these insides may be, because these are not ordinarily freely accessible to other than the possessor.

Finally, on the street after dark there are places close by the individual which are just outside his field of vision yet near enough to expose him rather severely to what might be lurking there.

Here, then, are three areas (and three lines that demark them) that must concern us: behind one's back, behind partitions, and behind darkness. The common feature is that inimical agencies can be there in "open hiding." They can be discovered by the subject without his having to pass through obstructions that are physical or even appreciably social. If these lurking agencies are predators, they can attack him with the same convenience. That dual possibility is what is meant by "lurk."

In many circumstances it seems that the subject can be (and remain) unconcerned about what lies beyond the lurk lines. If it is he himself who is vulnerable to attack, he might assume that the attackers would decline to risk so easy a discovery; if he is the

---

[52] Eric Parr, *Grafters All* (London: Max Reinhardt, 1964), p. 118.

attacker, that his potential victims would not commit themselves to so desperate a cover. In any case, situations occur in which the subject simply disattends places in which others might lurk, and others who might lurk there simply do not do so. But, of course, this gentlemanly arrangement can break down.

A central occasion for considering lurk lines is tied to the "sentry problem." Circumstances exist in which a sentry finds that the object of the enemy is to silence him before he can signal the alarm. A standard technique is for personnel of the other side to sneak up behind him and by means, say, of the knife-in-kidney, hand-over-nose-and-mouth technique, silence him permanently before he has a chance to give alarm.[53] There are other circumstances, of course, in which the object of enemy personnel is to bypass him in order to do damage at a further point. All of this means that the sentry role renders its player maximally vulnerable to lurk lines, providing something of a model for this kind of concern. Since the object of the enemy will be to move around or behind the sentry with as little sound as possible, the sentry must, if he is to be a wide-awake sentry, suspect the smallest sound behind him—such as the displacement of pebbles or the crunching of leaves—even to the point of imagining sounds that have not quite occurred, lest the sounds he now hears be the last ones he will ever hear. Exactly those sounds that everyone discounts and disattends—a cause for no alarm, mere background sounds—are for him matters of intense concern. That sort of concern can keep him very busy. Note, the blanket of minor sounds that the subject ordinarily attributes to "nature" is a cover that those who would employ stealth can rely on, thereby saving themselves from giving themselves away because of minor sound-making; it is the same blanket of incidental sounds that a subject who has been made wary by events can find himself suddenly attending.

The sentry problem, then, can be considered one extreme in regard to lurking; the "sniper problem" can be considered another. Houses and other buildings are typically treated as being of no im-

---

[53] The technique is outlined in Applegate, *op. cit.*, p. 460.

mediate concern by the individual in the street, something in which no danger can lurk, something out of bounds as a source of alarm. But of course windows can hide snipers, which means that the interior of buildings can become appended to streets as a lurk area. This becomes very evident during war or rebellion when a street of houses may have to be "cleaned out" one by one, cleaned out, that is, of lurkers. It is then, incidentally, that we can see most clearly how threatening the place behind a half-open pantry door can become.

As in the case of the furnished frame, lurk lines play a significant role in commercial fantasies. A few decades ago, jungle adventure stories were popular in which dangerous animals and hostile natives lurked around every turn of the path, and it was only because of friendly monkeys and their tree-top view that white heroes always managed to be warned in time, the color of the monkeys here being no restraint on their choice as allies. Modern thrillers employ the same theme, often with the hero lurking, as well as being lurked against. In almost every story, the hero finds reason to flatten himself up against the wall behind the curtain or to one side of the window out on the balustrade, fatefully carving out a lurk area by dint of his muscular strength, natural slenderness, and an ability to breathe very quietly and remain very still. (Incidentally, here we find a version of the sentry problem adapted for domestic fantasies. The hero, actively sought by bad men or mistaken good ones, sneaks up behind the heroine who had thought she was alone in a room, employs the hand-mouth technique but without addressing the kidney, waits for her eyes to shift their look from fear, then, assured of her temporary collaboration, frees her to not signal alarm.) Comedies of various sorts make the whole structure even more clear, as when the hero acts like a statue or learns about the enemy's plans by hiding under the conference table or, of course, takes cover under the bed. Comedy also locates the hero in a small room and then requires him to hide an inopportune visitor, then the one who made the first inopportune, then him, and so forth, until all imaginable lurk areas have been pressed into service, and the next person to be hid disorganizes the whole arrangement.

The lurk lines of articulation in *Umwelten* which are expressed in commercial fantasy are expressed also in children's play. It is children who try to sneak up behind their friends or await behind doors to say "boo." The night seeking that is done in hide-and-go-seek is an effective means of bringing a subject to a series of just those places that afford the others an ideal opportunity to lurk.

It should be expected that wherever comic characters or children find lurk lines to use, those undergoing acute distrust of their surround will find them, too. An example can be taken from that great American confession by Clifford Beers, which did so much to establish our stereotypes about how paranoid a paranoid could get:

> In my chamber of intermittent horrors and momentary delights, uncanny occurrences were frequent. I believed there was someone who at fall of night secreted himself under my bed. That in itself was not peculiar, as sane persons, at one time or another, are troubled by that same notion. But *my* bed-fellow—under the bed—was a detective; and he spent most of his time during the night pressing pieces of ice against my injured heels, to precipitate, as I thought, my overdue confession.[54]

But, of course, wherever child-like figures are set to lurk, or mental, demonic ones, there real figures could also find room. When real ones do, they provide a subject matter for retelling. The following comes from tales of the French underground and the Gestapo:

> Cyril Watney was at Bannes and learnt of what had happened [the German capture of two fellow resistors] from a Resistance man, named Bru, who had been to Brive. Bru warned him that the Germans were looking for him. Cyril knew he must disappear, but first he sent a signal to London, reporting Harry's misfortune and asking Baker Street to warn "Guguste" by radio not to return to Brive. Then, carrying his transmitter, Cyril moved to Figeac, where Madame Odette Bach put him up and hid his set in a coal hole.

[54] Clifford Whittingham Beers, *A Mind That Found Itself* (New York: Longmans, Green, 1908), p. 33.

A few hours after Cyril's arrival, SS men came to Odette's home, asking for "Michel," the terrorist from St. Cere. They stood on the threshold, while Cyril was hiding behind the open door. Odette Bach, with her five-year-old daughter Pierrette in her arms, assured the SS men that she had not noticed a stranger in the street. They went away, knocking at other doors.[55]

Lurk lines are of special interest in the study of public order because they seem to provide a delicate indicator of the social state of a community. Perhaps there are settlements in which the issue of lurking does not arise and the notion itself would be hard to come by unless children's games or commercial fantasy were drawn upon. In urban communities today, of course, this and other jungle themes are in the focus of concern, whether with warrant or not. Take, for example, the domestic version of the sentry problem. In walking along the street, the pedestrian must accept the condition that steps may be heard from behind approaching and overtaking him. In middle-class environments both the proper and likely response is for him to treat the sound as incidental, to be disattended. On many occasions, of course, the individual who acts as though he is disattending these sounds will be fully alive to them. In ghetto streets this concern seems more openly expressed. Here there seem to be more occasions when a user breaks cover and turns to check out all sounds of persons approaching from the rear. And this tack seems to be occurring increasingly in streets in general. Nor is space behind one's back the only lurk area that is obtaining awakened interest. Closed environments seem increasingly to be seen in terms of the lurk dangers they incorporate:

> The scattered positioning of high-rise towers in public-housing sites had produced access-paths to buildings which require the turning of sharp corners. Residents fear what awaits them around each turn. The circuitous access route is further complicated by the practice of locating shrubbery exactly at the turn in the path.
>
> The access-path from the project grounds to apartment building

[55] E. H. Cookridge, *Inside S.O.E.* (London: Arthur Barker, Ltd., 1966), pp. 338–339.

interior can be an equally threatening experience. The entrance lobby of the Columbus Houses project in Newark requires a double turn to bring one to the elevator waiting area. As a result, this area cannot be observed from the outside. Residents step into the building blind with no foreknowledge of what awaits them and once inside are out of view and earshot from the ground outside or from apartments within the building.[56]

A final point. Lurking as an *Umwelt* problem primarily involves individuals who are unacquainted, the assumption being that those who know each other are not likely to sneak up on each other except by way of joking—a joking, incidentally, that seems to testify to concern about lurk lines even in safe places. But there are two manifestations of the problem that involve those who are on familiar and trusted terms. The first concerns collusive betrayal. When a subject is present with others and in a state of talk with them, he employs the working assumption that negative views of him either will be expressed openly or suppressed, allowing him to know where he stands in regard to the encounter. By monitoring the faces of those with whom he is talking, he can check up on the maintenance of this rule and in effect enforce it. However, whenever there are more than two participants in the encounter or close-by non-participants, circumstances are established that enable this ruling to be breached by means of collusive gestures between persons other than the subject, he being the person against whom the collusion is sustained. The eye-to-eye channel between two individuals within which subtly focused facial expressions can be transmitted is so narrow that a three or more person configuration can hardly be policed fully by the man caught in the middle. Here, then, we have an issue of lurk lines, except it is not persons who are lurking but expressions of officially excluded judgments.

The second issue has to do with the greeting rule between acquainteds, the rule being that upon newly coming into sight of someone with whom one is acquainted, there is an obligation to make one's presence felt by extending a greeting. An incidental ef-

---

[56] Columbia Project, *op. cit.*, p. 15.

fect of this rule is that it ensures a subject protection from being observed or overheard unbeknownst to himself by an acquaintance. If for some reason an individual does not want to make full contact with a particular acquainted other, he can break the greeting rule and try to lurk his way through, try to steer a rapid course outside of the other's view while hoping to be able to muster an account should he be uncovered. The quite special self-conscious feeling one has during moments of such hiding suggests how deeply trained one is to greet and how desperately one can rely on the structure of one's *Umwelt* in order to achieve improper ends.

3. *Access Points:* Every *Umwelt*, howsoever closed off by walls, necessarily has points of routine access and impingement. Houses have front and back doors, ground-level windows, and often telephones. Apartment buildings have front lobbies. On the street, the individual will be conversationally accessible to strangers by virtue of request-for-an-audience signals which he is under some obligation to honor.

These points of access are, of course, restricted by convention from what is perceived as misuse. Telephones are engineered so that a ring must be given and answered before talking can occur; glancing into windows is allowed, but staring into them is generally defined as improper, as is, certainly, entering through an open one; doors have knockers and bells, and persons who do not share the fixed territory behind a door ordinarily are obliged to signal so that he who is inside is the one to open it; [57] strangers requesting a conversational hearing on the street are obliged to quickly offer acceptable grounds for the intrusion. But however protective, these conventional restrictions are largely conventional. Points of access can easily become points of alarm. When the doorbell rings at midday, housewives may feel a slight alarm, not having expected any calls. During off-call times for the telephone (say before nine

[57] The strength of this convention should not be underestimated. As Harvey Sacks has suggested to me in correspondence, our totalitarian fantasy of the harsh knock at the door at three in the morning contains little awareness of the fact that, after all, to use a knock, however harsh, is to acknowledge the territorial rights of the resident.

in the morning and after ten at night for adult members of the middle-class) a phone ringing may cause alarm. In some neighborhoods of some cities during some hours, any cross-color encounter between two unacquainted pedestrians can alarm one or both of them. And in cities like New York, apartments are seen as being very vulnerable, especially during an overnight absence of the resident, enough to produce significant developments in door locks and alarms,[58] in buzzer door-openers (that attempt to protect against the usual means of gaining hallway entree),[59] and in attack

---

58 See, for example, Joan Buck, "Your Own Defense Budget," *New York Magazine*, March 24, 1969, pp. 58–60; George Alexander, "A Nervous New Yorker's Guide to Safety Devices," *New York Magazine*, October 5, 1970, pp. 26–32.

59 The current state of feelings about doors is reflected in a recent two-page ad in *Time* (July 30, 1970) with a full picture of a swarthy man pressing an apartment lobby buzzer on one side and on the other the following:

WHO'S DOWNSTAIRS RINGING YOUR BELL?

A FRIEND?

OR THE BOSTON STRANGLER?

Before you press that buzzer, you'd better find out.

Burglars, con men and other low-life characters are trying all sorts of little tricks to get their feet in the door nowadays.

They'll say they have a telegram. (It's corny, but it works.) They'll swear they were recommended by a neighbor (whose name they saw on the bell). They'll even go as far as masquerading in overalls, pretending to be workers sent by "the landlord." (The Boston Strangler used this one.)

They're wise, all right. So if we want to stay healthy we've got to be even wiser—which is exactly what this ad is about.

Recently, a group of very wise, law-abiding citizens at our Automatic Electric subsidiary developed something that could put a lot of crooks on unemployment:

The Enterphone intercom—a lobby-to-apartment intercom unit that works through your telephone.

. . . .

When it's used along with a building's closed-circuit television setup, it becomes part of an electronic security system that lets you *see and hear* whoever's downstairs ringing your bell.

Let's say you're watching television when somebody presses the buzzer. With the Enterphone intercom your bell doesn't ring; your phone does. In short, distinctive bleeps. Before answering, you switch to your building's closed-circuit channel and get a good look at the mystery guest in the lobby. (And at his credentials, too, while you're at it.)

You can then pick up the phone, invite him up, and dial "6"—which electronically unlocks the downstairs door.

dog use.[60] It is also evident that the mails can become a source of harassing "poison-pen" letters and the telephone a source of obscene and threatening calls.

Points of access do, of course, subject individuals to vulnerabilities of a kind more subtle than mentioned so far. For example, it is a common practice of thieves to check by phone before breaking in, thus making sure that no one is home. They also accomplish the same purpose by appearing at the front door ostensibly selling insurance, magazines, or the like, should anyone answer.[61]

4. *The Social Net:* When an individual is in the open presence of others (and they are openly in his presence), he necessarily becomes vulnerable to them in certain standard ways in consequence of his character as a perishable organism and their character as an instrumentality. They can intend to rob him, assault him, sexually molest him, or block his free movement. (They can rely on innocuous appearance—on clothing that conceals weapons, and expressions that conceal intent—in order to position themselves to

---

If you don't like what you see and hear you can quickly dial the superintendent. Or the police.

Right now, the Enterphone intercom is available from General Telephone throughout our entire system. Residential closed-circuit TV isn't. But we're working on it.

Hopefully, they'll both be standard equipment in all apartment buildings someday. And maybe in private homes, too.

Until they are, though—or until other security measures are found—we at General Telephone and Electronics would like to pass along a couple of rules to safeguard you and your family.

Rule No. 1: Don't open your door to anyone unless you know who it is.

Rule No. 2: Never, never break Rule No. 1.

These concerns and devices ultimately spring from the fact that furnished frames have to have points of access, an issue first appreciated with full clarity by government organizations engaged in wartime, secret military work. Techniques first employed in these places are now, of course, becoming domesticated, such being one of the spinoff benefits of military industrial organization. Note, G. T. & E. makes no mention of picture-signature lapel cards, although for full apartment security these might be desirable, too.

[60] Jerrold J. Mundis, "Faster Than a Speeding Mugger, More Reliable Than a Cooping Cop . . . It's Your Very Own Attack Dog," *New York Magazine*, October 27, 1969, pp. 37–46.

[61] See Black, *op. cit.*, p. 94.

carry out these depredations.) They can entrap him into punishable admissions or deeds, or into actions he will come to find abhorrent, as when he responds unknowingly to encouragements from female impersonators. They can inveigle him into various kinds of confidence games. They can monitor him secretly by means of a camera or microphone concealed on their persons.[62] They can shadow or tail him. And if he is a control agent of some kind, they can hide contraband or stolen articles on their persons and employ one another as relays to rid a prime suspect of what he is suspected of.

As suggested, these fundamental risks of face-to-face interaction have been considerably appreciated by participants in daily interaction and by those who write about them. What is insufficiently appreciated is the bearing of "social" information on these contingencies.

I define information as social when it is about the informant

[62] The recent developments in monitoring equipment have been commented on widely in the popular literature. Less attention seems to have been given to the fact that listeners constitute monitoring devices, too. It is so much the case that conversation in a surround is assumed to be meant just for that place that when journalistic interviewing occurs, that is, an open effort to legitimate the carrying of statements from the place they were made to a distal world of newspaper and magazine readers, the person interviewed assumes that his flow of activity will be split in two, one part "for" the record, the other part "off" the record. I refer not merely to statements he makes that he specifically designates as being for or off the record, but also to his whole stream of small behaviors, almost all of which he will assume will be off the record. This split, then, is a fundamental rule regarding the frame for interview interaction. In the last five or six years, however, this rule has broken down in certain social circles, and interviewers have come to serve as monitoring devices for relaying what they witness of matters ordinarily held to be off the record. Subjects then find, in effect, that they have been spied on. The continued willingness of individuals to be interviewed in this manner usually is attributed to their desire for publicity and to the compensatory practice of being "on" in the sense of producing one's whole stream of behavior with the understanding that it may be recorded. There is an additional explanation. So deeply are these framing rules held that even when a subject is suspicious of a particular interviewer, he cannot help but split his activity into a part that might be relayed and a part that never would—or so he thinks.

himself and is conveyed to those in his immediate presence. Important here is information about the informant's social and personal identity, information about his intent or "projects of action," and information about his social relationships to others present, including especially those who obtain the information.

Now it appears that when an individual is present with others he assumes that a supply of social information will be available to him and that this will be adequate to allow him to judge whether or not he should be alarmed because of the set of persons in his immediate view—his "social net." Further, he anticipates that this source of information will enable him to act so as to avoid producing incidents which might themselves be alarming. And it seems to be a fact of social life that social information adequate in these terms is supplied him. What the individual needs in order to orient himself effectively to those around him he usually acquires, and he acquires it from them.

For the individual, then, it is these expectations regarding available social information that serve to limit the dangers contained in the social net around him, and typically it is these expectations which must be breached if his social net is to become a danger to him.

Take, for example, information about relationships.[63] There are rules about the civil inattention that passers-by owe each other, the greetings obligatory between the acquainted, and the signs of mutual orientation that members of a with owe each other. Therefore, the individual is assured considerable information about the relationships in his social net, information about the relationship of persons present to one another and to him. He will be able to know whether any two individuals are merely unacquainteds in the same gathering or unacquainteds who have struck up a momentary conversation, or acquainteds who have stopped to chat for a moment in passing, or individuals in the same with. In consequence, he will also know who among those present can act together as a team in collaborative activity, for teamwork assumes

---

[63] See "Tie-Signs," this volume.

team relationships and relationships ordinarily are publicized by "tie-signs" of various kinds.

The point is that the informing signs ordinarily available to the subject are exactly what will be manipulated by persons who are a source of alarm for him, whether their technique is to conceal relationships that exist or reveal relationships that do not exist. Without being able to conceal a collaborative structure behind the show of civil inattention that they extend to each other—a show appropriate between the unacquainted—pickpocket mobs could not steal, spies could not use the so-called "silent meeting" in order to exchange messages, the short-con involving two operators who ostensibly bump into each other could not be performed, and various forms of multi-person surveillance could not be employed. Without being able to mimic the ritual small talk that two unacquainted social equals exchange when chance proximity obliges it, two collaborating friends could less easily cover the passing of vital messages or documents between them. Without recourse to the mutual address of persons who know each other well, two unacquainted individuals could not cooperate in substantiating the false story of one of them. All of these machinations, note, hide behind the same set of appearances, those sustained in public places by civil fellow-users, both acquainted and unacquainted. Were there no such pattern of appearances, no such structure of mutual alignments recognized by all, the mischievous would have nothing to hide behind, and chicanery would grievously suffer.

The individual, then, needs to obtain information about the relationships of those in his surround, and ordinarily this information is made available to him through tie-signs of various kinds. Similarly, if he is to be at ease in a situation, he will require some information about the intent, the purpose, and the project of action of those in his presence, and this, too, is ordinarily made available to him.

In some cases the action of others may be quite transparent to the individual, either because he is conversant with the technique they employ, in the sense that one electrician can "follow" closely what another electrician is doing, or because the technique itself is not part of a complex skill, as when a customer can clearly see that what the soda fountain clerk is doing is putting a scoop of chocolate ice cream into a sugar cone. In other cases, say where esoteric technical skill is involved, the witness may not be able to follow in detail what it is that the technician is doing, but will know enough about the technology to be able to recognize more or less what the man is about—usually enough to know that no alarm is necessary. The same circumstances occur when a subject looks at someone walking in a businesslike manner on the street; the witness does not know where the walker is going or the nature of his specific purpose, but he feels that this activity can be located in a broad class of actions that are safe. All of these actions are, as it were, translucent—understandable enough to the witness for him to feel safe in the presence of the person performing them but not transparent enough to be followed in any detail. The sort of behavior that causes alarm, of course, is the kind that cannot be placed in a broad class, at least in a broad class of safe activities. Such opaque acts may not be threats in themselves but they leave the witness not knowing where the mind of the performer is, or what his purpose, and therefore not trustful of him. And here, of course, we find the obligation of those who find themselves being witnessed: their acts should not be opaque. One illustration, a Konrad Lorenz story, might be provided of the trouble caused to both performer and witness when minimal understandability is not present:

> One Saturday in June, I got off the train from Vienna at Altenberg station, in the midst of a gathering of bathers, such as often flock to our village at fine weekends. I had gone only a few steps along the street and the crowd had not yet dispersed when, high above me in the air, I saw a bird whose species I could not at first determine. It flew with slow, measured wing-beats, varied at set intervals by longer periods of gliding. It seemed too heavy to be a buzzard; for a stork, it was not big enough and, even at that height, neck and feet should have been visible. Then the bird gave a sudden swerve so that the setting sun shone for a second full on the underside of the great wings which lit up like stars in the blue of the skies.

The bird was white. By Heaven, it was my cockatoo! The steady movements of his wings clearly indicated that he was setting out on a long-distance flight. What should I do? Should I call to the bird? Well, have you ever heard the flight-call of the greater yellow-crested cockatoo? No? But you have probably heard pig-killing after the old method. Imagine a pig squealing at its most voluminous, taken up by a microphone and magnified many times by a good loudspeaker. A man can imitate it quite successfully, though somewhat feebly, by bellowing at the top of his voice "O-ah." I had already proved that the cockatoo understood this imitation and promptly "came to heel." But would it work at such a height? A bird always has great difficulty in making the decision to fly downwards at a steep angle. To yell, or not to yell, that was the question. If I yelled and the bird came down, all would be well, but what if it sailed calmly on through the clouds? How would I then explain my song to the crowd of people? Finally, I did yell. The people around me stood still, rooted to the spot. The bird hesitated for a moment on outstretched wings, then, folding them, it descended in one dive and landed upon my outstretched arm. Once again I was master of the situation.[64]

There is one element of social nets that warrants special attention. In orienting himself in public places, the subject accords a special status to those whose job is to keep supplies on hand, traffic moving, and everything in working order. Whatever the source of their pay, these "stocked characters" have a plant function, ensuring that a social order is maintained. Thus, in public places there are the police to appeal to when something goes wrong; there are street cleaners and road-repair men; there are newspaper vendors and doormen—routinely appealed to, of course, for informational services they are not paid to provide. These characters can be anywhere in public places and be of little interest, their freedom to be present being linked to the tendency of the user of the street to treat them as non-persons, mere background figures who function within a different frame of reference from co-users of the

---

[64] Konrad Z. Lorenz, *King Solomon's Ring* (London: Methuen & Company, 1957), pp. 45–46.

streets. And in consequence, of course, by use of the costumes and props of these stocked characters, villains can attack the whole of the public plant, effectively concealing alarming activities:

> MELBOURNE, AUSTRALIA—A gang of thieves stood in one of Melbourne's busiest streets last night, hammered a five-inch hole in the concrete wall of an antique dealer's shop and escaped with jewels worth $56,000.
>
> The men posed as construction workers on a new building going up beside the antique shop. They used a sledgehammer and crowbar to smash their way into the shop, then took oxyacetylene equipment in with them and cut open the office safe.[65]

> TOKYO—The bandit, about 22 years old, wearing the white helmet and black leather jacket of a traffic officer, rode a stolen white motorbike up to a bank car carrying bonus money for employees of the Toshiba Electric Co., 20 miles west of Tokyo.
>
> He told the unarmed bank men, from the Nippon Trust and Banking Co., that he had information that dynamite had been planted in the car.
>
> When the four got out, the bandit got in and drove away with the car and three metal boxes full of unrecorded yen banknotes worth $816,667.
>
> "He looked just like a policeman," said Eiji Nakada, the driver of the auto. "He said he had instructions from Koganei Police Station."[66]

Corresponding to the stocked characters that keep the public plant in running order, there is a set of functionaries who service domestic and office plants: electricians, plumbers, bug exterminators, telephone repairmen, meter readers, and television servicemen. These persons, like policemen, are allowed to initiate contacts and introduce definitions of the situation. Properly uniformed and certified, personnel of this kind are allowed to cut across the workday schedules of ordinary people and, in exchange for accepting something like non-person treatment, they are allowed the run of otherwise private places. Here, too, of course, we find a

[65] *Boston Traveller*, November 11, 1966.

[66] *Philadelphia Evening Bulletin*, December 10, 1968.

role that often is used as a cover by thieves, police agents, and rapists. Once in a building these impersonators can perform technical acts such as bugging a telephone—indeed, can do this with the assistance of the residents—because of the translucency of their work. One example might be cited:

> To 37 housewives in the Richmond and Taraval districts, Thomas Ahern seemed like any other Pacific Gas and Electric Company serviceman: smiling, polite and efficient.
>
> Too efficient, they learned later.
>
> Police said Ahern, a slender 28-year-old in white trousers, a blue windbreaker and a white cap, has been knocking on doors for the past month and telling housewives he must shut off the gas.
>
> "There is an emergency in the neighborhood," he would say.
>
> Then he would ask the women to wait by the gas meter, usually in the basement, to check the stoves and pilot lights.
>
> The helpful housewives would patiently wait by the meters for as much as half an hour, officers reported, before they would begin to wonder why the gas man hadn't returned.
>
> Upstairs they would find the drawers ransacked and all the loose money gone.
>
> The "gas man," of course, would also be gone.
>
> . . .
>
> The PG & E said Ahern was never one of its employees.[67]

In general, then, stocked characters and other caretaker types are accorded a license which those who have threatening intent find useful to exploit, this being done by impersonation. When the citizenry learns of these practices, alarm is felt. The individual may then come to feel that he has reason to doubt all those who come to keep his establishment in working order. Yet, in spite of these doubts, he will find it necessary to open up his door to these people, since he cannot operate his furnished frame without specialized help.[68]

---

[67] *San Francisco Chronicle*, November 20, 1963. For other examples of cooperation, see Dash, *op. cit.*, pp. 159, 185, 214–215.

[68] Well illustrated by the case of the Boston Strangler, who was known to gain access to apartments by acting like a maintenance man. Although

PART THREE: CONCLUSIONS

I *Connectedness*

1. In the first part of this paper it was suggested that if a subject is to be at ease in his surroundings of the moment—in his *Umwelt*—he need not find that things are as he expected them to be, only that, howsoever they are, he can be safe in withdrawing his attention from them. A special application of this theme must now be considered and can be because some principal kinds of alarm have been discriminated.

Given a subject's current project of action as a point of reference, given, that is, his current undertaking, intent, purpose, design or task, and given that this perspective is taken within an immediate surround and applied to it—given all this—one fundamental issue can be raised: the issue of connectedness.

Every subject can perceive a locally occurring event to be something occurring quite incidentally, something happening alongside his own unfolding course of action but not purposely engineered to affect the outcome of this action. (Such a design-unconnected event may, of course, be a well-designed part of someone else's independent course of action, and furthermore the subject may well exploit the anticipated occurrence of the event in realizing his own project; yet its incidental character remains.) In contrast, there is the event that the subject or others intendedly brings about because of its effect upon his course of action. Relative to the subject's project, then, there will be undesigned and designed events. For example, if the subject arranges to meet a friend in a particular crowded bar at 12:45 the next afternoon, and according to the bar clock he sees his friend approaching a minute after the

---

the whole city apparently became concerned with the issue of admitting maintenance men, almost everyone continued in one degree or other to do so, in a few cases with wariness which was short-lived.

appointed time, then I count as designed the fact of the co-occurrence of the two individuals at that place at that time. And I count as undesigned (relative to the subject) the fact that the bar was there that day, that the clock correctly told Eastern Standard Time, that particular other persons were present, and that the sun rose that morning, allowing that particular day to come about. Although these latter elements in the situation affect the individual and his design, and although he could hardly plan and execute his project without knowing about them and being able to count on them to occur as predicted, still, these elements are largely indifferent to whether or not he in particular carries out his design. For example, the bar owner may depend on the public using his bar as a place to meet, and he may indeed plan his facilities so as to encourage this practice, but ordinarily he does not adjust this plan to the requirements of any *particular* pair of meeters. And if he did, then he would become part of the designed features of the pair's plans.

The division between designed and undesigned is exhaustive and mutually exclusive. Ordinarily there will be in the individual's *Umwelt* more that is design-unconnected than design-connected.[69] In any case, the individual's ease within his *Umwelt* depends upon

[69] The question of how much of any particular scene is part of the individual's current design of action and how much undesigned is interesting. At least two variables can be mentioned. First, the more prestigeful and powerful the individual, the more the current surround enters the design of his activity. Note, for example, the difference between an ordinary person waiting in line for his coach air ticket and Frank Sinatra being awaited by his own airplane and crew to fly a route that he has determined, at a time he has established, and with a passenger list and menu he has specified. Whether a particular commercial passenger cancels out or not, the commercial flight goes to a designated place at a designated time (unless matters unconnected with the individual alter this, which has been said to happen occasionally). Sinatra cancels, however, and presumably his plane stays put. Second, whatever the individual's class and power level, his life-cycle rituals will involve occasions of relatively great design-connectedness. The best example is the wedding. The whole affair can be seen as oriented to and produced for the marrying couple. They are celebrities for the duration of the social occasion. If one or both fails to turn up, the whole flight must be canceled.

his knowing how this division is to be drawn at any particular moment. Thus, to continue with the example cited, whatever ease the individual manages to attain in the bar while meeting his friend is likely to be linked to his being able to assume, and with warrant, an anticipated division between designed and undesigned elements.

The individual, then, divides his *Umwelt* into the designed and undesigned, into project and setting, into the self-oriented and incidental. This division has significant corollaries.

First, the fact that the individual can feel that much of what is present in his surround has no active relation on its own to his current design (whether to further it or hinder it) provides him a ground for treating this part of his immediate environment as given, as something he can disattend safely. Often what he thus sees as neutral contains some or all of the persons present, persons who thereby require only civil inattention and involve themselves in his affairs only to the extent of according him the same courtesy. Whether, then, we deal with the inanimate or animate parts of the subject's *Umwelt*, we find that there is likely to be undesigned elements, and that he need but provide minimal carefulness to be secure in taking these elements for granted, as something to be disattended.

The second corollary. As suggested, the subject assumes that typically his current course of action is of no concern to the agencies—whether present or not—that are responsible for much of what is occurring around him. This assumption allows him a pacifying account for a broad class of events which otherwise would be alarming, events which he himself can attribute to some form or other of "fortuitousness" or credit as fortuitous when this imputation is advanced by others. To repeat, the great strength of belief the individual has in the indifference of much that is around him to his particular design allows him to believe in a special sense of "good" and "bad" fortune; he can believe that an event occurring in his *Umwelt* which has a fateful consequence for him need not have been planned with that in mind by anyone.[70]

---

[70] The strength of this belief is also seen in the contempt the individual is likely to manifest for those who openly attest to connections among the

Thus, however fateful the event turns out to be, at least he can quickly cease his alarm, for since no intent is to be imputed to the event, he can assume that no repetition is to be anticipated, that nothing is augured by what has occurred.

Varieties of this "meaninglessness" can be discriminated. "Luck" (good and bad) may be credited when something is lost or found, or trains run early or late with dramatic consequences for the individual's particular plan. "Pure accident" can occur when bodily harm is produced by or to the individual when (it is felt) he is in no way responsible. (Two cars that collide on an icy road can leave their drivers feeling that a pure accident is at work. A careless driver, on the other hand, tacitly engineers his own destruction, which, when accomplished, can be seen as "no accident"; but the particular person who happens to be the other party must see that although it may be no accident that someone was injured, it is pure bad luck that he happened to be the someone.) It is a "coincidence" when two old friends "bump into" each other; a "happenstance" when two unacquainted persons come into incidental social content and strike up a conversation that leads to a close relationship or mutually profitable business dealings. And there are lotteries and games of pure chance, these being devices specifically designed to bring into play in an organized way an ensured "undesignedness" between choices and outcomes.

2. The fundamental distinction that the individual draws between the designed and the undesigned provides the ground for another basic conception he brings to his surround, one that cuts across the first: the notion of contrivance. He knows that he himself can introduce an event into some other individual's *Umwelt* and disguise this event so that it appears (he hopes) to be unconnected to the other person's project when in fact it is, or appears to be design-connected when in fact it isn't. Since he is capable of contriving the world that others are in, he could hardly fail to see that his own world may be contrived by others. For this reason, if for no other, the subject can come to suspect the connections

---

unconnected, as in the espousal of "propitious" signs, horoscope readings, lucky charms, and the like.

among the events in his *Umwelt*. In sum: his ease in his *Umwelt* depends not merely on his being able to divide events around him into the designed and undesigned, but also on his being confident that these appearances are not merely contrived—unless, of course, it is he himself who has contrived them.

Whether the subject comes to suspect contrivance or not, there is some warrant for his doing so. Given the belief that he has in regard to fortuitousness, and given the fact that he is willing to discount certain otherwise alarming events on this ground, it is understandable that those who would trap him into acts he will come to see later as cause for alarm can employ the appearance of fortuitousness as a cover. They can arrange now for an event to happen later, which, when it does, will strike the individual as having occurred with no design, at least no design relative to him.

To wit: A pickpocket arranges to "accidentally" walk into his chosen victim, so that what follows, the flurry and touching of the remedial interchange, will momentarily expose the victim's pocket unguarded to a third pair of hands. An agent, desiring to obtain a plan for a harbor installation, learns where the plans are stored, who works in the office containing the locked files, which of these workers is vulnerable, and where that particular individual takes his morning coffee, and there happens to strike up a conversation with him, from whence a relationship is cultivated, leading to evenings out, successful (fixed) gambling, unsuccessful (fixed) gambling, the loan of money to pay gambling debts, and then the plans. And diplomat-agents are given the following advice concerning the preparation of normal appearances:

> It is recommended that intelligence officers take more frequent walks about the city at different times. Depending on his work load and the purpose for the walks, he can take walks after work, before work, and during his lunch hour. After he "accustoms" the counterintelligence service to such walks, the intelligence officer can use them later to support agent communications (posting or checking of signals), agent meetings, servicing dead drops, etc.[71]

[71] Oleg Penkovskiy, *The Penkovskiy Papers* (New York: Doubleday & Company, Inc., 1965; London: Fontana, 1967), p. 125.

A team of hijackers learn that two wage clerks draw a wage payroll from a bank every Thursday, that they hail the lead cab from the nearby rank, wait till it is at the bank steps, enter, and drive off to deliver the money. The clerks assume that the cabbie's sole relation to them derives from their being just another fare and that, therefore, they can use the cab, in effect, as an unmarked delivery car. On one Thursday as soon as they have gone into the bank to collect the money, three different individuals arrive separately (ostensibly unrelated to one another) and hire away all but one of the cabs, this one itself being fixed in the front position by appearing to be taken. When the clerks gesture for any next cab in line, it is this one that they get, one more deeply connected to their affairs than they had thought, as they soon find out.[72] The Los Angeles police, wanting to bug the premises of the bookkeeper of a suspect bookmaker, doctored reality in the following fashion, according to the late chief, William Parker:

> The investigating officers approached the owner of the premises and enlisted his cooperation. At the request of the officers, the owner, who lived in another county, wrote a letter to his tenants, stating that the time had arrived to make an annual termite inspection and stating that a termite contractor would call at a certain time. The police officers then hired a termite contractor, sufficiently familiarized themselves with the nature of his work so that they could plausibly appear to accompany and assist him, and went to the Glenville address. They were admitted by the bookkeeper. He and his wife and child were present in the building while the inspection was made and in fact engaged one of the officers in conversations about aspects of termite work. . . . While in the house, a listening device was secreted in the room. . . .[73]

A personal injury troupe finds a likely mark, plots his daily auto route, and then, at a convenient point, arranges for what looks like an accident. And the following:

> A couple of years ago, a bankbook burglar broke into an apartment in Manhattan and took a credit card with the victim's signature on it

[72] Parr, *op. cit.*, pp. 97–99.
[73] Quoted in Dash et al., *op. cit.*, p. 185.

and a bankbook showing deposits of eighteen thousand dollars. He left six hundred in cash in the drawer, and, sure enough, the victim needed some money the day after the burglary, took some of the cash there, and didn't notice the loss of his bankbook. Since that particular burglar didn't have either a wife or a girl friend to serve as an accomplice, he had rented office space a few days earlier and put an ad in the newspaper for a secretary, offering a handsome salary. The first girl to apply was hired, and her first chore was to go to the bank and withdraw some money. The practiced bank-book burglar doesn't create a fuss by closing an account; he just taps it for a judicious fraction—in this instance, for fifty-two hundred and fifty of the eighteen thousand dollars. The burglar had a withdrawal slip made out—signature and all—and he gave it to the girl along with the bankbook. As the girl left the office, so did her new employer. When she stepped out of the bank, he just happened to be passing by. On learning that she had got the money, he thanked her, took the bankbook, the identification, and the fifty-two hundred and fifty dollars, and told her to go back to the office. He never went back himself.[74]

So, too, when arrangements are made for an individual to find himself in the setting in which he that night engages in an activity for which he can later be blackmailed. And, of course, where games of pure chance or lotteries are involved, the problem is not to find some occasions of play that are fixed, but to find some that aren't.[75]

In all of these situations what we get is a "playing of the world backwards," that is, the contrivance of an apparently fortuitous

---

[74] Black, *op. cit.*, pp. 76, 79.

[75] There is an interesting paradox here. For example, in the numbers racket, the daily selection of the winning numbers is made up so as to maximally ensure no influence of the managers of the game upon the specific number selected. Items such as the second and third digit in the day's total bond sales are used. We have here, then, a kind of apotheosis of fortuitousness. But, of course, by bribing an executive in the bond clearing house, it has been possible to introduce design and connectedness—surely a heartening example of man's eternal effort to fight back the play of blind chance. See Danforth, *op. cit.*, "The Gentle Banker and His Big Fix: The Numbers Racket," pp. 318–326.

event which has alarming consequences for the individual. Interestingly, in the "big con" in which a whole social establishment may be put together to provide a few minutes of convincing background display, the mark is, in fact, as much the center of the design as any potentate could wish for, but, of course, the connectedness is only covert; if the operators are to succeed, they must convince the mark that he is but an incidental user of the place and that all the other individuals and artifacts present have a reason to be there independent of him, being involved in projects of action independent of his, that, in brief, they are merely alongside him.

The examples given of contrivance so far have an obvious bias. An individual whose world is played backward need not necessarily be disadvantaged by the result, alarming as the discovery of contrivance might be. In many courtships, for example, the earliest phase is accomplished by contrivance; one party finds that he has luckily happened to bump into the other party again, and it turns out that the other party had arranged to be there on an off-chance in an unadmitted effort, complete with a show of surprise, to help luck along. One further example might be added, one that suggests the scope that can be brought to the arranging of reality. When the British at the beginning of World War II began to develop sabotage techniques, camouflage, and other manufacture for intelligence and subversive purposes, the first expansion—from a carpenter's shop—was into premises in the back of the Victoria and Albert Museum:

> Those workshops and offices looked just like the ordinary mews they were supposed to be. To maintain secrecy, the walls of the museum were cut through into the mews, and the mews walls into the garages. Regularly every morning milk and newspapers were delivered. They were taken in at the different doors of what were ostensibly mews flatlets by specially selected A.T.S. girls, who would appear at the door dressed as ordinary British housewives in the middle of household chores: some with hair in curlers, others in apron or wearing a dressing-gown.[76]

---

[76] Bell, *op. cit.*, p. 20.

The point is now obvious. When a milkman delivers milk to the door and is greeted by a woman in curlers and dressing-gown, he can assume that the gown is on because of morning commerce of the kind he represents and therefore is not unconnected with his own project, namely, delivering the milk. But it is central to his notion of what the world is like that the curlers are there *in spite* of morning commerce and that the doorway itself was not cut into the wall on behalf of himself and the other tradesmen. He warrants a greeting, perhaps, but not a door.[77]

---

[77] The question arises as to just how elaborate contrivance can get. Taking the subject's current *Umwelt* as a point of reference, two dimensions must be explored: the synchronic, this bearing on the relation of one current element in his *Umwelt* to other current elements, and the diachronic, this pertaining to the relation of one element to what preceded it in time. The synchronic dimension seems the more readily accessible. Suggestions like the following can be made. Suspicious subjects seem to be calmed by the presence of a large number of persons of different sex, age, class and occupation, all apparently going about their separate businesses—differences in status apparently implying genuine unconnectedness. In consequence, police staking out an ambush lean toward the use of a whole troupe of differently disguised players. ("When Marighella's trusted bodyguard, Gaucho, appeared to case the rendezvous site, he saw two couples necking in a Chevrolet, laborers languidly unloading materials at a construction site, bricklayers working on an unfinished building across the street. . . . All [it turned out] were police. The fusillade lasted a full five minutes." *Time*, November 2, 1970, p. 21.) The diachronic dimension seems the more tricky and the more interesting. In playing a subject's world backwards, how far back can the contrivers go? And what structural limitations occur in this regard? Contrivers can make their plans by assuming a subject will follow his routines, and probably respond as predicted to a particular move, but to depend on being able to predict his reaction to the reaction to this reaction introduces almost too much margin of error. For example, in the story of the snaring of Penkovsky (Greville Wynne, *The Man from Moscow* [London: Hutchinson, 1967]), we read:

> A British Intelligence agent saw the Russian colonel sitting alone, saw the glass pause between table and lips, noted not once but on many evenings the faraway expression—and told London. And London, sensitive to the smallest oddities of behaviour, paused to reflect. . . .
>
> No regular British agent existed in the Soviet Union who was in the sort of position that might cross or have any connection with Penkovsky's career as an army officer. A regular agent, who might in any case be already known and marked by the Russians, could not move around to fit in with Penkovsky's movements without creating the most obvious suspicion.

It should now be plain that as the individual moves through the course of his day, the changing surround that moves with him is likely to contain many minor dealings with others that could have alarming significance for him. At many points he will be vulnerable to having his world played backwards. What makes this fate uncommon is not the difficulty of arranging it, *per se*, but the fact that most of those who might have a motive for making these arrangements do not think along these lines. And those who are willing and oriented lack the strategic information necessary in such designs: given what they want, they don't know who has it; given whom they know, they do not know what these potential victims can be separated from. Such stability as the individual has in his *Umwelt* derives in part from the fact that the right information is not in the wrong hands.[78]

> Someone new was needed. Someone who could travel in the Union without suspicion; who would be accepted at his face value for some bona fide work that he could be doing in Russia; who could be steered toward Penkovsky at the right time; who would not know till the last moment what his real mission was—since a perfectly natural behaviour could be achieved better by ignorance than by acting; and who, when he did know what was required, would have the experience to do whatever was necessary to assist Penkovsky (pp. 20–21).

Wynne then argues that he was re-recruited into intelligence because he appeared to be the sort of person whom Penkovsky would voluntarily talk to if he wanted to talk, and then placed in Penkovsky's orbit of incidental contact to await developments. Obviously, this sort of playing of the world backwards could only be done if the very high cost of playing the game and the very good chance of losing it were balanced by the gain that would result from the contrivance working—as, in this particular case, it apparently did.

If we shift our concern from contrivances aimed at the situation of particular subjects to those designed to influence political opinion, then the scope of the effort can become very large indeed. When a misguided, precipitous political act occurs which causes decisive reaction, questions are always raised, sometimes with warrant, concerning the possibility that the victims and not the enemy arranged the deed. A humbler example, yet with its own complexity, is the politician's practice of arranging for a confrontation in which exactly that obstreperous challenge occurs for which he has worked out a telling reply. The planted question at the press conference is the modest model.

[78] It is thus the case that whenever information about surrounds and fixed territories becomes *organized*, new vulnerabilities occur. If one tells

3. The possibility that the individual's world can be played backwards is matched to a degree by the possibility that it will be played forward improperly. Just as the individual assumes that the apparently incidental contacts he is now having with others in his *Umwelt* have not come about because of nefarious design, so he also assumes that the minor dealings that he is now having with persons passing on their separate ways will not be used by them to provide the bases for unanticipated costs to him later. In brief, he assumes that many of the involvements he sustains with those in his *Umwelt* will give way shortly to no connectedness at all.

The one example of this forward playing I want to consider is what in the criminal trades is called "fingering." The reference here is to the setting-up process whereby an individual with a minor or even fortuitous connection to a victim gives information gleaned during a contact with him to those who mean him harm, enabling them to be effective in a criminal action. (Here the contact itself is not a consequence of concealed design, but is opportunistically used against the victim with much the same result.) When an instance is examined in detail, we find that the mutual involvement of victim and finger was more consequential than the victim had thought it would be, or wanted it to be, and that he had been tacitly depending on such a restriction. For example, a messenger, florist, or bellhop can deal with hotel guests in a man-

---

the police that one will be away for a month, then someone definitely knows that one's house can be robbed leisurely. If the addresses of license number owners are organized so citizens who are sideswiped can write in to find out who the culprit was, then thieves similarly can discover the addresses of prosperous-looking couples. If art magazines list sales, then cultivated crooks can find out where good paintings are. Ships' passenger lists tell who will be away for the summer, and society columns organize information about who among the affluent will be at a ball on a particular evening. As a Scotland Yard spokesman was reported saying:

> "All a man needs . . . is a Sotheby's catalogue to find out what's in style and bringing high prices, the sales reports of the newspapers to show who's buying, a society magazine reporting who is taking vacations abroad and when, and the price of a railway ticket to the vacationer's country house."

Alfred Friendly, Times-Post Service London release in *San Francisco Chronicle Sunday Punch*, September 25, 1968.

ner that the guests will think is circumscribed to the service relationship, only to discover later after the investigation of the robbery of their rooms that the server's interest had more points of connection with them than they had assumed.[79]

Of course, law-abiding citizens are not alone in their vulnerability to fingermen; as earlier suggested, criminals are vulnerable in the same way and in much greater degree. Before citizens can be fingered, someone criminally inclined must incidentally discover something usable about them; criminals, however, need only be discovered planning or practicing their trade by someone ready for whatever reason to take the role of the good citizen, and in persons of that kind the world abounds. [80] Moreover, if a criminal is wanted by the police or by his competitors, his whereabouts alone comprises strategic information, and this can be acquired by anyone in any walk of life who knows what the culprit looks like and happens to see him, an extremely alarming condition. If a teammate or professional informer doesn't set him up, a passing stranger will. As suggested, criminal enterprise can be seen as a means of maximizing one's vulnerability to being set up by others. Only double agents seem more intent on ending up being strung along.

4. It is possible, then, for the minor contacts in the individual's *Umwelt* to have occurred for ominous reasons or, beginning fortuitously, to lead from there to ominous consequences. However, this actual vulnerability is not, I think, the important fact. What is important is this: given that an apparently undesigned contact can turn out in retrospect to have been the first visible move in a well-designed game being played against the individual, and therefore not incidental at all, and given, further, that a genuinely inci-

---

[79] Black, *op. cit.*, pp. 96, 99.

[80] And detective work can be seen to be, in appreciable degree, a device for exploiting informers. See, for example, Malachi L. Harney and John C. Cross, *The Informer in Law Enforcement* (2nd ed.: Springfield, Ill.: Charles C Thomas, 1968), and Jerome H. Skolnick, *Justice Without Trial* (New York: John Wiley and Sons, Inc., 1967), chap. 6, "The Informer System," pp. 112–113.

dental contact can be opportunistically exploited by bad characters—given all this—it follows that *any* current incidental contact that has so far not led to anything alarming might indeed do so. Every cab that turns up just when it is wanted might be driven by someone who is cause for alarm, someone who planned to appear to have happened by, or by someone who, in merely happening by, is nonetheless ready to exploit nefariously the trust his passengers will have to put in him. Any stranger over eighteen, any newish friend, could be a government agent; few citizens have reason to think they themselves have given cause for warranted or unwarranted surveillance, but many citizens have incidental contact with persons who do qualify for this attention, and someone else participating in this contact might therefore be there for peculiar reasons.

5. The notion of "merely someone who is present," of course, involves vulnerabilities itself. As already suggested, the subject, acting as a receiver of information about the relationships of those around him, can discern the following: persons he does not know who are extending him civil inattention; persons he does not know who have struck up talk with him on one ground or another; persons he knows; persons who do not know each other and are extending each other civil inattention; persons who had not known each other but are engaged in struck up talk; persons who had apparently known each other and have paused on their different courses for a moment's chat; persons together in the same with. These are the kinds of persons that can be in his net. This list specifies and exhausts, from one perspective, the possible "someones." But what in fact this list involves is a set of guises or appearances that can be suppressed or can be simulated and certainly have been for a variety of questionable purposes. Thus, it is precisely this list of possibilities that the wary subject comes to suspect. And what is thereby suspected is all the types of anyone's, all the someone's in his social net, in brief, everyone around him. The same list, of course, covers the guises he himself may enact in order to conceal alarming deeds of his own; indeed, as suggested, his

having used these guises in the past itself provides him all the instruction he might need—ensuring an appreciation of why to be suspicious, of what to be alarmed.

6. As an example of these issues regarding connectedness and the social net, look at a minor phenomenon: "second seeing." Although the subject often believes that he takes no notice whatsoever of the properly behaved strangers he passes on the street, we know this is not the case. He takes enough notice even of the most normal-appearing passers-by so that he and they can tacitly cooperate in the intricate business of avoiding collision. More to the point here, he also acquires and stores an impressive amount of identificatory information about them. This is borne out by the fact that under some circumstances if he and they see each other seeing each other, they can use this fact as an excuse for an acquaintanceship greeting upon next seeing that they have seen each other.[81] The acquisition of identificatory information is thus demonstrated when, upon the second seeing, the participants find that they call to mind a first, and therefore must have retained the memory of it all along.

The circumstances in which second seeings lead to acquaintanceship are "social"; the participants see from the context of their two seeings that they are appropriately placed socially for acquaintanceship. When acquaintanceship is not appropriate, the participants of a second seeing can treat the whole matter as happenstance, a fortuitous coming together, this being the understanding associated with the first coming together also. (Again, note, it is at their second meeting that the participants become alive to their having retained identificatory information concerning the first meeting.) Now if the places and character of these two meetings are discrepant, so that second seeings appear to be outside the compass of chance, then the subject is likely to feel alarm; he must consider the possibility, first, that the others have alarming designs in regard to him, and second, that they might think that he has

---

[81] Argued in "Tie-Signs," this volume.

such designs upon them. Thus, if it can be said that incidental, fleeting, anonymous contacts lay a base for later acquaintanceship, it can even more be said that they lay a base for later alarm.

I want to add two points about second seeings. First, in order to allay alarm upon such an occasion, the subject may break through to the others with a special smiling exchange, sometimes accompanied by words, whereby both parties openly admit through their expressions that an odd conjunction of events has occurred, that one might feel this were a base for alarm, but that really nothing but chance is amiss. The participants thereby "break frame"; they momentarily step out of their appropriate role as mutually disattending strangers, thereby providing an open acknowledgement of something that might otherwise leave lingering doubts, and an easy return to ordinary expectation regarding chance seeings.[82] Third seeings seem to be even more likely than seconds to evoke this sort of joking interchange.

The second point pertains to cover. The arts of surveillance involving "tailing" and "staking-out" depend crucially on a subject's willingness to treat first seeings as being entirely fortuitous—something that subjects are not always willing to do, since he who is tailed is likely to have reason to think that this might occur and to see in once-seen persons the possibility of nefarious design. But certainly second seeings have to be avoided in this line of work, expressed in the fact that the literature on surveillance is exceptional in giving explicit attention to the phenomenon of second seeing. It is thus, then, against the background of basic beliefs regarding happenstance and incidental contact that we are to appreciate the deviltry involved in what is called "rough shadowing":

---

[82] In public life there is a whole class of these little expression-interchanges involving momentary role release and a sort of jointly sustained collusion against a whole frame of reference. Thus, when a driver openly makes a minor mistake in traffic and momentarily ties up the passage of another motorist, he may, instead of trying to bluster it out or provide a gestured apology, glance into the eyes of the other driver and wink collusively or shrug, briefly incorporating the other in a jocular putdown of the traffic system and the motorist role.

> There are occasions when shadowing is intended to be discovered simply to scare the subject with knowledge that he has been found out and is being followed. "Rough" shadowing may be used, for example, with the man who is taking time off from business duties and whose boss is having him followed. The agent may brush against the culprit in the street and make an apology in order to draw attention to himself. "Next you get in the same elevator with him," Neville [chief of investigation at Pinkerton's] says, "and make sure he gets a good look at you. Later in the street you blow your horn and when he looks around you give him a wave or a smile. Twenty minutes later maybe you bump into him as he is coming out of a store or stand beside him at a counter as he makes a purchase. Eventually he realizes he's being followed and guesses why. Usually he stops taking time off and attends to his job again." Rough shadowing is frowned on by the courts, and the more reputable agencies use it with discretion. Others, however, carry it to extremes with mysterious phone calls and other minor terror tactics.[83]

To unravel the reasons why rough shadowing of a subject causes him alarm is to begin to lay out the way of being of the individual in his surround.

7. It is apparent, then, that the possibility, "passer-by incidentally glanced at," is a feature of the subject's *Umwelt* and one that can cause him alarm. The same could be said of the appearances, "someone striking up a conversation with oneself." A damaging critic of the automotive industry about to testify before a congressional committee suddenly finds that he is coming into incidental contact with attractive girls in the local drug store and supermarket, that conversation with them seems to be easy and seems to lead easily to further contact. With some warrant he feels that although this is the way in which relationships *can* begin, a nefarious design is at work in these particular cases.[84] So one of the possible categories of others in his *Umwelt* may well be spoiled for him.

---

[83] Willa Petscheck, "An Unblinking Look at the New York Private Eye," *New York Magazine*, November 23, 1970, p. 44.

[84] See, for example, *San Francisco Chronicle*, "Odd Shadowing of an Auto Critic," March 7, 1966, p. 17.

Presumably, then, he might find himself caught in the classical dynamics of suspicion: if one type of other (those with whom a conversation is struck up) is suspect, why not the other types? And if it is known that he has good cause to suspect some of his incidental others, will not other others feel that they might be suspected unjustly or feel he is concerned that they might feel that he wrongly feels they are to be suspected?

8. Suspicion, of course, cannot be reserved for the unacquainted or merely acquainted persons in one's social net. In his biography, Clifford Beers writes about how he treated kindly relatives who came to visit him in the hospital while he was (he later came to feel) quite mad:

> Relatives and friends frequently called to see me. True, these calls were trying for all concerned. I spoke to none, not even to my mother and father. For, though they all appeared about as they used to appear, I was able to detect some slight difference in look or gesture, and this was enough to confirm my belief that they were impersonators, engaged in a conspiracy, not merely to entrap me, but to incriminate those whom they imprisoned. It is not strange, then, that I refused to have anything to say to them, or permit them to come near me.[85]

Later, when he visits home:

> I could not believe that my relatives—if they were relatives—had not been informed of my presence in the city, and their words and actions upon my arrival confirmed suspicion and killed the faint hope I had briefly cherished. My hosts were simply the same old persecutors with whom I had already had too much to do. Soon after my arrival dinner was served. I sat at my old place at the table, and secretly admired the skill with which he who asked the blessing imitated the language and well-remembered intonation of my father's voice. But alas! for the family—I had imagined my relatives banished and languishing in prison, and the old home confiscated by the government![86]

---

[85] Beers, *op. cit.*, p. 57.
[86] *Ibid.*, p. 60.

Beers attributes these difficulties to his illness; and ill, apparently, he was. But it is not illness that creates the possibility of seeing the ordinary everything in an alarming light as a product of some conspiratorial plan; it is the nature of our *Umwelten* that makes them inevitably vulnerable to these sorts of rereadings. There is small chance that Beers' relatives, however enlightened and long-suffering, could have visited him or received him at home without their appearance of accepting him not giving way at various points. Inevitably it would have been possible to see that they were trying to act "natural" when indeed they did not feel it. And even if they had managed not to deviate from how they had treated him before his illness, it would be possible—as apparently it was—to see this as final evidence that a masquerade of some kind was in progress. For it is in the inevitable nature of appearing as if nothing is up that one is appearing exactly as one would were one trying to conceal a source of threat or a fear of it. And it is the inevitable consequence of purposely trying to act natural for the gentlest of reasons that one will produce just the kind of deception cues that would be produced were one's intentions evil and demonic.

9. Suspicion about normal appearances cannot, of course, be restricted to persons in the subject's presence; the physical objects and events around him can become suspect also. For these, too, can be fashioned in the guise of innocuous occurrences or fortuitously fateful ones, when in fact they are a contrived product of inimical design.

Whether, then, we look at the animate or inanimate elements of the subject's surround, much the same vulnerability seems to apply. The more innocent and the more normal things seem to the subject, the more he may feel he should be alarmed by the expertness of those who have designed the trap that has been set for him. (After all, the man who sees that his $600 in cash has not been touched in his dresser drawer feels he has found the best evidence that no thief has entered, but bankbook operators know this, too, so this best evidence could also be the worst evidence.) The subject may then cease to be able to discount anything as merely chance or incidental or routine. Whatever seems as it should be creates doubt just because of this appearance. Small deviations are singled out as evidence of total falseness. Even perfect appearances can be suspected.

It is theoretically possible, then, for the immediate environment around an individual to be transformed into something he must suspect, the suspicion falling on persons present, objects present, sounds and movements, and finally, on places not directly gazed at. When this suspicion occurs, say, during times of internecine warfare, then the individual may become anxious indeed, and what he becomes anxious for is not merely his safety but his situations: he ceases to be able to take for granted and discount and disattend the background features of the world around him. Normal appearance becomes, as it is, a broad cover under which persons and agencies may try to monitor him, approach him for attack, conceal things vital to him, attempt to make secret contact with him, and the like. His *Umwelt* becomes hot for him.

II *Summary*

1. It was suggested earlier that the life of many animals can be seen as oscillating between two radically different states, tranquility and mobilization, and that the capacity to be quietly on the lookout for signs for alarm is the mediating mechanism making it possible for these two states to approach each other closely in the same animal. Whenever, then, we find an animal idling his engine we can always ask what it will take to make him switch into high gear, and this we usually find is surprisingly small. That, after all, is the whole point of his alarm system. Behind this fact is something I think worth restating. In looking at the peace that usually obtains in public and semi-public places, in looking at persons quietly going about their business, we might find ourselves employing the standard imagery of a continuum that leads from these places and their people to places a little less secure and so on, until we are in the battlefield. Similarly, we could take the usual

view that the greater the sense of security, the less the chance of sudden eventfulness. But this temperate view indeed might be fundamentally wrong. Full calm may in nature be a very few steps away from full agitation. This seems true with lower animals and is quite probably true with man. Instead of contrasting various situations according to their degree of uneasiness, we might better ask of the most peaceful and secure what steps would be necessary to transform it into something that was deeply unsettling. And we cannot read from the depth of the security the number of steps required to reverse the situation. I am here arguing, note, for a distinction between the probability of alarm and its structural feasibility.

2. Four loci have been considered along which sources of alarm in the individual's *Umwelt* occur: the furnished frame, lurk areas, access points, and the social net. When things don't seem to be quite right and alarm is felt, it is along these lines that the signs and sources of alarm are distributed and articulated; it is along these lines that *Umwelten* can get shaky. These articulations, then, provide us with one version of the notion of structure. Note, in all cases where alarm results, a disruption has occurred in what the individual took to be the division in his world between the designed and the unconnected.

3. Individuals in modern society must jointly use fixed service equipment in public places and the fixed passageways leading to and from these places. A society such as ours could not afford the facilities found in public places unless this equipment were used there by streams of people. It is inevitable, then, that citizens must expose themselves both to physical settings over which they have little control and to the very close presence of others over whose selection they have little to say. The settings can bring disease and injury to those in them. And others present can introduce all the basic dangers inherent in co-presence: physical attack, sexual molestation, robbery, passage blocking, importunity, and insult. (Often these aggressions will take the form of "coercive exchange," namely, the giving up of something that one feels an ultimate claim to in exchange for a promise of no injury.)

The exposure necessary in public places is protected by laws as enforced by the presence or at least the "summonability" of the police. But this, of course, is a limited remedy. Many offenses in public places are not of the kind that are legally indictable. Those that are often can be approached with concealed weapons and intent, performed in a moment, and the performer can melt quickly into the crowd after the deed. If police alone had to be relied on to prevent this sort of crime, a good portion of the population would have to be employed in the constabulary. In any case, there always have been groupings in society which feel considerable need for protection from the police, not merely protection by them.

Exposure, of course, is made safe by additional means. Restrictions on who can use various public and semi-public facilities no doubt reduce risk; the price, of course, is immodest, being formal and informal segregation. Risk is also reduced by the fact that the offended party sometimes can walk away from the offense before it has fully involved him. And he can give the impression that he himself will fight back, a capacity and resolve that is ideally embodied in an attack dog. There is also the possibility that others present will lend the offended party a hand, raise a hue and cry, and serve as witnesses—this set of functions being a possibility lately despaired of in reportings of spectacular civic apathy. Further, there is the notion that although the individual is exposed to others, he is safe because in many connections the others have little to gain from an offense. Thus, every day thousands of pedestrians cross the street in front of thousands of stopped cars on the assumption that although a driver might well get away with a sudden attack, there is little profit to him in attempting it. Also, an argument can be made that as a consequence of upbringing in a family setting, the individual tends to exhibit sympathy and compassion for those who are in his immediate presence. (The counter is that although immediacy no doubt has a mollifying effect upon some aggressors, this basis of restraint very often proves entirely insufficient.) Finally, perhaps it can be claimed that individuals who together use a public place sustain some sort of tacit bargain or agreement to disavail themselves of the opportunities for various aggressions.

It is possible, then, to list some of the sources of social control in public places, but it is hard to have confidence that, even taken together, these are the relevantly effective ones. Whatever its causes, however, the surface character of public order can be identified. The inhibition of aggression routinely occurs, and some sort of civility usually is sustained. Individuals exert respectful care in regard to the setting and treat others present with civil inattention; mutual interference is avoided without much sign that an effort to do so is involved, and when accident or incident brings strangers into entangling contact, brief remedial interchanges are extended. Expressions of civility presumably serve to assure recipients that they are the target of either no intentions or honorable ones, and this apparently reduces alarm even though actual vulnerability remains.

4. The vulnerability of public life is what we are coming more and more to see, if only because we are becoming more aware of the areas and intricacies of mutual trust presupposed in public order. Certainly circumstances can arise which undermine the ease that individuals have within their *Umwelt*. Some of these circumstances are currently found in the semi-public places within slum housing developments and slum neighborhoods, and there is no intrinsic reason why some of these sources of alarm (as well as some additional ones) cannot come to be found in the residential community of the respectable classes, causing the fragile character of domestic settings to be evident there, too. Certainly the great public forums of our society, the downtown areas of our cities, can come to be uneasy places. Militantly sustained antagonisms between diffusely intermingled major population segments—young and old, male and female, white and black, impoverished and well-off—can cause those in public gatherings to distrust (and to fear they are distrusted by) the persons standing next to them. The forms of civil inattention, of persons circumspectly treating one another with polite and glancing concern while each

goes about his own separate business, may be maintained, but behind these normal appearances individuals can come to be at the ready, poised to flee or to fight back if necessary. And in place of unconcern there can be alarm—until, that is, the streets are redefined as naturally precarious places, and a high level of risk becomes routine.

As natural as it may be for us to do so, we cannot look to beasts to see what happens when things get brutish; nor will savages help particularly. Both these traditional sources of our disorder imagery are rather orderly in their natural state. That is embarrassing. We must look to urban civilizations and to any such time when danger or deprivation becomes acute. Here no better guide can presently be found than Claude Lévi-Strauss, who describes one of the things that can go wrong with surrounds, one way in which *Umwelten* can get heated up, even while he describes what it feels like to be thusly heated. At point is one of the lesser disorderings that can occur, a breakdown in civil inattention, a general cause for mild alarm, especially for those who are new to this state and at the same time well endowed with resources and feelings. I cannot improve on what Lévi-Strauss says, and close therefore by excerpting him:

> Every time I come out of my Calcutta hotel . . . I become the center of a ballet, which I would find comic, were it not so pitiful. One can pick out several entrances, each with a leading part:
>
> The shoe-shine boy dashing to my feet;
>
> The small adenoidal child rushing up with his: "One anna, papa, one anna!";
>
> The cripple, practically naked so that you can see in detail the knobs of his limbs;
>
> The pimp: "British girls, very nice . . .";
>
> The clarinet-dealer;
>
> The New Market porter, begging you to buy all his wares. . . .
>
> And finally the whole troupe of minor characters, touting rickshaws, taxis and gharries. . . . And then there is the cohort of shopkeepers, hawkers, peddlers, to whom your arrival may mean paradise: perhaps you will buy something. . . .

It would be tantamount to sacrilege even to be tempted to laugh or get irritated by all this. These grotesque gestures, these grimacing approaches—it would be idle to condemn them and criminal to mock them . . . All these despairing mimes have one origin—the haunting nightmare of hunger; . . . that hunger which gives a tragic intensity to the beggar's look as it meets your own through the metal bars of the first-class compartment, put there, like the armed soldiers crouching on the footboard, to protect you against that single mute supplication which could at any moment change into a screaming riot if the passenger's pity, overcoming his prudence, were to encourage the condemned to hope for alms.

. . .

Everyday life [in Southern Asia] appears to be a permanent repudiation of the very notion of human relationship. You are offered everything and promised everything; every ability is claimed, when not one is possessed. You are thus at the very outset compelled to deny in others that specifically human quality which makes possible good faith and a sense of contract and obligation. Rickshaw boys will offer to take you anywhere and everywhere, although they are more ignorant of the route than you yourself. . . .

The universal mendicancy is even more profoundly disquieting. One dare not meet a gaze frankly, for the simple satisfaction of making contact with another man; the slightest pause will be interpreted as weakness, as purchase for an importunity. . . . The higher they place me the greater their hopes that the nothing they ask of me will become something.

Thus they never dream of posing as equals. But this incessant pressure, this ingenuity, always alert to trick you, to deceive you, to get something from you by cunning, or falsehood, or theft, in the end become insupportable, even from human beings. And yet, how does one harden oneself? For—and this is the impasse—all these manoeuvres are different techniques of prayer. And it is because the fundamental attitude towards you is one of prayer, even when you are being robbed, that the situation is so utterly and completely unbearable.[87]

---

[87] Claude Lévi-Strauss, "Crowds," *New Left Review*, XV (May–June, 1962): 3–5.

[Appendix]

The Insanity of Place*

I

For more than 200 years now the doctrine has been increasingly held that there is such a thing as mental illness, that it is a sickness like any other, and that those who suffer from it should be dealt with medically: they should be treated by doctors, if necessary in a hospital, and not blamed for what has befallen them. This belief has social uses. Were there no such notion, we would probably have to invent it.

However, in the last twenty years we have learned that the management of mental illness under medical auspices has been an uncertain blessing. The best treatment that money has been able to buy, prolonged individual psychotherapy, has not proven very efficacious. The treatment most patients have received—hospitalization—has proven to be questionable indeed. Patients recover more often than not, at least temporarily, but this seems in spite of the mental hospital, not because of it. Upon examination,

* I am much indebted to Edwin Lemert and Sheldon Messinger and to Helen and Stewart Perry for help in writing this paper. It is reprinted with a few editorial changes from *Psychiatry: Journal for the Study of Interpersonal Processes*, vol. XXXII, no. 4 (November 1969). Copyright 1969 by the William Alanson White Psychiatric Foundation, Inc.

many of these establishments have proven to be hopeless storage dumps trimmed in psychiatric paper. They have served to remove the patient from the scene of his symptomatic behavior, which in itself can be constructive, but this function has been performed by fences, not doctors. And the price that the patient has had to pay for this service has been considerable: dislocation from civil life, alienation from loved ones who arranged the commitment, mortification due to hospital regimentation and surveillance, permanent posthospital stigmatization. This has been not merely a bad deal; it has been a grotesque one.

Consequently, in the last decade some important changes have been entertained regarding treatment of the mentally ill. There has been marked improvement in living conditions in mental hospitals, albeit no more so than in other backwashes of American society recently penetrated by secular conceptions of man's inalienable right to recreational facilities. More to the point, there has been some pressure to keep the potential patient in the community as long as possible and to return the hospitalized patient to the community as quickly as possible. The legal rights of persons accused of mental illness have been sharpened—in some states, such as California, to the point where involuntary commitment is quite difficult to arrange. And the notion is abroad that the goal is not to cure the patient but to *contain* him in a niche in free society where he can be tolerated. Where a niche is not available one is sometimes built, as in the institutions of family care and halfway house. And if this new approach places a burden on the patient's home, neighborhood, or work place, there is a current understanding of mental disorder to help justify this: since the patient has been put upon, since he is merely the symptom carrier for a sick set-up, it is only fair that the whole be made to share the burden; it is only fair that the patient and those with whom he is most involved be encouraged, preferably with psychiatric counsel, to work together to work things out.

Given the life still enforced in most mental hospitals and the stigma still placed on mental illness, the philosophy of community containment seems the only desirable one. Nonetheless, it is worth looking at some implications of this approach for the patient's various "others," that is, persons he identifies as playing a significant role in his life. To do this we must examine the meaning of the patient's symptoms for his others. If we do this we will learn not only what containment implies, we will learn about mental disorder.

Before proceeding, I want to introduce one issue and its concepts—an issue regarding the medical world and the doctor-patient relationship.

The ideal behind medical service is much like the ideal behind other legitimate services and, as in their case, is often realized. The patient comes to the doctor on his own, places himself in the doctor's hands, follows the doctor's orders, and obtains results which amply justify the trust and the fee.

Of course there are points of tension. The patient may not know of his need for service; knowing of his need, he may apply to charlatan servers; desiring medical service, he may not be able to afford it; affording it, he may shop around too much before settling on a particular physician; settling on one, he may not follow the advice he gets from him; following the advice, he may find his situation somewhat eased but not basically altered.

More at issue, the two-party dealings and two-party relationship between the doctor and his patient can become complicated in certain ways by other parties. For example: medical group-plans of various kinds can obscure the patient's view of the agency from which he obtains treatment; communicable diseases and suspect wounds oblige the physician to act for the community as well as for the patient. I will focus on one class of these third parties, the patient's daily circles: his service community, his work place, his friendships, and particularly his family.

Traditionally in medical service the patient's family has been given certain functions. For example, very commonly the family is expected to cooperate, to help out, to mobilize the domestic resources necessary to accommodate the special temporary needs of the patient. When the illness is major, the least the family will do is to use its car to bring the patient to the hospital and fetch him therefrom; at most, the household can become a hospital away from the hospital. Whatever the extent of the family help, the physician will usually have to communicate instructions to the helpers, directly or through the patient.

Another function of the family is guardianship. Adult members of the family can be openly called on to act for the patient, typically because he is below the age of discretion or beyond it, ratifying a medical decision ordinarily requiring the free consent of the person directly affected.

Furthermore, should the patient be a full-fledged adult and his situation desperate, the family may be brought into a secret relation with the doctor, who tells them facts about the patient's condition that they need to know for their own good or his, but that the physician feels he cannot on humanitarian or medical grounds tell the patient now. A kind of emergency guardianship is involved requiring collusion between the sick person's kin and the physician.

Here definitions might be justified. A "coalition" is a collaborative arrangement minimally between two parties who use it to control the environment of a third, the arrangement itself not being openly established and recognized in these terms. A "collusive net" or "collusive alignment" is a coalition aimed at one kind of control—the third party's definition of the situation.[1] No matter how many persons are actually involved in the various parties, only two basic roles are present: the two or more persons who collude—that is, the colluders; and the one or more persons whose definition of the situation is secretly managed, who might be called the "excolluded." Note that if collusion is to occur, the colluders must be in communication with one another, since independent response will not allow them to concert in the line they are maintaining. This collusive communication takes two forms: in one, the participants are not in the presence of the excolluded and

[1] For a recent treatment of family coalitions, see Jay Haley, "Toward a Theory of Pathological Systems," in *Family Therapy and Disturbed Families*, edited by Gerald Zuk and Ivan Boszormenyi-Nagy (California: Science and Behavior Books, 1967). A vivid treatment of collusion within the family is provided in the writings of Ronald Laing.

therefore need conceal only that they are in touch; in the other, the communication occurs in the immediate presence of the excolluded, typically by means of furtive signs. The first involves open communication between concealed persons, and the second, concealed communication between exposed persons.[2]

Collusion involves falseness knowingly used as a basis for action. Something of a conspiracy is therefore entailed, typically in regard to two fundamental matters. The first is reality. Collusion serves to maintain for the excolluded a definition of the situation that is unstable, one that would be disrupted and discredited were the colluders to divulge what they know, and were they to relax in their management of the evidence available to the excolluded. The second is relationships. The personal relationship that an excolluded individual feels he has in regard to each of the colluders would be undercut if he discovered that they have a collusive relationship to one another in regard to him.[3] The adulterous affair, that great training ground for off-stage acting, can be taken as a central example.

A collusive conspiracy of course may be quite benign, may be in the best interests of the person conspired against. Collusion is a normal and no doubt desirable part of social life. Children are raised by it, especially handicapped children. Everywhere egos are preserved by it and faces saved by it. More important, it is probably impossible for interaction to continue among three persons for any length of time without collusion occurring, for the tacit betrayal of the third person is one of the main ways in which two persons express the specialness of their own relation to each

---

[2] There is a parallel distinction in intelligence work between a clandestine operation and a covert operation, the first involving total concealment, the second concealment only of intent and method.

[3] Once someone begins to suspect collusion and has identified the members of the net, he will no longer be in a position to have his relation to them undercut. Lemert has suggested to me that an adversary process may then emerge, the excolluded attempting to prove publicly that there is a conspiracy against him, and the conspirators attempting to deny the evidence. Of course, a person can learn (whether correctly or not) that his suspicions were unfounded, and then re-credit his relationships.

other. Stable triads seem always to involve at least a little round-robin collusion, with each of the three possible pairs colluding, and each of the three participants serving a turn as the excolluded.

In ordinary medical practice, collusion is of no great issue. Perhaps this is so even in the case of the dying patient, where it is very likely that at least for a time he will be put on regarding his future, by the hospital staff if not by his family. As we will later see, it is in psychiatric care that collusion becomes a questionable and troublesome business.

II

We can begin to consider the insanity of place by reviewing and extending some elementary terms regarding the sociology of place.

The treatment that an individual gives others and receives from them expresses or assumes a definition of him, as does the immediate social scene in which the treatment occurs. This is a "virtual" definition; it is based upon the ways of understanding of the community and is available to any competent member, whether or not such interpretations are actually made and whether or not they are made correctly—that is, in the manner most others could be led to defend. The ultimate referent here is a tacit coding discoverable by competently reading conduct, and not conceptions or images that persons actually have in their minds. Note, a rounded definition requires a collation of relevant conduct and its interpretation, a task a lay person could do but have no reason for doing.

Virtual definitions of an individual may be "accorded"—that is, readable in the conduct of agencies seen as external to the individual himself. These definitions constitute the individual's "person." Corresponding to these accorded assumptions about him there will be virtually "acted" ones, projected through what is seen as his own conduct. These assumptions constitute the individual's "self." [4] Person and self are portraits of the same individual, the first encoded in the actions of others, the second in the actions of the subject himself.

The individual's acted definition of himself may be different in various ways from the definition accorded him. Further, the psychological relation he sustains to his accorded and acted definitions is enormously complex. He will certainly be unaware of some elements of these definitions and erroneously aware of others. He can be variously attached to such definitions as he is aware of, liking or disliking what he perceives is implied about him in his dealings with others, and inwardly accepting or rejecting these assumptions in various degrees. Also, he can employ various devices to press his desires regarding these assumptions about himself, or passively submit to definitions of himself that he feels are undesirable. As Cooley argued, the self-regarding sentiments such as pride and shame will be involved. When these various relations that an individual can have to what can be read about him become patterned and habitual, they can be called his "personality" or "character," comprising what we try to assess when we consider what an individual is really like, what he is essentially like, what he is like as a human being.

It should be plain now that the implicatory aspect of the individual's conduct has a very convoluted and recursive character. Even while his overall behavior can be read for the self-assump-

---

[4] See Kai T. Erikson, "Patient Role and Social Uncertainty—A Dilemma of the Mentally Ill," *Psychiatry* XX (1957): 263–274. The distinction between accorded and acted definitions of an individual follows Erikson's distinction between role-validation and role-commitment:

> For the purposes of this paper, it will be useful to consider that the acquisition of roles by a person involves two basic processes: *role-validation* and *role-commitment*. Role-validation takes place when a community "gives" a person certain expectations to live up to, providing him with distinct notions as to the conduct it considers appropriate or valid for him in his position. Role-commitment is the complementary process whereby a person adopts certain styles of behavior as his own, committing himself to role themes that best represent the kind of person he assumes himself to be, and best reflect the social position he considers himself to occupy (pp. 263–264).

tions which inform it, some of his minor gestures will convey what he feels about having a self that is defined in this way and what he feels about others' defining him as a given person; and these gestures in turn will be taken as part of his acted self by himself and others, which fact can in turn be taken into consideration in the assessment he or others make of him. The individual stakes out a self, comments on his having done so, and comments on his commenting, even while the others are taking the whole process into consideration in coming to their assessment of him, which consideration he then takes into consideration in revising his view of himself.[5]

Having considered the individual's person and his self, consider now their normative regulation. A social norm or rule is any guide for action recommended because it is felt to be appropriate, suitable, proper, or morally right. Three parties are involved: the person who can legitimately "expect" and demand to be treated in a particular way because of the rule; the person who is "obliged" to act in a particular way because of the rule; the community that supports the legitimacy of these expectations and obligations.

The treatment that is accorded anyone and that he accords others is typically regulated by social norms, and so also, therefore, are the delineative implications of these dealings. When, therefore, an individual becomes involved in the maintenance of a rule, he

---

[5] I do not think there is anything like an adequate version of these complications. Little help has been provided by pencil and paper students of the self who start with a subject's verbal description of himself, often based on his selection from verbal trait-lists, instead of starting with the serious ethnographic task of assembling the various ways in which the individual is treated and treats others, and deducing what is implied about him through this treatment. The result has been a trivialization of Cooley, Mead, and social psychology. The self acquires a hopelessly shifting status: in one sentence the student refers to the tacit coding of an individual's conduct, the assumptions in effect that the individual makes about himself, and in the next to a purely subjective mentalistic element—this itself having an inconstant referent. There is a failure to see that the term "conception" can radically shift in meaning, and that an individual's mental conception of self is merely his subjective and partial view of the effective conception he has of himself.

tends to become committed to a specific set of acted and accorded definitions of himself. If the rule obliges him to do something in regard to others, he becomes to himself and them the sort of person who would naturally act in this way, correctly delineated by what is expressed in this conduct. If the rule leads him to expect others to do something in regard to him, then he becomes to himself and them someone who is properly characterized by what is implied through this way of treating him. Accepting this delineation of himself, he must then make sure that through his treatment of others and their treatment of him the rule will be followed, allowing him to be what he feels he is.

In general, then, when a rule of conduct is broken, two individuals run the risk of becoming discredited: one with an obligation, who should have governed himself by the rule; the other with an expectation, who should have been treated in a particular way because of this governance. A bit of the definition of both actor and recipient is threatened, as is to a lesser degree the community that contains them both.

Having seen that rules of conduct are fundamental to definitions of a self, we must go on to see that they are just as fundamental to corporate social life. Put simply and quickly, the activities of any organization are allocated to members, and these activities are coordinated by being subsumed under (or being allowed to fall within or be covered by) various rules. Thus, many of the obligations and expectations of the individual pertain to, and ensure the maintenance of, the activities of a social organization that incorporates him.

Let me restate this general sociological position. Through socialization into group living, the individual comes in effect to make assumptions about himself. Although these assumptions are about himself, they nonetheless are delineated in terms of his approved relationship to other members of the group and in terms of the collective enterprise—his rightful contribution to it and his rightful share in it. In brief, these assumptions about himself concern his normatively supported place in the group.

The individual tends to organize his activity as if the single key to it all were the assumptions he makes about himself. He thus anticipates that his share of group expectations and obligations will be parceled out to him on the basis of (and as a confirmation of) his particular assumptions about himself. And by and large this self-organization of the individual's activity is effective because others in the group make more or less the same assumptions about him and treat him accordingly. Self and person coincide. His treatment of them and their treatment of him can be read as making the same set of assumptions concerning him, the same except for a difference in point of reference; and this set of assumptions will not be an incidental implication of the reciprocal treatment, but its key.

Here note that the expressive idiom of the individual's society and group will ensure that evidence of his assumptions about himself will be made available not only through his performing his main substantive obligations, but also through expressive means, comprising the way in which he handles himself while in the presence of others or while having dealings with them. Through quite minor acts of deference and demeanor, through little behavioral warning lights, the individual exudes assumptions about himself. These provide others with a running portent, a stream of expression which tells them what place he expects to have in the undertakings that follow, even though at the moment little place may be at stake. In fact, all behavior of the individual, insofar as it is perceived by others, has an indicative function, made up of tacit promises and threats, confirming or disconfirming that he knows and keeps his place.

III

With these elementary concepts to serve as a frame, turn now to a specific matter: the parallel drawn between medical and mental symptoms.

Signs and symptoms of a *medical* disorder presumably refer to underlying pathologies in the individual organism, and these constitute deviations from biological norms maintained by the homeostatic functioning of the human machine. The system of reference here is plainly the individual organism, and the term "norm," ideally at least, has no moral or social connotation. (Of course, beyond the internal pathology there is likely to be a cause in the external environment, even a social cause, as in the case of infectious or injurious situations of work; but typically the same disorder can be produced in connection with a wide variety of socially different environments.) But what about *mental* symptoms?

No doubt some psychoses are mainly organic in their relevant cause, others mainly psychogenic, still others situational. In many cases etiology will involve all of these causal elements. Further, there seems no doubt that the prepatient—that is, the individual who acts in a way that is eventually perceived as ill—may have any of the possible relations to intentionality: he may be incapable of knowing what he is doing; or he may know the effects of his acts but feel unable to stop himself, or indifferent about stopping himself; or, knowing the effects of certain acts, he may engage in them with malice aforethought, only because of their effects. All of that is not at issue here. For when an act that will later be perceived as a mental symptom is first performed by the individual who will later be seen as a mental patient, the act is not taken as a symptom of illness but rather as a deviation from social norms, that is, an infraction of social rules and social expectations. The perceptual reconstituting of an offense or infraction into a medical, value-free symptom may come quite late, will be unstable when it appears, and will be entertained differently, depending on whether it is the patient, the offended parties, or professional psychiatric personnel doing the perceiving.[6]

---

[6] Of course, some personal conditions, such as loss of memory or intense anxiety or grandiose persecutory beliefs, are very quickly shifted from offense to symptoms, but even here it is often the case that social rules regarding how a person is properly to orient himself or feel about his situation may be what are initially disturbed.

This argument, that mentally ill behavior is on its face a form of social deviancy, is more or less accepted in psychiatric circles. But what is not seen—and what will be argued in this paper—is that biological norms and social norms are quite different things, and that ways of analyzing deviations from one cannot be easily employed in examining deviations from the other.

The first issue is that the systems regulated by social norms are not biological individuals at all, but relationships, organizations, and communities; the individual merely follows rules or breaks them, and his relation to any set of norms that he supports or undercuts can be complex indeed—as we shall see, more of a political issue than a medical one.

The second issue has to do with the regulative process itself. The biological model can be formulated in simple terms: deviation; restorative counteractions; reequilibration (associated with the destruction or extrusion of the pathogenic agent); or disorganization, that is, destruction of the system. A realistic picture of social regulation is less tidy.

The traditional sociological answer to the question of regulation and conformance is found in the normative sense of the term "social control" and the corrective cycle that presumably occurs when an offense takes place.

As suggested, through socialization the individual comes to incorporate the belief that certain rules are right and just, and that a person such as himself ought to support them and feel remorse and guilt if he does not. He also learns to place immediate value on the image that others might obtain of him in this regard; he learns to be decently concerned about his reputation.

Taking the notion of personally incorporated norms as central, one can distinguish three basic forms of normative social control. First, and no doubt most important, there is "personal control": the individual refrains from improper action by virtue of acting as his own policeman. Finding that he has acted improperly, he takes it upon himself to admit his offense and volunteer such reparative work as will reestablish the norms and himself as a man respectful of them.

Second, there is "informal social control." When the individual begins to offend, the offended parties may warn him that he is getting out of line, that disapproval is imminent, and that deprivations for continuation are likely. As a result of this more-or-less subtle warning, amplified and sustained until the offense is corrected, the offender is brought to his senses and once again acts so as to affirm common approved understandings. As Parsons has remarked, this corrective feedback is constantly occurring in social life, and is in fact one of the main mechanisms of socialization and learning.[7]

Third, the threat that an offender introduces to the social order is managed through "formal" social sanction administered by specialized agents designated for the purpose. Criminals certainly break social rules, but there is an important sense in which they do not threaten the social order, and this by virtue of the risk they accept of apprehension, imprisonment, and harsh moral censure. They may find themselves forced, as we say, to pay their debt to society—the price presumably adjusted to the extent of the offense—which in turn affirms the reasonableness of not breaking the rules at all. In any case, they often try to conceal the act of breaking the law, claim to be innocent when accused, and affect repentance when proven guilty—all of which shows that they know the rules and are not openly rebelling against them. Note that the efficacy of informal and formal social control depends to a degree on personal control, for control that is initiated outside the offender will not be very effective unless it can in some degree awaken corrective action from within.

Personal control, informal control, and formal control are the moral means and the main ones by which deviations are inhibited or corrected and compliance to the norms is assured. But taken together, these means of control provide a very narrow picture of the relation between social norms and social deviations.

For one thing, the agencies of control that have been reviewed can be as effective as they are not because of the offender's moral concern, but because of his expediential considerations. The good

[7] Talcott Parsons, *The Social System* (New York: The Free Press, 1951), p. 303.

opinion of others may be sought in order to render these persons vulnerable to exploitation. A fine may be viewed not as a proclamation of guilt but as a routine cost to be figured in as part of operating expenses.[8] The point here, of course, is that often what looks like automatic and dependable conformance is to be expected from the actor only over a strictly limited range of costs to him.

Further, the norms may be upheld not because of conscience or penalty, but because failure to comply leads to undesired, unintended complications which the offender was unaware of when first undertaking his offensive action.[9]

But even this expanded base for normative social control provides a partial view. The control model that is implied—a model that treats social norms somewhat like biological norms—is itself too restrictive. For when an offense occurs it is by no means the case that sanctions are applied, and when negative sanctions or penalties *are* applied, or when unanticipated penalizing consequences occur—that is, when the corrective cycle is begun—it is by no means generally true that diminution of the deviation results.

When the offense occurs, the offended parties may resolve the situation simply by withdrawing from relevant dealings with the offender, placing their social business with someone else. The threat of this sort of withdrawal is, of course, a means of informal social control, and actual withdrawal may certainly communicate a negative evaluation, sometimes unintended. But the process just as certainly constitutes something more than merely a negative sanction; it is a form of management in its own right. As we shall see, it is just such withdrawal which allows those in a social con-

---

[8] When the agencies of control take the same expediential view, then we might better speak of social direction rather than social control. It is thus, for example, that a subsidy policy directs crop allocation without reliance on the factor of moral sensibility.

[9] This is a functionalist argument. See, for example, S. F. Nadel, "Social Control and Self-Regulation," *Social Forces* XXXI (1953): 265–273.

tact to convey glaringly incompatible definitions and yet get by each other without actual discord.

If the offense is such as to make legal action possible, the offended person may yet desist (and withdraw) for practical reasons which sharply limit the application of formal control: the cost and time required to make a formal complaint and appear in court; the uncertainty of the legal decision; the personal exposure involved in taking official action; the reputation that can be acquired for being litigious; the danger of reprisal later by the offender.

There are still other contingencies. The individual who offends expectations can prevail, causing his others to accept him on his new terms and to accept the new definition of the situation that this implies. Children growing up in a family are constantly engaged in this process, constantly negotiating new privileges from their keepers, privileges which soon come to be seen as the young person's due. Some of the mutinies that occur in schools, prisons, and ghettos illustrate the same theme. The social changes produced by the labor movement and the suffragette movement provide further examples.

And even when withdrawal from the offender or submission to him does not occur, social control need not result. The negative moral sanctions and the material costs of deviation may further alienate the deviator, causing him to exacerbate the deviation, committing him further and further to offense. And as will be later seen, there may be no resolution to the discord that results thereby. The foreign body is neither extruded nor encysted, and the host does not die. Offended and offender can remain locked together screaming, their fury and discomfort socially impacted, a case of organized disorganization.

These limitations on the social version of the homeostatic model are themselves insufficient, for they are cast in the very assumptions that must be broadened. The issue is that the traditional social control approach assumes an unrealistically mechanistic version of the social act, a restriction that must be relaxed if the close analysis of social control is to be achieved.

As the law suggests, our response to an individual who physically performs an offensive act is radically qualified by a battery of interpretive considerations: Did he know about the rule he was breaking, and if so, was he aware of breaking it? If he did not appreciate the offensive consequences of his act, ought he to have? And if he did anticipate these offensive results, were they the main purpose of his act or incidental to it? Was it within his physical competence to desist from the offense, and if so, were there extenuating social reasons for not doing so?

The answers to these questions tell us about the actor's *attitude* toward the rule that appears to have been violated, and this attitude must be determined before we can even say what it is that has happened. The issue is not merely (and often not mainly) whether he conformed or not, but rather in what relationship he stands to the rule that ought to have governed him. Indeed, a significant feature of *any* act is what it can be taken to demonstrate about the actor's relation to such norms as legitimately govern it.

However, the actor's attitude toward a rule is a subjective thing; he alone, if anyone, is fully privy to it. Inevitably, then, an important role will be played by the readings others make of his conduct, and by the clarifying expressions that he contributes, whether to ensure that a proper purpose is not misinterpreted or an improper one is not disclosed. It follows, for example, that if a deviator is suitably tactful and circumspect in his violations, employing secrecy and cover, many of the disruptive consequences of the violation in fact will be avoided. A particular application of the rules is thwarted, but the sanctity of the rule itself is not openly questioned.

A reorientation is therefore to be suggested. An actual or suspected offender is not so much faced with an automatic corrective cycle as with the need to engage in remedial ritual work. Three chief forms of this work are available to him: accounts, apologies, and requests. With accounts he shows that he himself did not commit the offense, or did it mindlessly, or was not himself at the time, or was under special pressure, or did what any reasonable man would have done under the circumstances;[10] with apologies he shows that if indeed he had intended the offense, he now disavows the person that he was, bewails his action, repents, and wants to be given a chance to be what he now knows he should be; with requests he seeks the kind of offer or permission which will transform the act from his offense into the other's boon. With this ritual work, with explanations, propitiations, and pleas, the offender tries to show that the offense is not a valid expression of his attitude to the norms. The impiety is only apparent; he really supports the rules.

Once we see that ritual work bears on the very nature of social acts and considerably loosens what is to be meant by social equilibrium, we can readdress ourselves to the crucial difference between medical symptoms and mental symptoms.

The interesting thing about medical symptoms is how utterly nice, how utterly plucky the patient can be in managing them. There may be physical acts of an ordinary kind he cannot perform; there may be various parts of the body he must keep bandaged and hidden from view; he may have to stay home from work for a spell or even spend time in a hospital bed. But for each of these deviations from normal social appearance and functioning, the patient will be able to furnish a compensating mode of address. He gives accounts, belittles his discomfort, and presents an apologetic air, as if to say that in spite of appearance he is, deep in his social soul, someone to be counted on to know his place, someone who appreciates what he ought to be as a normal person and who is this person in spirit, regardless of what has happened to his flesh. He is someone who does not *will* to be demanding and useless. Tuberculosis patients, formerly isolated in sanitaria, sent home progress notes that were fumigated but cheerful. Brave little troops of colostomites and ileostomites make their brief appearances disguised as nice clean people, while stoically concealing the hours of

[10] A discussion of accounts is available in Marvin Scott and Stanford Lyman, "Accounts," *American Sociological Review* XXXIII (1968): 46–62.

hellish toilet work required for each appearance in public as a normal person. We even have our Beckett player buried up to his head in an iron lung, unable to blow his own nose, who yet somehow expresses by means of his eyebrows that a full-fledged person is present who knows how to behave and would certainly behave that way were he physically able.

And more than an air is involved. Howsoever demanding the sick person's illness is, almost always there will be some consideration his keepers will *not* have to give. There will be some physical cooperation that can be counted on; there will be some task he can do to help out, often one that would not fall to his lot were he well. And this helpfulness can be *absolutely* counted on, just as though he were no less a responsible participant than anyone else. In the context, these little bits of substantive helpfulness take on a large symbolic function.

Now obviously, physically sick persons do not always keep a stiff upper lip (not even to mention appreciable ethnic differences in the management of the sick role); hypochondriasis is common, and control of others through illness is not uncommon. But even in these cases I think close examination would find that the culprit tends to acknowledge proper sick-role etiquette. This may only be a front, a gloss, a way of styling behavior. But it says: "Whatever my medical condition demands, the enduring me is to be dissociated from these needs, for I am someone who would make only modest reasonable claims and take a modest and standard role in the affairs of the group were I able."

The family's treatment of the patient nicely supports this definition of the situation, as does the employer's. In effect they say that special license can temporarily be accorded the sick person because, were he able to do anything about it, he would not make such demands. Since the patient's spirit and will and intentions are those of a loyal and seemly member, his old place should be kept waiting for him, for he will fill it well, as if nothing untoward has happened, as soon as his outer behavior can again be dictated by, and be an expression of, the inner man. His increased demands are saved from expressing what they might because it is plain that he has "good" reasons for making them, that is, reasons that nullify what these claims would otherwise be taken to mean. I do not say that the members of the family will be happy about their destiny. In the case of incurable disorders that are messy or severely incapacitating, the compensative work required by the well members may cost them the life chances their peers enjoy, blunt their personal careers, paint their lives with tragedy, and turn all their feelings to bitterness. But the fact that all of this hardship can be contained shows how clearly the way has been marked for the unfortunate family, a way that obliges them to close ranks and somehow make do as long as the illness lasts.

Of course, the foregoing argument must be qualified. In extreme situations, such as the military, when it can be all too plain that the ill person has everything to gain by being counted sick, the issue of malingering may be seriously raised and the whole medical frame of reference questioned.[11] Further, there is the special problem caused by illness directly affecting the face and the voice, the specialized organs of expression. An organic defect in this equipment may be a minor thing according to a medical or biological frame of reference, but it is likely to be of tremendous significance socially. There is no disfigurement of the body that cannot be decorously covered by a sheet and apologized for by a face; but many disfigurements of the face cannot be covered without cutting off communication, and cannot be left uncovered without disastrously interfering with communication. A person with carcinoma of the bladder can, if he wants, die with more social grace and propriety, more apparent inner social normalcy, than a man with a harelip can order a piece of apple pie.

With certain exceptions, then, persons have the capacity to expressively dissociate their medical illness from their responsible conduct (and hence their selves), and typically the will to do so. They continue to express support of the social group to which they belong and acceptance of their place therein. Their personality or character will be seen to remain constant in spite of changes

[11] Here see the useful paper by Vilhelm Aubert and Shelden Messinger, "The Criminal and the Sick," *Inquiry* I (1958): 137–160.

in their role. This means that the illness may tax the substantive resources of the group, make tragic figures of well members, but still not directly undermine the integrity of the family. In brief, ritual work and minor assistance can compensate for current infractions because an important part of an infraction is what it can be taken to symbolize about the offender's long-range attitude toward maintaining his social place; if he can find alternate ways of conveying that he is keeping himself in line, then current infractions need not be very threatening. Note that the efficacy here of excusing expressions (with the exceptions cited) is due to the fact that medical symptoms involve behavior which is either not an infraction of social norms at all—as in the case of internal tumors of various kinds—or only incidentally so. It is the incidental side effects of the physical deviation that disqualify the person for compliance. When an amputee fails to rise to greet a lady, it is perfectly evident that this failure is only an incidental and unintentional consequence of his condition; no one would claim that he cut off his legs to spite his courtesies. Almost as surely, his disqualification for jobs that require rapid movement can be seen as a side effect of his deviance and not its initial expression. He is a deviator, not a deviant. Here is incapacity, not alienation.

Now turn to symptoms of mental disorder as a form of social deviation. The most obvious point to note is that since there are many kinds of social deviation that have little to do with mental disorder, nothing much is gained by calling symptoms social deviations.[12]

The position can be taken that mental illness, pragmatically speaking, is first of all a social frame of reference, a conceptual framework, a perspective that can be applied to social offenses as a means of understanding them. The offense, in itself, is not enough; it must be perceived and defined in terms of the imagery of mental illness. By definition one must expect that there always will be some liberty and some dissensus in regard to the way this frame-

[12] I omit considering the popularists who have tried to establish the psychogenesis of everything that is interesting, from crime to political disloyalty.

work is applied. Many important contingencies are known to be involved, some causing the imagery to be applied to psychologically normal behavior with the consequence of reconstituting it into a mental symptom. But given this necessary caveat, we can ask: In our society, what is the nature of the social offense to which the frame of reference "mental illness" is likely to be applied?

The offense is often one to which formal means of social control do not apply. The offender appears to make little effort to conceal his offense or ritually neutralize it. The infractions often occur under conditions where, for various reasons, neither the offended nor the offender can resolve the issue by physically withdrawing from the organization and relationship in which the offense occurs, and the organization cannot be reconstituted to legitimate the new self-assumptions of the offender—or, at least, the participants strongly feel that these adaptations are not possible. The norms in question are ones which frequently apply and which are constantly coming up for affirmation, since they often pertain to expressive behavior—the behavior which broadcasts to all within range, transmitting warnings, cues, and hints about the actor's general assumptions about himself. Finally, with the exception of paranoia of primary groups (*folie à deux*, *trois*, etc.), the offense is not committed by a set of persons acting as a team, but rather—or so it is perceived—by an individual acting on his own. In sum, mental symptoms are willful situational improprieties, and these, in turn, constitute evidence that the individual is not prepared to keep his place.[13]

---

[13] Although much of mental symptomatology shares these offense features—thereby allowing us to answer to the argument that mental symptoms are not merely any kind of social deviation—it is the case that many social deviations of the situational kind do not qualify as signs of mental illness. We have been slow to learn this, perhaps because mental wards once provided the most accessible source of flagrant situational improprieties, and in such a context it was all too easy to read the behavior as unmotivated, individually generated aberrancy instead of seeing it as a form of social protest against ward life—the protest having to employ the limited expressive means at hand. In the last few years the non-psychi-

One implication of the offense features I have mentioned should be stressed. Mental symptoms are not, by and large, *incidentally* a social infraction. By and large they are specifically and pointedly offensive. As far as the patient's others are concerned, the troublesome acts do not merely happen to coincide partly with what is socially offensive, as is true of medical symptoms; rather these troublesome acts are perceived, at least initially, to be intrinsically a matter of willful social deviation.

It is important now to emphasize that a social deviation can hardly be reckoned apart from the relationships and organizational memberships of the offender and offended, since there is hardly a social act that in itself is not appropriate or at least excusable in some social context. The delusions of a private can be the rights of a general; the obscene invitations of a man to a strange girl can be the spicy endearments of a husband to his wife; the wariness of a paranoid is the warranted practice of thousands of undercover agents.

Mental symptoms, then, are neither something in themselves nor whatever is so labeled; mental symptoms are acts by an individual which openly proclaim to others that he must have assumptions about himself which the relevant bit of social organization can neither allow him nor do much about.

It follows that if the patient persists in his symptomatic behavior, then he must create organizational havoc and havoc in the minds of members. Although the imputation of mental illness is surely a last-ditch attempt to cope with a disrupter who must be, but cannot be, contained, this imputation in itself is not likely to resolve the situation. Havoc will occur even when all the members are convinced that the troublemaker is quite mad, for this defini-

---

atric character of considerable symptomlike behavior has become much easier to appreciate because situational improprieties of the most flagrant kind have become widely used as a tactic by hippies, the New Left, and black militants, and although these persons have been accused of immaturity, they seem too numerous, too able to sustain collective rapport, and too facile at switching into conventional behavior to be accused of insanity.

tion does not in itself free them from living in a social system in which he plays a disruptive part.

This havoc indicates that medical symptoms and mental symptoms are radically different in their social consequences and in their character. It is this havoc that the philosophy of containment must deal with. It is this havoc that psychiatrists have dismally failed to examine and that sociologists ignore when they treat mental illness merely as a labeling process. It is this havoc that we must explore.

IV

The most glaring failure to organize conduct in accordance with assumptions about himself that others accept is to be found in those dramatic cases where the individual, perceived to be in a state of disorganization as an actor, accords himself a personal biographical identity not his own or temporarily reconstitutes himself in accordance with age, sex, and occupational categories for which he does not qualify. Often this is associated with the individual's imputing quite grandiose personal properties to himself.[14] He then makes some effort to treat others accordingly and tries to get them to affirm this identification through their treatment of him.

Note that mental hospitals can manage such diffusions and distortions of identity without too much difficulty. In these establishments much of the person's usual involvement in the undertakings

[14] Corresponding to these expressed overreachings, there will be alterations in the overreacher's subjective sense of himself. Here a very useful paper was contributed by Josiah Royce titled, "Some Observations on the Anomalies of Self-Consciousness," helpfully brought to attention in an abridged reprinting in Edgar Borgatta and Henry Meyer's *Sociological Theory* (New York: Alfred Knopf, 1961). Since Royce's statement in 1895, progress in this area has been modest.

of others and much of his ordinary capacity to make contact with the world are cut off. There is little he can set in motion. A patient who thinks he is a potentate does not worry attendants about their being his minions. That he is in dominion over them is never given any credence. They merely watch him and laugh, as if watching impromptu theater. Similarly, when a mental hospital patient treats his wife as if she were a suspect stranger, she can deal with this impossible situation merely by adjusting downward the frequency and length of her visits.[15] So, too, the office therapist can withstand the splotches of love and hate that the patient brings to a session, being supported in this disinvolvement by the wonderfully convenient doctrine that direct intercession for the patient, or talk that lasts more than fifty minutes, can only undermine the therapeutic relationship. In all of these cases, distance allows a coming to terms; the patient may express impossible assumptions about himself, but the hospital, the family, or the therapist need not become involved in them.

Matters are quite different, however, when the patient is outside the walls of the hospital or office—outside, where his others commit their persons into his keeping, where his actions make authorized claims and are not symptoms or skits or something disheartening that can be walked away from. Outside the barricades, dramatically wrong self-identification is not necessary in order to produce trouble. Every form of social organization in which the patient participates has its special set of offenses perceivable as mental illness that can create organizational havoc.

One very important organizational locus for mental symptoms consists of public and semipublic places—streets, shops, neigh-

---

[15] A mental hospital in fact can be defined functionally as a place where persons who are still rightfully part of our daily lives can be held at bay and forced to wait for our occasional visits; and we, instead of sharing existence, can ration it. Of course, patients often can manage to hold their kinsmen at bay, too, simply by declining to meet them off the ward or by becoming upset when they visit. However, the cost of this rejection can be very high—for example, loss of an opportunity to get off the ward for a time and to obtain minor supplies. Further, what the patient can hold off is not life with his loved ones, but visits.

borhoods, public transportation, and the like. In these places a fine mesh of obligations obtains which ensures the orderly traffic and co-mingling of participants. Modes of personal territoriality are delineated, and respect for their boundaries is employed as a key means of ordering mutual presence. Many classic symptoms of psychosis are precise and pointed violation of these territorial arrangements. There are encroachments, as when a mental patient visiting a supermarket gratuitously riffles through a shopper's cart, or walks behind the counter to examine what is contained there, or openly advances her place in the checkout line, or leans into an ongoing conversation not her own, or addresses a midpassage statement to someone who has not been brought into a state of talk. There are self-contaminations involving exposure or befoulment, as when a patient is denudative, or too easily invites conversational contact from others, or speaks aloud shameful admissions, or smears himself with half-eaten food, or openly toys with his mucus, or takes dirty objects into his mouth. There are "hyper-preclusions," as when a patient declines to acknowledge any conversational overture, or shies away from passing glances, or fights off a medical examination, or will not let go of small personal possessions.

From this brief look at public places and social order among the unacquainted,[16] turn to closer social organization involving sustained obligations among sets of acquainted persons. First, formal work organizations. For this I propose to review Edwin Lemert's study of mental patients with paranoid complications whose trouble appeared to be focused on the job.[17]

Lemert dates the trouble-career of each member of his sample

---

[16] I have made a more extended effort along these lines in *Behavior in Public Places* (New York: The Free Press, paper edition, 1966) and *Interaction Ritual* (New York: Anchor Books, 1967).

[17] Edwin M. Lemert extensively studied 31 cases involving paranoid complications: 23 in southern California, 6 in northern California, and 2 miscellaneous cases. "Paranoia and the Dynamics of Exclusion," first published in *Sociometry* XXV (1962): 2–20, and reprinted in his *Human Deviance, Social Problems, and Social Control* (Englewood Cliffs, N.J.: Prentice-Hall, 1967).

by suggesting that each had been subjected to a loss, or threat of loss, of status, on or off the job, for which apparently no compensatory alternative could be found. Apparently such an individual can respond by declining to exert control over himself, and by resisting the informal control attempted by others. His willingness to play the game while on the job declines. He begins to intrude into the decision territory of subordinates and makes improper demands upon them, by implication subordinating them to his sphere of operation. He declines to return confidences with equals, thus leaving them with unreciprocated and insecure relations to him. He becomes insulting and arrogant, failing to show expected consideration for the feelings of the others, while exhibiting an improperly elevated view of himself. He attempts to arrogate to himself informal privileges which are part of the status symbolism of the group and otherwise allocated. He attempts to use markers of place without having the place that is customarily marked by them.

The conduct so far cited violates the informal rules for the management of personal place. We see in this a simple interdependency between the actor and his others, where the disturbed boundary is the one between the actor and these others. But in addition to these direct disturbances there are some indirect ones. Given the actor's membership in a work-group which is itself a segment in the total organization, we find he is in a position to disrupt the boundary relations of his segment to other segments. For example, he overrides group cleavages, threatening the working relationship between them. And he exposes the informal power structure, jeopardizing its relationship to the overarching official structure. He uses formal and official means to force his fellows to consider his demands directly, if only because he has forced higher officials to attend to his instituted complaints.

Plainly, then, the actor's failure to keep his place has disruptive consequences for his work associates, undermining their sense that a common understanding concerning everyone's social place exists and is a viable guide for daily activity. An important part of Lemert's analysis is his consideration of the sequence of events that is set in motion by this initial disturbance.

In order to cope with the troublesome colleague, the others avoid him physically when possible and exclude him from joint decisions and joint ventures. This very exclusion begins to color these excluding events, bringing a new meaning to them. When his workmates find that face-to-face interaction with him is unavoidable, they employ a humoring, pacifying, noncommittal style of reply which serves to damp the interaction as much as possible without giving him obvious cause for complaint. In order to be better prepared for what he might do, they may spy on him, in any case coming together in his absence to share their reaction to his latest move, pool their information, consider his next move, plot out together their next move, and in general celebrate the special solidarity that antagonism to him has created. A countergroup sustained through gossip is thus formed, with him as the negative focus. He becomes the center of distraction.

In consequence of this freeze-out, the actor, recipient now of no corrective feedback, may be forced to relatively violent outbursts as a means of making some impression upon the glossily opaque shell that others have constructed around him. They in turn may find it necessary to form a collusive net so as to inveigle him into receiving psychiatric attention.

Two implications of Lemert's analysis may be suggested. First, a system of informal social control can easily go awry. Tact and secrecy can have the ultimate consequence of constructing a real paranoid community for the paranoid. Secondly, until the individual is hospitalized, or until his reputation becomes widespread so that no one takes his actions seriously (and this latter form of encapsulation is found in large-scale social organizations), his symptoms have a very disruptive effect; it is a great deal to ask that members of the organization respond with understanding and support—it's a wonder, in fact, that organizations are as tolerant as they are.

I have sketched the relation between mental symptoms and two forms of social organization—public order and formally organized work places. Turn now to the final unit of organization to be considered, the domestic or family establishment.

V

Approach the family—say in the American middle-class version—through conventional sociological terms. When we examine its internal functioning, its internal social economy, we find a legitimated distribution of authority, material resources, work, and free time. There is the obligation of each member to care for and protect the others, insofar as they are in need of this help and a member is able to provide it. There is a normatively established allocation of respect, affection, and moral support. Some common values and special ways of doing things will be maintained. Knowledge of the family biography will be shared, along with memory of joint experiences. A crisscross of personal relationships will be sustained. A common care will be exerted (by all but the very young) so that the damage that could easily occur to the household through fire, water, soiling, and breaking will not occur. And each member will be trusted by the others not to exploit any of the lethal instrumentalities readily available in the house for harming himself or the others. Finally, as the special feature of the family as a social organization, each member commits his own feelings and involvements to what he takes to be the personal interests and personal plight of each of the others.

If the behavior of any one member, especially that occurring in the presence of other members, is examined closely, it reveals an expressive style that affirms this allotting of obligations. The maintenance of this style by each member gives the other members constant assurance that their expectations will be lived up to and that things are as they should be. In brief, the activity of each member tends to express that he knows what his social place is in the family and that he is sticking to it. Of course, if an individual member has medical difficulties, he is likely to make extra demands, but part of the safety here is due to the ritual work he engages in which neutralizes these demands as threats to the family's normative order, ensuring constancy to the members' sense of what the ill individual is like as a personality. Nonmedical crises, such as the lengthy absence of a member for military service, can similarly be handled, provided only that appropriate ritual work is done.

Turning to the external economy of the family, we find something similar. Resources which have value in the external environment are budgeted among the members in a conserving and perceivedly equitable manner. The fund of private information about the family possessed by the members is preserved, and a united, somewhat false front is maintained before the world—as if there were a family information rule. Finally, the relationships and work/school obligations that link individual members to outside persons and organizations comply with established jurisdictional rulings whereby the family retains some rights. In any case, the family member is pulled out of the family space only by real organizations and real persons who have made a real place for him. In brief, nonfamily claims on family members are limited and regularized.

The maintenance of the internal and external functioning of the family is so central that when family members think of the essential character, the perduring personality of any one of their numbers, it is usually his habitual pattern of support for family-organized activity and family relationships, his style of acceptance of his place in the family, that they have in mind. Any marked change in his pattern of support will tend to be perceived as a marked change in his character. The deepest nature of an individual is only skin-deep, the deepness of his others' skin.

In the case of withdrawals—depressions and regressions—it is chiefly the internal functioning of the family that suffers. The burden of enthusiasm and domestic work must now be carried by fewer numbers. Note that by artfully curtailing its social life, the family can conceal these disorders from the public at large and sustain conventional external functioning. Quiet alcoholism can similarly be contained, provided that economic resources are not jeopardized.

It is the manic disorders and the active phases of a paranoid kind that produce the real trouble. It is these patterns that constitute the insanity of place.

The beginnings are unclear and varied. In some cases something causes the prepatient—whether husband, wife, or child—to feel that the life his others have been allowing him is not sufficient, not right, and no longer tenable. He makes conventional demands for relief and change which are not granted, perhaps not even attended. Then, instead of falling back to the *status quo ante*, he begins his manic activity. As suggested, there are no doubt other etiologies and other precipitating sequences. But all end at the same point—the manic activity the family comes to be concerned with. We shall begin with this, although it is a late point from some perspectives.

The manic begins by promoting himself in the family hierarchy. He finds he no longer has the time to do his accustomed share of family chores. He increasingly orders other members around, displays anger and impatience, makes promises he feels he can break, encroaches on the equipment and space allocated to other members, only fitfully displays affection and respect, and finds he cannot bother adhering to the family schedule for meals, for going to bed and rising. He also becomes hypercritical and derogatory of family members. He moves backward to grandiose statements of the high rank and quality of his forebears, and forward to an exalted view of what he proposes soon to accomplish. He begins to sprinkle his speech with unassimilated technical vocabularies. He talks loudly and constantly, arrogating to himself the place at the center of things this role assumes. The great events and personages of the day uncharacteristically evoke from him a considered and definitive opinion. He seizes on magazine articles, movies, and TV shows as containing important wisdom that everyone ought to hear about in detail right now.

In addition to these disturbances of rank, there are those related to the minor obligations which symbolize membership and relatedness. He alone ceases to exercise the easy care that keeps household equipment safe and keeps members safe from it. He alone becomes capricious in performing the little courtesy-favors that all grown members offer one another if only because of the minute cost of these services to the giver compared to their appreciable value to the recipient. And he voices groundless beliefs, sometimes in response to hallucinations, which imply to his kin that he has ceased to regulate his thought by the standards that form the common ground of all those to whom they are closely related.

I repeat that the claims and actions of the ill person are not necessarily bizarre in themselves, merely bizarre when coming from the particular patient addressing himself to his particular family. And bizarreness itself is not the issue. Even when the patient hallucinates or develops exotic beliefs, the concern of the family is not simply that a member has crazy notions, but that he is not keeping his place in relationships. Someone to whom we are closely related is someone who ought not to have beliefs which estrange him from us. The various forms of grandiosity can have the same significance.

The constant effort of the family to argue the patient out of his foolish notions, to disprove his allegations, to make him take a reasonable view—an argumentation so despaired of by some therapists—can similarly be understood as the family's needs and the family's effort to bring the patient back into appropriate relationship to them. They cannot let him have his wrong beliefs because they cannot let him go. Further, if he reverses his behavior and becomes more collected, they must try to get him to admit that he has been ill, else his present saneness will raise doubts about the family's warrant for the way they have been treating him, doubts about their motivation and *their* relationship to him. For these reasons, admission of insanity has to be sought. And what is sought is an extraordinary thing indeed. If ritual work is a means of retaining a constancy of image in the face of deviations in behavior, then a self-admission that one is mentally ill is the biggest piece of ritual work of all, for this stance to one's conduct discounts the greatest deviations. A week of mayhem in a family can be set aside and readied to be forgotten the moment the offender admits he has been ill. Small wonder, then, that the patient will be put under great pressure to agree to the diagnosis, and that he may give in, even though this can mean that he must permanently lower the conception he has of his own character and must never again be adamant in presenting his views.

The issue here is not that the family finds that home life is made unpleasant by the sick person. Perhaps most home life is unpleasant. The issue is that meaningful existence is threatened. The definitions that the sick person tacitly accords the family members are less desirable than the ones they had before and imply that the family members are less connected to him than they had thought. If they accept this revision, then meaningful organization can be re-achieved, as happens, for example, when family cult-formation occurs or *folie à ménage*. But if they do not, there is trouble.[18]

Let me repeat: the self is the code that makes sense out of almost all the individual's activities and provides a basis for organizing them. This self is what can be read about the individual by interpreting the place he takes in an organization of social activity, as confirmed by his expressive behavior. The individual's failure to encode through deeds and expressive cues, a *workable* definition of himself, one which closely enmeshed others can accord him through the regard they show his person, is to block and trip up and threaten them in almost every movement that they make. The selves that had been the reciprocals of his are undermined. And that which should not have been able to change—the character of a loved one lived with—appears to be changing fundamen-

[18] Theories of *gemeinschaft* argue that intimates must agree on basic beliefs or break up their relationship, and that, by implication, the willingness of a skeptical member to come around is motivated by a desire to maintain relationships. But there are, of course, exceptions to the rule of agreement. The model here in social science literature is Mr. Keech, who quietly went about his usual business while Mrs. Keech at home was publicly organizing for the end of the world. See Leon Festinger et al., *When Prophecy Fails* (New York: Harper Torchbooks, 1964), esp. pp. 38–39.

tally and for the worse before their eyes. In ceasing to know the sick person, they cease to be sure of themselves. In ceasing to be sure of him and themselves, they can even cease to be sure of their way of knowing. A deep bewilderment results. Confirmations that everything is predictable and as it should be cease to flow from his presentations. The question as to what it is that is going on is not redundantly answered at every turn but must be constantly ferreted out anew. And life is said to become like a bad dream—for there is no place in possible realities for what is occurring.

It is here that mental symptoms deviate from other deviations. A person who suddenly becomes selfish, heartless, disloyal, unfaithful, or addicted can be dealt with. If he properly shows cause or contrition he can be forgiven; if he is unrepentant but removable he can be redefined. In either case, his others can come to terms with him, in the sense that the expressions he gives off concerning his definition of himself and them are indications that confirm the relationship they feel they now have to him. The grammaticality of activity is sustained. A patient's mental symptoms, however, are something his others cannot come to terms with. Neither he nor they withdraw from the organization or relationship sufficiently to allow his expression to confirm what his status implies. Thus his behavior strikes at the syntax of conduct, deranging the usual agreement between posture and place, between expression and position.

The domestic disorganization created by the ill person points up an important fact about social control in a unit like the family. Any grown member of the family can leave the household against the will and advice of the family, and, except for exacting financial claims against him, there is nothing that the family can do about it. The power of the leavetaker is especially strong if he departs properly, through channels as it were, with an appropriately staged announcement of intentions. On the other side, there are circumstances (varying in America from state to state) in which a family can have a member removed bodily to a place of detention. However, when, for whatever reason, neither of these forms of socially recognized departure occurs, the family and its household prove to be vulnerable in the extreme. For then the standard notion of social control effected through a corrective cycle becomes quite untenable. The simple fact is that when an offender is disapproved of and punished, and warned what will happen if he persists, it is tacitly assumed that he will be sufficiently committed to the life of the group, and to sustaining those who presume authority in it, to *voluntarily* take the sanction to heart and, whether in good grace or bad, desist from the particular offense. If the family offender elects not to heed the warning, there is then really nothing effective that can be done to him. Sheer manhandling that is not responded to by tacit cooperation requires the full effort of at least two strong adults and even then can only be managed in brief spurts—long enough to remove someone from a house, but not much longer. Even merely to stand watch and guard over a person requires more than a household can usually manage for very long. And the household itself can hardly be run if everything that might be damageable or dangerous must be kept out of an adult's reach.

Households, then, can hardly be operated at all if the good will of the residents cannot be relied on.[19] Interestingly, it is right at the moment of punishment and threat, right when the offender presumably has additional reasons for antagonism, that the family is most clearly dependent on his self-submission to family authority. Punitive action forces the offender either to capitulate and lose face, or to disabuse his opponents of their belief that they have power over him. Just when he is most angry at them he must see that he alone can save their illusions concerning their control over him. Negative sanctions within the context of a household, then,

[19] A useful recent description of the structural contingencies of disciplining an unwilling family member is provided in Louise Wilson, *This Stranger, My Son* (New York: G. P. Putnam's Sons, 1968). Mrs. Wilson describes in some detail what a child diagnosed as paranoid schizophrenic can accomplish with the domestic equipment at hand. A full picture is also available in the Bettelheim accounts of the Sonia Shankman Orthogenic School, but in this case, of course, the care that requires the staff's full-time effort *is* their official full-time job. The consequences of attempting discipline of a family member old enough to go to the university but not quite old enough to be defined as independent is beautifully available in the ugly Russier case.

constitute a kind of doomsday machine, forcing the last available opportunity to avoid a breakdown of order upon the stronger of the two parties, who must act as if he is the weaker. Obviously, on occasion he will not be considerate. This vulnerability of family organization is reinforced by the fact that the offender may well give less consideration to his own bodily welfare and his own interests than those who must control him.

I have considered some of the disorganizational consequences of the patient's failure to support the internal order of the family. It is, however, when the family's external functioning is considered that the full derangement is seen.

The social place of a family in the community at large is a matter of some delicacy, based as it is on personal and informal control that exposes the family to a thousand possible markets for its various resources—markets which the family itself must deal with prudently if it is to maximize its own long-range interests as these are conventionally defined. It is this circumspection, ordinarily self-imposed, that the active patient transcends.

Misplaced enterprise occurs. Family monies are squandered on little examples of venture capitalism. Grand services and equipment are bought or contracted for, nicely illustrating the democratic, accepting attitude of those who sell things and the personal control that all of us ordinarily maintain.[20] Bargains advertised in the newspaper are ordered in excessive quantity by phone.[21] The occupational and age-grade structure is dipped into far enough down to find commandeers and hirelings for expansive private projects. An unnecessary office or industrial layout is grafted onto the household. The patient finds that his ordinary job is cramping

---

See *The Affair of Gabrielle Russier* (New York: Alfred P. Knopf, 1971), and the fine introduction to it written by Mavis Gallant.

[20] Admittedly, there are some limits due to formal social control. A thirteen-year-old cannot go down to his friendly Ford dealer and negotiate the purchase of a new Mustang, although a few years later he can. Similarly, although almost any adult can at will set a real estate agent to work, earnest money will eventually be needed.

[21] See Roueché's case study, "Ten Feet Tall," *The Incurable Wound* (New York: Berkeley Books, 1958). Roueché provides useful details regarding the overreaching social behavior of a man enjoying a brief manic episode due to the side effects of cortisone treatment.

and gives it up or is fired.[22] A flurry of projects is initiated. A press of occupation occurs.

Contacting is accelerated. The telephone is increasingly used. Each call becomes longer and more calls are made. Favorite recipients are called more and more frequently. When the hour renders local calls a gross violation of informal rules, long-distance calls are made into acceptable time zones; when the hour prevents even these, night telegrams are dispatched.[23] A flood of letter-writing may occur.

Participation is broadened. Assistance is volunteered to persons and organizations undesirous of receiving it from this quarter—the patient appreciating that an offering is a warrantable means of making contact with the recipient. Public life is entered through its least guarded portals: participation in volunteer work; letters to politicians, editors, and big corporations; celebrity hunting; litigation. Critical national events, such as elections, war policy statements, and assassinations, are taken quite personally. Personal appearances on radio and television may be sought; press conferences and press releases may be engineered. Perceived slights in public places lead to scenes and to the patient's making official complaints to officials.

---

[22] A manic patient who can become too large for his home can similarly become too large for his job. Starting with a commendable increase in enthusiasm for his work, he begins to offer fellow workers wanted help and advice, extends this to what is seen as interference in the spheres of others, and finally takes to giving unauthorized directives and acting as a spokesman for his work-organization when he is away from it. During this process of becoming a self-appointed boss, he begins to arrogate to himself more and more equipment, space, and subordinate help. And since his private business and convivial enterprise have greatly expanded and are coming to be very ill-received at home, he shifts more and more of these activities to the work-place, spends more and more time during and after work thus engaged, and soon violates the very delicate norm governing the penetration of private interests into work. He promotes get-togethers of work personnel, and embarrasses status divisions by trying to bring together for conviviality everyone at work who is remotely within his social reach.

[23] Monthly telephone bills that are twenty times normal have an interesting story to tell. Telephone companies, however, are scrupulously detached in these matters. Theirs is not to wonder why but only to collect.

Associating is intensified. Neighbors are dropped in on at unsuitable hours. Parties are arrived at first and left last. There may be a surge of home entertainment that is unstabilizing: properly related friends attend until other commitments cause them to defect; newly formed friends are substituted, but each set wears out more quickly than the last, requiring recruitment from less and less suitable sources; ultimately the gatherings become socially bizarre. Semi-official, public-spirited purposes for home gatherings are increasingly employed, this providing some warrant for the patient's inviting persons he has merely heard about, and for aggregations of persons of widely different social rank. Invitation lists are extended right up to the last minute, as if there were a need to be in touch with all acquaintances and to pack the environment with people. Evenings of commercial recreation and weekend outings are organized repeatedly, involving much recontacting and also the mustering of unacquainted persons into one venture.

Finally, relating is expanded. Courtesy introductions and offhand referrals by others are followed up and made something of, acquaintanceship is presumed upon, and presuming requests are made across affinal lines to spouses of friends. "Middlemanning" occurs, the ill person attempting to bring into contact persons perceived as having use for each other. The functional specificity of service relations is breached. Advice is proffered to and asked of service personnel on many matters; the use of reciprocal first-naming is suggested; social invitations are extended. Corresponding to this diffusion, personal friends are loaded with service requests and enrolled in schemes and projects. Occasional workers, hired by the patient to help in projects, will be transformed into friends to fill the gap that has developed, but these will now be friends who can be ordered to come and go, there resulting a kind of minionization of the patient's social circle.[24] Minor shortcomings in services received from long-utilized professionals, tradesmen, and repairmen lead to run-ins and the immediate establishment of new service connections. Family secrets are confidentially divulged at informal

[24] A form of social organization sometimes bred by very high office; this is best illustrated today, perhaps, in the Hollywood entourage.

gatherings to persons who are merely acquaintances. Newly formed friends are enthusiastically praised to the family, giving the impression that the patient's capacity for deep involvement is being exercised capriciously. If the patient is single, unsuitable mating may threaten to occur across age, race, or class lines; if married, then unsuitable re-mating. And some sexual promiscuity may occur of the kind that can be realized at will because it trades on marked status differences. In all of this, the patient either takes advantage of others or places others in a position to take advantage of him, in either case to the deep embarrassment of his family.

A general point can be detected here about the patient's rage for connectedness and position. Since his movement from his allotted place is to be accomplished entirely by the power of self-inclination, two spheres will be in easiest reach for him. One consists of local persons who are appreciably beneath him socially and who are willing to be approached at will because the association can mean some kind of economic gain or social enhancement. The other sphere consists of powerful and well-known personages. Of course, only the most vicarious and attenuated contact can be made with these notables, the channels here being fan letters, telegrams, attendance at personal appearances, unaccepted party invitations, and the like. Nonetheless, when actual social connections become disturbed and insufficient, these figures are there; they acquire a startling immediacy and come to serve as points of reference for self-organization.

The patient, then, is free to move in two directions: downward by means of social trade-offs; upward by means of vicarious or abortive contact. Interestingly, the more trouble at home, the greater the need to move into the lives of friends; the more this is done, the more the second circle will close itself off by virtue of being overtaxed; the more this occurs, the more fully does the patient take flight into unsuitable alliances and vicarious ones. Further, what remains of an inner circle tends to be alienated by what the patient attempts in the next concentric ring; what is there developed is undermined by his antics in a still wider circle. Tentative expansion outward thus reduces what is already possessed, and sharply increases the need to consolidate the new circle. With all of these forces working together, an explosion of dealings results. There is a flight into the community.

Without taking the time to examine in detail any of these overreachings, or to consider the clinical hypothesis that the patient may be seeking every possible external support for an internal state that is collapsing, let it only be said that so far as family organization is concerned, what happens is that the boundary between it and the community is threatened. In the extreme, the family as a unit that holds itself off from the environing world is forcibly washed away, the members literally displaced from the domestic establishment by a flood of nonmembers and by the sick person's organizational activity.

Note that the community context of family life is such that this sort of diffusion is always possible. The patient does not construct his own avenues of access; he merely uses excessively devices available to anyone in his position. To appreciate this fact, we must look at the community as a system of fences and gates, a system for regulating the formation and growth of social relationships.

A relationship cannot form unless two persons can come into personal contact of some kind (whether face-to-face or mediated), and a relationship cannot develop unless its members can interact over a period of time.

Contact itself is organizationally facilitated in certain basic ways. Contemporary social organization provides that places of residence and work can be reached by phone, telegraph, letters, and personal visits. The necessarily common use of public and semipublic facilities, especially the streets, brings a wide variety of persons within face-to-face reach of one another. The institution of acquaintanceship (established often through introduction) confers preemptive contact rights. Because of such devices, a very wide potential exists for contact, and through contact the development of relationships.

This potential, in turn, is sharply curtailed by various factors. We do not know the appearance or address of many of those we might want to be in touch with. We are bound by rules which proscribe our initiating talk with unacquainted others except on various good grounds. We are likely to be ignorant of where and when those social occasions will occur where those whose acquaintance we seek will be present, and presence itself allows for the initiation of talk. Knowing where and when, we may not be qualified by money, membership, or invitation to go. Beyond this, there are all the devices used for blocking contacts: disguise of personal appearance, avoidance of public places, nonlisting of telephone numbers, the stationing of gatekeepers to intervene at places of residence and work, segregation by cost and ecology, and so forth.[25] But note, these various blocks to association cannot be allowed to be complete. Any door that *completely* keeps out undesirables also keeps out some desirables; any means of completely shutting oneself off also shuts out contacts that would be profitable. After all, relationships that come to be close can be traced back to an overture or introduction; service dealings which prove satisfactory can be traced back to an unknown client's or customer's appearing on the telephone; successful projects, to nothing more substantial than announced intentions; valuable publicity for a celebrity, to one among the many phone calls he receives; a warning that one has dropped one's wallet, to a stranger who accosts one on the street. Who knows from whom the next phone call or letter will be and what it will be about? The most careful screening in the world must still expose someone on the staff to *anyone* who bothers to try to make contact. Presentments have to be given a moment's benefit of the doubt, lest that which will come to be desirably realized will not have been able to begin. We must always pause at least for a moment in our oncoming rejection of another in order to check the importuner out. There is no choice: social life must ever expose itself to unwarranted initiatings. A screening device would have no functional value if the only persons who got through it were the persons who got to it.

Mechanisms for facilitating and restricting relationship formation are reinforced by formal legal control, in the sense that per-

---

[25] These devices are most fully used by the famed, apparently in part because they can least rely on the probability that interested members of the public will lack detection information about them.

sons who decline to be drawn into certain negotiations can be forced to do so by the law, as can those who decline to desist from certain importunings. Much more important, the mechanisms are reinforced by personal control and informal control, resulting in a tacit social contract: a person is obliged to make himself available for contacting and relationship formation, in return for which others are obliged to refrain from taking advantage of his availability. He incidentally can retain the illusion that he does not cut people off; they, that they would not be rejected.

This contract of association is made viable by the allowance of prognosticative expression. An open and friendly address conveys that overtures will be welcomed; a wary and stiff mien, that importunement will result in open rejection. Anyone wending his way through his daily round is guided not only by self-interest but also by these expressions. He avoids accepting subtle invitations that might lead to unsuitable associations and avoids transgressing where subtle warnings have been issued. He keeps to the straight and narrow. He handles himself ungenerously because on all sides there is something to lose.

It is understandable, then, why the patient finds himself in a disruptable world. Merely by jeopardizing a little more than persons like himself are usually willing to do—through exposing himself either to unsuitable relationships or to insulting rejection—he is in a position to penetrate all social boundaries a little. Whosoever the other, there will always be good reasons to warrant relating to him, and therefore a cover, however quickly discreditable, for the beginning of interaction with him.

A final comment. The manic activity I have described is obviously located in the life of the privileged, the middle and higher classes.[26] I think this apparent bias in selecting illustrations is war-

---

[26] Some empirical evidence for this argument is provided in August Hollingshead and Fredrick Redlich, *Social Class and Mental Illness* (New York: John Wiley & Sons, 1958), p. 288.

For an analytical illustration, consider an extreme comparison: a black wino and a blond model, he in rough clothes and she in the style of the upper middle-class. Compared their public situation—the passage of each

ranted. Social resources must be possessed before they can be handled in the manner that has been considered. Therefore mania would seem to be a disease of persons with social advantages—money, lineage, office, profession, education, sexual attractiveness, and a network of social and familial relationships. Perhaps impoverished expansionists, having few goods to exchange for being taken seriously, are soon forced to make ludicrous presentations, and transform everyone around them into skeptical ward attend-

---

across, alongside, or toward the paths of unacquainted others. Consider the eye practices each must face from these walkers-by.

The wino: A walker-by will take care to look at him fleetingly if at all, wary lest the wino find an angle from which to establish eye-to-eye contact and then disturb the passage with prolonged salutations, besmearing felicitations, and other importunements and threats. Should the wino persist in not keeping his place, the discourtesy of outright head-aversion may be necessary.

The model: A walker-by will fix her with an open gaze for as many moments as the passage will allow without his having to turn his head sharply. During this structured moment of staring he may well be alert in fantasy for any sign she makes interpretable as encouraging his attentions. Note that this helter-skelter gallantry remains very well in check, no danger to the free flow of human traffic, for long ago the model will have learned her part in this ceremony, which is to conduct her eyes downward and unseeing, in silent sufferance of exposure.

Against this structural view of the public situation of the beast and the beauty (illustrating the boundaries of civil inattention), consider the consequence to each of being apparently possessed by an unsuppressed urge to enter into dealings.

Of himself the wino can make a mild nuisance, but nothing much more disarraying than that is likely to be allowed him. The more he rattles the bars of his cage, the more hurrying-by will be done by visitors to the zoo. Social arrangements are such that his screaming right into the face of an unacquainted other may only complete his treatment as someone who does not exist. The friendly model, in contrast, will find that suddenly there are a hundred takers, that strangers of both colors, three sexes, and several age groups are ready to interrupt their course for an adventure in sociability. Where'er she smiles, relationships begin to develop. A wino leaves a narrow trail of persons more fully busying themselves with their initial plans. A manic beauty may not get far enough to leave a trail. She opens up a world that then closes in on her. She clots and entangles the courses of action around her. The more delicate and ladylike, the more she is the peril the Victorian manuals should have warned the city about.

ants. Thus it could be argued that the well-stationed are prone or at least overrepresented; the insanity of place is a function of position.

I have already touched on some features of the family's response to life with the patient. Members feel they are no longer in an easefully predictable environment. They feel bewildered by the change of character and personality that has occurred. Moreover, since the dramatic change has come to a person they feel they should best be able to characterize, cognition itself becomes an issue; the very principles of judgment by which one comes to feel that one knows character and is competent to judge it can become threatened. Consider now some further aspects of the family's response.

One issue concerns the structure of attention. Put simply, the patient becomes someone who has to be watched. Each time he holds a sharp or heavy object, each time he answers the phone, each time he nears the window, each time he holds a cup of coffee above a rug, each time he is present when someone comes to the door or drops in, each time he handles the car keys, each time he begins to fill a sink or tub, each time he lights a match—on each of these occasions the family will have to be ready to jump. And when it is not known where he is or it is known that he is behind a locked door, an alert will have to be maintained for any hint of something untoward. The possibility that the patient will be malicious or careless, that he will intentionally or unintentionally damage himself, the household, or the others, demonstrates that standard household arrangements can be full of danger; obviously, it is the presumption of conventional use that makes us think that these conventional arrangements are safe.[27]

---

[27] Professionals who manage the actively suicidal are acutely alive to the unconventional lethal possibilities of domestic equipment; indeed, in published case records detail is provided. Less clearly appreciated, perhaps, is that a person with *any* type of actively expressed mental disorder can unhinge the meaning of his domestic acts for the other members of the family. What would ordinarily be an uneventful household routine can come to be seen as a deed through which the patient may intentionally or unintentionally damage the equipment at hand, the persons nearby, or himself.

Three points are to be made concerning the family's watchfulness. First, households tend to be informally organized, in the sense that each member is allowed considerable leeway in scheduling his own tasks and diverting himself in his own directions. He will have his own matters, then, to which he feels a need to attend. The necessity, instead, of his having to stand watch over the patient blocks rightful and pleasurable calls upon time and generates a surprising amount of fatigue, impatience, and hostility. Second, the watching will have to be dissimulated and disguised lest the patient suspect he is under constant surveillance, and this covering requires extra involvement and attention. Third, in order to increase their efficiency and maintain their morale, the watchers are likely to engage in collaboration, which perforce must be collusive.

The family must respond not only to what the patient is doing to its internal life, but also to the spectacle he seems to be making of himself in the community. At first the family will be greatly concerned that one of its emissaries is letting down the side. The family therefore tries to cover up and intercede so as to keep up his front and theirs. This strengthens the collusive alignment in the family against the patient.

As the dispute within the family continues and grows concerning the selves in whose terms activity ought to be organized, the family begins to turn outward, first to the patient's kinsmen, then to friends, to professionals, to employers. The family's purpose is not merely to obtain help in the secretive management of the patient, but also to get much needed affirmation of its view of events. There is a reversal of the family information rule. Acquaintances or other potential sources of aid who had once been personally distant from the family will now be drawn into the center of things as part of a new solidarity of those who are helping to manage the patient, just as some of those who were once close may now be dropped because apparently they do not confirm the family's definition of the situation.

Finally, the family finds that in order to prevent others from giving weight to the initiatory activity of the patient, relatively distant persons must be let in on the family secret. There may even be necessity for recourse to the courts to block extravagances by conservator proceedings, to undo unsuitable marriages by annulments, and the like. The family will frankly allow indications that it can no longer handle its own problems, for the family cat must be belled. By that time the family members will have learned to live exposed. There will be less pride and less self-respect. They will be engaged in establishing that one of their members is mentally ill, and in whatever degree they succeed in this, they will be exposing themselves to the current conception that they constitute the kind of family which produces mental illness.

While the family is breaking the informational boundary between itself and society—and an appeal to a therapist is only one nicely contained instance of this—it may begin to add some finer mesh as well as some spread to its collusive net. Some of the patient's telephone calls are tapped and some of his letters opened and read. Statements which the patient makes to different persons are secretly polled, with consequent exposure of incongruities. Experiences with the patient are shared in a widening circle in order to extract and confirm patterns of impropriety. Discreetly planned actions are presented to the patient as unplanned spontaneous ones, or disguised to appear as if originating from a source still deemed innocent by him. This conspiracy, note, is an understandable result of the family's needing very much to know the patient's next move in order to undo it.

A review of the family's response to the patient easily suggests that members will find much cause to feel angry at him. Overlaid, however, there will be other feelings, often stronger. The damage the patient appears to be doing, especially in consequence of his overreachings outside the family, is seen to hurt his own interests even more than those of the rest of the family. Yet for the family this need not produce grim satisfaction or help to balance things out; rather, matters may be made worse. As suggested, it is the distinctive character of the family that its members not only feel responsible for any member in need, but also feel personal identification with his situation. Whenever the patient is out alone in the community, exposed and exposing himself to what can be perceived as a contamination of his self and a diminution of his character, whenever the patient must be left alone at home, exposing himself as well as the household to intended and unintended dangers, the family will know anxiety and fear.

It has been suggested that a family with mania to contend with is likely to form a collusive net, the patient being excolluded.[28] Now turn and take the point of view of the patient.

The family's conspiracy is benign, but this conspiracy breeds what others do. The patient finds himself in a world that has only the appearance of innocence, in which small signs can be found —and therefore sought out and wrongly imputed—showing that things are anything but what they seem. At home, when his glance suddenly shifts in a conversation, he may find naked evidence of collusive teamwork against him—teamwork unlike the kind which evaporates when a butt is let in on a good-natured joke that is being played at his expense.[29] He rightly comes to feel

---

[28] If the patient is an adult, the consequences for children are especially painful. In order to protect the young from the imperious demands of the patient and from the conception of the patient that would result were his acts taken as serious ones, the young may have to be recruited into the net. This will also facilitate the collusion by reducing the number of others from whom its operation must be concealed. The children may accept this invitation, decline it, or, if careful enough, give each side the impression that its view is being supported. Whatever the response of the young, adult solidarity is clearly broken and idealization of adults undermined. Children's insubordinate treatment of the ill person can result, the other adults being unable to reinforce demands of the patient. Further, the more the ill person becomes a source of unwarranted demands upon the young, the less the other adults feel they can exert parental discipline where discipline is due.

[29] For this the patient requires no special perceptiveness, sometimes attributed to the insane. It is an empirical fact that in our society the furtive signs through which a collusive alignment is maintained against someone who is present are often crude and easily available to the excolluded. Ordinarily the colluders do not discover that they have been discovered because the excolluded wants to support the surface appearance that he is not so unworthy as to warrant this kind of betrayal. Paradoxically, it is exactly such a surface definition of the situation that the colluders require in order to have something to undercut. I want to add that colluders very often de-

that statements made to him are spoken so as to be monitored by the others present, ensuring that they will keep up with the managing of him, and that statements made to others in his presence are designed and delivered for his overhearing. He will find this communication arrangement very unsettling and come to feel that he is purposely being kept out of touch with what is happening.

In addition, the patient is likely to detect that he is being watched, especially when he approaches some domestic device which could be used to harm himself or others, or which is itself valuable and vulnerable to harm. He will sense that he is being treated as a child who can't be trusted around the house, but in this case one who cannot be trusted to be frankly shown that he is not trusted. If he lights a match or takes up a knife, he may find as he turns from these tasks that others present seem to have been watching him and now are trying to cover up their watchfulness.

In response to the response he is creating, the patient, too, will come to feel that life in the family has become deranged. He is likely to try to muster up some support for his own view of what his close ones are up to. And he is likely to have some success.

The result is two collusive factions, each enveloping the other in uncertainties, each drawing on a new and changing set of secret members. The household ceases to be a place where there is the easy fulfillment of a thousand mutually anticipated proper acts. It ceases to be a solid front organized by a stable set of persons against the world, entrenched and buffered by a stable set of friends and servers. The household becomes a no-man's land where changing factions are obliged to negotiate daily, their weapons being collusive communication and their armor selective inattention to the machinations of the other side—an inattention difficult to achieve, since each faction must devote itself to reading the other's furtive signs. The home, where wounds were meant to be licked, becomes precisely where they are inflicted. Boundaries are broken. The family is turned inside out.

---

cline to stage their collusion as discreetly as they could. As in many other occasions of false behavior, the manipulators half want their dupe to be aware of what is really thought of him.

We see, then, that the domestic manic breeds, and is bred in, organizational havoc, and that this havoc is all too evident. Yet here clinical reports have been very weak. I venture a Durkheimian account.

It is frequently the case that hospitalized patients who have behaved at home in the most exotic and difficult fashion are taken back into the family upon release from the hospital, and that however tentatively they are received, they are given some sort of trial acceptance. Also, it is quite generally the case that before hospitalization, the feeling of the family that the troublesome one is mentally ill will come and go: with each outburst the family will have to face anew the idea that mental illness is apparently involved, but with each moment of the patient's wonted and tranquil behavior, sharp new hope will be experienced by the family—hope that everything is coming back to normal. This readiness to oscillate, this resilience of hope on the family's part, should not be taken particularly as evidence of good will or resistance to bad-naming. In other circumstances, I'm sure, most families would be quite ready to form a rigid and stereotyped view of an offender. But the fact is that there is no stable way for the family to conceive of a life in which a member conducts himself insanely. The heated scramble occurring around the ill person is something that the family will be instantly ready to forget; the viable way things once were is something that the family will always be ready to re-anticipate. For if an intellectual place could be made for the ill behavior, it would not be ill behavior. It is as if perception can only form and follow where there is social organization; it is as if the experience of disorganization can be felt but not retained. When the havoc is at its height, participants are unlikely to find anyone who has the faintest appreciation of what living in it is like. When the trouble is finally settled, the participants will themselves be unable to appreciate why they had become so upset. Little wonder, then, that during the disorganization phase, the family will live the current reality as in a dream, and the domestic routine which can now only be dreamt of will be seen as what is real.

VI

Return now to the earlier discussion of collusive elements in the medical role. Return to the doctor's dilemma.

The traditional picture of mental hospitalization and other psychiatric services involves a responsible person, typically a next of kin, persuading, dragging, conning, or trapping the patient-to-be into visiting a psychiatrist. A diagnostic inspection occurs. It is then that the psychiatrist is likely to begin his collusion with the next of kin, on the grounds that the patient cannot be trusted to act in his own best interests, and that it will not do the patient any good to learn the name and extent of his sickness.[30] The patient, of course, is likely to feel betrayed and conspired against; and he may continue to until he is well enough to see that the collusive action was taken in his own best interests.

The great critics of the collusive management of the mental patient have been the psychoanalysts. They act on the assumption that if a real relationship is to be developed with the client, one allowing the therapist and client to work together profitably, then this relation must not be undercut by the therapist's engaging in collusive communication with the client's responsible others. If contact is necessary between therapist and patient's kin, then the kin should be warned that the patient must know what has taken place, and what in substance the therapist said to the kin. Therapists realistically appreciate that information about the patient put into the hands of his loved ones might well be used against him. This communications policy cuts the therapist off from many sources of information about the patient, but there is an answer in

[30] Surely this practice is not entirely a bad thing, since this information can deeply affect the patient's view of himself, and yet diagnoses seem to vary quite remarkably, depending on the prevailing diagnostic fashion and the tastes of the practitioner.

the doctrine that the patient's trouble is in his style of projecting and relating, and that this can be well enough sampled by means of what is disclosed during private sessions. A parallel can be noted here to what is called hotel anthropology.

I am suggesting that therapists, especially of the psychoanalytical persuasion, appreciate the collusive implication of their contacts with the third party and go far in protecting the patient from this collusion. However, by this very maneuver they help consolidate another collusive relationship, that between themselves and the patient in regard to the responsible others. The practice of trying to get at the patient's point of view, the effort to refrain considerably from passing obvious moral judgments, and the strict obligation on the patient's part to betray all confidences if these seem relevant—all these factors in conjunction with the privacy of the therapeutic setting ensure collusive coalition formation to a degree unappreciated even by the next of kin. (Whereas ordinary relationships give rise to collusive coalitions, the therapeutic situation is a collusion that gives rise to a relationship.) This resembles a domestic handicapping system, whereby the weakest team in the family tournament is given an extra man. Let me add that collusion for hire seems a rum sort of business to be in, but perhaps more good is done than harm.

What has been considered can be reduced to a formula. Traditionally the psychotic has been treated through a collusive relation between his therapists and his family and ends up excolluded into the mental hospital, while the neurotic (who is so inclined and can afford it) has been treated to a collusive relation with his therapist against his family or boss and remains in the community.[31]

There is a collusion, then, for psychotics who end up in a men-

---

[31] Admittedly in recent times some therapists have attempted to treat the same patient in and out of the hospital, in which case the usual alignments are not possible; some have engaged in "family therapy"; and some have attempted a flexible open relationship of access allowing for private and family sessions with the same patient. But even these arrangements, I think, do not prevent collusion problems.

tal hospital and for neurotics who stay in the community—the psychiatrist being constrained to engage in one or the other form, depending on his patient and, beyond that, his type of practice. What is to be considered here, however, is the collusion arising when psychotics of the manic kind are managed in the community.

First note that the therapeutic or patient-analyst collusion will have shortcomings. Private talks with the patient will not tell the therapist what is happening to the family or what its urgent needs are. This is indicated by the fact already suggested that psychotherapists have provided hardly any information about the organizational meaning of illness for the units of social organization in which the illness occurs. In any case, since the patient is likely to continue his troublesome activity unabated after beginning therapy, the family will feel that the therapist has become a member of the patient's faction. This is no small matter. The patient's domestic opponents find themselves pressed to the wall of sanity, having to betray a loved one lest his uncharacteristic assumptions about himself make their life unreal. Their social place is being undermined, and the standards they have always used in judging character and identity are in question. The failure of any other person to confirm their view of the patient, even when this failure merely means declining to take sides, adds weight to the hallucinatory possibility that they might be wrong and, being wrong, are destroying the patient. And persons distant from the family will certainly fail to confirm the family's position. A fact about the wider community must here be appreciated. Unless the patient is very ill, those who know him little—even more, those who know him not at all—may not sense that anything is wrong, and with good reason; at least for a time, all they may notice is that an individual is more friendly and outgoing, more approachable than he might be. Those in the community who *do* develop doubts about the patient are likely to be tactful enough to refrain from directly expressing them. After all, easing themselves out of contact with the troublesome one is all that is necessary. The worst that can happen to them is that they will briefly have to face how conditional their concern for another is—conditional on his being willing to withdraw in response to suggestions and hints.

The other type of psychiatric collusion may not be much better. If the family has psychiatric assurance that it is the patient who is crazy and not the family members, this mitigates somewhat their need for confirmation of their position from friends and associates, and in turn mitigates their flight into the community. But in order to contain and discipline the patient, and through this to preserve the possibility of reestablishing the old relationships later, they will feel compelled to tell him he is not himself and that so says the psychiatrist. This won't help very much. The family will almost certainly have to use this club. It won't, however, be the right one. The patient will feel that the family members are concerned not about his illness, but about their pinched status. And the patient by and large will be right. The patient then must either embrace the notion of mental illness, which is to embrace what is likely to be a destructive conception of his own character, or find further evidence that his close ones have suddenly turned against him.

In summary, the physician finds that he must join the family's faction or the patient's, and that neither recourse is particularly tenable. That is the doctor's dilemma.

VII

In this paper an attempt has been made to sketch some of the meanings of mental symptoms for the organization in which they occur, with special reference to the family. The argument is that current doctrine and practice in psychiatry have neglected these meanings. To collapse the warfare of social place in a troubled family into such terms as "acting out" or "manic" keeps things tidy, but mostly what such terms accomplish is the splendid isolation of the person using them. A concept such as "hyperactivity," which psychiatrically denotes precisely the behavior I have been considering, seems to connote some sort of mechanical malfunctioning with little suggestion of the social overreachings that are actually involved.

A final complication. Throughout this paper I have spoken of the mentally ill patient and his mental symptoms. That was an optimistically simple thing to do. Medical symptoms and mental symptoms, so-called, are radically different things. As pointed out, the malfunctioning that medical symptoms represent is a malfunctioning of the human organism and only very rarely constitutes an elegant denial of social functioning. However impaired physically, the medically ill person can almost always express that he is not intentionally and openly opposing his place in the social scheme of things. So-called mental symptoms, on the other hand, are made up of the very substance of social obligation. Mental symptoms directly express the whole array of divisive social alignments: alienation, rebellion, insolence, untrustworthiness, hostility, apathy, importunement, intrusiveness, and so forth. These divisive alignments do not—in the first instance—constitute malfunctioning of the individual, but rather disturbance and trouble in a relationship or an organization. We can all largely agree that everything should be done to patch up bodies and keep them alive, but certainly not that social organizations of all kinds should be preserved. Further, as already suggested, there are a multitude of reasons why someone who is not mentally ill at all, but who finds he can neither leave an organization nor basically alter it, might introduce exactly the same trouble as is caused by patients.[32] All the terms I have used to describe the offensive behavior of the patient—and the term "patient" itself—are expressions of the viewpoint of parties with special interests. Quotation marks would have been in order, but too many of them would have been necessary.

[32] An implication is that those who come to the attention of psychiatry are a very mixed bag. Given current admission procedures, and given the current patient-load of nonanalytical office practitioners, I don't see how it is possible for psychiatrists to know whether or not it is mental illness that underlies the symptom with which they are dealing. Not knowing what they are dealing with, they understandably have small success in dealing with it.

The conventional psychiatric doctrine makes a place, of course, for psychiatry. The argument goes that an individual can appear more or less normal to those in his family, his work place, or his neighborhood, and really, underneath it all, be what is called a very sick guy—one who needs some help. The prepatient and his intimates can refuse to see that anything fundamental is wrong, when to a professional eye it is plain that he is, as they say, quite sick. By the time the prepatient and his others appreciate that something is wrong, he may—the psychiatric argument goes—be very sick indeed. By that time his close others are likely to be penalizing him in all sorts of ways for his illness, and blaming him for something that they probably helped to produce. The solution is to catch things early, before symptoms become florid, the personality deteriorates, and irreparable damage has been done.

This conventional view, however, can be fatefully wrong, and wrong both for the patient and his others. For when someone not in a hospital has a manic episode, the following possibilities should be considered.

On the one hand, there may be very little wrong with the offender's psychobiological equipment. The psychological significance of the trouble for him may be relatively superficial and may, in fact, be partly understandable in terms of his changing relation to those outside the troubled organization. After all, the mess that the manic makes does not come out of his head. It comes from the vulnerabilities of domestic and community organizations to persons with social resources to expend.[33] On the other hand, those

[33] Similarly, we should appreciate that depression is not something that can be fully understood by looking inside the patient. It seems to me that depressed persons come to appreciate consciously how much social effort is in fact required in the normal course of keeping one's usual place in undertakings. Once an individual feels a little less outgoing than usual for him, a very large part of his social universe can easily become attenuated, simply because such a universe is partly sustained at the constantly exercised option of the actor. At many contact points in the individual's daily round, his others will be on the lookout for signs of disaffection and be ready to begin to withdraw from him in order to protect their own reception. A small hint that he has become less inclined toward them can begin a general letting go of him. It might be added that while the classic notion of

who must contain the manic in their social organization may, because of his social behavior, find themselves fighting for their social lives. The social significance of the confusion he creates may be as profound and basic as social existence can get.

The most disruptive thing a well organism can do is to acquire a deadly contagious disease. The most disruptive thing a person can do is fail to keep a place that others feel can't be changed for him. Whatever the cause of the offender's psychological state—and clearly this may sometimes be organic—the social significance of the disease is that its carrier somehow hits upon the way that things can be made hot for us. The sociological significance of this is that social life is organized so that such a way can be found for it.

The manic is someone who does not refrain from intruding where he is not wanted or where he will be accepted but at a loss to what we see as his value and status. He does not contain himself in the spheres and territories allotted to him. He overreaches. He does not keep his place.

But more than place and the self it affords are involved. The manic does not accept tactful treatment as an exchange for not pressing too far. And he not only fails to keep the place which he and his others had allocated to him, but declines, apparently willfully, to engage in the ritual work that would allow his others to discount this failure.

In response, his others feel that his character and personality have suddenly changed, that he is no longer himself, and no longer

---

manic-depressive cycles is no longer put forward in psychiatry—the current view being that one of the two modes predominates—it is the case that many manics experience periods of marked depression when to face any moment in the day requires a terrible effort. Again the plight of finding everything just too much of a drag is not to be attributed solely to an intrapsychic factor, but also to the fact that social place is organized so that some special effort is always required to maintain it. Given that much of social life is organized in terms of personal control and informal control, conditions are present for multiplying in every direction a slight increase or decrease in outgoingness. Depression and mania necessarily become ready possibilities, and not surprisingly often in the same person.

himself in a way that disallows his close others from being what they feel they must be. Unfitting his self to his person, he unfits the persons of those around him to their selves. Wherever his dealings go, disarraying follows.

The manic declines to restrict himself to the social game that brings order and sense to our lives. Through his antics he gives up "his" self-respect, this being the regard we would allow him to have for himself as a reward for keeping a social place that may contain no other satisfaction for him.

The manic gives up everything a person can be, and gives up too the everything we make out of jointly guarded dealings. His doing so, and doing so for any of a multitude of independent reasons, reminds us what our everything is, and then reminds us that this everything is not very much. A somewhat similar lesson is taught by other categories of troublemaker who do not keep their place.

Index

Index